STRATHCLYDE UNIVERSITY LIBRARY
30125 0035
KV-119-912

ANDERSONIAN LIBRARY
WITHDRAWN
FROM
LIBRARY
STOCK
UNIVERSITY OF STRATHCLYDE

NEW DIRECTIONS FOR PRODUCT TESTING AND SENSORY ANALYSIS OF FOODS

F
N
P

JOURNALS AND BOOKS IN FOOD SCIENCE AND NUTRITION

Books

NEW DIRECTIONS FOR PRODUCT TESTING AND SENSORY ANALYSIS OF FOODS, H. R. Moskowitz

PRODUCT TESTING AND SENSORY EVALUATION OF FOODS, H. R. Moskowitz

ENVIRONMENTAL ASPECTS OF CANCER: ROLE OF MACRO AND MICRO COMPONENTS OF FOODS, E. L. Wynder *et al.*

FOOD PRODUCT DEVELOPMENT IN IMPLEMENTING DIETARY GUIDELINES, G. E. Livingston, R. J. Moshy, and C. M. Chang

SHELF-LIFE DATING OF FOODS, T. P. Labuza

RECENT ADVANCES IN OBESITY RESEARCH, VOL.III, P. Bjorntorp, M. Cairella, and A. N. Howard

RECENT ADVANCES IN OBESITY RESEARCH, VOL. II, G. A. Bray

RECENT ADVANCES IN OBESITY RESEARCH, VOL. I, A. N. Howard

ANTINUTRIENTS AND NATURAL TOXICANTS IN FOODS, R. L. Ory

UTILIZATION OF PROTEIN RESOURCES, D. W. Stanley, E. D. Murray and D. H. Lees

FOOD INDUSTRY ENERGY ALTERNATIVES, R. P. Ouellette, N. W. Lord and P. E. Cheremisinoff

VITAMIN B_6: METABOLISM AND ROLE IN GROWTH, G. P. Tryfiates

HUMAN NUTRITION, 3RD ED., F. R. Mottram

DIETARY FIBER: CURRENT DEVELOPMENTS OF IMPORTANCE TO HEALTH, K. W. Heaton

FOOD POISONING AND FOOD HYGIENE, 4TH ED., B. C. Hobbs and R. J. Gilbert

POSTHARVEST BIOLOGY AND BIOTECHNOLOGY, H. O. Hultin and M. Milner

THE SCIENCE OF MEAT AND MEAT PRODUCTS, 2ND ED., J. F. Price AND B. S. Schweigert

Journals

JOURNAL OF FOODSERVICE SYSTEMS, O. P. Snyder, Jr.

JOURNAL OF FOOD BIOCHEMISTRY, H. O. Hultin, N. F. Haard and J. R. Whitaker

JOURNAL OF FOOD PROCESS ENGINEERING, D. R. Heldman

JOURNAL OF FOOD PROCESSING AND PRESERVATION, D. B. Lund

JOURNAL OF FOOD QUALITY, M. P. de Figueiredo

JOURNAL OF FOOD SAFETY, M. Solberg and J. D. Rosen

JOURNAL OF TEXTURE STUDIES, M. C. Bourne and P. Sherman

JOURNAL OF NUTRITION, GROWTH AND CANCER, G. P. Tryfiates

NEW DIRECTIONS FOR PRODUCT TESTING AND SENSORY ANALYSIS OF FOODS

by

Howard R. Moskowitz, Ph.D.

MOSKOWITZ/JACOBS, INC.
VALHALLA, NEW YORK
and
TASC GROUP, INC.
EVANSTON, ILLINOIS

FOOD & NUTRITION PRESS, INC.
WESTPORT, CONNECTICUT 06880 USA

FOOD & NUTRITION PRESS, INC.
Westport, Connecticut 06880 USA

ISBN: 0-917678-18-4
Library of Congress Catalog Card Number: 84-72988

Printed in the United States of America

DEDICATION

I dedicate this book lovingly to my dear wife Mary, who helped me develop, test, validate, and market the technologies discussed in these chapters. Over the years she has continually encouraged me to apply the technologies to business problems, and to expand the horizon beyond basic research into applied product testing.

PREFACE

I wrote this book to share with readers my vision of the future. Product testing and sensory analysis have grown in scope and popularity over the past twenty-five years. Today, most companies use one or another form of testing, either with consumers or with in-house experts. Products go forward at the R&D and marketing stages, based upon the opinions generated by subjective consumer or expert panel tests. As a consequence we see more and more reliance on procedures for the early evaluation of products, prior to the marketplace. The evaluations serve both as guidance for development, and as fail-safe mechanisms to guard against product disaster.

Although we daily witness the continuing growth of testing, much of the testing has become routinized. Indeed, in many companies, sensory evaluation and product testing at both the market research and R&D level has become little more than a clerical function. Procedures have become standardized, weighted down with corporate norms and guidelines. The innovative approaches have often disappeared under the weight of recommended or required methods.

Technology and science cannot advance without new frontiers, and without the creativity that originally led to its birth. This book presents an array of technologies, uniquely appropriate to product testing, culled from the solution of practical problems. Rather than concentrating on traditional methods, the book emphasizes new techniques, currently in use by marketing researchers, marketers, and advanced researchers in sensory analysis. In a sense, therefore, this book presents the author's vision for the next fifteen years—where product testing and sensory analysis should go to maximize its utility for solving the practical, business-oriented issues which daily arise in corporations.

HOWARD R. MOSKOWITZ

CONTENTS

Section III. Using the Data for Technical and Marketing Guidance

OVERCOMING OBJECTIONS TO NEW TECHNOLOGY—INSIGHTS AND RECOMMENDATIONS

INTRODUCTION

Ask any consultant about the barriers to success, and inevitably the discussion will end up with the "people issue." Technology, no matter how powerful, useful, and valid, can never succeed if the target audience of consumers (managers, sensory analysts) refuses to accept it. Literature about the technology can appear in the scientific journals, *ad infinitum,* but it takes the acceptance from the practitioner and those with real-world problems to endow the technology with a life of its own. In the words of many, "if the technology promises so much, why doesn't everyone use it?"

To achieve success in product testing and sensory analysis by introducing new ideas, one first has to achieve acceptance. This chapter deals both with the barriers to acceptance, and with some techniques of overcoming those barriers. To those who have patience and persistance, success inevitably follows, especially if the technology truly "works" and provides a useful, valid service. To those without patience, and who want a quick "payout," success may rear its head for a short while, but quickly retreat. New ideas demand love, care, persistance and patience. Success comes, but only after trials.

UNCOVERING THE BARRIERS TO ACCEPTANCE

Sensory analysis and product testing do not have the glory that their counterparts do, such as advertising evaluation, simulated test marketing, etc. Most managers on the corporate side use product testing and sensory analysis as tools to evaluate mundane questions, such as "does the new product differ from the old product?" or "does my new entry win significantly versus the market leader?" These questions constitute the bread and butter of product testing. However, they do not partake of the excitement generated by other research tools, such as test market simulators, which project the market share and volume of new product entries, or of the Nielsen numbers, which provide an idea of the actual share of market enjoyed by the different products in the category. Traditionally, managers have relegated product testing and sensory analysis to a ho-hum existence, necessary to evaluate products but nonetheless a cut-and-dried service, which one performs on a day in, day out basis. In effect, the ultimate consumer of the research, namely the manager, has come to perceive product testing as a clerical affair, best conducted "by the book," according to a prescribed set of standards, replete with a history of normative data for comparison, and certainly not the proper area for innovative thinking.

SPECIFIC BARRIERS TO ACCEPTANCE

This section deals with the types of barriers that one may encounter during the course of introducing the product testing technology described in this book.

People Just Can't Taste More Than Two Products Without Becoming Fatigued

Over the decades, marketers have come to accept the dictate of marketing research regarding consumer abilities to taste products. In the typical informal inspections (cuttings and tastings in some companies), the marketing director, product manager and other assorted parties rapidly evaluate a whole array of alternative prototypes, as well as competitive products. They do this quickly, unscientifically, with little rest time between samples. Take a movie of the activity, without the sound, and it looks like a disciplined beginning, with everyone tasting the products daintily, and with care. After a while, however, the participants in this tasting lose the discipline, and simply taste at will, going back and forth, comparing new samples to old samples, devising hypotheses, tasting samples, and discarding the hypotheses, only to start with new ones. Ask the participants how they feel about the products, and eventually the answer comes out that they have lost track of the products, that they do not remember the products, and that their sensitivity has just simply disappeared.

In traditional marketing, research managers get used to receiving paired comparison data (e.g., A beats B on overall liking, but B tastes sweeter). Marketing researchers run innumerable paired comparison tests using outside field services. Respondents or participants in these tests simply have to indicate (after tasting products) which product in the pair they prefer, which has a stronger taste, etc. The sheer popularity of the paired comparison method adds to one's skepticism that panelists can actually evaluate more than two products without losing their sensitivity. If so (goes the unstated, but underlying thinking) then why do we limit panelists to tasting only two products? As logic would inexorably have it, we limit the panelists because, we conclude, they probably can't discriminate beyond the two that we provide them. (Otherwise, why did we limit these to two in the first place?)

The chapter on validating the test procedures shows how one can dispel this myth of panelist inability, by systematically varying the formulations, and then correlating attribute ratings with formula concentration. Once managers understand the implication of these correlations, they recognize that panelists can and do discriminate, even after testing 10-20 prototypes. The manager must see these statistics, and must feel comfortable with the field work before accepting the data. No amount of intellectual discourse can take the place of actual experience with multiple product testing. Managers and marketers may want to believe, but they feel comfortable only after having the actual experience of looking at the panelists tasting the products, and then seeing the results. With systematic formula variations it becomes possible to demonstrate validity, and remove this barrier to technology.

Okay, It Sounds Good In Theory—But Can You Really Do This In The Field

Marketing researchers and sensory analysts usually spend little time with panelists. The typical field interview consists of a short mall intercept. The interviewer, desirous of making the quota for the project (namely, a certain number of qualified participants), goes after the most likely prospects in a well-trafficked mall, asking the prospective respondent a few questions, and then if the panelist qualifies, inviting the person to participate in a short interview. In sensory analysis, conducted with in-house panelists, much the same occurs, but in a different guise. The panel leader has the job of recruiting a set number of individuals in the company (or university) to participate in a taste test. Participants may qualify because they consume the product on a regular basis, or because company policy dictates that all company employees must participate in at least 2-3 such tests per month, as part of the terms of employment.

In all of these situations we have to recognize the existence of tradeoffs. The interviewer or panel leader has to acquire sufficient data from the requisite panelists. In turn, the panelists have to decide whether they would like to participate in this test, or go on doing what they have been doing. Individuals who become involved in their daily activities, or shoppers who want to keep shopping, refuse to participate, or participate grudgingly with an eye on the clock.

If we look at the consequence of this behavior, we see the following:

(1) A harassed interviewer who has to fill his or her quota

(2) Panelists, many of whom do not want to participate, but do so only because of overt or covert pressure to do so

(3) A limited slot of time to accomplish the interview, because other activities demand attention and because the interview has low priority and low importance in the mind of the panelist or respondent (no matter what the company policy dictates).

It should come as no surprise, therefore, that the interviews which last the least amount of time seem best to the outside observer, while the interviews lasting 20 minutes or longer, with the unwilling participant, degenerate into a contest of "watch the clock and get the data as fast as possible."

To overcome this problem, and to instill confidence into longer interviews requires a change in field procedure. One has to prerecruit participants to spend an extended period of time evaluating the product. Rather than relying on the traditional one-on-one interview in a mall, it becomes necessary and efficient to prerecruit a bank of individuals (e.g., 25 or so) to participate for an extended, 2-4 hour session. During the session, the panelists have a chance to evaluate an entire array of products in a relaxed fashion. Rather than rushing to do something else, the panelists participate with most paying full attention. They will receive money for their participation, and the screening earlier insures that each panelists would have the available hours to spend in the test.

To insure improved field work also requires a choreographed test procedure. The careful researcher will lay out the activities that a panelist has done during the test. These include orientation (learning about the scales, and questionnaire), product receipt and evaluation and data checking. Table 1 shows a choreography for a beverage test, from start to finish. Notice that:

(1) The test allows up to 50 panelists to participate

(2) Interviewers monitor the panelists

(3) Other interviewers dispense the product

(4) Each step in the pattern proceeds sequentially

(5) The panelists generally proceed at their own pace

(6) Sufficient checks and balances exist in the test to guard against problems, in terms of panelist motivation, or errors in product selection

(7) Tremendous efficiencies of scale exist in the test procedure. The panelists participate for 4 hours, evaluating 20 products, as well as pro-

viding attitude and usage information. This constitutes a total of 50 (people) × 4 (panelist hours) = 200 panel hours, condensed into a centrally planned and controlled four-hour session

(8) The marketing researcher or sensory analyst can monitor the entire session, rather than relying upon the field service to execute the study

(9) The arrangement makes it easy to spot poor interviewers, and reward excellent ones. It also becomes possible to spot poor respondents or panelists during the course of the session (e.g., those who have little or no interest in the task)

(10) One can validate the screening of participants by administering a screening questionnaire at the test site. This insures that the panel represent what the manufacturer wants, rather than the panelists comprising a convenience sample, recruited at a mall, to fill a quota.

A choreographed procedure, with sufficient interviewers and panelists starts off with the appearance of disarray, as all the panelists sit down, and wait for the session to begin. After a few minutes, however, all becomes quiet. Panelists concentrate on the task, do not talk to each other, and proceed assiduously to complete the alloted test. Such sessions work as well with children as with adults. Most importantly, however, once managers and marketers see the test in action they quickly realize that a field service can easily run such a test, collecting consumer data on many products. Marketers and managers then feel comfortable, because they have seen a smoothly executed study. Their innate biases against evaluating many products eventually disappear because the field service and marketing researcher (or sensory analyst) has actually performed the task. Disbelief in the consumer's ability turns around 180 degrees, into recognition of what one might truly accomplish, using the new technology.

It Works On Beverages, But Certainly Not On My Product

A certain sense of joy pervades managers who work with products; the joy that their product somehow differs from all other products in the universe, that their products suffer unique problems. Each category of products has unique characteristics, and indeed the problems pervasive to one category and difficult to solve may dissolve away into minor issues in another category.

To someone who wants to close his or her eyes and ears to new approaches, what a wonderful excuse this category uniqueness makes. After all (or so goes the thinking) "the technology proposed sounds wonderful. It probably works on beverages, but not alcoholic ones. Or if it works on alcoholic beverages, then my product has some other unique twists, which makes it difficult (if not impossible) to apply the technology."

TABLE 1
EXAMPLE OF CHOREOGRAPHING A 4 HOUR BEVERAGE TEST WITH 50 CONSUMERS

Part A—Setup requirements

Personnel—1 moderator (interviewer)
—10 attending interviewers (1 for each 5 panelists)
—3 interviewers to dispense product and check temperature of beverage

Physical Requirement—1 large room (30×40 minimum)
—tables to store product
—10 tables, accommodating 6 people per table (5 panelist plus attending interviewer)

Part B—Actual Sequence Of Activities

1. Panelist prerecruited 1 week prior to test, qualified, invited to attend
2. Panelists all show up, ready for the 4 hour session
3. Moderator introduces panelist to task
4. Panelists go through orientation exercise (evaluating area of circles)
5. Attending interviewer checks panelist ratings for comprehension
6. Moderator shows panelist the beverage questionnaire, explains terms
7. Panelist begins with first product in a unique randomized order
8. Panelist gets product from dispensing area, returns to seat
9. Panelist rates the product on attributes
10. Panelist shows ratings to attending interviewer who asks several questions
11. Panelist disposes of products and waits 5 minutes
12. Panelist repeats steps 7-11 for next product
13. After panelist finishes 7 products, panelist waits 10 minutes
14. Steps 7-11 repeated, for sets of 7 products, followed by a longer wait
15. Time between samples—7 minutes (approximately)
16. Total time to evaluate 20 products—approximately 4 hours
17. At each step of the process, panelist ratings checked by interviewer

How can one get the manager to deal more directly with the situation, and to look at the technology as an aid to answering problems. Certainly, demeaning the concern about the uniqueness of a problem, and engaging in confrontation head on seems one answer to the problem. The over-ambitious consultant, strongly believing in the new technology, might engage in an ongoing battle, head to head, against the manager who firmly believes that his or her category possesses unique problems. Direct confrontation does not work. It only makes the participants on both sides more defensive, and less willing to listen to each other.

An alternative method, often quite useful, consists of simply throwing up one's hands at the immense difficulty of solving this uniqueness problem. After all, if the problem facing the manufacturer seems so overwhelming, so large, and so unique, how can the consultant (who truly wants to help) dare bring in the technology? Perhaps just leaving the manager alone with the problem would prove more productive. Clinical psychologists call this "paradoxical intervention." If, indeed, the problem with the category (e.g., beer) looms so large, and seems so unique, then in reality this problem does not allow a solution, even by the new technology. Certainly, the older, more traditional methods don't work either. The manager's solution is to choose a random course of action, and punt.

By pursuing a strategy of "paradoxical intervention," the marketing researcher accomplishes two objectives.

(1) The client (generally a manufacturer) feels that someone appreciates his problem. After all, to the manufacturer the uniqueness of his or her product seems quite real, and the problems and challenges quite large.

(2) By stopping any attempt to convince the manufacturer that the new technology can help, and by suggesting a more random strategy, the marketing researcher confronts the underlying problem quite directly. If the manufacturer (client) continues to aver that no approach works, then in effect he or she has to use techniques that seem outdated and useless, and which admittedly cannot solve the problem. During the course of the meeting between the client and the market researcher, the researcher has removed his or her new technology even from consideration. The client manufacturer has nothing to fight against, nothing to deny, and thus has to again face the problem of what to do with his or her product, which causes so much grief and aggravation. The meeting becomes more constructive, because neither side tries to convince the other of the correctness of their respective positions.

Quite often meetings during which the consultant researcher withdraws the technique from consideration, rather than fighting for its acceptance, prove eminently productive. If not forced to listen to a technology, but rather invited to consider the technology in a respectful manner, most concerned manufacturer clients will listen. After all, they do care about their product, and do want to do the best. They may not want to feel pushed into adopting a new technology from a high pressure salesman, but they also want to accomplish their business goals, and will do so by using a nonthreatening technology.

Sounds Great—A Black Box—I'd Buy It—But Not Now

People have mixed feelings about new technology. Buying involves emotion, and buying research and research techniques involves just as much emotion as buying tangible products. For most people on the client side, buying entails some risk, if not directly financial, then in terms of one's position in the corporation.

As a further corollary in research, whether marketing research or sensory analysis, people buy what they understand. They may listen to presentations involving new technologies, and enjoy these presentations, but if the technique comes off as a "black box," with the presenter unable or unwilling to simplify matters, then the client will often not purchase the service or incorporate the ideas into his or her approaches.

New technologies often involve statistics, modeling, and novel approaches not currently in the client's repertoire of experience. How does the honest researcher, trying to market the technology, overcome the fear of the black box? Quite often the client listening to a presentation does not even recognize that the technology involves black box procedures, but simply feels uncomfortable, because he or she does not fully understand everything presented. In a meeting, to show ignorance of a technique or lack of understanding constitutes a business "no-no" for the manager, so that the lack of understanding never gets resolved, and the technology never gets adopted.

In corporations, the marketing researcher or sensory analyst endeavoring to promote the new technology will inevitably meet up with a host of individuals from different departments. Each individual has a unique background and responds to a unique set of needs. In product testing, evaluation and optimization, marketing, sensory analysis, marketing research, statistics, and advertising look at the data. Quite often representatives from all of these departments sit in on the presentation. To some, the procedures seem quite simple; to others the procedures resemble a complex of mathematical equations bound up by the cords of incomprehensibility.

To achieve acceptance demands that the technology answer questions, not that it present a black box approach. Clients do not buy technology; they buy answers to questions that impact their business careers. A successful presentation of the technology might best begin with business issues needing a solution. All manufacturers face these business issues. Commencing one's presentation with a problem, rather than with a technique humanizes the technology. The consultant researcher now recognizes the problems, which confront his or her client. The technology becomes the instrument to solve the problem, rather than remaining on an intellectual pedestal, the creation of a mind(s) not connected with real world issues.

A secondary step in presenting the model consists of listing the activities the panelists perform, the reasons for those activities, and the type of data that emerges from the evaluation. At each step of the way, the consultant researcher has to tie-back the data or activities to the problem.

Approaches without a tie-back to problems do not sell, except to those who enjoy methodology for the sake of intellectual stimulation.

The final step consists of presentation of technical issues to those involved with technical aspects of procedure. Prior to this step, however, the consultant has clearly related the technology to problems, has shown what occurs in the execution of the procedures, and how the data answers specific questions. Only afterwards, does it become relevant to deal with technical aspects, such as statistical designs, regressions, modeling, measures of variability, etc.

We can sum this section up in a simple phrase "Sell the solution to a problem, not the technique by itself." Problems always crop up, techniques come and go.

Sounds Good—But We Have To Solve Real Problems And This Seems Too Academic

A strange division seems to exist between manufacturers involved in the day to day evaluation of products, and academics or scientists involved in the sensory and market analysis of products. Reading scientific journals can leave one with the impression that the methods described just simply cannot work, given the day to day problems and exigencies needed in the business community. Certainly (or so goes the feeling) with enough time and money the marketing researcher or sensory analyst would like to do the best job possible. However, time tables and budget constraints continually rear their heads. The new technology seems interesting, and could solve the problem, but not right now. The marketing researcher has to stamp out fires, and attend to the basics. Perhaps later on, when one has time, resources, experimental budget (and interest!) one could explore the new technology, and try it out. Right now, avers the corporate client, we have to satisfy the demands currently in-house. The time just doesn't seem right to try anything new, possibly next year (or, even more realistically, probably never).

One's appeal to workload, and to the academic nature of new technology, can simply overwhelm any new technology. Who wants to assume the burden of possibly disrupting ongoing business, simply to sell a technology? An appeal to business pressures, and the corollary, this technology seems too academic for right now, spells the death knell for the new approach. The covert message states, "I'm up to my ears in reality, so don't make me think, don't give me anything to distract my attention, because in reality I feel perfectly satisfied with the way I deal with problems."

Of all barriers to new technology, this barrier presents the most formidable one. The messages contained in the statement, "it seems academic, and I have to deal with reality," carry with them numerous hidden meanings. The potential client has dismissed the technology because it does not seem appropriate to a business climate. The client further has dismissed the entire meeting, because of the pressing issues involved in running the day-to-day work. By hiding behind the guise of a harassed employee and a desk piled high with papers, the potential client has set the stage to go back to what he or she usually does. After all, (or so goes the covert thinking) "at least I can deliver what they expect of me. If, I should diverge from my path, even a jot, I might fail because time will run out and I will not accomplish even what I can do today."

In reality, one cannot expect individuals with this attitude to really care about new technology. Their interest focuses on maintaining the status quo and their desks bespeak busy, harassed existences. They have difficulty accomplishing anything new, because they have to run around making sure that all goes well doing things the "old way." They muddle through, go home early, and feel confident that their activities serve the company best. They serve by occupying themselves with busy work. They fail to rise beyond middle level management because they simply do not have the time to make their job more productive and more efficient.

As negative as this prognosis seems, fortunately this particular barrier eventually goes away. Individuals too busy to try new ideas get shunted off to the side. They not only discriminate against one new idea; they discriminate against all new ideas. They stay doing the same work year after year, while others, more interested in the goals than in the busy work, ascend into decision making positions. Eventually these busy bees, with no time for new ideas and with a disdain for improved technology, either wake up and change, remain in a job where they can do little damage, or wander from company to company, seeking refuge from the future, and from a world of innovation with which they cannot cope.

We Tried It Five Years Ago And We Had Some Problems With It

All too often technology takes years to develop properly. No new technology emerges in perfect form, like Venus, emerging full form and in perfection from the head of Jupiter. Also, no one really has 100% new ideas. Technology develops in a slow, laborious fashion, with errors, blind alleys, charlatans, and a modicum of truly dedicated apostles.

Inevitably, corporate clients have problems with technology. Nothing destroys one's enthusiasm quite as much as hearing that a potential client "tried the approach sometime back, but had problems with it, and so shelved it." One usually discovers that:

(1) The person who had the experience has no idea when he or she tried the procedure

(2) No records exist regarding the project

(3) If the project did actually occur, the problems may bear little or no resemblance to the complaints now voiced

(4) The person who had the problem with the technique no longer works for the company.

An appeal to previous negative experience constitutes a very strong defensive ploy. After all, how can the consultant researcher really expect the client to purchase the technology, when the client (and presumably the consultant) knows fully well that the technology simply cannot work. One never needs to show evidence that the technology fails. The consultant has to prove and continually re-establish validity. The in-house client doesn't have to prove anything. A simple statement of dismissal suffices. In actuality, in-house clients do have this power to dismiss technology, and do not have to marshall evidence to support their position. Even if their recollection proves faulty, it doesn't matter. By the time they, or someone else, recognizes that the previous problem actually did not exist, or did not relate to the current technology, the damage has already occurred. The new technology has lost credibility.

To overcome this barrier takes patience; patience to wait out the negative individual. Other members of the corporation, if exposed to the concept and the technology, may "spark" to it and not pay attention to the disgruntled historian of failures. Word of mouth does wonders to overcome negative experience. If people talk about the technology in positive terms, then the complaint that it failed to work previously loses impact. The social reinforcement of hearing that a technology works, from one's peers in the same company or other companies, acts as a remarkable revitalizing agent. Suddenly, the technology no longer bears resemblance to the method that failed previously. People become more accepting, and will forgive the previous errors, because now they see other people using the techniques and reaping the benefits. Indeed, old errors turn into war stories. Failures now become critical anecdotes one can use to demonstrate how far one has come with the technology.

Sounds Great—But Are You Using The Right Dependent Variable

Marketing researchers and product testers work with various subjective measures. One key set of measures incorporates hedonics; whether purchase intent, or overall liking. These variables constitute matters of opinion. In reality the relation between stated purchase intent and actual purchase behavior may not resemble a straight line. Knowing how to relate consumer attitude ratings to market behavior (e.g., volume purchase) constitutes an important link that makes product testing technology a valuable tool in the hands of a marketer.

The foregoing paragraph presents the positive side, namely, one's recognition that the marketer should relate test scores to actual market behavior. The paragraph can also take on an ominous tone. To a critic of new technology, only a perfect measure of market behavior will satisfy his criteria of validity. In the most extreme case, the technology has no validity at all unless the ratings of liking accurately predict trial for a product, repeat and market share. Any performance less dramatic means that the technology simply has no place in his or her repertoire of tools.

A consultant trying to sell a new product testing technology always has the temptation to over-promise in order to get the technology tried. Trial begets repeat, and without trial no one at the manufacturer will ever know what the technology can accomplish.

To a skilled critic who wants to devastate the technology, this eagerness on the part of the technology salesman comes as a blessed gift. One simply has to demand more and more from the technology, and then extract promises of increasing levels of performance. Rather than the technology finding use in screening and optimizing the new product prototypes for later test, the technology now has to predict, quantitatively, performance in other tests, or performance in the marketplace. The critic and the consultant lose sight of the fact that the technology has limitations. The critic wants to guide the technology sufficiently far out on a limb so that any imperfections in the technology, any limitations, and any executional errors cannot but destroy the entire procedure. The consultant trying to introduce the technology may fall for this trap, in his or her eagerness to sell the procedure.

The way around this barrier consists of limiting the promise of the technology to a couple of easily accomplished goals. Even if the technology can accomplish miracles, no one wants to hear about them. The best strategy consists of under-promising the benefits, and over-delivering the results. Let the client manufacturer learn about the additional benefits by insight, rather than having the consultant promise them, and possibly fail to deliver.

This section was suggested by Barry Tannenholz.

We Need to Get Everybody On Board

In sensory analysis, and to a lesser extent in marketing research, the professionals do not control the budget. Often, they have little money that they can truly call "discretionary." Much of their budget goes towards routine, service testing. Indeed, quite often the budget sets the entire department outlook.

Inevitably, when decisions require committee approval, little new occurs. Committees of management, especially those at middle management level, do not have the technical expertise to judge new technology. All too often the proponent of a new technology in-house has the least years of service. Young people, full of ideas, enthusiasm and vision, want to try new approaches. Middle management, satisfied that they have arrived, manage to quell that enthusiasm by invoking the bureaucracy. Rather than allowing the novice some freedom to explore, middle management demands consensus to diffuse responsibility. No one ever seems to worry about capturing glory, except the innovators, but everyone likes to avoid risk.

Unfortunately, this situation pervades all companies. As a consequence, the new technology cannot appear overly technical, because the decision makers (not the utilizers) will not understand it. Instead, middle management opts for possibly weaker techniques that they can understand, and which they can explain to their superiors.

In sensory analysis, as one example, only recently have researchers begun to use modeling techniques, using experimental design, regression, and optimization. Over the years, sensory analysts have confined themselves to descriptive analysis; training panels to describe their sensory impressions, on one or another scale. When asked about the utility of the pictures that emerge from the procedures, few know the final utility of the techniques. Some say that product developers use the descriptive profiles to help them improve the product. Others, with more candor, say that middle and upper management likes pictures, and that in itself suffices to validate the approach. The simple (but potentially less powerful) techniques get everyone on board.

To counter the problem of group decision-making demands someone willing to take a risk, to try something new, and to innovate. Usually the younger researchers and sensory analysts, just out of school or with a few years background, play this role. These individuals, and the ambitious middle and upper management look towards the positive aspects of new technology. They don't worry about group consensus. If the technology works, they want to use it and place their trust in a management looking for results, rather than looking for hypotheses to explain consumer behavior (the so-called analysis paralysis).

AN OVERVIEW

This prologue presents common barriers to new technology from the point of view of consumer research and sensory analysis. However, the problems alluded to, the personality types, and the approaches transcend product testing and sensory analysis. They apply to all areas of science, some more than others. Unfortunately, with research, one has reports to show for the final product, not actual products themselves. Thus, in the end, validity truly remains a matter of opinion. Those willing to take risks and to try new technology will eventually succeed, because they will produce better products. Those not willing to try new ideas will eventually fail, or end up in the same position, for the rest of their life, where they can watch the action from the sidelines, and wonder why in the world people seem so interested in this technology anyway.

The remainder of this book deals with new approaches, designed to advance the cause and utility of product testing in an applied environment. Hopefully, readers will come away with a renewed sense of excitement at the opportunities which present themselves with the new technology of product testing and sensory analysis.

SECTION I.
The Measurement Tools

CHAPTER 1

MEASURING THE IMPORTANCE OF ATTRIBUTES TO CONSUMERS

INTRODUCTION

This chapter deals with the relative importance of attributes. To many researchers, the problem of measuring relative importance seems fairly straightforward; simply ask the consumers to rank attributes in order of importance, from most important to least important. (These investigators also believe that one can ask the consumers to scale relative importance, using a numerical scale.) The average rank or average scale value reflects the degree of importance.

Do consumers truly know the relative importance of attributes, however? If the investigator performs the experiment, he or she will quickly determine the following:

(1) Given a large list of attributes, some of which represent liking ratings (e.g., liking of flavor), and others which represent sensory characteristics (e.g., sweetness), the liking ratings always come out on top, as the most important attributes.

(2) The sensory attributes tend to come out in the middle or below.

(3) If the researcher has, by chance, included some negative attributes (e.g., bitterness), these tend to come out at the bottom of the importance list.

The foregoing results continue to appear, time after time. The consistency of the ranking of attributes done in this fashion provides a pleasant feeling of comfort and "reliability", until the researcher begins to inquire about the meaning of the results. What does a moderate importance rating attached to the attribute of "sweetness" truly mean to a panelist? One can conclude that to most individuals a "good flavor" should have high priority, but what about "sweetness". How can one ask about the "importance of sweetness"?

Methods For Measuring The Relative Importance of Attributes—Overview

This section provides an overview to measuring relative importance, prior to a case history.

We will deal with the following procedures, each of which measures one or another aspect of relative importance:

Direct Rating Of Importance
Annoyance Rating
Correlation With Overall Liking
Quantitative Relation Between Liking and Attribute Rating

Direct Rating of Importance

Consumers have little or no trouble assigning direct ratings of importance. One simply has to ask them to do so, using either a rating scale or a ranking scale. Table 1.1 shows the relative importance of attributes, for a variety of foods, developed by the rating procedure.

One key result which clearly emerges from Table 1.1 concerns the high level of importance assigned to the liking attributes, and to the image attributes. As noted in the introduction to this chapter, these "motherhood" types of attributes always score on top. Consumers rate overall quality, nutrition, etc., as the most important dimensions of a product. On the other hand, they consistently downrate the importance of the sensory attributes.

A user of these data may feel tempted to generalize, and say that the consumers do know what they want. On the other hand, upon deeper reflection, one might wish to ignore this ranking. Possibly individuals can rank order attributes such as "liking" (e.g., liking of flavor scores higher in importance than liking of texture, or liking of aroma). However, when it comes to the nonevaluative, sensory attributes, the direct rating or ranking of attribute importance loses its meaningfulness. The direct rating procedure cannot handle the nonevaluative sensory dimensions.

Relative Importance Measured By "Annoyance Ratings"

Consumers have an easier time rating importance when the investigator presents them with a concrete situation to evaluate. For instance, by asking consumers how "annoyed" they would feel if they had purchased a product that tasted "too sweet" (e.g., a beverage), the researcher can indirectly measure importance. Presumably, the more annoyed the panelist feels about the product defect, the more important the attribute.

TABLE 1.1
RELATIVE IMPORTANCE OF ATTRIBUTES
BY DIRECT RATING*

	Attribute**	Still Fruit Beverage	Whole Wheat Bread	Candy (Adult Bar)
H	Good Flavor	85	79	64
E	Nutritious/Wholesome	56	87	39
D	High Quality	68	82	57
O	Fresh	60	91	60
N	Made By A Reputable Manufacturer	45	84	70
I	Familiar	42	62	61
C	Good Aroma	40	70	44
	Good Texture/Mouthfeel	39	59	59
	Good Appearance	38	53	51
	Good Color	32	55	54
S	Sweet (Right Level)	28	41	60
E	Tart (Right Level)	19	N.A.	N.A.
N	Color (Right Level)	15	51	54
S	Aroma (Right Strength)	15	60	39
O	Texture (Right Amount)	18	74	55
R	Bitter (Right Amount)	N.A.	N.A.	21
Y	Off-Taste (Right Amount)	11	12	12

Scale Definition For Relative Importance:

*0 = Not Important 100 = Extremely Important
**Specific wording may change as appropriate
N.A. = Not Applicable

Test Specifics: Panel = Adults (3 separate tests, 50 adults per test)
All conducted in the New York Market

A key benefit which emerges from the rating of "annoyance" consists of the ability to measure the criticality of "overshooting" versus "undershooting" a target. One can ask panelists to rate annoyance for "too much sweetness", as well as annoyance for "too little sweetness", both relative to what the panelist wants. The ratings reflect relative importance. Furthermore, delivering too much may not generate as much annoyance as delivering too little.

Panelists find the annoyance rating procedure easy to comprehend. The researcher presents them with a single statement about a product problem. The panelists have little or no trouble reacting to this problem and their ratings provide a measure of relative importance.

Table 1.2 presents an array of annoyance ratings, obtained in this manner for the frozen pizza category. Note that one can provide the panelist with several levels of product defects (e.g., much too much versus too much, or just too much). The numbers in Table 1.2 thus represent relative importance.

TABLE 1.2
RELATIVE IMPORTANCE MEASURED BY ANNOYANCE

CATEGORY—FROZEN PIZZA

Evaluative (Liking) Dimensions

Poor Appearance	64
Poor Aroma	68
Poor Taste/Flavor	78
Poor Texture	71
Low Quality	84

Sensory Dimensions

	Much Too Little	Too Little	Just Right	Too Much	Much Too Much	
Crust						
Soggy	87	42	0	29	38	Crisp
Thin	54	21	0	24	46	Thick
Sauce						
Light	53	31	0	24	39	Dark
Bland	57	38	0	29	40	Spicy
Cheese						
Flavor	62	34	0	31	52	
Amount	81	57	0	12	29	
Size						
Small	69	42	0	17	34	Large

Test Conditions

Panel = 100 Adults (Eating & Rating Products At Home, Then Rating Annoyance)

Scale: (0 = No Annoyance, 100 = Extreme Annoyance)
(The higher the annoyance rating, the more important the attribute)

Key conclusions one can reach from the importance ratings as obtained by annoyance include the following (Table 1.2).

(1) Consumers show a hierarchy of importance levels.

(2) Generally, taste and flavor dominate, followed by texture and

appearance. Defects in flavor usually (but not always) outweigh defects in texture and appearance.

(3) The range of annoyance ratings can often exceed 30 points (on a 0-100 point annoyance scale).

(4) The annoyance ratings do not necessarily show symmetry. For instance, "too little cheese" outweighs "too much cheese". Quite often, the asymmetry can become quite pronounced.

TABLE 1.3
HOW DIFFERENT SEGMENTS OF THE POPULATION RATE ANNOYANCE OF PRODUCT DEFECTS
CATEGORY = POTATO & GRAIN FLAVORED SALTED SNACKS

				Adults	
	Total*	Adults (½ Total)	Teens (½ Total)	Flavor Oriented** (½ Adults)	Health Oriented** (½ Adults)
Appearance					
Poor Appearance	54	[61	47]	64	58
Color Too Dark	39	42	37	45	39
Color Too Light	35	31	39	32	30
Looks Too Greasy	63	[72	54]	59	85
Aroma					
Poor Aroma	59	[64	54]	66	62
Aroma Too Strong	51	53	49	54	52
Aroma Too Weak	45	48	42	51	45
Taste					
Poor Taste	75	76	74	76	76
Too Salty	78	[83	73]	[77	89]
Not Salty Enough	59	[52	66]	56	48
Potato Flavor Too Weak	62	64	62	66	62
Potato Flavor Too Strong	67	68	66	67	69
Texture					
Poor Texture	68	[74	62]	73	75
Too Dry	57	53	61	53	53
Too Greasy	74	[79	69]	[74	84]
Too Thin	35	36	35	[32	40]
Too Thick	48	[42	54]	43	41

TEST CONDITIONS

*100 Panelists (New York, Chicago)

**Obtained from a separate questionnaire where panelists described their hierarchy of food values.

[61 47] All bracketed values denote key differences among subgroups in terms of annoyance ratings.

One can also segment consumers on the basis of category usage, or other variables, and measure relative annoyance. Table 1.3 presents the results of a study on snack chips which shows that the annoyance ratings may vary, depending upon the particular subgroups in the population. Individuals do differ, and have different value systems. These differences affect annoyance ratings.

Relative Importance Measured By Correlations With Acceptance

Quite often researchers correlate attribute ratings with overall liking or with purchase intent. The correlation coefficient provides a measure of the degree to which two variables covary in a linear fashion. The Pearson correlation (R) varies from a low of −1 (denoting perfect inverse relation), through 0 (denoting no linear relation at all), and upwards to +1 (denoting a perfect linear relation).

Table 1.4 presents the results of some of these correlation analyses, performed for a variety of categories. As one can easily see, the liking rating overall often shows the highest correlation with partwise attribute liking

TABLE 1.4
HOW OVERALL LIKING CORRELATES WITH ATTRIBUTE LIKING AND SENSORY ATTRIBUTES

	LIKING ATTRIBUTES				SENSORY ATTRIBUTES	
	Appearance	Aroma	Taste/ Flavor	Texture/ Mouthfeel	Flavor* Intensity	Texture* Intensity
Soup	0.87	0.83	0.97	0.90	0.44	0.57
Sausage	0.84	0.82	0.88	0.92	0.61	0.71
Pizza-frozen	0.90	0.89	0.97	0.94	0.39	0.74
Snack chips	0.90	0.78	0.97	0.88	0.58	0.81
Iced tea	0.50	0.87	0.90	0.95	0.76	0.23
Cheese pasta sauce	0.48	0.73	0.96	0.77	0.43	0.31
Cake-raisin	0.43	0.25	0.97	0.82	0.64	0.42

*Specific attribute varies with the particular product

Test Conditions: 7 Studies. About 60 people per study (category users). Each panelist rated between 4 and 15 products (depending upon the particular study) using a 0=100 scale.

ratings (e.g., liking of taste/flavor). However in the same studies we find that overall liking does not vary in a clear fashion with the simple sensory attributes of perceived flavor intensity, with sweetness, with sensory texture variables, etc.

Correlation coefficients assume that there exists a linear relation between acceptance and an attribute. The correlation coefficient measures the strength of that linear relation. The researcher assumes that the attributes showing the strongest linear relation with overall acceptance constitute the most important attributes, whereas those which do not show the linear relation do not play a significant role in acceptance, and thus have lesser importance.

Attractive as the correlation coefficient seems, it has two basic flaws:

(1) The correlation coefficient measures the existence of a *linear* relation between attribute rating and acceptance. It does not measure the

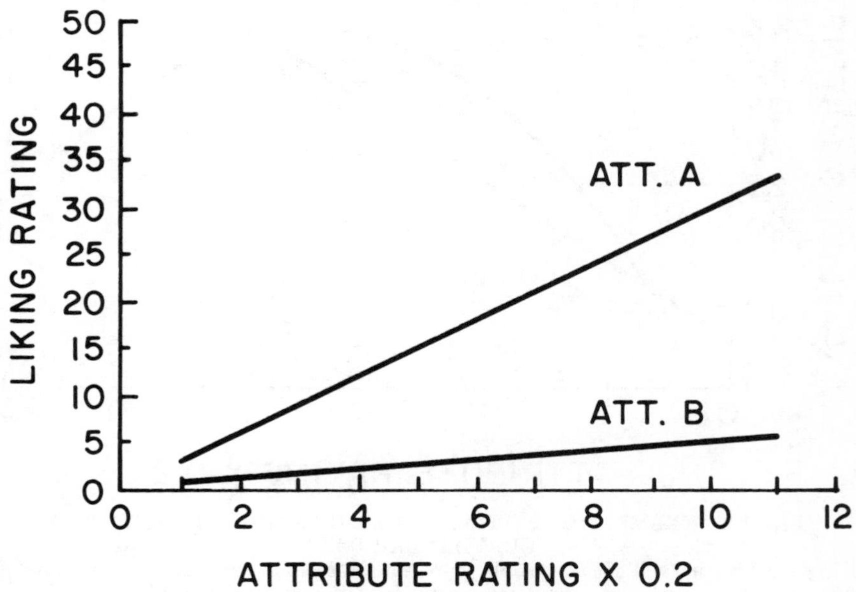

FIG. 1.1. COMPARISON OF TWO LINEAR RELATIONS BETWEEN ATTRIBUTE LEVEL AND LIKING.

Both relations exhibit the same correlation (+1.0) between liking and attribute level. However, attribute A generates a steep line, whereas attribute B generates a flatter line. We infer that attribute A exhibits more importance, because small changes in A correspond to larger changes in liking.

degree to which acceptance varies in a quantitative manner with changes in attribute level. Two variables can exhibit equal correlation with acceptance. However, changes in one variable may correspond to very large changes in acceptance, whereas the same magnitude of changes in the second variable may correspond to relatively small changes in acceptance (Fig. 1.1).

(2) The relation between attribute level and acceptance may not necessarily follow a straight line. If so, then the correlation coefficient used as an index of the strength of a linear relation may mislead the user. For instance, if liking covaries with perceived sweetness according to an inverted U-shaped curve (Fig. 1.2), then a straight line fitted to essentially curvilinear data will generate an incorrect measure of importance.

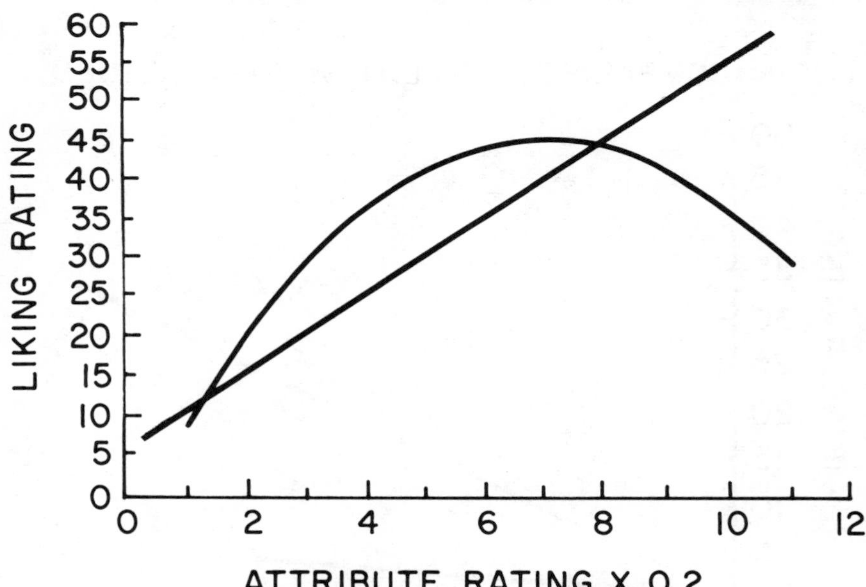

FIG. 1.2. EXAMPLE OF FITTING A STRAIGHT LINE TO ESSENTIALLY CURVILINEAR DATA.
The straight line will not adequately represent the relation between the two variables, and may provide incorrect information about the trend.

Relative Importance By Linear Equations Between Attribute Level and Acceptance

Suppose that the researcher has an opportunity to measure consumer responses to a variety of attributes, all of which appear to vary in a linear fashion with overall acceptance. For instance, the attributes thus measured may constitute overall liking, as well as liking of appearance, liking of aroma, liking of taste, liking of texture, etc. Each attribute correlates 0.9 or higher with overall acceptance. The high correlations between these attributes and overall liking suggests that the attributes all play a major role in influencing acceptance. However, do they play an equal role?

To answer this question, one might wish to plot the ratings of overall liking versus the ratings of the attributes, in a scatter plot, similar to that shown in Fig. 1.1. Or, equally valid, one can develop a straight line equation relating overall attribute rating as the dependent variable, versus the attribute ratings, each of which in turn becomes the independent variable. The equation for a straight line relating two variables appears as (Eq. 1.1):

$$\text{Overall Acceptance} = A + B\ (\text{Attribute Rating}) \qquad (1.1)$$

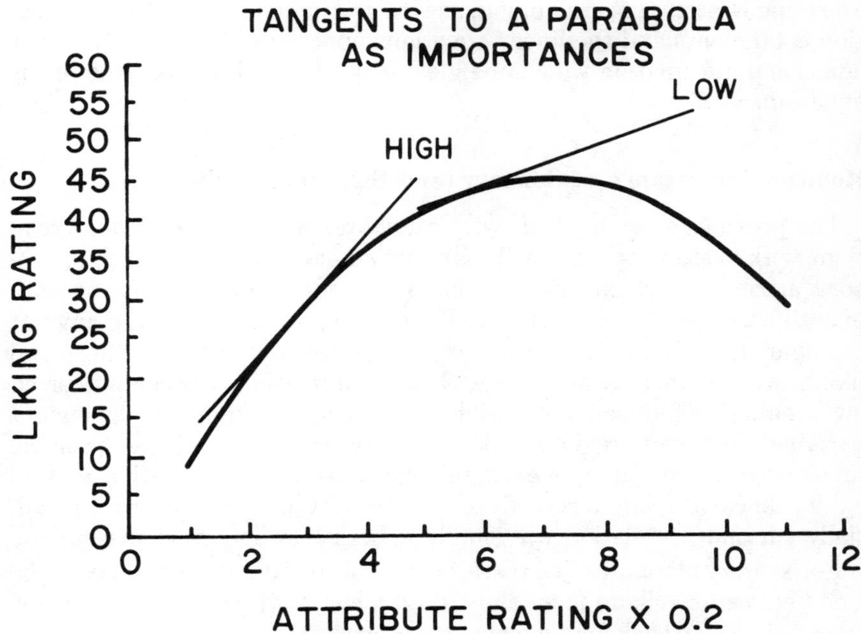

FIG. 1.3. EXAMPLE OF PARABOLIC (CURVILINEAR) RELATION BETWEEN ATTRIBUTE LEVEL AND LIKING.
Here the tangent to the curve (namely, the derivative) provides the measure of importance.

Looking at Fig. 1.1 or at the slope of the straight line (B), we can priorize the attributes in importance using the size of the linear slope. Those attributes showing the steepest linear slope possess the highest importance. Small changes in these attributes correspond to large changes in the rating of acceptance. In contrast, those attributes showing the shallowest linear slope possess the least importance, because large changes in the independent variable correspond to relatively small changes in overall acceptance.

The linear regression which generates a measure of importance by its slope has an advantage over the correlation coefficient. The linear regression approach provides a quantitative measure of the degree to which acceptance changes with attribute change. If, in fact, there does exist a significant linear relation between attribute level and acceptance, for a variety of measures, then the linear slope can differentiate among the attributes, all of which may show equally high correlation. In contrast, the correlation coefficient limits itself strictly to the strength of a linear relation, but not to the quantitative nature of that linear relation.

Table 1.5 shows a database of attributes, for a meat sausage product. The panelists rated overall liking, as well as attribute liking. The correlation coefficients and the linear equations appear in Table 1.5. Note the additional information which one gleans by having developed the linear equation.

Relative Importance of Sensory (and Similar) Attributes

The previous sections dealt with attributes which exhibit linear relations with overall acceptance. What importance should we attach to sensory attributes, which often exhibit inverted U-shaped relations with overall acceptance? For instance, if we systematically vary the amount of sugar in coffee, and instruct consumers to rate both sweetness and liking, we will uncover an inverted U-shaped relation between perceived sweetness (the independent variable), and overall liking (the dependent variable). As noted previously, neither the correlation coefficient nor the linear regression line applies in this case, because the relation fails to exhibit linearity. Any forced fit of the straight line relation to an essentially curvilinear relation will simply generate an incorrect measure.

For sensory attributes, the researcher must consider the curvilinear relation between attribute level and liking, when trying to quantify importance. If we step back for a moment to reconsider the meaning of a straight line as a measure of importance, we can develop the following definition: "Relative importance of an attribute corresponds to the magnitude of change in acceptance (or other criterion variable) which occurs with unit changes in the independent variable". Given this definition, we can now

TABLE 1.5
(A) PARTIAL DATABASE OF SAUSAGE PRODUCTS

Product	Like Total	Like Appear	Like Color	Like Aroma	Like Flavor	Like Spicy	Like Salty	Like Smoky	Like Texture
201	39	48	36	46	55	50	46	27	48
202	13	18	20	23	10	12	12	17	16
203	38	65	44	57	51	47	52	46	65
204	32	57	47	26	25	35	31	38	38
205	29	40	37	42	55	50	36	42	51
206	37	74	49	55	61	52	46	45	69
207	42	63	40	60	67	60	52	55	62
208	26	58	35	47	35	50	29	42	39
209	20	28	31	33	12	12	10	16	36
210	47	61	55	52	54	60	55	52	71
211	43	65	45	67	60	55	47	50	71
212	49	71	59	65	72	78	65	69	81
Importance Rating	--	55	57	61	77	65	79	66	71

(B) CORRELATIONS AND EQUATIONS RELATING OVERALL LIKING TO ATTRIBUTE LIKING

Attribute Liking	Correlation (R)	Overall Liking = A + B (Attribute Liking)
Appearance	0.84	0.53
Color	0.88	0.89
Aroma	0.82	0.62
Flavor	0.88	0.46
Spiciness	0.89	0.51
Salty	0.96	0.62
Smoky	0.84	0.59
Texture	0.92	0.53

Conclusions

1. Unit increases in color acceptance generate the highest marginal increases in liking.
2. The direct rating of importance does not parallel the correlations with liking, or the slope of the line relating attribute liking to overall liking.

Test Conditions

40 panelists (Southfield, Michigan) each rating 12 sausages in rotated order, and rating them using a 0-100 scale. Then each panelist rated importance of attributes on a 0-100 scale.

develop a measure of importance for all types of variables; those which show linear relations with acceptance, and those which do not.

Figure 1.3 shows a prototypical curve relating acceptance to attribute level. Note that the definition above does not limit itself to a straight line. Rather, it pertains to any systematic relation between two variables. If the relation follows an inverted U-shaped parabola, how can we measure unit changes in sensory attribute level? For a straight line, the unit change equals the slope of the line, which remains constant. However, for nonlinear relations, such as that shown in Fig. 1.3, we do not have a straight line.

From basic calculus, we can measure the rate of change of one variable (e.g., overall acceptance) as a function of the change of another variable (e.g., sensory attribute), by computing the first derivative of the function. For a straight line defined by the following equation (Eq. 1.2):

$$\text{Acceptance} = A + B\ (\text{Attribute Level}) \tag{1.2}$$

we define the first derivative as (Eq. 1.3):

$$B = \text{slope of the line} \tag{1.3}$$

In the more complicated case, where a parabola governs the relation, we can define the relation by the following equation (Eq. 1.4):

$$\text{Acceptance} = A + B\ (\text{Attribute}) + C\ (\text{Attribute})^2 \tag{1.4}$$

We can derive this relation by straightforward, curve-fitting procedures, where the dependent variable equals the acceptance rating, and where we use two independent variables (the attribute and the squared value of the attribute).

The first derivative, or rate of change of acceptance with respect to the attribute, looks like the following (Eq. 1.5):

$$B + 2C\ (\text{Attribute}) \tag{1.5}$$

The foregoing equation tells us that the rate of change of liking with respect to the attribute (namely, the relative importance value) does not remain constant, as it did for the simple linear case (where it equalled B, a constant). Rather, relative importance changes as the attribute level changes. Depending upon the coefficients of the equation and on the value that the attribute assumes, the relative importance value can increase, decrease, or even become zero.

A glance at Fig. 1.3 will reveal why this occurs. If we draw the tangent or slope at any point, we will find that the tangent changes. At the optimum point, the tangent appears as a flat line, or slope of 0. Miniscule changes at the optimum level correspond to virtually no change in acceptance. On the other hand, as we diverge further and further from the optimum, the absolute value of the slope or tangent at that level grows increasingly larger, suggesting that small changes in an attribute at those less-than-optimal points will correspond to substantial changes in acceptance.

The foregoing analysis thus suggests that, for the sensory attributes, relative importance obeys different rules, compared to attributes which exhibit linear relations with acceptance. Depending upon the optimally acceptable level for that attribute, the attribute may exhibit a great deal of importance, or very little importance.

As an example of the measurement of relative importance by means of the absolute value of the derivative, consider the results shown in Table 1.6. The panelists rated the flavor intensity of a cherry flavored beverage

TABLE 1.6
PARTIAL DATABASE—CHERRY CARBONATED BEVERAGE

Product	Like Overall	Darkness	Aroma	Sweet	Tart	Cherry Flavor	Off Taste	Quality	Natural
1	63	40	49	57	60	68	45	52	48
2	57	37	39	63	42	55	47	46	43
3	42	44	49	41	67	66	50	39	40
4	50	44	52	48	55	55	51	39	39
5	57	39	43	56	57	68	49	45	43
6	55	41	41	68	44	60	45	47	44
7	50	38	46	44	60	58	46	46	48
8	52	42	42	47	49	46	46	46	41
9	53	40	42	60	55	63	43	43	42
10	53	38	42	60	45	54	51	40	33
11	41	39	44	35	70	62	57	31	39
12	44	41	45	42	47	46	41	42	40
13	60	35	38	60	53	63	43	53	48
14	51	38	35	63	45	53	48	44	40
15	45	37	37	42	60	53	47	42	40
16	46	41	40	48	46	43	46	43	40
17	58	38	44	55	56	64	44	44	44
18	53	37	40	53	52	51	41	46	44
19	53	38	50	55	61	58	46	48	44
20	51	38	38	51	53	56	45	44	42
21	54	42	38	61	46	57	43	48	37
22	29	42	45	31	61	47	56	32	37
23	50	38	40	53	70	72	54	45	42
24	38	38	39	53	38	36	53	30	28
25	58	39	41	58	56	63	49	49	48

Test Conditions: 100 panelists. 2 Markets (Omaha, Jacksonville)
Each panelist evaluated 15 of 25 prototypes in randomized order, using a 0-100 scale.

using a 0-100 point rating scale. For each of 25 beverages, the panelists assigned profile ratings to overall liking, sweetness, tartness, flavor intensity, and other attributes respectively. Table 1.6 shows the database generated for this study. Note that the products differ in terms of attribute ratings. Table 1.7 shows the equations relating each attribute to overall acceptance, as well as the first derivative of the equation. In most instances that we need a quadratic function (namely, a parabola) to relate liking to an attribute. Thus, for these attributes relative importance will vary as a function of the attribute level. The bottom of Table 1.7 shows the relative importance values at five different attribute levels. We use the absolute value of the first derivative to eliminate negative numbers, so that importance always take on positive values.

TABLE 1.7
(A) EQUATIONS RELATING SENSORY ATTRIBUTES TO OVERALL LIKING—ON AN ATTRIBUTE BY ATTRIBUTE BASIS

CHERRY FLAVORED DRINKS

Schematic Equation: $\text{Liking} = K_0 + K_1\,(\text{Attribute}) + K_2\,(\text{Attribute})^2$

Parameters	K_0	K_1	K_2	Multiple R^2
1. Sweetness	−31.3	2.67	−.020	.66
2. Tartness	−56.9	4.17	−.040	.20
3. Cherry Flavor	−21.2	2.14	−.015	.33

(B) RELATIVE IMPORTANCE = ABSOLUTE VALUE OF THE FIRST DERIVATIVE OF LIKING WITH RESPECT TO ATTRIBUTE

Schematic Equation: $\text{Importance} = \left| K_1 + 2K_2\,(\text{Attribute}) \right|$

Relative Importance (Numbers In Table)

Attribute	Level				
	30	40	50	60	70
1. Sweetness	1.47	1.07	0.67	0.27	0.13
2. Tartness	1.77	0.97	0.17	0.63	1.43
3. Cherry Flavor	1.24	0.94	0.64	0.34	0.04

Note: | | = Absolute Value

Researchers in food science and marketing know that acceptance does not simply vary as a function of one attribute alone. Instead, everyday observation will quickly reveal that acceptance varies as a function of two or more independent variables. For instance, consider the case of coffee, to which one adds both sugar and milk. As the amount of sugar increases, acceptance first increases, peaks, and then drops down. Similarly, as the amount of milk increases, acceptance again follows an inverted U-shaped curve. Furthermore, when we add these two variables simultaneously to coffee we find that the sugar and milk in the coffee interact with each other. The optimum level for sugar developed in the presence of a low level of milk may differ (often substantially) from the optimum sugar level in the presence of a high level of added milk. The relation follows a surface, rather than a curve. The surface appears like a mountain, shown schematically in Fig. 1.4

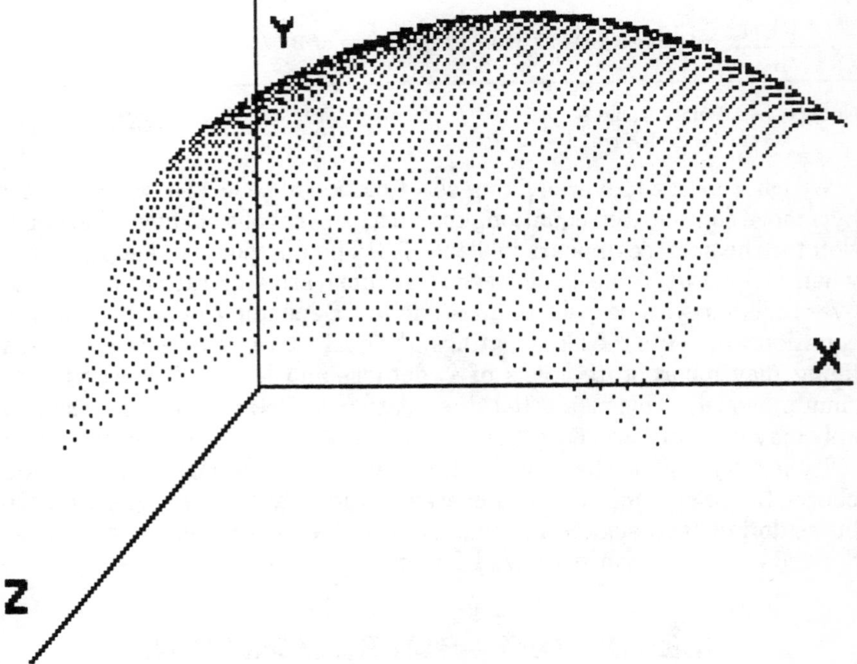

FIG. 1.4. EXAMPLE OF A SURFACE RELATING ATTRIBUTE LEVEL TO LIKING.
Here the tangent to the surface (namely, a line or a plane) provides the measure of importance.

TABLE 1.8
STANDARD EQUATION RELATING ACCEPTANCE TO ATTRIBUTE (OR FORMULA) LEVEL
—2 VARIABLES (A, B)—

Liking $= K_1A + K_2B$	(Linear)
$+ K_3AB$	(Cross Term)
$+ K_4A^2 + K_5B^2$	(Squares or Parabolic Terms)

Rate of Change of Liking With Respect to Attributes:

(1) With respect to "A" (Holding B constant)

$$\frac{\delta \text{ Liking}}{\delta A} = | K_1 + K_3(B) + 2K_4(A) | \} \text{ Importance of A}$$

(2) With respect to "B" (Holding A constant)

$$\frac{\delta \text{ Liking}}{\delta B} = | K_2 + K_3(A) + 2K_5(B) | \} \text{ Importance of B}$$

Note: $| \, |$ = Absolute Value
δ = partial derivative

We can represent overall liking as a function of several attribute levels by a more complicated equation, known as a parabolic surface. The equation for the surface appears in Table 1.8. The key point to keep in mind when looking at Table 1.8 concerns the derivative or rate of change of overall liking with respect to an attribute. Depending upon the specific equation which fits the liking ratings, the derivative for sweetness versus liking may incorporate levels of sweetness and levels of cherry flavor simultaneously. This means that the relative importance of sweetness not only may vary with sweetness level, but also with level of other attributes.

Table 1.9 presents the equation for overall liking versus sweetness and cherry flavor strength for the beverage. Note that the two sensory attributes do interact, suggesting that the relative importance of sweetness depends as well upon perceived flavor.

CASE HISTORY—STICK MARGARINES

Background

In order to illustrate some of the principles underlying the measurement of relative importance we will consider a case history pertaining to

TABLE 1.9
LIKING OF CHERRY FLAVORED BEVERAGE

—A Equation Using Sweetness and Cherry Flavor
—B Relative Importance at Various Levels

(A) Liking = −60.5 + 2.16 (Sweetness) − 0.03 (Sweetness^2)
+ 1.38 (Cherry) − 0.02 (Cherry^2)
+ 0.025 (Sweetness × Cherry)
($R^2 = 0.88$)

(B) Relative Importance of Sweetness =

| 2.16 − 0.06 (Sweetness) + 0.025 (Cherry) |

RELATIVE IMPORTANCE OF SWEETNESS
(Numbers in Body of Table)

		CHERRY LEVEL			
		40	50	60	70
	40	0.76	1.01	1.26	1.51
	50	0.16	0.41	0.66	0.91
SWEETNESS	60	0.44	0.19	0.06	0.31
LEVEL	70	1.04	0.79	0.54	0.29

RELATIVE IMPORTANCE OF CHERRY FLAVOR

Relative Importance of Cherry Flavor =

| 1.38 − 0.04 (Cherry) + 0.025 (Sweetness) |

		CHERRY LEVEL			
		40	50	60	70
	40	0.78	0.38	0.02	0.42
	50	1.03	0.63	0.23	0.17
SWEETNESS	60	1.28	0.88	0.48	0.08
LEVEL	70	1.53	1.13	0.73	0.33

Note: | | = Absolute Value

stick margarine. The details of this case provide the reader with an idea of how one can give priority to attributes in a variety of ways.

The Fryman Corporation manufactures stick margarines, and has done so for the past fifty years. Over that period it has introduced a number of different products into the market. Tastes for margarine have changed since Thomas Fryman began business in the mid 1930's. Consumer awareness of salt as a key health factor generated a large business in low salt and salt-free margarines. Tom Fryman, son of the founder, developed a number of entries in the margarine market, as well as developing a relatively prosperous co-packing operation (private label) for supermarkets.

TABLE 1.10
ARRAY OF TEST FORMULATIONS FOR STICK MARGARINE STUDY

Prototype	Flavor Type	Flavor Level	Color Level
1	A	H	H
2	A	H	M
3	A	H	L
4	A	L	H
5	A	L	M
6	A	L	L
7	B	H	H
8	B	H	M
9	B	H	L
10	B	L	H
11	B	L	M
12	B	L	L
13	C	H	H
14	C	H	M
15	C	H	L
16	C	L	H
17	C	L	M
18	C	L	L
19-20 CONTROLS	[in-market products]		
	A,B,C = 3 Different Margarine Flavors	High Vs. Low	High, Medium, Low

In 1978 the marketing group at Fryman Corp. decided to market a reduced salt product. In order to do so they commissioned three well-established flavor houses to supply them with improved prototype margarine flavors, to which R&D at Fryman Corp. would add different levels of salt, in an attempt to keep a low salt level, but at the same time maximize consumer acceptance.

Early development work suggested the need to test an array of different product formulations, representing various flavor types and levels, along with different salt levels. The total number of prototypes came to 18, along with two controls (see Table 1.10).

Test Specifics

The test required a home use evaluation of the products, to insure that the consumers would serve the margarine products to the family, as well as cook with it. Furthermore, for many products, home use testing allows the consumer to experience the product in a variety of contexts. Margarines (and other additives) enjoy use in baking, cooking, as a spread on breads/crackers, as well as a flavor enhancer for vegetables.

The consumers comprised margarine users in four markets. Altogether, 200 consumers participated. Each consumer evaluated 4 margarines, over a 4 week period. This generated a total of 800 evaluations (200 consumers × 4 products = 800 ratings), or approximately 40 ratings per product. Although in conventional marketing research terms a base size of 40 seems low, in terms of "representativeness", the early stage nature of this study (a screening evaluation) and the large number of prototypes needed for testing provided a valid rationale to minimize the total panel size. Otherwise, as the marketing research director realized, the cost to field the study could become too expensive.

In order to accomplish the test objectives, the director of marketing research recommended that field services from four markets spread across the U.S. and recruit the consumers to participate, with a total of 65 per market (to end up with 50). Furthermore, the director of marketing research recognized that she could secure the best possible data if prior to the actual home use evaluations the panelists who would participate could have a chance to evaluate one stick of margarine under supervised conditions. In this way the panelist would understand the scale, understand the attributes, and an attending interviewer could answer any questions which arose.

Margarines possess a variety of sensory characteristics. In order to tap these characteristics, the marketing research director suggested a list of attributes which would encompass appearance, aroma, taste/flavor, texture, and image evaluations. The final set of attributes used for the evaluation appears in Table 1.11. Each panelist rated the attributes using one of two scales. For liking attributes, the panelist used an anchored scale, beginning at 0 (to denote dislike extremely), going through 50 (to denote neutrality), and then going up to +100 (to denote like extremely). For the remaining attributes, the panelists used a similar 0-100 point anchored scale, beginning at 0 (to denote none of the characteristic at all present in the margarine sample) up to 100 (to denote an extreme amount). The anchored scale allows for discrimination, and reduces any ambiguity in the evaluations. Panelists find the scale easy to understand and to use, and can assign ratings using the scale, for a wide variety of attributes.

TABLE 1.11
LIST OF RELEVANT ATTRIBUTES FOR
STICK MARGARINE STUDY

Appearance
- Liking
- Color Depth
- Smooth vs. Rough

Aroma
- Liking
- Strength
- Buttery

Taste/Flavor
- Liking
- Buttery
- Salty
- Sweet
- Cheese-Like
- "Fresh"

Mouthfeel/Texture
- Liking
- Oily
- Coats Mouth
- Melts Slowly vs. Quickly
- Light vs. Heavy
- Smooth vs. Grainy/Lumpy

Overall/Image
- Liking
- Purchase Intent
- Unique
- Nutritious
- High Quality
- Margarine-Like vs. Butter-Like

TABLE 1.12
ATTRIBUTE RATINGS OF STICK MARGARINES*

	LIKING					IMAGE				SENSORY					
Product	Overall	Color	Aroma	Flavor	Texture	Quality	Unique	Nutritious	Natural	Oily	Buttery	Light	Yellow	Hard	Sweet
101	57	63	66	60	67	68	66	55	66	59	64	66	67	57	50
102	62	53	60	62	61	62	56	57	59	69	70	68	59	71	43
103	44	55	58	54	60	60	63	53	66	59	65	65	60	58	40
104	60	52	56	54	62	61	49	46	58	66	67	65	51	64	65
105	59	56	63	62	66	64	55	47	62	61	67	69	56	64	48
106	75	56	66	69	69	68	55	55	66	63	67	66	52	61	49
107	51	54	59	56	61	71	65	58	66	62	64	63	55	65	43
108	58	61	55	61	60	67	61	57	65	68	62	61	66	68	58
109	72	49	64	63	55	67	58	52	66	63	69	63	54	61	53
110	63	57	58	61	59	60	51	53	59	76	67	66	56	76	63
111	69	49	55	64	56	59	49	44	58	64	65	69	59	59	56
112	45	61	56	52	58	66	60	51	60	69	61	61	59	69	41
113	61	64	62	66	66	66	61	55	60	70	57	61	59	71	57
114	66	48	60	56	62	64	56	51	64	67	69	75	48	65	49
115	68	49	58	63	59	59	53	46	63	56	65	68	56	59	65
116	59	63	62	57	69	71	71	57	68	56	66	66	67	54	55
117	68	56	64	64	66	67	58	59	67	62	59	65	58	64	59
118	70	55	66	68	65	65	59	47	64	66	71	76	50	64	44
Importance**	62	67	66	89	76	94	35	93	75	22	74	81	59	31	64

*Only data from the 18 test prototypes appears in this table.
**For liking ratings, panelists scaled importance of good color, etc.
For sensory ratings, panelists scaled right level of yellowness, etc.

Data Base Of Ratings

The data base of ratings appears (in part) in Table 1.12. The key observations to make include the fact that the panelists appeared able to discriminate among the various samples. Furthermore, note the direct rating of "importance assigned using a 0-100 point scale.

Developing Measures of Relative Importance— Direct Rating Of Importance

This section develops and considers the different measures of importance. The first measure considered comprises the direct ratings, which appear again in Table 1.12. Note the following:

(1) The attribute liking ratings and the image ratings score highest in terms of relative importance on a direct rating basis.

(2) The sensory attributes score intermediate in terms of relative importance. [The actual question that the panelist answered consisted of the following phrase "Please rate how important you feel that the manufacturer deliver a margarine with the right amount of . . . (e.g., sweetness). 0 = not important, do not care, 100 = extremely important, care very much"].

(3) The negative sensory attributes (e.g., has an oily texture) score very low. This leads one to believe that when it comes to sensory attributes the consumers have an extremely difficult time understanding the concept of "relative importance" as an attribute that they have to scale. They automatically assign a value to the sensory characteristic that they would find most acceptable.

Correlation Of Attribute Rating With Overall Liking

The second analysis consists of the correlation between overall liking and each attribute. To do this we look at all of the prototypes tested (Table 1.12), on a product by product basis, for each attribute, and then correlate the attributes with overall liking. These correlations appear in Table 1.13, in the third column (column 1 shows the attributes, column 2 the direct rating of importance). Note the pattern, which we discussed previously; the partwise liking ratings and the image ratings correlate highly with overall acceptance. On the other hand, a simple linear correlation fails to demonstrate any importance for many of the sensory attributes, although it does suggest that perceived sweetness and lightness may exhibit some degree of importance.

Straight Line Equations Relating Attribute Liking to Overall Acceptance

The third analysis consists of developing straight line relations between

TABLE 1.13
COMPARISON OF MEASURES OF RELATIVE IMPORTANCE STICK MARGARINE

Attribute	Self-Rated Importance	Correlation with Liking	Linear Slope Relating Attribute Liking to Overall Liking
Liking of			
Color Appearance	67	−0.40	−0.68
Aroma	66	0.41	0.93
Taste/Flavor	89	0.78	1.39
Texture	76	0.10	0.24
Sensory			
Oily	22	0	0
Buttery	74	−0.16	−0.24
Light	81	0.43	0.89
Yellow	59	−0.42	−0.66
Hard	31	0	−0.12
Sweet	64	0.43	0.46

overall liking and the liking of each attribute. These straight line equations also appear in Table 1.13, in the fourth column (showing the slope). The straight line relation suggests that unit increases in acceptance of flavor correspond to fixed increases in overall acceptance. The rank order of importance of attributes developed by the straight line method differs from the rank order developed by the correlation, for the following reasons:

(1) Two attributes may exhibit similar correlation coefficients versus overall liking, but yet exhibit different slopes. If so, then according to the correlation coefficient, these two attributes should exhibit the same relative importance. On the other hand, according to the linear slope, they will exhibit different relative importance values.

(2) Attributes which exhibit low R values, or low slopes (these generally go together) probably do not exhibit any linear relation with acceptance at all. By using only the correlation coefficient the investigator knows only some of the story. By developing the straight line equation, the relation becomes clearer, however, because the investigator can get a better feeling as to the magnitude of the relation between attribute level and acceptance.

Developing Curves Relating Attributes Level and Liking

This section provides the reader with an additional example of how relative importance varies with attributes, in a continuously changing fashion. Table 1.13 suggests that most of the sensory attributes fail to vary in a simple straight line fashion with overall liking, and so according to conventional measures their relative importance value plunges. The liking attributes emerge as most important.

For the various sensory attributes, we can develop a parabolic surface relating attribute level, the square of attribute level and pairwise interactions to overall acceptance. This equation appears in Table 1.14. The equation provides the reader with an idea of how liking might vary in a nonlinear fashion with attribute level and with interactions among attribute levels. In addition, and to make comparison easier between the linear and the nonlinear models, we have put the R squared values for the linear model next to the results in Table 1.14. In this way, the reader can see how much more one can accomplish by relating liking to attributes by nonlinear (e.g. parabolic) curves.

TABLE 1.14
EQUATION RELATING OVERALL LIKING OF STICK MARGARINE TO SWEETNESS YELLOWNESS, OILINESS

$$\text{Liking} = -273.62 + 13.49\,(\text{Sweetness}) - 0.0932\,(\text{Sweetness})^2 - 0.0077\,(\text{Yellow})^2 + 0.0208\,(\text{Oiliness})^2 - 0.0507\,(\text{Sweetness}) \times (\text{Oiliness})$$

$R^2 = 0.76$ (All terms significant in the equation) (quadratic equation)

Relative Importance

Sweetness = $|\ 13.49 - 0.1864\,(\text{Sweetness}) - 0.0507\,(\text{Oiliness})\ |$

Yellowness = $|\ -0.0154\,(\text{Yellowness})\ |$

Oiliness = $|\ 0.0416\,(\text{Oiliness}) - 0.0507\,(\text{Sweetness})\ |$

Liking = $91.9 + 0.48\,(\text{Sweetness}) - 0.74\,(\text{Yellowness}) - 0.26\,(\text{Oiliness})$
$R^2 = 0.39$ (linear equation)

Note: | | = Absolute Value

The first observation to emerge from Table 1.14 concerns the improvement in the predictability of overall liking by using linear and square terms in the equation. This means that, for the most part, the sensory attributes behave in a curvilinear fashion versus overall liking (e.g., as the attribute increases, liking first increases, then peaks at an optimum, and then decreases). Thus, simply using the straight line model will not do justice to the sensory attributes, despite their importance.

The second observation concerns the relative importance value. The previous sections suggested that to develop a measure of relative importance we have to measure the rate of change of liking with respect to the attribute level (namely, the slope or tangent), at a specific attribute level. Furthermore, the rate of change will not remain constant throughout the total range. To accomplish the objective of measuring the rate of change, we compute the first derivative, which appears in Table 1.14 as well.

TABLE 1.15
RELATIVE IMPORTANCE OF SWEETNESS, OILINESS AND YELLOWNESS BASED UPON RATE OF CHANGE OF LIKING VERSUS ATTRIBUTE LEVEL*

SENSORY ATTRIBUTE LEVEL			IMPORTANCE OF ATTRIBUTE*		
Sweet	Yellow	Oily	Sweet	Yellow	Oily
40	40	40	4.01	0.62	0.36
40	40	60	2.99	0.62	0.47
40	40	80	1.98	0.62	1.30
40	60	40	4.01	0.92	0.36
40	60	60	2.99	0.92	0.47
40	60	80	1.98	0.92	1.30
40	80	40	4.01	1.23	0.36
40	80	60	2.99	1.23	0.47
40	80	80	1.98	1.23	1.30
60	40	40	0.28	0.62	1.38
60	40	60	0.74	0.62	0.55
60	40	80	1.75	0.62	0.29
60	60	40	0.28	0.92	1.38
60	60	60	0.74	0.92	0.55
60	60	80	1.75	0.92	0.29
60	80	40	0.28	1.23	1.38
60	80	60	0.74	1.23	0.55
60	80	80	1.75	1.23	0.29
80	40	40	3.45	0.62	2.39
80	40	60	4.46	0.62	1.56
80	40	80	5.48	0.62	0.73
80	60	40	3.45	0.92	2.39
80	60	60	4.46	0.92	1.56
80	60	80	5.48	0.92	0.73
80	80	40	3.45	1.23	2.39
80	80	60	4.46	1.23	1.56
80	80	80	5.48	1.23	0.73

*Using the absolute value of the first (partial) derivative at that sensory profile

Finally, to get a feeling of relative importance, we have selected three different sensory levels for each attribute, and computed the numerical value of the derivative at each level, which appears in Table 1.15. From Table 1.15, the reader can assign rank orders of relative importance to the various attributes. However, one must bear in mind that the relative importance of attributes will vary, depending upon the relation between attribute level and liking, and depending upon the level of the attribute. Two attributes may have equal importance at one point on the intensity scale, but diverge dramatically at a much higher or much lower attribute level.

An Overview To The Margarine Study

The examples just cited for margarine suggest a variety of ways of developing measures of relative importance. One can see, however, that no single measure suffices. Depending upon the particular operation used to develop relative importance measures, the attribute importance will vary.

Rather than trying to develop a single measure, the margarine manufacturer has to recast the question into a different form. One key question concerns the relative impact of different product problems of defects. Which product problems will most dramatically diminish acceptance? By correlating attribute liking with overall liking (or by fitting a straight line to the relation), we can answer that question, and put the different attribute liking into a single order.

Another question that the manufacturer might ask concerns the importance of sensory attributes as they quantitatively affect acceptance. To do this requires the development of the curvilinear relation between attribute level and overall liking. At that point, it becomes a straightforward task to measure how liking changes with attribute level, provided one knows the attribute level and the magnitude of change. The researcher can now compare sensory attributes to each other (provided the researcher does know the level of each attribute).

Both approaches, developing measuring straight line relations versus developing curvilinear relations, differ dramatically from the rated level of attribute importance. The former (curve fitting) considers the behavioral relation between attribute level and liking. The latter (rated importance) considers an attitudinal measure; the panelist's own reaction, which may or may not accord with actual behavior.

A SECOND CASE HISTORY—WHEAT CHIPS

The Dougherty Corporation manufactures a variety of snack foods.

During the past five years senior management, led by Pat Dougherty, daughter of the founder and current president, made a conscious decision to pursue new opportunities in the snack food industry, concentrating their efforts on salted snacks (e.g., wheat and rye chips).

A detailed marketing research evaluation of the current market, for needs and gaps, revealed interest in a "health-oriented" salted snack category. Consumers said that they wanted the flavor of conventional chips, but that at the same time they wanted other health-oriented benefits, e.g., low calorie.

R&D developed a variety of prototypes for the snack chip, which provided various product benefits that could support a health positioning. Some of the product variants included salt reductions, oil/fat reductions, vitamin fortification and improved grain blends to capitalize on the allure of natural grain products.

TABLE 1.16
KEY ASPECTS FOR THE SNACK CHIP STUDY

A. STIMULI

16 snack chips systematically varied in color, cook process, oil

B. ATTRIBUTES

Appearance: Liking, Darkness, Size, Thickness

Aroma: Liking, Strength

Taste/Flavor: Liking, Overall Intensity, Salty, Off Taste

Texture: Liking, Crispy, Oily

Overall: Liking, Purchase Intent, Freshness

All attributes scaled using a 0-100 point scale, anchored at both ends.

C. ACTIVITIES

Panelists pre-recruited to participate.

Panelists show up, ready for a 4 hour session.

Panelists learn to use 0-100 point scale through a warmup exercise.

Panelists evaluate 12 products, on attributes.

Each panelist evaluates the products in a unique order.

Panelists rate ideal snack chip on same attributes.

Panelists rate annoyance for product defects.

Panelists fill out an attitude and usage questionnaire on snacks.

Table 1.16 presents the test specifics, including attributes, number of products and activities during the evaluation. Note that after having an opportunity to rate each of the products on an extended list of attributes, the panelists then rated the degree to which they would feel "annoyed" if the product had specific defects. They rated annoyance using a 0-100 point scale, where zero represented "not annoyed" with the product defect, whereas 100 represented "extremely annoyed" with the product defect.

Results Of Annoyance Rating Of Entire Panel

The average annoyance ratings appear in Table 1.17. Keep in mind that attributes which annoy panelists represent attributes to which the panelist attends, and which influence acceptance. In contrast those attributes which fail to annoy the panelists represent attributes without any dramatic importance, whatsoever. Defects, or failure to achieve an optimum level, in the minds of these panelists, do not reduce acceptance.

Several key trends emerge from the results shown in Table 1.17:

(1) Attributes do exhibit different levels of annoyance or relative importance. Panelists seem able to differentiate attributes on the basis of annoyance.

(2) As one might expect, flavor problems lead the list, suggesting that defects in flavor attributes would generate the greatest negative reaction. Thus, flavor appears to represent the most important dimension (or set of dimensions), followed by texture.

(3) The panelists rated four levels of defects (much too much, slightly too much, slightly too little, much too little). The pattern of annoyance ratings suggest an asymmetry in annoyance. For flavor, under-delivering a specific sensory attribute generates more negatives than over-delivering.

(4) Depending upon the specific attribute, slightly too much may either generate almost as much annoyance as does "much too much" or much less annoyance. For some attributes, a little defect generates as much annoyance as a severe defect. In contrast, for other attributes (e.g., saltiness) the greater defect (under- versus over-delivery on that attribute) the greater the annoyance, and the more important the problem.

Do Different Subgroups In The Population Generate Similar Patterns

In this study on snack chips, the researcher had an opportunity to "break out" the annoyance ratings into ratings assigned by consumers of different ages (e.g., teen versus adult), and different markets (e.g., east coast versus midwest). To what extent do these different consumers exhibit different profiles of annoyance? Asked in another way, do these consumers exhibit different hierarchies of importance?

TABLE 1.17
ANNOYANCE RATINGS FOR SNACK CHIPS—FULL PANEL*

Appearance	
Much Too Small	65
Too Small	48
Too Large	20
Much Too Large	25
Much Too Thin	31
Too Thin	25
Too Thick	42
Much Too Thick	57
Much Too Light	25
Slightly Too Light	22
Slightly Too Dark	42
Much Too Dark	74
Taste/Flavor	
Far Too Salty	71
Slightly Too Salty	34
Not Quite Salty Enough	59
Far Too Little Salt	73
Much Too Strong Wheat Flavor	60
Slightly Too Strong Wheat Flavor	32
Slightly Too Weak Wheat Flavor	40
Much Too Weak Wheat Flavor	72
Texture	
Much Too Dry	44
Too Dry	28
Too Oily	37
Much Too Oily	81

Scale: 0 = No Annoyance
100 = Extreme Annoyance At Defect

*Panel Size = 100

As part of the study, the panelists had to fill out an attitude and usage questionnaire, which probed their food preferences, their health interests, and classified them by their age, sex, occupation, etc. This type of information can prove helpful in dividing a consumer panel into smaller, possibly more homogeneous groups. Based upon the responses to the questions, the researcher divided the panel into three sets of subgroups; by age (younger versus older), by market (east coast versus midwest) and by self rated health concern (high concern with health versus low concern with health).

Table 1.18 shows the average annoyance rating assigned to several appearance, flavor and texture attributes. Note that in Table 1.18 we have the attributes listed down the side. Each column in Table 1.18 corresponds to a specific subgroup of consumers in the population.

As we can see from Table 1.18, the annoyance values do vary from one consumer group to another. To the marketing research and to R&D, these differences suggest that at least on an attitudinal basis consumer segments do differ from each other. What health-oriented consumers feel important, non-health oriented consumers may rate as unimportant.

USING RELATIVE IMPORTANCE MEASURES IN SENSORY QUALITY CONTROL WORK

Background

This section deals with the use of measures of relative importance to quantify the seriousness of differences between prototype products and target products. These target products may represent either in-market products that a manufacturer wants to imitate or reproduce, or the target products may constitute the gold standard or best plant run of a product.

Typically, manufacturers try to achieve a standard of quality that leads to consumer loyalty. In most manufacturing operations, quality slippage can occur in any of a dozen or more different points in the operation. If the manufacturer can measure the sensory (or physical) characteristics of the target product and the prototypes emerging from the manufacturing stages, it becomes possible to quantify departures from the desired product. On the other hand, one does not necessarily know whether these departures constitute true problems, or simply minor differences to which a consumer might attend, but which in the total scheme make little or no difference to acceptance.

A Case History—Nut Snacks

The Moon Corporation manufactures nut snacks, comprising of processed, high quality nuts, prepared in a specially developed sweet and salty

TABLE 1.18
ANNOYANCE RATING—BY SUBGROUPS

	User Group		Age of Consumer	
	Brand A	Brand B	Adult	Teen
Appearance				
Much Too Small	63	67	65	65
Too Small	51	46	51	45
Too Large	22	19	23	17
Much Too Large	32	21	29	22
Much Too Thin	33	30	32	30
Too Thin	26	24	25	25
Too Thick	45	40	47	36
Much Too Thick	58	56	65	48
Much Too Light	29	23	25	26
Slightly Too Light	26	18	22	23
Slightly Too Dark	44	41	40	44
Much Too Dark	73	74	71	76
Taste/Flavor				
Far Too Salty	71	71	71	71
Slightly Too Salty	38	32	36	33
Not Quite Salty Enough	61	58	60	57
Far Too Little Salt	73	73	74	72
Far Too Strong Wheat Flavor	61	59	70	50
Slightly Too Strong Wheat Flavor	36	28	35	27
Slightly Too Weak Wheat Flavor	37	43	38	42
Much Too Weak Wheat Flavor	68	76	84	60
Texture				
Much Too Dry	47	43	40	49
Too Dry	31	27	28	28
Too Oily	35	38	36	38
Much Too Oily	80	82	81	81

Scale: 0 = No Annoyance
100 = Extreme Annoyance At Defect

sauce. The nuts emerge from the process with a unique, highly acceptable flavoring. Over the past seven years, the Moon Corporation has developed eleven snack products using this process and has seen its franchise and profits grow by a factor of 5000%.

As one part of its product development and quality assurance program, the Moon Corporation has a sensory panel comprising 10 judges rate the sensory characteristics of the nut products. These judges have had sufficient experience with the products so that they generate reliable data. Furthermore, their ratings correlate with objective physical measures. For instance, quite often they detect texture problems, in terms of "crunchiness". Generally these deviations also reveal themselves as changes in objective measures of "texture" as well. Over the years, since the inception of the program, Richard Moon, the president and founder, has come to rely upon the panel as a key tool in quality.

Given the reliability and validity of the panel ratings, the only remaining question for Richard Moon concerned the relative importance of departures. The panel ratings for various production runs versus that of the gold standard appears in Table 1.19. Note the differences between the production runs and the gold standard. Do these differences mean changes in acceptance? Should Bonnie, the quality control director at the Moon Corporation "pull" these products, or in fact do the departures from the gold standard reflect relative insignificant variations?

Approach

In order to answer the foregoing questions, Moon commissioned a study in which consumers rated the same products as the experts had rated. The consumers evaluated the products, rating each on a battery of attributes. Afterwards, the consumers rated the relative importance of departures from their ideal product by means of annoyance ratings. These ratings of relative importance also appear in Table 1.19.

In looking at the ratings shown in Table 1.19, one can do the following analyses:

(1) Evaluate the magnitude of difference between the "gold standard" product and the prototype. This measures the deviation, but it does not indicate the importance of that deviation.

(2) Look at the relative importance of the deviation, as rated by level of annoyance. The consumers rated the degree to which they felt annoyed for departures of attributes from the ideal (or, here, from the gold standard). These ratings of annoyance provide the quality control director with a better sense about which departures may lead to product problems, and which may not.

TABLE 1.19
DEPARTURES OF NUT SAMPLES FROM THE GOLD STANDARD AND THE CRITICALITY OF THOSE DEPARTURES (VIA ANNOYANCE RATINGS)

	ATTRIBUTES RATED BY CONSUMERS				
	Darkness	Solid Color	Flavor Level	Oiliness	Hardness
Annoyance Rating	45	39	71	48	53
Gold Standard Rating	58	84	64	37	59
Product A					
Profile rating	42	21	91	49	33
Difference from gold standard	16	63	27	12	26
Relative criticality*	7	24	19	5	13
Product B					
Profile rating	36	41	39	61	79
Difference from gold standard	22	43	25	24	20
Relative criticality*	9	16	17	11	10

*Defined as the product of three terms: difference between the product and the gold standard (absolute), relative importance via annoyance, and the decimal 0.01 as a multiplier

(3) Judge criticality by combining departures from the gold standard with relative annoyance to obtain a single index number.

AN OVERVIEW

Consumers do behave as if the attributes of products possess different levels of relative importance. One can measure importance using a variety of techniques, including self-rated importance of attributes, correlations with liking, degree of annoyance, or rate of change liking with actual level of the attribute.

In any product development program, researchers should keep in mind two ways to think about relative importance:

(1) Relative importance of different sense dimensions. Here, one should focus attention on either liking of the attributes (e.g., liking of appearance, liking of aroma, liking of taste/flavor, liking of texture), or else self-ratings of importance (namely, estimated importance of good flavor versus good appearance, versus good texture versus good aroma). For these liking attributes, panelists have a fairly good idea of relative importance. They seem to know whether or not flavor possesses more importance than texture. However, the consumers probably rank order the sense dimensions in a very general fashion, and not on specific attributes within a sense dimension.

(2) Relative importance of attribute levels. Here, we find that consumers probably cannot accurately rate relative importance. One cannot easily explain the meaning of "importance" for a sensory attribute (e.g., importance of sweetness intensity). In this case, the researcher can use one of two techniques. The first consists of developing a curve relating attribute level to liking and then determining the change in liking corresponding to a unit change in attribute level. The second consists of presenting consumers with specific product defects and measuring their stated degree of annoyance. High levels of annoyance correspond to high importance levels, whereas low levels of annoyance correspond to low importance levels.

REFERENCES

AHTOLA, O. T. 1975. The vector model of preferences: An alternative to the Fishbein model. J. Marketing Res. *12,* 52-59

BECKWITH, N. E. and LEHMANN, D R. 1975. The importance of halo effects in multi-attribute models. J. Marketing Res. *12,* 265-275.

CLYDESDALE, F. M. 1984. The influence of colour on sensory perception and food choices. In *Developments In Food Colours—2* (J. Walford, ed.), Elsevier Applied Science Publishers, London, 75-112.

CSISZAR, J. 1949. Comparative butter scorings using various score systems. XIIth International Dairy Congress, Stockholm, *4,* 470-479.

EHRENBERG, A. C. 1953. On Plank's rational method of grading food quality. Food Technol. *7,* 188.

FENTON, F. A. 1957. Judging and scoring milk. U.S. Department of Agriculture, Farmer's Bulletin, *2111,* 1-20.

FISHBEIN, M. 1963. An investigation of the relationship between beliefs about an object and attitudes toward that object. Human Relations *16,* 233-240.

HARPER, R. and BARON, M. 1950. Studies of the nature of subjective judgments in cheese-grading. J. Dairy Res. *17,* 329-335.

HARPER, R. 1950. Some psychological aspects of craftsmanship in dairying. J. Occupational Psych. *24,* 230-238.

HAUSER, J. R. and URBAN, G. T. 1979. Assessment of attribute importances and consumer utility functions: von Neumann-Morgenstern theory applied to consumer behavior. J. Consumer Res. *5,* 251-262.

HEELER, R. M., OKECHUKU, C. and REID, S. 1979. Attribute importance: contrasting measurements. J. Marketing Res. *16,* 60-63.

HOLBROOK, M. B. and HUBER, J. 1979. Separating perceptual dimensions from affective overtones: An application in consumer aesthetics. J. Consumer Res. *5,* 272-283.

HOPKIN, J. W. 1950. A procedure for quantifying subjective appraisals of odor, flavor and texture of foodstuffs. Biometrics *6,* 1-16.

HUTCHINGS, J. B. 1977. The importance of visual appearance of foods to the food processor and the consumer. In: *Sensory Properties Of Foods* (G. G. Birch, *et al.* ed.) pp. 27-40. Applied Science Publishers, Rippleside.

JAKOBSEN, F. 1949. Rational grading of food quality. Food Technol. *3,* 252-254.

LEARSON, R. J. and RONSIVALLI, L. J. 1969. New approach for evaluating the quality of fishery products. Fish. Indus. Res. *4,* 249-259.

MACHER, L. 1957. Evaluation of beer by points and by comments. Brauwelt *97B,* 373-383.

MAKOWER, R. U. 1950. Methods of measuring the tenderness and maturity of processed peas. Food Technol. *4,* 403-408.

MCFAYDEN, S. C., STILES, M. E., BERG, R. T. and HAWKINS, M. H. 1973. Factors affecting consumer acceptance of meats. Canad. Inst. Food Technol. J. *6,* 219-225.

MOSKOWITZ, H. R. 1981. Sensory intensity versus hedonic functions: Classical psychophysical approaches. J. Food Quality, *5,* 109-138.

MOSKOWITZ, H. R. 1984. Relative importance of sensory factors to acceptance: Theoretical and empirical analyses. J. Food Quality *7,* 75-90.

MOSKOWITZ, H. R. and CHANDLER, J. W. 1977. New uses of magnitude estimation. In: *Sensory Properties Of Foods* (G. G. Birch *et al.* ed.), Applied Science Publishers, Rippleside, 189-209.

NESLIN, S. A. 1981. Linking product features to perceptions: Self-stated versus statistically revealed importance weights. J. Marketing Res. *18,* 80-86.

SHEPPARD, D. 1955. Description terms and points systems for rating food qualities. Food Res. *20,* 114-117.

SZCZESNIAK, A. S. 1971. Consumer awareness of texture and of other food attributes. J. Texture Stud. *2,* 196-206.

SZCZESNIAK, A. S. 1972. Consumer awareness of and attitudes to food texture. II. Children and teenagers. J. Texture Stud. *3,* 206-217.

SZCZESNIAK, A. S. and KAHN, E. L. 1971. Consumers' awareness of and attitudes to food texture. I. Adults. J. Texture Stud. *2,* 280-295.

TARVER, M. and SCHENK, A. M. 1958. Statistical development of objective quality scores for evaluating the quality of food products. Development of the scoring scales. Food Technol. *3,* 127-131.

TILGNER, D. J. 1964. How to improve sensory quality scoring procedures by objective weighting. Food Manuf. *39,* 34-39.

WEISS, J. 1972. Results of investigations on the influence of possible sensory quality criteria on sensory quality of apple juice. Confructa *17,* 68-76.

WEITZ, B. and WRIGHT, P. 1979. Retrospective self insight about the factors considered in product evaluations. J. Consumer Res. *6,* 280-294.

WIESMAN, C. K. 1971. Identifying and controlling product quality attributes—using preference taste panels. Food Prod. Devel. 21-22.

CHAPTER 2

TESTING FOODS ON A BLIND VERSUS BRANDED BASIS

INTRODUCTION

In much of the scientific literature associated with sensory analysis and product testing, we read of "blind" product tests. Consumers have the opportunity to evaluate the products without benefit of identification. This identification might constitute minimal information, such as the product name, or might comprise an extensive amount of information, such as the name, the package, and either advertising and/or point of purchase promotion material.

The marketing researcher, marketer and sensory evaluation expert can learn a lot by comparing the profiles of products tested on a blind versus on a branded basis. Consumers who assign attribute ratings to products without knowing the identification of the products often dramatically change their ratings when they know the identification of the product.

This chapter presents a detailed case history of blind versus branded product evaluation, using instant coffees as the category.

CASE HISTORY—INSTANT COFFEES

Background

In the U.S., the instant coffee market constitutes an extremely competitive product category, with a limited number of major entries and a limited number of manufacturers. The manufacturers spend a great deal of money on product development, on advertising and on promotion. In the marketer's terms, instant coffees represent a "high involvement category". Consumers know what they like and often vocally and forcefully make their brand preferences known.

The study reported below took into consideration a total of 13 U.S. instant coffee products, some caffeinated, others decaffeinated. Interest focused on the profile of attribute ratings one would obtain from consumers, who evaluated the coffees three ways: blind (no identification at all), by image (name alone) and branded (with full identification, including bottle, point of purchase promotional material, etc.).

TEST SPECIFICS

Instant Coffees Tested In The Study

Table 2.1 presents a list of the instant coffees tested in this study. Note that the list of coffees adequately covers the range of available coffees in the U.S. market.

TABLE 2.1
PRODUCTS TESTED IN THE INSTANT COFFEE STUDY

COFFEE	TYPE	MANUFACTURER
Maxwell House	Regular	General Foods
Maxim	Decaf.	General Foods
Brim	Decaf.	General Foods
Yuban	Regular	General Foods
Sanka	Decaf.	General Foods
Taster's Choice	Regular	Nestle
Taster's Choice	Decaf.	Nestle
Nescafe	Regular	Nestle
Nescafe	Decaf.	Nestle
Sunrise	Chicory	Nestle
Folger's	Regular	Proctor & Gamble
High Point	Decaf.	Proctor & Gamble
Kava	Acid Free	Borden Foods

Attributes Evaluated By Consumers

In order to develop the database for comparing blind and branded ratings, the research director who organized the study selected a set of 27 attributes, shown in Table 2.2. Note that some of these attributes pertained to acceptance, some to nonevaluative sensory dimensions (e.g., perceived flavor strength), whereas other attributes probed "image" dimensions. These image dimensions constitute more complex characteristics of products, calling into play sensory, liking and cognitive reactions to the product. Attributes requiring the panelist to rate "appropriateness" for specific usage occasions represent just such image dimensions.

TABLE 2.2
PHASES OF COFFEE EVALUATION AND ATTRIBUTES RATED IN EACH PHASE

PHASE I—EVALUATION OF THE COFFEE POWDER	
Liking	Liking of Appearance
Sensory	Darkness
Sensory	Fine vs. Grainy
Sensory	Strength of Aroma
Liking	Liking of Aroma
PHASE II—EVALUATION OF THE COFFEE (WITHOUT ANYTHING ADDED)	
Sensory	Amount of Oily Film
Sensory	Darkness of Coffee
Sensory	Strength of Aroma in Cup
Liking	Liking of Aroma in Cup
PHASE III—ADDITION OF MILK, SWEETENER, ETC. TO COFFEE	
Liking	Purchase Interest
Sensory	Strength of Flavor
Sensory	Smoothness of Flavor
Sensory	Bitterness
Image	Fresh Brewed Taste
Sensory	Aftertaste
Liking	Liking of Aftertaste
Image	Richness of Flavor
Image	Perceived Amount of Caffeine
Image	Suitability for After-Meal Drink
Image	Perceived Quality
Image	Hearty/Robust
Image	Familiarity with Coffee
Image	A Coffee to Wake Up To and Get Started With
Image	A Coffee to Linger Over and Savor Its Taste
Image	A Coffee to Sit With and Just Relax
Image	A Coffee to Serve to Guests
Liking	A Coffee that the Respondent Would Want to Switch To

Scale Used

To facilitate data collection, the research director suggested a simple, anchored 0-100 point scale. Panelists have little or no trouble understanding the use of a 0-100 scale. To insure comprehension, the field service director actually conducting the evaluations had the panelists participate in a short, warmup exercise, in which the panelists rated the perceived area of geometrical shapes, using the 0-100 scale. (Such warmup exercises serve two purposes. First, they relax the consumers. Consumers do not necessarily know what to expect when they embark on a product evaluation test. A short experience with a bank of geometrical shapes for which they have to rate perceived size, relaxes the panelists and gives them confidence. Second, the interviewer can discover those particular panelists who have difficulty with numbers, usually a small percentage of the panel in general.)

TABLE 2.3
PANELIST ACTIVITIES DURING THE INSTANT COFFEE AUDIT STUDY

One week prior to study, an interviewer recruited the panelists.
The panelists had to drink instant coffee.
By pre-arrangement, half the panel comprised men, the other half comprised women.

At the session:

Step 1— Orientation in scaling by a short warmup exercise (evaluation of circles for perceived area).

Step 2— Evaluation of first product (blind test basis)

Phase 1—Evaluation of coffee powder
Phase 2—Evaluation of the prepared, black coffee
Phase 3—Evaluation of coffee after sweetener, whitener added

Step 3— Panelist ratings check for consistency and comprehension by an attending interviewer.

Step 4— Steps 2-4 repeated. Each panelist evaluated a randomized 9 products of the full set of 13.

Step 5— Attitude and usage questionnaire answered. The questionnaire dealt with coffee purchase and usage habits.

Step 6— Coffee names rated on full set of 27 attributes, without presence of coffee product. Each panelist rates the same 9 of 13 coffees, on an "image" basis.

Step 7— Lunch served.

Step 8— Panelists rate the same 9 coffees (of 13), on a branded basis. They spooned out the coffee from the actual jars, prepared it, and rated it in the same way that they had rated the "blind" product (Step 2-4).

Step 9— Panelists paid and dismissed.

Activities During The Test

The activities followed a carefully choreographed sequence, as described in detail in Table 2.3. Note that in view of the extensive number of coffees included in the test, the sessions required a total of 7 hours. Fielding studies of this type requires weekend tests, when the panelists can devote a full day of their time. (One can shorten the test to several hours, by testing fewer products, both blind and branded.)

Initial Results—How Do The Coffees Rate Overall Blind Versus Branded Versus Image

Do coffee ratings for overall acceptance differ on a branded versus blind

TABLE 2.4
COMPARISON OF BLIND AND BRANDED RATINGS OF COFFEES ON PURCHASE INTENT (0-100 SCALE)

	Blind	Branded	Image (Name Only)	Impact of Brand (Branded—Blind)
Maxwell House	37	59	63	22
Folgers	42	56	62	14
Taster's Choice (Regular)	39	54	57	15
Nescafe (Regular)	37	41	40	4
Maxim	29	46	47	17
Sunrise	38	35	37	−3
Yuban	40	42	44	2
Kava	27	25	34	−2
High Point	39	43	40	4
Sanka	36	49	49	13
Taster's Choice (Decaffeinated)	42	52	52	10
Nescafe (Decaffeinated)	45	43	40	−2
Brim	40	50	48	10

basis? Table 2.4 shows that they do. Coffees such as Maxwell House Instant do not score highly on a blind basis but do extraordinarily well branded, in terms of purchase intent.

As Table 2.4 shows, the branding effect varies from coffee to coffee, with the effect probably a function both of the basic level of acceptance of the coffee "blind", and the amount of advertising which goes into developing a high quality brand image.

In this study the researchers also tested the consumer reaction to "image", defined as the name of the coffee alone, without benefit of package or product. Most consumers had some degree of familiarity with the coffees, due to the high involvement nature of the category. We find from Table 2.4 (last column) that the image or name generates similar ratings of acceptance as does the branded product. The implication which emerges suggests that for the instant coffee category, image and brand may override actual product acceptance per se. Knowledge of the product identity may suffice to turn a modestly acceptable instant coffee into a highly acceptable one.

Attribute Profiles—Entire Panel

In this coffee "category audit" the consumers had a chance to rate many relevant dimensions on the 0-100 scale. We can compare the scale ratings, on a blind versus a branded basis to determine which attributes vary dramatically.

As an example of the results, consider the profiles for three major "regular" coffees, shown in Table 2.5. These coffees include Maxwell Instant, Taster's Choice Regular and Folger's. Table 2.6 shows the profiles for three decaffeinated coffees; Sanka, Taster's Choice Decaffeinated and High Point.

Note that the image characteristics most affected by advertising (e.g., high quality, good for waking me up and getting me started) show the greatest susceptibility to branding. The sensory characteristics (e.g., strength of flavor) also show some susceptibility to branding, but not as much. Finally, keep in mind that the products vary in the effect of branding. Some coffees such as Sanka and Maxwell House, show much greater sensitivity to brand identification.

Do Users of Brands Show Enhanced Branding Effects

The instant coffee study contained ratings assigned by a wide spectrum of coffee consumers. Thus, it became feasible to segment the data into reactions from different user groups. The consumer panel allowed the researcher to look more in depth at four different user groups, each of

TABLE 2.5
COMPARISON OF BLIND AND BRANDED RATINGS
FOR 3 MAJOR REGULAR INSTANT COFFEE BRANDS

	MAXWELL HOUSE			FOLGERS			TASTER'S CHOICE		
	Blind	Branded	Brand Effect	Blind	Branded	Brand Effect	Blind	Branded	Brand Effect
Appearance									
Darkness	47	60	+13	70	75	+ 5	29	43	+14
Fine vs. Grainy	53	53	0	67	67	0	67	66	– 1
Aroma (Dry)									
Strength	39	56	+17	52	67	+15	57	63	+ 6
Liking	41	55	+14	47	59	+12	45	51	+ 6
Aroma (In Cup)									
Strength	48	63	+15	59	66	+ 7	52	61	+ 9
Liking	43	58	+15	51	59	+ 8	48	55	+ 7
After Drinking									
Flavor Strength	49	65	+16	60	68	+ 8	56	61	+ 5
Smooth	48	59	+11	48	58	+10	49	55	+ 6
Richness	42	59	+17	50	62	+12	46	55	+ 9
Amount/Caffeine	41	58	+17	49	59	+10	40	54	+14
Heavy/Robust	42	62	+20	51	61	+10	44	56	+12
Wake Up	38	59	+21	43	57	+14	43	52	+ 9
Linger Over	33	52	+19	38	51	+13	35	46	+11
Purchase	37	59	+22	42	56	+14	39	54	+15

TABLE 2.6
COMPARISON OF BLIND AND BRANDED RATINGS FOR 3 KEY DECAFFEINATED INSTANT COFFEE BRANDS

	SANKA			HIGH POINT			TASTER'S CHOICE DECAFFEINATED		
	Blind	Branded	Brand Effect	Blind	Branded	Brand Effect	Blind	Branded	Brand Effect
Appearance									
Darkness	54	63	+ 9	57	73	+16	31	44	+13
Fine vs. Grainy	49	60	+11	58	54	– 4	64	64	0
Aroma (Dry)									
Strength	39	52	+13	43	55	+12	45	53	+ 8
Liking	39	46	+ 7	45	44	– 1	46	52	+ 6
Aroma (In Cup)									
Strength	52	60	+ 8	51	57	+ 6	54	58	+ 4
Liking	43	50	+ 7	45	47	+ 2	46	53	+ 7
After Drinking									
Flavor Strength	52	58	+ 6	54	57	+ 3	51	59	+ 8
Smooth	47	53	+ 6	47	51	+ 4	54	57	+ 3
Richness	42	50	+ 8	44	48	+ 4	47	53	+ 6
Amount/Caffeine	42	22	–20	44	35	– 9	37	19	–18
Heavy/Robust	39	50	+11	44	48	+ 4	45	53	+ 8
Wake Up	36	39	+ 3	42	38	– 4	41	42	+ 1
Linger Over	31	40	+ 9	35	37	+ 2	37	44	+ 7
Purchase	36	49	+13	39	43	+ 4	42	52	+10

which comprised 40 or more individuals: users of Maxwell House, Folger's, Taster's Choice and Sanka. The 40 + consumer base provided a sufficient number of ratings to insure a reliable sample.

It should come as no surprise that panelists "uprate" their own brand. Table 2.7 shows the ratings of acceptance for each brand, on a blind versus a branded basis, for the users of the brand versus the full panel.

TABLE 2.7
HOW INSTANT COFFEE USERS RATE THEIR OWN PRODUCT
(Attribute = Purchase Intent)

Maxwell House Users Rating Maxwell House	
Blind	32
Branded	74
Brand Effect	+42
Total Panel Rating Maxwell House	
Blind	37
Branded	59
Brand Effect	+22
Folgers Users Rating Folgers	
Blind	42
Branded	66
Brand Effect	+24
Total Panel Rating Folgers	
Blind	42
Branded	56
Brand Effect	+14
Taster's Choice Users Rating Taster's Choice	
Blind	40
Branded	72
Brand Effect	+32
Total Panel Rating Taster's Choice	
Blind	39
Branded	54
Brand Effect	+15

Some key observations emerging from Table 2.7 include the following:

(1) On a blind basis, consumers may or may not like their own brands.

(2) The degree of liking of a blind product may depend upon two things; a basic degree of liking of one's product and a recognition of one's product (blinded) leading to a partial branding effect. This occurs especially strong for Folger's (which has dark crystals and which Folger's users can recognize).

(3) The brand effect shows specificity. The jump in acceptance due to branding occurs for one's own product and rarely affects other products in the category. Thus, for instant coffee, the repeated advertising reveals its effect in a specific, targeted fashion.

We can obtain some further understanding of the brand effect by considering how a particular user group (Instant Maxwell) rate the characteristics of their own coffees and a competitor (Folger's). Table 2.8 shows the ratings of the coffees on both a blind and a branded basis. As Table 2.8 clearly shows, the branding effect, and the enhancement due to the consumer's actual usage, occurs for sensory attributes as well as for acceptance. Those sensory attributes most subject to the branding effect include the flavor attributes. Appearance attributes (darkness of granules) show the least brand effect. We might tentatively conclude that branding has a greater effect for the more nebulous sensory impressions of flavor, and lesser impact on the concrete sensory impressions of product appearance.

Do All Consumers Show Similar Sensitivity To Branding

The previous sections revealed that the overall panel of consumers showed strong brand sensitivity, especially to the better known instant coffees. Furthermore, the user segments showed dramatic sensitivity to branding. Does this sensitivity apply to all consumers? What about consumers with different "value structures" (e.g., consumers who shop for convenience and price, rather than for flavor)?

As part of the instant coffee study, the consumers filled out an attitude and usage questionnaire which probed some of their values. Questions in the attitude and usage portion dealt with relative importance of flavor versus price. From this question, it became possible to isolate a group of consumers who shopped primarily for price versus a larger group of consumers who shopped for flavor. Another question in the attitude and usage portion of the study involved brand loyalty. It became possible to isolate individuals who stated that they often switched versus those who stated that they felt themselves highly brand loyal to one product.

Do these consumer segments, which differ in their psychological atti-

TABLE 2.8
HOW INSTANT MAXWELL HOUSE USERS RATE THEIR OWN PRODUCT (BLIND VS. BRANDED) AND HOW THEY RATE FOLGERS (BLIND VS. BRANDED)

	INSTANT MAXWELL HOUSE			FOLGERS		
	Blind	Branded	Brand Effect	Blind	Branded	Brand Effect
Dry In Cup						
Like Appearance	48	70	+22	60	66	+ 6
Darkness	82	72	+10	64	73	+ 9
Aroma Strength	46	65	+19	47	67	+20
Aroma Liking	45	66	+21	46	60	+14
Prepared Black						
Darkness	61	74	+13	72	74	+ 2
Aroma Strength	52	71	+19	55	65	+10
Aroma Liking	45	71	+26	49	57	+ 8
Prepared With Additives						
Purchase Interest	32	74	+42	41	56	+15
Flavor Strength	52	71	+19	55	71	+16
Smoothness	46	66	+20	42	55	+13
Better	44	36	− 8	37	43	+ 6
Fresh Brewed	37	61	+24	37	56	+19
Aftertaste	52	44	− 8	50	45	− 5
Liking of Aftertaste	32	48	+16	38	40	+ 2
Richness	42	68	+26	46	62	+16
Amount of Caffeine	45	59	+14	44	55	+11
For After Meals	35	69	+34	41	58	+17
Quality	40	71	+31	44	62	+18
Hearty	41	71	+30	43	64	+21
Wake Up	34	71	+37	37	55	+18
Linger Over	27	67	+40	33	47	+14
Sit & Relax	28	69	+41	33	48	+15
Serve To Guests	29	71	+42	35	50	+15

tudes, show similar types of brand sensitivity? Table 2.9 shows the rating of overall acceptance for the various groups. Note that those individuals who call themselves flavor shoppers show substantially less absolute brand sensitivity than those individuals who call themselves "price shoppers". Furthermore, from other data in this study, it emerged that those who call themselves "brand loyal" show greater branding effects than those who call themselves "switchers". Thus, to some extent, brand value varies as a function of one's attitudes toward the category, in addition to varying as a function of the coffee in particular and one's brand purchase history.

TABLE 2.9
HOW TWO ATTITUDINAL SEGMENTS OF COFFEE CONSUMERS RATE INSTANT COFFEES—BLIND VS. BRANDED

	FLAVOR ORIENTED			PRICE ORIENTED		
Coffee	Blind	Branded	Brand Effect	Blind	Branded	Brand Effect
Maxwell House	39	57	+18	42	51	+ 9
Folgers	42	56	+14	39	57	+18
Taster's Choice (Regular)	42	55	+13	23	53	+30
Nescafe (Regular)	38	39	+ 2	37	39	+ 2
Maxim	31	45	+14	25	47	+22
Sunrise	37	34	− 3	28	11	−17
Yuban	41	44	+ 3	42	32	−10
Kava	25	25	0	25	22	− 3
High Point	38	45	+ 7	38	34	− 4
Sanka	37	49	+12	31	43	+12
Taster's Choice (Decaffeinated)	42	49	+ 7	39	57	+18
Nescafe (Decaffeinated)	44	43	− 1	54	42	−12
Brim	38	51	+13	44	43	− 1
Average Brand Effect*			(7.5)			(12.1)

*Computed by taking the mean of the absolute values of the brand effect

AN OVERVIEW—COFFEES

Consumers do not buy products on a blind basis. Rather, they buy products that they have heard about or used previously. Much of the product testing work involves blind product evaluation, in which the researcher makes every effort to remove sources of product identification. For product alterations (e.g., changed level of components), this works fine because the product would have the same brand name for both treatments.

When evaluating the comparative acceptance or sensory properties of different products, however, researchers and marketers should test the products both blind and branded. Testing products blind provides only half the picture. The results on a blind basis may not emerge on a branded basis. Yet, testing products branded alone may fail to highlight intrinsic product differences because the branding effect overshadows other product characteristics.

Unfortunately, most product manufacturers do not develop data banks of information such as that shown above for instant coffees. Manufacturers field many tests with products, some blind and others branded, and can weave together the data from the different tests to develop hypotheses and tentative conclusions about the effect of branding. Regrettably, however, the data from these disparate tests comes from different panels of consumers, from studies implemented for a variety of different reasons, using different (and often not comparable) stimuli, with different lists of attributes. The task of weaving this aggregation of data together to provide a coherent picture requires talent and faith to bridge many gaps in the database. In contrast, studies in which the researcher provides both sets of blind and branded stimuli to the same individual, with the same scale and with the same attributes, can go a long way towards alleviating the problem.

Key benefits for an integrated data base, such as that developed for instant coffee, include the following.

(1) An understanding of the performance of all key products in the category, blind and branded.

(2) An understanding of the effect of the brand, on the total panel and on users of the specific products.

(3) A measure (over time) of changes in product acceptance, branded acceptance and the gap between the blind product performance versus the branded product performance (blind product supported by imagery and advertising).

CASE HISTORY—PASTA SAUCES—TRACKING PRODUCTS OVER TIME

Background

The Schimoler Foods Company manufactures a variety of tomato based products, and has done so since 1953. Starting from a small, one plant factory operation located in Texas, Schimoler Foods grew into a multimillion dollar concern. In 1971, a major U.S. conglomerate bought a controlling share of Schimoler Foods, and took its pasta sauce national, with a great deal of fanfare and ensuing success.

Schimoler Foods markets three major lines of pasta sauce; a conventional, tomato based product, a meat flavored product, and a full zesty, hearty, spicy tomato flavored product. Since its acquisition by the multinational conglomerate, Schimoler Foods has consistently advertised these three products on prime-time television, varying the level of advertising and varying the trade promotions on a year-by-year basis.

In 1974, Gregory Schimoler, son of the founder and then (as now) chief executive officer, recommended that his marketing research staff evaluate product acceptance, primarily on a blind basis, both for the Schimoler products and for major competitors. Schimoler wanted to measure his products' strengths and weaknesses to insure ongoing product consistency and acceptance. After three years with the program, Schimoler noticed that his products had changed in quality with consumer acceptance decreasing. Other competitor brands showed mixed patterns. Some increased, some decreased (Table 2.10)

During the initial marketing evaluation of the data after year 1 (1974), the marketing research director, Michael Merrier, suggested that consumers evaluate the pasta sauces both blind and branded, rather than just branded alone. Merrier recognized that whereas product acceptance might vary from year to year because of the nature of the product formulation, the effect of advertising could effectively cancel out the variation. By testing the pasta sauces both blind and branded, the marketing group could develop an idea of changes in product acceptance (and real characteristics), with versus without the impact of identification.

Table 2.11 presents the results of the blind versus branded evaluations for all the years (1978-1984) for the plain (red) pasta sauce. We also see the media dollars and promotion dollars spent by the competitors and by the Schimoler Company during that period.

Key insights emerging from Table 2.11 include the following:

(1) The Schimoler product declined in overall acceptance, on a blind basis, first rapidly, and then erratically (during the past several years). Recently it began to increase in acceptability.

(2) The competitors have tended to vary erratically in their blind product acceptance during the same period, not systematically, and not equally (either from year to year, or across products). This change in acceptance reflects product development activity which probably modified the product composition. Competitor A has showed the strongest and most consistent acceptance.

(3) The Schimoler product remained high in branded acceptance, despite variations in blind acceptance. We see here the great deal of brand equity developed for the Schimoler products, with this equity offsetting the decrease in quality.

(4) At the same time we see a gradual increase in branded product acceptance for one competitor, (A) suggesting that manufacturer A may have begun to reap the benefits of advertising and promotion programs.

Evaluations of products on a blind versus a branded basis helps the manufacturer track changes in product acceptance, based upon pure sensory cues (blind testing), as well as changes in product acceptance, based upon a combination of product and image cues (branded testing). Furthermore, one can correlate the brand impact with advertising dollars, as Table 2.12 shows, to develop a quantitative relation between advertising expenditure, and brand value. We can do this for Schimoler and its competitors' products. Table 2.12 shows the equation produced from the following ingoing assumption:

Brand value for the year depends upon advertising expenditures and promotion expenditures for the previous years. Here we hypothesize that the previous year's activity influences the current year's product test data.

AN OVERVIEW TO BLIND VERSUS BRANDED TESTING

This chapter presents a more comprehensive approach to the standard product evaluation. Traditional testing, concerning blind product tests alone, may provide incorrect information about products, vis-à-vis actual market performance. Consumers consume products which stimulate sensory characteristics. However, and just as important, these products also carry along with them emotional and cognitive "baggage" built up from consumer experience and advertising.

A testing program comprising blind versus branded products quickly provides the marketer and the product developer with an idea of which specific factors drive product acceptance. Do consumers attend to the product and disregard the advertising? Do both product and brand identification contribute equally to product acceptance and image characteristics? Or in fact, does branded evaluation, and the presence of imagery, overwhelm the product's sensory characteristics and thus dominate and drive acceptance? Only a systematic testing program can reveal which alternative governs a product.

Finally, by systematic evaluation of blind versus branded products over a period of several years, the marketer and quality control manager can develop norms for the product, tested under both blind and for branded

TABLE 2.10
HOW ACCEPTANCE AND TWO SENSORY ATTRIBUTES (FLAVOR STRENGTH, CONSISTENCY) VARY ON A YEAR-BY-YEAR BASIS FOR PASTA SAUCE
(NUMBERS IN TABLE = MEAN RATINGS FROM PANELS)

CODE/MANUFACTURER/VARIETY	1974 (50 Panelists)	1975 (61 Panelists)	1976 (48 Panelists)	1977 (67 Panelists)
Acceptance				
A—Schimoler (Red)	67	61	60	58
B—Schimoler (Meat)	78	70	68	69
C—Schimoler (Mushroom)	75	65	67	62
D—Competitor A (Red)	44	49	61	66
E—Competitor B (Red)	53	57	52	58
F—Competitor C (Red)	61	60	69	74
Flavor Strength				
A—Schimoler (Red)	55	52	50	49
B—Schimoler (Meat)	72	68	69	66
C—Schimoler (Mushroom)	64	60	61	57
D—Competitor A (Red)	37	41	57	64
E—Competitor B (Red)	59	63	61	64
F—Competitor C (Red)	59	56	67	68

TABLE 2.10 (Continued)
HOW ACCEPTANCE AND TWO SENSORY ATTRIBUTES (FLAVOR STRENGTH, CONSISTENCY) VARY ON A YEAR-BY-YEAR BASIS FOR PASTA SAUCE
(NUMBERS IN TABLE = MEAN RATINGS FROM PANELS)

CODE/MANUFACTURER/VARIETY	1974 (50 Panelists)	1975 (61 Panelists)	1976 (48 Panelists)	1977 (67 Panelists)
Consistency/Thickness				
A—Schimoler (Red)	45	47	51	46
B—Schimoler (Meat)	57	59	52	49
C—Schimoler (Mushroom)	58	55	50	47
D—Competitor A (Red)	36	45	62	63
E—Competitor B (Red)	50	53	48	55
F—Competitor C (Red)	63	59	64	69

Note: All panelists rated each attribute on a 0-100 point anchored scale

TABLE 2.11
PROFILE OF RED PASTA SAUCE BY YEAR
—Blind Vs. Branded Acceptance
—Brand Effect (Brand-Blind)
—Advertising Dollars (TV, Radio) and Print (Newspapers)

	1975	1976	1977	1978	1979	1980	1981	1982	1983	1984
Schimoler										
Liking (Blind)	61	60	58	55	56	58	61	67	69	71
Liking (Branded)	67	69	73	74	77	74	75	78	71	75
Brand Effect	+6	+9	+15	+19	+21	+16	+14	+11	+2	+5
TV/Radio $	3.2	2.5	2.9	3.1	3.2	3.1	3.4	2.9	2.9	2.9
Print $	2.1	1.7	2.6	2.5	2.8	2.9	3.1	3.0	3.1	3.2
Competitor A										
Liking (Blind)	49	61	66	68	72	75	72	73	71	75
Liking (Branded)	56	59	64	61	65	68	69	73	75	77
Brand Effect	+7	+2	+2	−7	+5	7	−3	0	+4	+2
TV/Radio $	1.1	1.2	1.1	0.9	1.1	1.2	1.1	1.4	1.6	1.7
Print $	0.2	0.3	0.2	0.4	0.1	0.2	0.3	0.7	0.8	1.1

TABLE 2.11 (Continued)
PROFILE OF RED PASTA SAUCE BY YEAR
—Blind Vs. Branded Acceptance
—Brand Effect (Brand-Blind)
—Advertising Dollars (TV, Radio) and Print (Newspapers)

	1975	1976	1977	1978	1979	1980	1981	1982	1983	1984
Competitor B										
Liking (Blind)	57	52	58	61	60	57	53	49	51	49
Liking (Branded)	64	66	65	68	71	66	70	64	66	65
Brand Effect	+7	+14	+7	+7	+11	+9	+17	+15	+15	+16
TV/Radio $	0	0	0	0	0	0	0	0	0	0
Print $	1.1	1.4	1.2	1.5	1.3	0.9	1.4	1.6	1.5	1.8
Competitor C										
Liking (Blind)	60	69	74	65	68	71	68	66	71	65
Liking (Branded)	68	74	78	77	73	74	72	77	72	74
Brand Effect	+8	+15	+4	+12	+5	+3	+4	+11	+1	+9
TV/Radio $	3.8	4.3	4.6	4.1	4.1	3.2	4.6	3.8	4.1	3.7
Print $	1.2	1.4	1.7	2.0	2.1	2.3	2.7	2.6	2.8	2.9

Note: All dollar expenditures shown on a relative basis by year's consumer price index.

TABLE 2.12
EQUATIONS SHOWING HOW BRANDED ACCEPTANCE RELATES TO BASIC PRODUCT ACCEPTANCE, (BLIND) AND DOLLARS SPENT TO ADVERTISE THE PRODUCT

%Change in Branded Liking = Rating (This year vs. last year)	PRODUCER			
		COMPETITOR		
	SCHIMOLER	A	B	C
Constant	4.83	−0.42	1.76	−0.08
% Change in "Blind" Liking Rating (This year vs. last year)	−0.72	0.72	0.56	0.01
% Change in TV ($) (Last year vs 2 years ago)	0.45	0.07	0.07	0.21
% Change in Print ($) (Last year vs. 2 years ago)	−0.30	0.04	−0.08	−0.03
R^2	0.44	0.49	0.44	0.76

Conclusions

Schimoler Foods— TV advertising a key in increasing branded liking. Blind liking not key.
Competitor A— Blind Liking Key.
Competitor B— Blind Liking Key.
Competitor C— TV Advertising Key.

conditions. One begins to get a feel for the types of scores products achieve in the category and can detect departures in acceptance, in either the upwards or the downwards direction. Finally, it becomes possible to uncover potential problems with a product in the market, when the product itself fails to generate sufficient acceptance blind, but where the branded product maintains acceptance. In that case, if one leaves the product problem uncorrected for a sufficiently long time, eventually the branded acceptance score will suffer as well. The testing procedure thus serves as an early warning system for product problems in the marketplace.

REFERENCES

ARCHIBALD, R. B., HAULMANN, C. A. and MOODY, C. E., JR. 1983. Quality, price, advertising, and published quality ratings. J. Consumer Res. *9,* 347-356.

ANDREWS, I. R. and VALENZI, E. R. 1971. Combining price, brand, and store cues to form an impression of product quality. Proceedings, 79th Annual Convention, American Psychological Association, 649.

DAY, G. S. 1969. A two-dimensional concept of brand loyalty. J. Advertising Res. *9,* 29-35.

JACOBY, J., OLSON, J. C. and HADDOCK, R. A. 1971. Price, brand name, and product composition characteristics as determinants of perceived quality. J. Appl. Psych. *55,* 577.

LAWRENCE, R. J. 1973. Consumer brand choice—a random walk? J. Marketing Res. *12,* 314-324.

GRAHN, G. L. 1969. NBD model of repeat-purchase loyalty: An empirical investigation. J. Marketing Res. *6,* 72-78.

MOSKOWITZ, H. R. and JACOBS, B. 1980. Ratio scaling of perception vs. image: Its use in evaluating advertising vs. product delivery. In: Current Issues & Research in Advertising (J. H. Leigh and C. R. Martin Jr., ed.) pp. 59-95. University of Michigan, Div. of Res., Ann Arbor, MI.

MAKENS, J. C. 1965. Effect of brand preference upon consumers' perceived taste of turkey. J. Appl. Psych. *49,* 261-263.

McCONNELL, J. D. 1968. The development of brand loyalty: An experimental study. J. Marketing Res. *5,* 13-19.

MONROE, K. B. 1976. The influence of price differences and brand familiarity on brand preferences. J. Consumer Res. *3,* 42-49.

MOSKOWITZ, H. R. 1979. Mind, body and pleasure: An analysis of factors which influence sensory hedonics. In: *Preference Behavior And Chemoreception* (J. H. A. Kroeze, ed.) pp. 131-148. Information Retrieval Ltd., London.

WHEATLEY, J. J. and CHIU, S. Y. 1977. The effects of price, store image, and product and respondent characteristics on perceptions of quality. J. Marketing Res. *14,* 181-186.

WHEATLEY, J. J., WALTON, R. G. and CHIU, S. Y. 1977. The influence of prior product experience, price and brand on quality perception. In: *Advances In Consumer Research,* Vol. 4. Association for Consumer Research, Ann Arbor, MI.

CHAPTER 3

MEASURING CONSUMER DISCRIMINATION ON ATTRIBUTES

INTRODUCTION

Product testers, marketing researchers and sensory analysts like to use many different attributes in their questionnaires. The attributes probe different areas of product characteristics. Typically, the researcher operates under the unspoken dictum that "the more the better."

Quite often questionnaires filled out by interviewers or consumers require that the panelist rate his or her reactions on 20 or more attributes. Besides requiring a great deal of panelist attention, such lengthy questionnaires may generate less valid data for the attributes appearing at the end of the questionnaire.

How does a research measure the "utility" of the various attributes? Do all attributes show equal ability to discriminate among products, or do some attributes discriminate better than do others? If the researcher can effectively measure discrimination ability among attributes, it becomes possible to pare down the number of attributes to a limited but more effective few. How to measure discrimination constitutes the topic for this chapter.

MEASURING DISCRIMINATION ABILITY

The first issue concerns the actual ability of an attribute to discriminate among products. Some attributes may do a better job than others in separating the products. However, despite the fact that products show wide ranges on some attributes and narrow ranges on others, the researcher has to keep the following issues in mind.

(1) The variability across products must achieve a moderate to high level. The attribute should generate inter-product variability, so that some products score low versus others which score high. On an absolute numerical basis, the scale thus must separate products.

(2) At the same time the variability across people must not become so high as to overshadow the variability across products. Stated somewhat differently, the scale must generate true product differences, and relatively low people differences within a product.

The Concept Of Analysis Of Variance

Statisticians who evaluate product differences often use techniques known generically as analysis of variance (or ANOVA). The ANOVA procedure decomposes the variability of ratings in a data set into components. Some of the variability occurs because of true product differences. Other variability emerges from random or error variability, separate from differences due to products. The analysis of variance techniques partition the variability in the data into the various contributors or sources of variation.

A CASE HISTORY USING THE ANOVA METHOD FOR MEASURING DISCRIMINATION

Palmer & Co., manufacturers of bread and rolls recently embarked on a program of line expansion. Under the leadership of its president, Steven Palmer, the company began to diversify its product line by an aggressive policy of product development.

During the course of research, it quickly became clear that one could instruct consumers to evaluate baked goods (e.g., bread and rolls) on a wide variety of attributes. For some attributes, the marketing researcher found a great deal of discrimination across products. For other attributes evaluated in the same session, the discrimination across products simply did not emerge.

Researchers at Palmer & Co., who had not done a great deal of research in the past, suggested that, prior to embarking on a long term, systematic consumer evaluation of products, they should evaluate the utility of the large attribute list. The marketing research director, Bill Rhia, recommended that based upon this research he would retain the most discriminating attributes, and eliminate the least discriminating ones.

Test Design

The test design required that the panelists rate a total of 6 different prototypes, each a variation on a basic butter roll. The panelists rated each butter roll on a wide variety of attributes. Table 3.1 shows the attributes (listed down the side). Note that the sequence of activities parallels the general test designs discussed in the previous chapters, namely, the panelist spends several hours evaluating a variety of products, on a variety of attributes.

Results

Table 3.1 also presents the averages, and the typical standard deviation for the various products, on the various attributes. As Table 3.1 shows, panelists can and do discern differences among the products using the 0-100 point scale, and seem to have little difficulty doing so.

TABLE 3.1
DATABASE FOR SWEET BUTTER ROLL STUDY

	Product						Typical Standard Deviation	F Ratio* Analysis of Variance
	101	102	103	104	105	106		
Appearance								
Liking	74	68	61	70	54	56	27	3.56
Large	75	63	73	81	60	55	20	11.99
Rich	66	71	66	69	49	57	25	4.65
Like/Shape	74	66	60	70	58	54	26	3.57
Aroma								
Liking	71	75	73	72	68	67	21	0.86
Strength	67	67	66	67	68	64	21	0.16
Flavor								
Liking	72	69	68	69	68	72	21	0.22
Buttery	58	61	54	57	61	70	25	1.82
Texture								
Liking	72	69	71	67	66	76	25	0.81
Hard/Outside	73	66	78	76	71	68	24	1.22
Hard/Inside	57	51	62	59	59	58	28	0.65
Moist	65	70	65	73	66	80	25	2.34

$$*\text{F Ratio} = \frac{\text{Variability Among Products}}{\text{Error Variability}} \quad \text{(5,216 Degrees of Freedom)}$$

Error Variability = Random Error + Panelist Differences

Panel = 42 consumers (category users, each rating all 6 prototypes)

In order to measure discrimination, the statistician at Palmer & Co. recommended running a one-way analysis of variance on the attributes. In this way, one could determine the degree to which the various attributes differentiated among the 6 prototypes.

Recall that the one-way analysis of variance partitions the variability into two sources; differences due to products, and random differences or error variability (generally due to panelist or intersubject differences). Table 3.1 also lists the results from the one-way analysis of variance, namely, the F ratio, which represents the ratio of two variabilities (due to product differences due to error). The higher the F ratio, the greater the discrimination among the products, on the scale.

Table 3.1 clearly indicates differences among attributes in terms of their discrimination ability. The sensory attributes vary, with appearance attributes exhibiting the most discrimination and the aroma attributes exhibiting the least discrimination. The liking attributes exhibit substantially lower discrimination. The reduced discrimination occurs because individuals differ among themselves in what they like. Thus, the denominator, representing "error" variability, really comprises two sources of variation; true error (random variation) and actual differences due to different points of view adopted by the different consumers.

HOW DISCRIMINATION ON ATTRIBUTES VARIES WITH EXPERIENCE

Background

The previous section illustrated a method for assessing discrimination ability on an attribute by attribute basis. This section shows how the researcher can use this procedure to compare different groups of consumers.

The Bellomy Group, Inc. owns several wineries in upper New York State. Over the past twelve years, it increased production of its varietal wines by an average of 30% per year. At the same time, its wines have achieved acceptance by a wide variety of consumers and wine experts.

As part of his product development program, Lacy Bellomy, the owner and chief executive officer, requires all members of his staff to participate in a six month "in-house" course on wine tasting. During this period, the participants become accustomed to wine tasting, learn the language and the nuances and generally become more or less "expertized" in the sensory analysis of wine.

Wine tasting at the Bellomy Group does not proceed in an informal, haphazard manner. Rather, at each session, the panelists sit down to evaluate about 3-4 wines, rating each on a variety of attributes using a scale. Originally, the scale used for each attribute consisted of a series of words, denoting gradations of a characteristic. In 1972, however, Lacy Bellomy suggested that the panelists use an anchored line scale and put their ratings as marks on the line. This procedure eliminated the use of numbers, but for subsequent analysis the project leader in sensory evaluation had to transform the line marks to a number equivalent to percentage of the scale used (from 0% at the low end, to 100% used at the high end).

Test Procedures

Although the sensory analyst at the Bellomy Group did not acquire the data discussed here as part of a specific study, the routine nature of the procedure for testing generated quite a substantial volume of data. The relatively constant test conditions and the frequent evaluation periods by the same people, of the same wines, allowed the generation of a matrix of ratings useful for this topic of experience versus discrimination.

Table 3.2 shows the test setup, in terms of the panelist activities and lists the attributes.

The data used for the analysis consisted of the following.

(1) Ratings on 6 sensory attributes, representing key dimensions for wine.

TABLE 3.2
SET UP FOR WINE TASTING STUDY

Panelists—	Experts at the winery (N = 10) and other employees from experts (N = 10).
Activity—	Panelists evaluate 2 wines per day for 4 days (total of 8 wines) Wines vary by variety All panelists use simple consumer terminology *but* experts re-define those words using their own terms as well.
Attributes—	Aroma Intensity Full Bodied Flavor Sweet Tart Bitter Astringent
Sample of Wines—Local varietal reds.	
Scale—	0-100 anchored at both ends
—	1 replicate per panelist per wine

(2) Ratings by a total of 20 individuals, 10 of whom had worked at Bellomy for 3 years or more, and who had familiarity with wine and wine testing (so-called "experts"). The remaining 10 had just joined the staff, either as food science professionals, or as clerical staff. None of the latter 10 had ever had any experience in wine tasting in particular, or in descriptive sensory evaluation in general.

Parenthetically, the reader should note that the sensory analyst balanced the total panel size. The original data base consisted of attribute ratings assigned by more than 45 people, over a six month period of time. However, in order to insure equal numbers of panelists in the "experienced" versus "non-experienced" groups, the sensory analyst matched individuals, to generate 10 matched individuals in each of two groups.

Results—Ratings of Wines on Attributes

Table 3.3 shows the results of the study, in terms of ratings of 8 wines on the six attributes, by the total panel and by the two subgroups (experience, nonexperienced/consumer). The mean ratings suggest slightly more differentiation among wines by the experienced panelists. However, we do not know the degree to which the experienced panelists show an increased level of discrimination.

The sensory analyst performed two sets of analyses of variance (both, one-way ANOVA); one for the experienced panel on each of the attributes and one for the nonexperienced panel. These values also appear in Table 3.4. They provide the reader with a measure of discrimination. Recall that the higher the F ratio, the greater the variation across products (namely, a measure of discrimination), and the smaller the random, or error variability. As Table 3.3 shows, the experienced panelists do generate higher F ratios. On the other hand, for some attributes, such as sweetness, the F ratios (or discrimination level) shown by nonexperienced panelists almost reaches that exhibited by experienced panelists. For attributes such as astringency, however, the experienced panelists show substantially more discrimination.

Probing Deeper Into The Reasons For Discrimination

The analysis of variance technique partitions the variability into the contributory sources; total variation, variation due to product differences and variation due to random error. We can use this partition to tell us more about our two groups of panelists and why they exhibit different results in the ratings. Do the more experienced panelists show higher discrimination ability because they see larger differences among the same wines? Or, do they discriminate better because these experienced panelists agree with each other (reducing the random error variability), but see no greater differences than do nonexperienced panelists. Both hypotheses could generate enhanced discrimination, but for different reasons. The former (perception of larger differences) means a change in perception, as a result of experience. The latter suggests a change in the use of the language.

TABLE 3.3
DATABASE OF RATINGS FOR WINE (EXPERTS & CONSUMERS) AND RESULTS OF A ONE-WAY ANALYSIS OF VARIANCE

Wine Number	Panel Group	Aroma Intensity	Full Bodied	Sweet-ness	Tart-ness	Astrin-gent	Bitter-ness
101	EXP.	42	48	33	69	86	63
	CON.	54	73	27	60	90	85
102	EXP.	42	51	37	47	78	71
	CON.	54	76	56	55	85	79
103	EXP.	53	63	29	53	71	65
	CON.	54	67	39	69	78	69
104	EXP.	51	52	46	71	81	64
	CON.	54	62	36	50	78	75
105	EXP.	43	43	43	64	63	56
	CON.	51	48	32	60	73	65
106	EXP.	51	58	33	58	68	46
	CON.	47	47	41	75	83	74
107	EXP.	44	40	59	65	85	65
	CON.	50	59	59	55	86	70
108	EXP.	45	39	57	63	66	52
	CON.	50	61	49	61	75	59
F Ratio From 1 Way Analysis Of Variance							
EXPERT		.57	1.59	1.99	1.02	2.79	1.51
CONSUMER		.09	1.55	1.56	.85	1.21	1.64

Degrees of freedom for analysis of variance
Between products—7 (8 Wines Tested)
Within (Error)—72
10 panelists, 8 wines, 1 judgment per panelist per wine

Table 3.4 presents the source of variance tables for each of the attributes for the two groups. Note that the table provides two measures; total sum of squares (effectively, the variation across all products and panelists), and the sum of squares and variability due to products (here, the larger the more the products differ).

Since the total sum of squares partitions into the variation due to products versus the variation due to error, we can look at the proportion of total variation (total sum of squares) due to product differences. The first ratio in Table 3.4 (sum of squares due to products, divided by total

TABLE 3.4
IN-DEPTH EVALUATION OF DISCRIMINATION—
WINE STUDY

A. BASIC TABLE FOR ANALYSIS OF VARIANCE

Source Of Variation	Sum Of Squares	Degrees Of Freedom	Mean Square	F Ratio
Between Products:	X	7	X/7	[X/7]/[Y/64]
Within Products (Error):	Y	64	Y/64	
Total	X+Y	71		

B. PROPORTION OF TOTAL VARIABILITY
DUE TO PRODUCT DIFFERENCES

	EXPERTS			CONSUMERS		
	Total Sum Of Squares [A]	Sum of Squares Due To Product Differences [B]	Ratio [B/A]	Total Sum Of Squares [A]	Sum of Squares Due To Product Differences [B]	Ratio [B/A]
Aroma Intensity	24897	1311	0.05	63004	497	0.01
Full Bodied	30815	1875	0.06	58763	7691	0.13
Sweet	54239	8820	0.16	67160	8846	0.13
Tart	50177	4528	0.09	57642	4390	0.08
Astringent	26488	5654	0.22	22054	2324	0.11
Bitter	36823	4689	0.13	32895	4534	0.14

sum of squares) shows us the proportion of variability due to product differences. Note that the experts do show a greater proportion of their variability explained by product differences, and less explained by error variation. Thus, we conclude (at least initially) that for the Bellomy program, discrimination improves because the participants "see more differences" among products, after participating. Note that we would reach the same conclusion using the F ratio. Looking at the sum of the squares for total variation versus variation due to product differences gives us a better insight into the data.

Another appropriate analysis consists of comparing the sum of the squares due to product differences. For aroma intensity and astringency, the experts show much greater variation across products than do consumer, nonexpert panelists.

AN OVERVIEW

The discrimination test procedures discussed here show that, indeed, attributes differ in the degree to which they can discriminate between products. The wine study also showed that panelists use the attributes in different ways. Expert panelists perceive greater differences among products using attributes, than do consumer panelists (at least for many, if not all of the attributes scaled).

Marketing researchers and product testers in R&D always look for those attributes which differentiate among products. In terms of "communication theory", attributes which discriminate carry "signals". Attributes which do not communicate carry "noise". The results from these two case histories show that the researcher can perform statistical analyses on the variability of ratings, for each attribute separately. The analysis, which partitions the variation of ratings into that due to products versus that due to error, will quickly reveal which attributes discriminate, and which do not. The reader should keep in mind, however, that the same attribute can perform differently in two contexts—whether different product categories (e.g., aroma intensity in bread versus wine) or for the same category rated by two different types of panelists (e.g., experts versus consumers).

REFERENCES

AMERINE, M. A. 1948. "Triangular" taste testing. Wine Rev. *16,* 10-12.

AMERINE, M. A. and OUGH, C. S. 1964. The sensory evaluation of Californian wines. Lab. Practice. *13,* 712-716.

BRADLEY, R. A. 1964. Applications of the modified triangle test in sensory difference trials. J. Food Sci. *29,* 668-672.

GRIDGEMAN, N. T. 1970. A re-examination of the two-stage triangle test for the perception of sensory differences. J. Food Sci. *35,* 87-91.

MULLER, J. and ROUSSEAU, D. 1972. A study of the discriminatory behavior of consumers in a double triad comparison taste test. Psychologia Africana *14,* 2, 103-110.

PURSELL, E. D., SANDERS, R. E. and HAUDE, R. H. 1973. Sensitivity to sucrose in smokers and nonsmokers: A comparison of TSD and percent correct measures. Perception and Psychophysics, *14,* 34-36.

SARAY, T., URBANYI, G. and DOBRAY-HORVATH, E. 1972. Test methods and evaluation procedures for the determination of the sensory properties of foodstuffs. Acta Alimentaria (Hungary) *1,* 279-295.

WREN, J. J. 1972. Taste-testing of beer for quality control. J. Inst. Brewing *78,* 69-75.

CHAPTER 4

VALIDATING PANEL RATINGS

INTRODUCTION

The relative recency with which product testing and sensory analysis has entered into the marketing and technical communities sometimes engenders a credibility problem. Marketing researchers, used to testing two or three products among large samples (hundreds of consumers), often do not understand how panels comprising 30-100 individuals can possibly provide valid information, projectible to the entire consumer population. On the other hand, R&D product developers, accustomed to the accuracy and reliability of objective or instrumental measurements, question the validity of "subjective ratings". "How", they ask, "can such an intrinsically variable organism such as the human being, provide reliable quantitative data?"

This chapter deals with the topic of validating panel ratings, using a variety of different methods. In the end, however, validity truly remains a matter of opinion. One can gather evidence, weigh it, and then decide, but the validity of the results rests on the opinions of those who look at the data. No one can prove ultimate validity. However, the assiduous and honest investigator can marshall arguments and evidence which show that the ratings assigned by panelists do, in fact, correspond to expectations generated either by previous tests, or by analytical measurements of stimulus properties.

CATEGORIES OF VALIDITY

Scientists recognize several categories of validity:

(1) Face validity. Does the test measure what it should measure?

(2) Convergent validity. Do different test measures lead to the same conclusion? If they do, then we conclude that the measures in fact quantify the same basic property.

(3) Construct validity. Do the measures actually quantify the underlying mechanisms which we assume to operate? (e.g., do sweetness ratings actually measure sweetness)

(4) Predictive validity. Do the ratings obtained with a small sample of consumers project to a much larger sample?

FACE VALIDITY AND PANEL RATINGS

Face validity refers to the validity that people intuitively perceive. For instance, in a product test designed to measure acceptance, researchers use a variety of different acceptance measures. These include ratings of purchase intent (likelihood of buying), overall acceptability, degree of switching, etc.

These attributes correspond to performance in the language used by marketers. Product tests (whether conducted with large samples, or with small church group panels) often use these acceptance measures. These measures add face validity to the test. The marketer feels comfortable that the test measures overall acceptance in a variety of ways.

As simple as the concept of face validity seems (namely, the test should look like it measures what it says it measures), matters become extremely fuzzy as the requirements for the test change. For instance, in the simplest of cases, one presents the panelist with two samples and asks the panelist to choose which sample he or she likes more. This time honored method of paired comparison testing provides the gold standard for acceptance measurement. Marketing strategies live and die by the results of direct preference testing. Researchers have designed innumerable field procedures to insure valid field executions of these preference tests. And, indeed, in many companies, the final "go, no-go" decision pertaining to a product rests upon the results of the direct preference test. However, does a "win" against competition (blind or branded) correspond to ultimate success in the marketplace? That is not really known.

In order to insure face validity, the researcher who designs the questionnaire should include questions which probe the relevant attributes. In a product test, the researcher can instruct panelists to rate sensory characteristics (objective evaluations of the amount of an attribute), as well as acceptance characteristics (degree of liking, including overall acceptance and attribute acceptance). In this way, the questionnaire possesses face validity, because it probes what it should probe, namely, consumer reactions to the various attributes of a product.

From time to time, researchers use attributes and questions which do not possess face validity. Attributes include those which deal with the "personality" of the type of individual who uses the product, or attributes pertaining to more complex characteristics, such as "high quality" and "unique". These attributes have face validity in the marketing sphere, because they can help marketers better understand consumers' psychological reactions to the product. However, in the stream of product development and testing, these attributes certainly possess limited face validity.

Virtually, all manufacturers include in their questionnaires attributes which upon first glance seem to have face validity, but which upon further probing do not. For instance, for beverages, the attribute "natural", and the attribute "refreshing" continue to appear. Researchers argue that these two attributes do have validity because the researchers have used them for so long, in test after test. However, in reality, these two attributes do not possess validity, because neither the research investigator nor the panelist can accurately define the attributes in more than a general sort of way. Similar problems arise in the evaluation of other stimuli, such as meat, where attributes such as "high quality" come into play. Researchers and marketers often base decisions on these attributes, but in actuality the attributes really have little or no face validity. What does the term "high quality" actually mean in the evaluation of a sausage product? If the term pertains to acceptance, then why not use the term "liking" or "purchase intent"?

CONSTRUCT VALIDITY

Another form of validity required in product testing consists of "construct validity". We define construct validity as follows: "The test measures existing, and valid underlying subjective processes". For instance, in beverage evaluation, construct validity would evidence itself if the ratings of perceived sweetness match or correlate with actual levels of sweetener in the beverage. Scientifically, we know that perceived sweetness varies in a lawful manner with sweetener level (all other attributes held constant). By showing this correlation for the test data, the researcher can demonstrate that the test procedures possess construct validity.

Demonstrating Construct Validity For Systematically Varied Formulations

If the product developer systematically varies the formulations, so that the formula components do not correlate with each other, one can easily demonstrate that the panelists validly rate the products. One needs only to correlate perceived intensities of key attributes with the formula variables.

As an example of construct validity, consider the experiment described in Table 4.1, where the product developer generated an array of fish sticks. The test formulations systematically varied in terms of level of spice in the batter coating, the size of the fish sticks (in terms of length) and the thickness of the batter remaining on the fish (a function of certain process variables).

TABLE 4.1
A. SPECIFICS OF STUDY INVOLVING FISH STICKS

(1) R&D systematically varied 3 formula variables:

—Amount of Batter (Breading)
—Spice Level
—Size of Fish Stick (Length)

(2) Panelists evaluated the 15 fish sticks over a 4-hour period on 30 attributes.

(3) Panelists used a 0-100 scale.

(4) A total of 30 panelists participated.

B. SIMPLE CORRELATIONS OF SENSORY ATTRIBUTE RATINGS WITH R & D FORMULA VARIABLES

Consumer Sensory Variables Attributes	R & D VARIABLES		
	Amount of Batter/Breading	Level of Spice	Size of Fish Stick
Appearance			
Amount of Crust	0.72*	0.12	-0.42
Crispiness	0.59	0.05	0.13
Thickness	-0.04	-0.12	0.24
Size	0.19	0.05	0.88*
Flavor			
Spicy	-0.21	0.55*	0.15
Fish Flavor	-0.12	0.36	0.27

*Correlations demonstrating that the panelists perceive the systematically varied formula variables.

In this study, the panelists rated each of 15 fish sticks on a variety of attributes, including sensory, acceptance and "image" attributes. The bottom of Table 4.1 shows the sensory attributes.

To demonstrate validity, we can correlate the attribute ratings with the independently varied physical formulations (Table 4.1). Note that, in most instances, we find reasonably high correlations between what R&D produced and what the consumers perceived. In order to insure validity, however, we must use the ratings of "perceived intensity" (e.g., perceived length of the fish stick, perceived level of spiciness). We cannot use liking ratings because we do not know, for sure, that liking of an attribute increases with the physical level, in a straight line fashion. We feel confident, however, that perceived intensity should increase in a linear fashion (or at least in a continuous fashion) with physical formula level.

CONVERGENT VALIDITY

Advances in the soft sciences (namely, those dealing with subjective behavior, rather than physical variables) often derive their validity from the convergence of different techniques. If the techniques generate similar conclusions, the researcher can feel assured that the methods have validity because they do generate the same results.

For product (and concept) testing, one can demonstrate convergent validity in a variety of ways. For instance:

(1) Two different types of scales generate similar results,

(2) Two different measuring systems generate similar results (e.g., direct preference by choosing one of two as the more preferred, versus inferring preference by means of a scale).

Quite often, product testers and sensory analysts judge the validity of a test or study by convergent validity, but do not recognize that they do so. In a product test, the panelists can rate a wide variety of different attributes, as well as choose the most preferred product. The panelist might have to scale overall liking, as well as liking of specific sensory characteristics. Generally, overall liking "follows" or tracks liking of flavor and texture. When this happens, the researcher feels assured that the panelists have provided "consistent" data (namely, expected patterns of responses from different attributes). Furthermore, panelists should prefer the product they rate higher on liking.

From time to time tests fail to show convergent validity. For instance, one may perform a test in which the panelists first have to demonstrate their ability to discriminate by means of a "triangle test" (two products identical, one different, with the requirement to choose the "odd" sample). Afterwards, the panelist has to select which product he or she likes most from a set of products, which had originally appeared in the triangle test.

Convergent validity fails when the panelists exhibit definite, statistically significant preferences for one of the products, but still show no significant ability to discriminate between the preferred product and the nonpreferred product.

CASE HISTORY—BEER

The Herstein Company brews a number of beers, in the midwest U.S. During the past twelve years, its president, Morris Herstein, instituted a battery of test procedures to improve product quality and, thus, to insure and maintain consumer satisfaction. These procedures included difference testing, expert and consumer profile ratings of attributes, and preference tests. During the first six months of the research and testing program, Herstein carefully developed a system to assess the validity of the testing program.

In order to validate the results of the tests, Herstein recognized that the testing program had to satisfy two objectives.

(1) The ratings had to track known physical variations of the stimuli. Beers comprising higher levels of bittering agents should taste more bitter. This constituted construct validity.

(2) The consumer measures had to demonstrate validity. However, no one at the brewery really knew the mind of the consumer. Thus, to demonstrate validity required several different test methods. By demonstrating that the various methods led to the same conclusions, Herstein felt that he could provide the necessary evidence for the validity of the "taste" tests.

Initial Approach—Developing The Panel Tasks

Early in the program, Herstein recognized that he had to acquire a bank of reliable, normative data. Furthermore, to demonstrate validity, these data had to address sensory characteristics of beer. Although the Herstein Company had previously conducted consumer taste tests, virtually all of these tests constituted simple preference tests, wherein the panelists drank two beers (either at home or at the central R&D laboratory), and told an interviewer which of the two he or she preferred. This simplistic preference test did not generate data needed to demonstrate validity.

In order to demonstrate validity, Herstein suggested that the panelists in the product testing program have an opportunity to scale each beer they tried on a variety of attributes including both sensory and acceptance measures. These attributes would constitute the product "signature".

In addition to the attribute rating procedure, Herstein also suggested that the panelists undergo discrimination and difference tests, to determine the difference between pairs of beers. According to the brewmaster, the beers in the test should vary, ranging from pairs that would seem almost identical to pairs that would seem virtually worlds apart. Accordingly, products similar to each other should score "low" on perceived difference. Panelists should confuse them in a discrimination test.

After much discussion, Herstein recommended a battery of tests which comprised the following.

(1) Discrimination testing by triangle tests, to measure the "confusability" of pairs of beers.

(2) Direct ratings of dissimilarity between pairs of beers, to measure overall difference.

(3) Profile ratings of each beer on a list of 7 sensory characteristics and 3 acceptance characteristics.

TABLE 4.2
PROFILES OF EIGHT BEER SAMPLES

	BEER SAMPLE							
	101	102	103	104	105	106	107	108
Overall								
Like Overall	67	63	54	58	55	55	52	50
Purchase Intent	52	48	44	46	44	48	37	41
Quality	48	45	40	45	44	45	40	40
Sensory								
Darkness	60	60	58	46	48	47	50	48
Aroma Strength	58	59	55	58	59	54	53	57
Flavor Strength	57	56	55	46	48	49	52	52
Richness	54	47	51	43	46	42	45	46
Biting/Astringent	56	67	55	70	70	77	61	72
Bitterness	50	63	53	59	51	63	43	53
Aftertaste	45	49	43	46	41	45	47	40

Results From The Consumer Panel

The testing protocol took approximately 2 months to complete, with a total of 8 beers and 30 consumer panelists. Table 4.2 shows the profile results, and Table 4.3 shows the discrimination and difference test results.

Key trends which emerge from the panel studies include the following.

TABLE 4.3
BEER EVALUATIONS
DIRECT RATINGS OF DISSIMILARITY
BETWEEN PAIRS OF DIFFERENT BEERS*

BEER PAIR	101	102	103	104	105	106	107	108
101								
102	44							
103	36	38						
104	62	54	48					
105	45	56	38	39				
106	57	49	38	35	46			
107	54	72	47	54	40	52		
108	41	51	31	39	34	42	38	

PERCENT OF TIME (×100) THAT PANELISTS
CORRECTLY DISCRIMINATED TWO BEERS ON THE
TRIANGLE TASTE TEST**

BEER PAIR	101	102	103	104	105	106	107	108
101								
102	56							
103	33	33						
104	81	61	61					
105	55	59	39	37				
106	59	46	35	39	48			
107	41	93	50	63	48	63		
108	35	71	36	34	39	41	42	

*0 = Identical, 100 = Very Different
**Chance probabilities (random guessing = 33)

(1) For profile ratings, perceived overall favor intensity correlates highly with darkness and flavor richness (Table 4.4). This correlation confirmed what the brewmaster and Herstein had recognized through informal observation, namely, that to consumer panelists the more bitter the beer, the stronger the flavor.

(2) The darkness of the beer also correlated highly with perceived flavor intensity and with objective measures of light transmittance (data not shown). These correlations again suggested validity because of the recognition that many dark beers do have stronger flavors. Furthermore, the

very high correlation between perceived darkness and objective measures of darkness (via light transmission measures) strongly reaffirmed the validity of the technique.

(3) Although the panelists scaled overall liking, liking of flavor and purchase intent, as well as scaling "high quality" on their questionnaire, these attributes correlated highly with each other. Yet, the actual magnitudes of the ratings differed. According to Herstein, the high correlation suggested that overall liking, purchase intent and perceived quality measured the same underlying consumer dimension. The differences in the ratings meant that the panelists did not actually copy the ratings of overall liking into the ratings of purchase intent or quality. Rather, the panelists appeared to rate the attributes one at a time. The high correlation among pairs of attributes, coupled with dissimilar numerical values suggested validity.

(4) Products exhibiting different sensory profiles also showed high ratings of overall dissimilarity, when panelists directly rated perceived dissimilarity (Table 4.3). Keep in mind that the panelists profiled the beers during one test occasion and rated perceived dissimilarity or difference on another test occasion. Furthermore, keep in mind that the profile procedure requires the panelist to assess individual attributes, whereas the task of rating perceived dissimilarity requires the panelist to act as an integrator of all the information available. Yet, it appears that the larger

TABLE 4.4
CORRELATION OF KEY ATTRIBUTES WITH LIKING, FLAVOR INTENSITY, DARKNESS

	Liking	Flavor Intensity	Darkness
Acceptance			
Overall Liking	1.00	0.46	0.66
Quality	0.86	0.03	0.45
Purchase Intent	0.84	0.26	0.23
Sensory			
Darkness	0.66	0.92	1.00
Aroma Strength	0.54	0.03	0.21
Flavor Strength	0.46	1.00	0.92
Richness	0.52	0.81	0.83
Biting	−0.33	−0.69	−0.73
Bitterness	0.26	−0.16	−0.01
Aftertaste	0.52	0.23	0.36

the difference in the profile between two products, the greater the perceived dissimilarity. Figure 4.1 presents the relation between perceived dissimilarity and the average, absolute difference between pairs of beers, on the nonevaluative sensory attributes. Note the high correlation.

(5) The results of the triangle test also suggest that pairs of products scoring low on overall difference (namely, dissimilarity) or which generate similar sensory profiles tend to generate higher confusability scores, and vice versa. Panelists have a more difficult time telling apart beers which to them seem similar qualitatively or which have similar profiles of sensory characteristics (Fig. 4.2).

These results confirmed the validity of Herstein's test panel procedures. The reader should keep in mind that, although one does not possess any external criterion of validity (other than correlations between sensory attributes and physical variables), the data generate patterns which exhibit a great deal of consistency. Products which seem similar overall do have

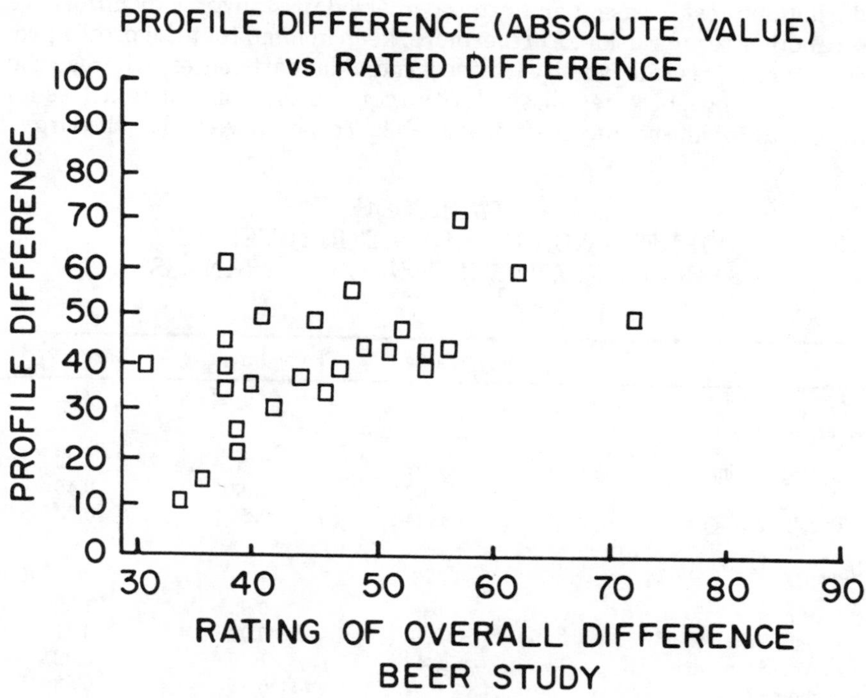

FIG. 4.1. COMPARISON OF DIRECT RATINGS OF OVERALL DIFFERENCE BETWEEN PAIRS OF BEERS VERSUS THE ABSOLUTE DIFFERENCE IN THE PROFILE BETWEEN THE SAME PAIR OF BEERS.

similar profiles. Panelists confuse these similar products more often than they confuse dissimilar products. Finally, with products which consumers like, they tend to rate high on purchase intent.

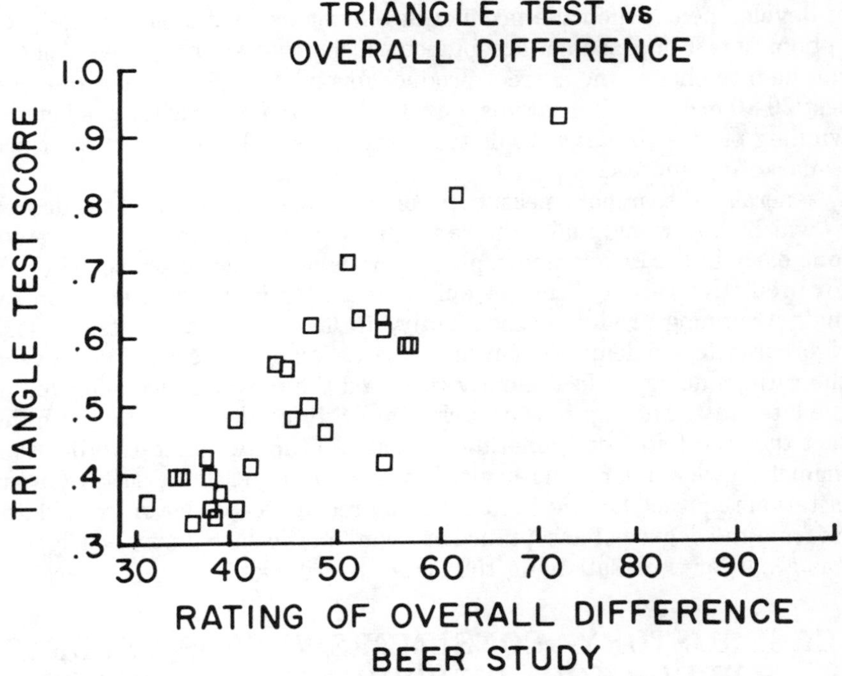

FIG. 4.2. COMPARISON OF DIRECT RATINGS OF OVERALL DIFFERENCE BETWEEN PAIRS OF BEERS VERSUS THE PROBABILITY OF CORRECTLY DIFFERENTIATING THE SAME TWO BEERS BY A TRIANGLE TEST.

PREDICTIVE VALIDITY

Predictive validity, or the ability of one set of results to predict another, constitutes the "summum bonum" or ultimate goal for all product testing. Indeed, most marketers and manufacturers look at the product testing procedures as a pre-test to predict ultimate performance in the free marketplace. Products which perform well in product testing should perform well in the market, all other factors held constant.

Quite often, researchers perform a series of product tests, beginning with small scale, in-house panels, then going to small church panels in a local neighborhood, and then finally to large scale, home-use panels, and even to test markets or test market simulators. Hopefully, the results in an early test will agree with the results in a more expensive, larger scale, later test.

Researchers in all fields search for predictive validity. In the early phases of development, when the product developer has available a variety of options, a test of consumer acceptance which possesses predictive validity can help to choose the correct product formulation. If, in fact, one can test 20-30 product alternatives inexpensively and accurately predict the winning product in larger scale tests, then this ability can help to insure a marketing success.

Generally, researchers measure predictive validity in terms of the degree to which they would make the same decision, on the basis of two tests (one early in the development phase versus one later). A loose criterion for predictive validity requires only that a winning product early on remain a winning product subsequently, in the larger scale tests. A more rigorous criterion demands that there exist a quantitative relation between the ratings achieved in the early test, and the performance achieved in the later test. The rigorous or stringent criterion does not stop with the fact that the two tests generate the same ultimate qualitative decision (namely, a winner early on remains a winner later on). Rather, the rigorous criterion requires that one predict the degree of acceptance or "win" later on from the degree of acceptance or "win" in the early test. Clearly, one has a harder time satisfying the rigorous criterion.

CASE HISTORY—CONSUMERS VERSUS EXPERTS AS PREDICTORS OF PRODUCT ACCEPTANCE

The Kaplan Corporation manufactures smoked meats of various types and has done so for the past forty five years. Recently, its new president and grandson of the founder, Robert Kaplan, attended a seminar series on consumer and expert panel development. The sponsors of the seminar series introduced the concept of expert panelists to augment one's analytic capabilities.

The possibility of using in-house experts to "predict" ultimate consumer acceptance intrigued Kaplan. In order to determine the feasibility of developing the in-house predictive capability, he designed the study shown in Table 4.5. In that study, the panelists would comprise three groups; experts trained in descriptive analysis, consumers from a local church panel (so-called Research Guidance Panel, or RGP) and consumers who would use the products at home, on a one time basis. All three groups would rate acceptance and sensory characteristics of the products.

TABLE 4.5
SPECIFICS OF A STUDY TO INTER-RELATE EXPERTS, LOCAL CHURCH GROUP PANELS, AND BROAD SCALE CONSUMER HOME USE PANELS

Category—	Spicy Bologna (varied in spice type and level)
Panels—	Experts—6 in-house R&D experts trained in the Flavor Profile Method.
—	Church Group—25 consumers, who evaluated the products in a 3 hour, pre-recruit test session (one evening).
—	Broadscale Consumer Test—100 consumers, total of 3 geographically dispersed markets. Each consumer tested 3 of the 6 prototypes for 1 week per sample (total of a 3 week home use test).
Attributes	(Same attributes used by all panelists)
	Liking/Overall Darkness of Color Strength of Aroma Liking of Flavor Saltiness Pepperiness (hotness) Spiciness Liking of Texture Fattiness Hardness

At the end of the training period, Kaplan implemented the study. The consumers (experts, local church panel, extended home use panel) tested six products and generated the ratings shown in Table 4.6.

Key Trends

The results from the study, as shown in Table 4.6, suggest the following.

(1) The liking ratings assigned by the home use panel correlated fairly well with the liking ratings assigned by the church panel (RGP). The correlation, achieving a value of 0.83 (out of a perfect 1.0), suggests that winning meats selected by the church panel will also "win" or achieve high acceptance when rated by the home use, consumer group (Table 4.7).

(2) In terms of size of ratings, however, the church group (RGP) and the home use consumer group generate different numbers. Both groups used a 0-100 point scale, but the church group assigned higher numbers.

TABLE 4.6
ATTRIBUTES OF SPICY BOLOGNA RATED BY THE THREE PANELS

Sample	Total	Total Like	Dark-ness	Like Flavor	Salty	Pep-pery	Spicy	Like Texture	Fatti-ness	Hard-ness
201	EXP	—	34	—	37	39	23	—	46	37
201	CON	36	38	38	32	41	20	37	47	41
201	RGP	60	42	58	56	54	46	50	61	54
202	EXP	—	41	—	47	37	46	—	39	43
202	CON	41	36	39	39	44	42	40	42	39
202	RGP	47	44	49	54	55	55	54	53	52
203	EXP	—	31	—	46	38	28	—	53	45
203	CON	39	35	38	36	45	25	34	50	44
203	RGP	60	37	57	47	56	36	53	66	55
204	EXP	—	55	—	60	35	26	—	48	48
204	CON	21	54	23	58	41	23	26	46	44
204	RGP	29	65	31	67	55	34	38	55	58
205	EXP	—	38	—	38	44	27	—	53	42
205	CON	41	34	39	32	44	21	38	48	40
205	RGP	65	44	63	49	58	38	53	69	56
206	EXP	—	34	—	42	43	30	—	49	42
206	CON	39	31	38	36	43	24	35	46	41
206	RGP	64	40	60	44	52	43	52	60	52

EXP = Expert Panel
RGP = Research Guidance Panel (Local Church Group).
CON = Broad Scale, Multi-Market, Consumer Test (Home Use).
All numbers on the same 0-100 point scale.
Experts did not rate "liking" (total, flavor, texture).

Thus, in terms of a stringent criterion, the local church group test did not accurately predict the absolute value of consumer acceptance. The research director at the Kaplan Co. recommended developing an equation that would relate or predict ratings assigned by the home use panel, from liking ratings assigned by the church group. The equation appears below (Eq. 4.1 and 4.2):

$$\text{Home Use Ratings} = A + B\ (\text{Church Group Ratings}) \qquad (4.1)$$

$$\text{Home Use Ratings} = 11.35 + 0.46\ (\text{Church Group Ratings}) \qquad (4.2)$$

(3) Both the experts and the church group panel predicted the sensory profile assigned by the home use panel, although to different degrees.

TABLE 4.7
INTERCORRELATIONS AMONG THE THREE PANELS ON ATTRIBUTE RATINGS FOR SPICY BOLOGNA

	Expert—Consumer	RGP—Consumer	Expert—RGP
Liking	—	0.83	—
Darkness	0.89	0.94	0.98
Like/Flavor	—	0.91	—
Salty	0.97	0.79	0.69
Peppery	0.31	0.42	0.06
Spicy	0.98	0.35	0.57
Like/Texture	—	0.91	—
Fattiness	0.92	0.84	0.85
Hardness	0.59	0.64	0.53

In Net

Kaplan concluded from this study that one could validly predict large scale consumer acceptance from ratings assigned by smaller group of consumers (RGP). For most sensory characteristics, both experts and RGP fared equally well in predicting the attribute profile assigned by the home use group to the six meat samples. For some attributes (e.g., perceived spiciness) experts and the RGP disagreed, and this one group (e.g., experts) better predicted the consumer ratings.

AN OVERVIEW

This chapter dealt with issues pertaining to validity. Validity consists of the agreement of one's observations with other data, whether these data constitute objective physical measures, or other measures made by different techniques, at a different time.

Understandably, in a soft science such as product testing or sensory evaluation, validity may take on some elusive qualities. One does not necessarily have a standard of correctness against which to quantify validity. In some instances, validity may mean simply that when the researcher repeats the study, using a different sample, in a home use test (the most natural or ecologically valid sample) the observations made previously with the small test sample hold up, and one would come to the same decision. For the more scientific minded, validity can emerge if the ratings for sensory characteristics track known physical formulations.

Finally, one should distinguish between validity and reliability. Reliability constitutes the ability to repeat the same measure under two different conditions, or at two different times. Neither measure may have validity. Validity, in contrast, consists of the agreement between one's observation in the test and some other standard of correctness or criterion, assumed to possess validity or truth.

REFERENCES

BASS, A. R. and FIRESTONE, I. J. 1980. Implications of representativeness for field and laboratory research findings. Amer. Psychol. *35,* 463-464.

BRINBERG, D. 1982. Validity concepts in research: An integrative approach. In: *Advances In Consumer Research,* Vol. 9. (A. Mitchell, ed.), Association For Consumer Research, Ann Arbor, MI.

BYRNE, D., GOLIGHTLY, C. and CAPALDI, E. J. 1963. Construction and validation of the food attitude scale. J. Consult. Psych. *27,* 215-222.

CALDER, B. J., PHILLIPS, L. W. and TYBOUT, A. M. 1982. The concept of external validity. J. Consumer Res. *9,* 240-244.

ENIS, B., COX, K. and STAFFORD, J. 1972. Students as subjects in consumer behavior experiments. J. Marketing Res. *9,* 72-74.

FERBER, R. 1977. Research by convenience. J. Consumer Res. *4,* 57-58.

GRANBOIS, P., and SUMMERS, J. 1975. Primary and secondary validity of consumer purchase probabilities. J. Consumer Res. *4,* 31-38.

HEELER, R. and RAY, M. L. 1972. Measure validation in marketing. In: *Advances In Consumer Research,* Vol. 3. (B. B. Anderson, ed.), Association For Consumer Research, Cincinnati, OH.

HOWARD, A. 1973. Taste panel technique. I. Reproducibility, reliability, and validity. Food Res. Quarterly *32,* 80-84.

LYNCH, J. G., JR. 1982. On the external validity of experiments in consumer research. J. Consumer Res. *9,* 225-239.

PERYAM, D. R. 1957. Factors affecting the accuracy and reliability of sensory tests. American Society For Quality Control Transactions, 675-685.

PERYAM, D. R. and HAYNES, J. G. 1957. Prediction of soldier's food preferences by laboratory methods. J. Appl. Psychol. *41,* 2-6.

PESSEMAIER, E. A., BURGER, P., TEACH, R. and TIGERT, D. 1971. Using laboratory brand preference scales to predict consumer brand purchased. Management Sci. *17,* 371-385.

PILGRIM, F. J. and KAMEN, J. M. 1963. Predictors of human food consumption. Sci. *139,* 501-502.

SAWYER, A., WORTHING, P. and SENDAK, P. 1979. The role of laboratory experiments in test marketing strategies. J. Marketing *43,* 60-67.

SCHUTZ, H. G. 1971. Sources of invalidity in the sensory evaluation of foods. Food Technol. *25,* 249-253.

CHAPTER 5

FATIGUE ANALYSIS— HOW MANY PRODUCTS CAN AN INDIVIDUAL REALLY TEST?

INTRODUCTION

Over the years, product testers have informally developed a lore about what panelists can and cannot do in testing often without empirical supporting evidence. One recurring topic in this lore consists of the belief that consumers simply cannot test more than just a limited number of samples. Beyond that number, these researchers feel the consumer's ability to differentiate among products significantly diminishes.

In contrast to this dismal view of the panelist's sensory capacities, we find just the opposite from psychophysical studies on sensory perception. In many research studies published in the archival scientific literature, investigators report that they present the panelists with a wide array of stimuli (e.g., sweetener solutions, odorants). These stimuli vary in concentration and in quality. Yet, time after time, the panelists seem able to discern differences among the samples. Furthermore, their ratings track the known physical levels. Indeed, researchers have even shown that one can reliably generate the same slopes relating physical concentration and sensory intensity rating from one study to another (Marks 1974; Stevens 1975).

Given the disparity between what panelists seem easily able to do in basic scientific studies and what investigators believe they cannot do (according to the prevailing opinions in product testing), how do we evaluate the panelist's ability to test many stimuli? Can we discover that number of samples after which the panelist's ability to discriminate significantly diminishes?

FOUR APPROACHES TO TESTING SENSORY FATIGUE

This chapter presents four approaches to testing and quantifying so-called fatigue in product testing (which presumably emerges during the course of testing an array of samples).

(1) Measure the variability of the ratings on a position by position basis. Here, we focus interest on the standard error when the panelist tests a product the first time, second time, third time, etc., in an extended series.

(2) The relation between order and rating. Do we find a correlation, or indeed any sort of relation at all between the order of trial (first, second, . . .) and the magnitude of the rating?

(3) The average rating assigned for the first set of trials versus the average rating assigned for the last set of trials. Comparisons will indicate whether a numerical change in the magnitude of the ratings occurs during the evaluation.

(4) The existence of significant order effects, by means of a two way analysis of variance. The two way ANOVA looks at the variability generated by product, by order of testing and by their interaction. It provides the researcher with a measure of the statistical significance (if any) of the order effect.

HOW THE VARIABILITY OF THE RATINGS CHANGES WITH NUMBER OF PRODUCTS TESTED

Background

For this first analysis, we focus attention on the variability of the ratings, as indexed by the standard error of the means.

In the study discussed here, panelists evaluated coconut patties, varying in composition. A total of 100 panelists participated. Each panelist had an opportunity to rate every patty on a series of 15 attributes, covering appearance, aroma, taste/flavor and texture characteristics. Furthermore, each of the 5 patties appeared equally often in every one of the 5 test positions, providing 20 ratings per patty per position.

The coconut patty study provides us with an opportunity to look at the effect of position on the variability of the ratings. Table 5.1 presents the mean ratings and the standard errors for these ratings, for six attributes, on a position by position basis. Note that we have combined the products together to generate one overall rating, recognizing that they do differ. However, here we focus interest only on the overall variability of the ratings. To do so requires that we not take into account individual products *per se*.

Table 5.1 reveals the following.

(1) The variability of the ratings differs, on an attribute by attribute basis. The highest variability occurs with the "liking" ratings. This should come as no surprise, since we know that individuals differ more among themselves in terms of what they like, than they differ in their sensory perceptions.

(2) On a position basis, the first product tried generates the highest variability. The variability diminishes considerably in the second position. Although the actual size of the standard error bounces around in positions 2-5, it rarely reaches the magnitude that it achieved in the first position. This leads us to conclude that the variability in the ratings for these five products does not increase as the panelists continue to evaluate products.

(3) The variability of ratings in the fourth and fifth positions (where we might expect fatigue to occur) does not differ appreciably from the variability in the second and third positions. Again we conclude that little fatigue has occurred. Had fatigue begun to set in, with panelists unable to discriminate we might have expected to observe some noticeable change

TABLE 5.1
MEAN RATING AND STANDARD ERROR FOR COCONUT PATTIES RATED IN 5 POSITIONS (FIRST TO FIFTH)

	Position 1		Position 2		Position 3		Position 4		Position 5	
	Mean	S.E.	Mean	S.E.	Mean	S.E.	Mean	S.E.	Mean	S.E.
Liking	52	6.6	48	5.9	50	5.8	47	5.7	46	5.9
Darkness of Cover	78	4.5	74	4.2	75	4.4	70	4.4	73	4.5
Aroma Strength	46	5.6	41	4.9	44	5.3	43	5.1	44	5.1
Sweetness	68	5.8	63	5.1	66	4.9	66	4.8	67	5.2
Coconut Flavor	82	4.6	80	4.1	80	3.9	78	4.2	83	4.1
Hardness	58	4.4	61	3.8	60	3.8	58	3.9	62	4.1

Data comes from the average rating assigned to five coconut patties, each tested equally often in each of the five positions. The numbers in the table show the average rating assigned to the five patties and the average standard error achieved by the five patties.

S.E. = Standard error of the mean.

in variability. That change might appear as either a decrease (suggesting that panelists could see no differences and rated all products in the middle of the scale), or an increase (suggesting that they could see no difference and thus randomly assigned numbers).

We conclude from this initial study that the variability of ratings does not dramatically change over repeated testings, at least for five products. The high variability achieved by the products tested in the first position also should spark some interest. Often researchers rely on the first product tested (the first "monadic") to make their marketing decision because they feel that the first product has encountered the least bias in the test. They feel that this first rating should reflect the panelist's true feelings about the specific product. Yet, these results (which mirror numerous other results of a similar type) suggest that the first product in a sequence shows the greatest variability. Possibly panelists have a poorly established frame of reference against which to rate the products. Only after trying a product and rating it can they establish the proper frame of reference. Quite possibly, then, a better test technique might consist of presenting consumers with a "training" product. The panelists would then evaluate the product for "practice" but the researcher would not use the ratings in the analysis. The first product establishes a frame of reference for subsequent evaluations.

THE RELATION BETWEEN ORDER TRIED AND RATING

Background

For this second analysis, we focus interest on trends between order tried (e.g., 1st, 2nd, 3rd) and the rating. Do any trends exist? For instance, if we correlate liking ratings with order tried, for the same product, do we find a consistent drop or increase in liking rating, as a function of order?

For this analysis, let us consider the evaluation of grape jellies. The Wick Corporation manufactures a line of grape jellies. Tom Wick, its president, recommended the development of an in-house testing program to evaluate the various alternative jelly formulations. However, before embarking on the actual evaluation phase, Wick wanted to measure the ability of panelists to evaluate jelly products. He reasoned that it would make no sense for panelists to evaluate 5-10 products, if they indeed lost their sensitivity to product differences after the second or third tasting. For jellies, which have a cloying sweet taste, this issue became even more relevant because of the fear of ongoing sensory fatigue.

To measure ongoing discrimination ability, Wick commissioned a study on reactions to a variety of different jellies. The panelists in that study comprised jelly users (ages 18-35). The panelists rated ten different grape jellies on a series of sensory and liking characteristics. In total, 100 panelists participated. For every jelly sample, the panelists rated sensory, acceptance and quality characteristics. In addition, the test design insured that every panelist would test each jelly in a totally randomized order, and that each of the ten jelly samples would appear equally often (10×) in each of the ten order positions.

TABLE 5.2
RATINGS OF FIVE GRAPE JELLIES ON FOUR ATTRIBUTES BY ATTRIBUTE, AND POSITION (10 RATINGS PER POSITION)

	Summary Results			Ratings by Each Position in the Test									
	Mean	Mean Pos. 1-5	Mean Pos. 6-10	Position 1	2	3	4	5	6	7	8	9	10
Liking													
Jelly A	40	37	43	34	32	43	43	35	39	42	45	42	51
Jelly B	49	47	50	37	54	48	45	52	54	43	53	43	61
Jelly C	41	41	41	30	48	45	37	46	27	41	36	57	45
Jelly D	48	42	53	34	29	67	44	40	51	30	51	65	69
Jelly E	54	57	51	54	48	75	57	52	46	56	66	43	45
Darkness													
Jelly A	63	61	65	62	65	60	67	52	68	59	73	68	58
Jelly B	61	64	58	70	71	53	63	67	66	56	55	52	65
Jelly C	55	52	57	59	50	61	36	58	56	52	61	59	60
Jelly D	61	59	63	55	41	67	65	68	61	63	71	66	56
Jelly E	66	67	66	67	66	63	72	67	69	75	76	58	55
Sweetness													
Jelly A	62	64	60	63	68	72	51	66	66	58	73	51	53
Jelly B	65	69	61	57	78	75	64	75	73	52	62	54	67
Jelly C	62	64	61	52	65	68	66	71	68	57	62	54	65
Jelly D	53	52	55	48	49	54	57	54	54	45	59	68	51
Jelly E	65	63	68	67	60	44	68	76	57	75	80	76	55
Flavor													
Jelly A	63	65	62	71	64	69	59	64	59	67	80	48	58
Jelly B	60	59	61	47	60	73	54	64	72	50	58	59	66
Jelly C	66	65	67	47	78	61	66	77	74	77	64	56	65
Jelly D	49	48	51	49	53	50	46	44	45	40	56	56	60
Jelly E	60	59	62	52	50	71	61	63	50	66	71	69	55

Pos. = Position

Table 5.2 shows the rating for five of the jellies on four attributes, as a function of position. Note that we cannot discern any particularly clear pattern between attribute rating and position. However, on average, the five jellies do differ from each other quite considerably.

In order to better discover the relation between order of testing and attribute rating, Wick suggested fitting either a straight line or a curve (e.g., parabola) to the data. The rank order of trial (1-10, first through tenth) would act as the independent variable and the rating of the attribute for the product would act as the dependent variable. A straight line relation with a statistically significant correlation or slope (either positive or negative) would demonstrate a significant order effect. An insignificant relation based upon the correlation or the slope would demonstrate no significant order effect. Table 5.3 shows no general order effect based upon a supposed linear relation between order of trial and attribute rating, for either product prototype. However, liking does increase slightly with position.

The relation between attribute rating and order of trial might not necessarily follow a straight line. Sometime during the course of the evaluation, fatigue might occur, which would change the ratings. Until that point, however, the ratings would remain the same. To evaluate the existence of the fatigue effect requires a nonlinear relation, such as that shown by the parabola. Here we posit the existence of a systematic relation between order of trial and attribute rating, but recognize that the relation need not follow a straight line. Table 5.3 shows, however, little or no general effect of position, either linear or nonlinear relation as measured by the R^2 values, leading Wick to conclude that the panelists could evaluate 10 jellies without undue order bias or fatigue. The reader should keep in mind, however, that in the jelly study, at least 8 minutes elapsed between products, to insure recovery from the previous evaluation. If the researcher bunches the evaluations together, and by so doing minimizes the time for recovery, this reduced recovery time may, in fact, generate significant fatigue and show up as a significant order effect.

AVERAGE RATINGS FROM THE FIRST HALF VERSUS THE SECOND HALF OF THE TEST

Background

The third analysis consists of an evaluation of the ratings assigned by panelists for the first five versus the second five tastings. Keep in mind that the panelists who rated the jellies made ten evaluations in total. Do the ratings from the first five evaluations correspond to the ratings from

TABLE 5.3
PARAMETERS OF MODELS RELATING ATTRIBUTE RATINGS TO POSITION

			LINEAR POSITION EFFECT			PARABOLIC POSITION EFFECT			
Jelly	Attribute	=	K_0 +	K_1 (Position)	R^2	K_0 +	K_1 $(Position)^2$ +	K_2 $(Position)^2$	R^2
A	Liking		32.8	1.42*	0.56	34.4	0.63	0.07	0.57
B	Liking		43.7	0.97*	0.17	43.1	1.26	-0.03	0.17
C	Liking		36.3	0.88	0.09	40.8	-1.32	0.20	0.12
D	Liking		32.8	2.76*	0.30	41.3	-1.49	0.39	0.34
E	Liking		59.9	-1.03	0.10	51.9	2.97	-0.36	0.17
A	Darkness		61.8	0.25	0.02	61.4	0.46	-0.02	0.02
B	Darkness		68.1	-1.16*	0.24	73.1	-3.61*	0.22	0.29
C	Darkness		51.2	0.72	0.08	58.8	-3.03	0.34	0.19
D	Darkness		54.9	1.16*	0.16	41.8	7.74	-0.60	0.43
E	Darkness		69.7	-0.55	0.06	57.8	5.47*	-0.54*	0.43
A	Sweetness		68.2	-1.11*	0.16	62.7	1.64	-0.25	0.21
B	Sweetness		71.7	-1.10*	0.12	65.9	1.78	-0.26	0.17
C	Sweetness		63.5	-0.12	0.01	53.9	4.67*	-0.43*	0.27
D	Sweetness		48.9	0.9 *	0.18	47.0	1.89	-0.09	0.19
E	Sweetness		59.6	1.13	0.09	52.9	4.50	-0.31	0.13
A	Flavor		69.1	-0.94	0.11	67.3	-0.06	-0.08	0.11
B	Flavor		57.5	0.51	0.03	51.6	3.47	-0.27	0.09
C	Flavor		64.7	0.32	0.01	49.6	9.40*	-0.82*	0.39
D	Flavor		45.5	0.81*	0.15	58.1	-5.52*	0.58*	0.64
E	Flavor		55.4	0.98*	0.12	47.8	4.94*	-0.36	0.23

* = T value (exceeds 1.0 in absolute value, showing significance).

Although some coefficient do achieve statistical significance, the R^2 values generally do not exceed 0.40, meaning that position of the product explains at most 40% of the variability in a product rating (across various positions).

the second five? If we find a systematic change, we can conclude that there probably does exist some type of order effect, even though we cannot pick up that effect from the variability of the ratings, nor discover it by relating the product ratings to the position number in the test. In essence, this third analysis represents a looser criterion for order effect. We simply want to find out whether the ratings assigned at the beginning of the test session differ from those assigned at the end of the session.

Approach

For this analysis, we have looked at the various products separately, on four attributes, as shown in Table 5.2. The table shows the average ratings for the first five positions, vs. those for the second five positions. Note that these ratings come from different panelists, and thus to some extent we confound the order effect with the panelist effect. (In this jelly evaluation study, the same panelist could not rate the same jelly in each of the ten positions). As Table 5.2 shows, however, we see relatively little effect for the first versus the last five positions. In some cases we do find an effect, e.g., the liking rating tends to increase. However, the order effect differs in direction and magnitude from one jelly product to another. We conclude, therefore, that even if an order effect does exist for the evaluation of the jellies, it does not make itself clearly evident.

USING ANALYSES OF VARIANCE TO MEASURE ORDER EFFECT

Background

The final approach used to assess the effect of order and the ability of panelists to detect differences in an extended test consists of measuring the variability due to product differences versus the variability due to order differences. Ideally, if no order effect exists, then we should find most of the variability in the data attributable to product differences and virtually no variability ascribable to order differences. On the other hand, if order of evaluation plays a role (so that fatigue or burnout does occur), we should expect to find a significant effect due to order, possibly lower in magnitude than that due to product, but still significant.

Approach

We will use the analysis of variance technique, this time using the Two Way Analysis Of Variance (2-Way ANOVA). The analysis of variance partitions the variability of the ratings into contributions provided by known variables (here product, position of tasting, interaction of product

× position and error). For the 2-Way ANOVA we can look at the ratio of three sources of variability: product or position or product × position versus the error variability or unexplained variability. These generate three F ratios.

If we develop analysis of variance tables for the different attributes, we can measure the F ratios for product, for order, and for the interaction of product and order. The higher the resulting F ratio, the more likely there exists a significant difference among products (or position). For instance, if we discover high F ratios for product, but low F ratios for position, then we conclude that there exists significant differences among the products on the attribute, but relatively little significant difference in terms of the position of testing.

The reader should keep in mind that the analysis of variance does not look for a systematic pattern between order of trial (1st, 2nd, . . . , 10th) and rating. Rather, it just looks to see whether the variability ascribable to order to evaluation generates a significant amount of variability. If order does generate the variability, we conclude that there exists an order effect.

TABLE 5.4
RESULTS OF TWO-WAY ANALYSES OF VARIANCE
TO EVALUATE POSITION EFFECTS—JELLY

	F Ratio		
Attribute	Product	Position	Product × Position
Liking	4.13	1.54	1.12
Purchase	2.82	0.54	1.34
Like Color	2.11	0.43	1.01
Darkness	2.58	0.74	1.03
Like Taste	3.69	0.92	1.09
Sweetness	3.68	0.48	1.16
Flavor	10.44	0.32	1.42
Aftertaste	4.73	1.67	0.99
Like Aftertaste	1.71	0.73	1.22
Like Texture	2.43	0.44	1.39
Hardness	4.24	0.82	0.79
Runny	4.57	0.89	0.96
Dissolves Fast	1.84	0.53	0.91
Natural	3.64	1.55	0.91
Unique	3.69	1.27	1.18

Note: High F ratios mean greater effects.
Number of Products = 10
Number of Positions = 10

We do not know the nature of the effect, but we can conclude that ratings differ from each other (for the same product and attribute), depending upon the position in the test series (1st, 5th, etc.).

Results

We ran the 2-Way ANOVAS for the various attributes, and computed the F ratios, which appear in Table 5.4

The analyses of variance clearly show that the products differ from each other, as we expect. Consumers can and do pick up differences among the ten grape jelly samples. However, standing in sharp contrast to the product differences, we see little or no effect of order. This means that for the evaluations of jelly, we would probably make the same decision for products tested in the first position as for products tested in the second position. The magnitudes of the ratings do not change. Finally, Table 5.4 shows a slight interaction of product × position. We conclude that the products show similar behaviors to each other. In other words, we do not find that some of the jelly samples exhibit strong sensitivity to order, whereas others do not.

GENERAL DISCUSSION OF BURNOUT AND FATIGUE

This chapter has concentrated on only two products; coconut patties and jellies, to evaluate the existence and magnitude of sensory fatigue and burnout. In neither case have we found the fatigue or burnout to exist, to any noticeable degree. Why then, from researcher to researcher, does one continue to hear the statement that consumers cannot discriminate among products, if they test more than 3 or so products? Why then do we find the pervasive belief in the panelist's inability to discriminate, when both basic researchers and applied product testers can clearly demonstrate the absence of any noticeable order effect?

Boredom

One source of fatigue comes from panelist boredom. Product testing does not exactly thrill the vast majority of panelists who participate in it. Possibly a participant might become interested enough to volunteer for a study and then find the first one or two samples interesting to test. However, after a few samples, the panelist already understands the system, knows what to expect and finds the procedure routine and uninteresting. At this point, resistance to further participation sets in.

Anyone watching a child who loses interest in a task quickly notices that the child becomes bored and says that he/she feels "tired" and "unable to continue". A similar phenomenon rears its head in product testing. Boredom generates a feeling of fatigue, but a psychological fatigue, and loss of interest, rather than sensory fatigue. All too often the bored panelist complains that he or she "cannot tell the differences between samples". This complaint of fatigue represents a socially acceptable way of complaining about the boring task. Researchers and product testers might feel insulted if the panelist complains that the task has become boring, but it seems perfectly correct and acceptable (indeed almost admirable) to complain that one has lost one's sense of taste or smell.

Too Little Time Between Samples

In many conventional taste tests, too little time elapses between samples. Indeed, one need only observe informal "cuttings" (namely, in-house taste evaluations by marketing and R&D staff) to realize that many of the complaints of fatigue arise because the participants try one product after another. Quite often, those in charge of product development and marketing complain that they simply lose track of the products and can no longer remember the first few products, after evaluating 4-5 samples. All too often, however, these same individuals incorrectly evaluate the products. Rather than allowing several minutes to elapse between stimuli, they taste one right after the other. They try to remember each sample and compare it to the previous samples. Such a strategy does not work particularly well, whether one evaluates graphics, aromas, tastes or even concept statements. To achieve greater discrimination requires that panelists evaluate each product by itself, on a scale, without trying to recall all previous products that they have tried.

Motivating Panelists And Reducing The Fatigue Factor

A motivated panelist, who can participate in a product testing session for an hour or more can provide a relatively large amount of data, often free of fatigue. In contrast to the traditional taste test which uses unmotivated panelists for a short period of time, this author recommends using previously recruited consumer panelists, who participate for an extended period. The period may last up to 4 hours in a single day and the total participation may go on for 3-4 days to generate the extensive period of participation.

If we look at the product test session as a "factory" to generate data, we can measure the output of this factory over time. At the start of the session, the panelist does not know what to do. The interviewer loses time orienting the panelist. Generally, the initial ratings have lower reliability than do the later ratings. In the middle of the test session the panelist performs at peak capacity and provides the best information. Towards the end, the panelist begins to prepare for the end of the session and the performance quality may decrease slightly.

If we pursue this analogy further, comparing the short test sessions (e.g., 10-20 minutes, in an R&D laboratory or in a mall) versus extended previously recruit tests, we quickly find that the short tests provide a smaller ratio of "productive" time of interviewing to "total interview time". In a 20 minute test, the first five minutes, or 25%, may not generate as good data as the remaining 15 minutes. In contrast, in a 4 hour test (240 minutes), allowing for 10 minutes of orientation in the beginning and 10 minutes at the end generates a total of 220/240 or more than 90% productive time.

The key thing to keep in mind, therefore, from this chapter concerns the utility of extended sessions, where the panelists do not have to rush through the evaluations at a rapid pace. By previously recruiting the panelists and paying them, the product tester can generate substantially better data. Furthermore, a relaxed session allows the product tester to space out the samples, reducing the potential sensory fatigue. The monetary remuneration further works to maintain ongoing interest and involvement, militating against boredom. By following this approach, one substantially reduces the risk of fatigue and decreases the burnout so often described by researchers as a ubiquitous phenomenon which plagues product testing.

REFERENCES

BENDIG, A. W. 1955. Rater reliability and "judgmental fatigue", J. Appl. Psych. *39,* 451-454.

BENDIG, A. W. 1957. Rater reliability and "judgmental demoralization", J. Appl. Psych. *41,* 66-68.

BRADLEY, J. E., WALKER, C. T. and PERYAM, D. R. 1954. Influence of continued testing on preference ratings. In: *Food Acceptance Testing Methodology.* National Academy of Sciences, National Research Council.

KAMEN, J. M., PERYAM, D. R., PERYAM, D. B. and KROLL, B. J. 1969. Hedonic differences as a function of number of samples evaluated. J. Food Sci. *34,* 475-479.

KAMENETZKY, J. 1959. Contrast and convergence effects in ratings of foods. J. Appl. Psych. *43,* 47-52.

LAUE, E. A., ISHLER, N. H. and BULLMAN, G. A. 1954. Reliability of taste testing and consumer testing methods. I. Fatigue in taste testing. Food Technol. *8,* 387-388.

WARD, A. C. and BOGGS, M. M. 1951. Comparison of scoring results for two and four samples of corn per taste session. Food Technol. *5,* 219-220.

CHAPTER 6

MEASURING THE COMMUNICATION PROFILE OF PACKAGES

INTRODUCTION

The previous sections have dealt with the evaluation of actual products, whether tested blind or branded. Can we apply the same approaches to the evaluation of packages? Do packages communicate information about the product, and if so how can the product tester and sensory analyst uncover that information?

Traditional package research attempts to determine whether the consumer likes or dislikes the package, whether the package stands out on the shelf, etc. Rarely do researchers attempt to determine what characteristics of a product a package communicates. From time to time, one or another researcher may run a study in which consumers have to describe the "personality" which goes along with a specific package. Consumers do intuit differences among packages which reveal themselves in personality attributes.

This chapter deals with the evaluation of packages, from three viewpoints.

(1) Does the consumer like or dislike the package, and if so, then how much?

(2) What sensory characteristics does the package promise (if any)?

(3) What personality or image characteristics go along with the package, if any?

RESEARCH DESIGNS FOR PACKAGE EVALUATION

The research designs covered in this chapter parallel the designs discussed in the previous chapters. Only the stimuli differ (here the stimuli comprise packages, and occasionally products). In general, the researcher selects a series of packages to evaluate, including test packages and "control" packages (for comparisons). The panelists profile each of the packages on a wide variety of characteristics. Panelists may or may not have an opportunity to evaluate products at the test session. If they do, then the panelists profile the products on the same attributes and use the same scale that they used to evaluate the packages.

CASE HISTORY—CEREAL PACKAGES VERSUS CEREAL PRODUCTS

Background

This case history concerns the evaluation of cereal packages and products for dry ready-to-eat cereals. The Eberts Co. manufactures a line of these dry cereals and competes in an ever-tightening market, against a host of larger companies with greater budgets for advertising and promotion. In view of the requirement that the cereal packages both communicate the proper messages and generate acceptance, Pat Eberts, president and founder, commissioned an evaluation of the various product packages. For this particular study, she focused on adult-oriented products.

Research Approach

Previous work at the Eberts Co. had primarily concentrated on measuring the visibility of the package on a store's shelf versus other dry cereals. Eberts recognized the need for evaluating what the package communicated, so that the package development groups might have an opportunity to improve the packages and thus perhaps increase share.

To accomplish the research objective, the marketing research director commissioned a study in which the panelists (category users) would first have an opportunity to evaluate two different dry cereals on a variety of attributes. This initial exposure to the cereals would provide the panelists with a frame of reference. Later during the session, the panelists would then evaluate 6 different cereal packages, first without identification of the brand name (package alone, no brand or manufacturer), and then the same packages (in a different order), this time with the manufacturer and brand name. The panelists would have a chance to scale each of the stimuli (2 cereals, 12 packages), both on the same set of attributes.

The test design outlined above allows the researcher and marketer to accomplish a number of objectives simultaneously.

(1) Evaluate the acceptance of the products, as conveyed by the package.

(2) Evaluate the acceptance of the products, as conveyed by the package, and the brand name.

(3) Develop a profile of attribute expectations generated by the package, without versus with the brand name and cereal name provided.

(4) Determine which particular characteristics generate the acceptance score.

(5) Determine whether or not the expectations generated by the package lie in the range of delivery provided by the product. (Data not shown.) (Since, however, in this study the panelists did not evaluate all of the 6 products but only 2 of 6, we would use the comparison of product versus package for qualitative guidance only and not draw hard and fast conclusions about package promise versus product delivery).

Results—Profile Of The Packages (Blind)

Table 6.1 shows the profiles of the various packages, without identification (BL) versus with identification (BR). Note that the panelists had had previous experience evaluating two actual cereal products, so that we can anchor their expectations of the product (from package evaluation) back to the ratings of the actual cereals.

Table 6.1 reveals the following trends.

(1) Panelists can and do differentiate among the packages, both without benefit of brand name and cereal and with benefit of the brand name and cereal.

(2) We see the greatest differentiation on the attributes of acceptance, nutrition, etc. We can tie these differences back to the pictures on the box. Table 6.1 provides a short description of each package type (at the bottom).

(3) The differentiation among packages becomes even clearer when the researcher provides the panelist with information about the manufacturer and type of cereal in the box.

(4) In terms of ratings of the expected sensory properties of the product, we see less differentiation among packages, on a blind basis, than we see for liking and image/performance attributes.

(5) However, in terms of branded package evaluation, where panelists knew the type of cereal in the package and the manufacturer, we see a great deal of differentiation.

Key Conclusions—Eberts Package Study

We conclude from this study that packages can and do differ from each other and that they convey these differences to panelists, primarily on the dimensions of acceptance and image/performance. Panelists react to the packages by showing different degrees of liking. However, panelists

TABLE 6.1
RATINGS OF SIX CEREAL PACKAGES ON ATTRIBUTES COMPARISON OF BLIND AND BRANDED RATINGS

EXPECTATIONS OF THE CEREAL FROM THE PACKAGE	A		B		C		D		E		F	
	BL	BR	BL	BR	BL	BR	BL	BR	BL	BR	BL	BR
Overall Liking	45	62	51	58	49	61	43	32	39	28	46	40
Appearance												
Like Appearance	42	59	41	52	48	65	42	39	36	32	46	49
Darkness	38	42	40	50	36	42	36	54	53	64	47	57
Piece Size	36	33	32	25	59	63	52	43	61	68	34	31
Unusual Shapes	46	29	41	34	43	48	46	47	63	75	39	36
Like the Shape	36	48	38	44	58	63	52	52	35	38	40	41
Aroma												
Like the Aroma	51	57	53	60	53	58	51	39	45	42	44	39
Fruity	42	34	38	28	29	34	36	49	36	47	46	69
Strength	36	36	38	34	32	37	35	51	46	59	51	70
Taste/Flavor												
Like Taste	46	59	42	54	57	59	44	38	31	25	39	28
Sweet	43	32	39	36	31	26	52	69	59	75	46	58
Fruity	39	35	34	31	28	33	45	59	34	43	41	82
Spicy	33	21	39	25	31	19	33	43	38	47	43	69
Rich	39	47	36	43	45	51	41	38	31	38	32	36
Texture												
Like Texture	57	61	55	63	53	62	56	59	47	51	53	59
Crunchy	53	59	53	52	59	74	55	59	57	53	57	53
Crispy	52	63	53	54	51	57	52	56	55	53	57	57
Image												
For Adult	43	73	47	59	61	78	48	19	31	15	41	27
For Child	56	44	46	40	31	25	47	79	57	78	46	78
Gimmicky	37	21	36	18	42	31	46	64	59	81	47	69
Nutritious	39	52	42	61	62	69	39	41	42	31	38	34

Generalized descriptions of the cereal target audience

Cereal A—Regular Wheat Flakes	Adult Oriented
Cereal B—Rolled Circles (Oats)	Adult Oriented
Cereal C—Shredded Wheat Type Cereal	Adult Oriented
Cereal D—Circular Fruit Flavored Ball	Child Oriented
Cereal E—Chocolate Spaceman	Child Oriented
Cereal F—Fruit Flavored Loops	Child Oriented

Panel = 50 women with children (Chicago). Each used an anchored 0-100 point scale to rate the packages both without and with identification of manufacturer and brand.

BL = Without identification
BR = With identification (name, manufacturer)

do not necessarily exhibit strongly defined expectations about the sensory characteristics of the products contained in the package unless the package specifically emphasizes the dimensions (e.g., fruit flavor).

By putting a brand and a cereal name on the package it becomes possible to engender specific sensory expectations about the product. Whether these expectations parallel the delivery of the product remains for other testing. However, it appears that once the panelists know the type of product in the package they do have some expectations about what the product should taste like and how they will perceive its texture.

HOW DO PACKAGE ELEMENTS GENERATE SPECIFIC EXPECTATIONS ABOUT PRODUCTS

The previous section dealt with the evaluation of qualitatively different packages. This section deals with the evaluation of similar types of packages, whose elements vary, either in a nonsystematic (but quantifiable) method or in a systematic pattern. This section looks at the relation between package elements and consumer ratings. Does there exist a relation between components of a food package and expectations or communications generated by those elements? If so, how can the product tester ferret out these relations and use them to improve package development?

CASE HISTORY—ROSE WINES

Rose wines come in a variety of different types of bottles, varying in color, shape, cap versus cork and label. The Burkhart Corporation of Ohio imports wines from around the world, and supplies a large and increasing number of stores as customers. Jay Burkhart, founder of Burkhart Corp., noticed that from time to time many of his customers (package store owners) requested certain wines and not others. Upon further inquiry, he found that his customers (who did not actually drink many of the wines they stocked) felt that some wines connoted "high class" products, whereas others connoted "middle of the road" products.

To better understand what characteristics of the product generated these perceptions, Burkhart hired a marketing research agency in central Ohio to evaluate consumer reactions to rose wines on a package basis only. The motivating factor behind the study concerned the potential relation between package characteristics and consumer expectations or impressions about the product. By understanding this relation (if a relation actually did exist), Burkhart recognized that he could improve the sales effectiveness of his customers. Furthermore, in terms of his own business, Burkhart recognized that with this information he could supply wines whose packages supported the quality image that he promised and the pricing that he recommended.

Research Specifics

In order to develop the best database, Burkhart and his research group recognized that they would have to test a wide variety of rose bottles, varying in quality, package design, etc. Table 6.2 lists the various bottles in terms of the product characteristics. By performing a "content analysis" on the bottle and label, the research group uncovered the basic physical dimensions along which the rose bottles varied. These included size, height, cap type, origin of market (e.g., French versus U.S.), etc. Parenthetically, this content analysis constitutes a valuable exercise because it forces the researcher and the marketer alike to pay attention to the competitive frame in its entirety. All too often in product research and marketing, those most deeply involved in the key decisions pay attention only to one or two key competitors and fail to look at other competitors that might not do as well as the market leader, which nevertheless provide many positive characteristics that consumers desire.

TABLE 6.2
CONTENT ANALYSIS OF BOTTLES
FOR ROSE WINES

Wine Bottle	Bottle Size	Type of Cap	Origin of Wine	Bottle Color	Neck Wrap	Label Type
1	Large	Screw	France	Green	No	Simple
2	Small	Cork	USA	Brown	Yes	Ornate
3	Large	Cork	USA	Green	Yes	Ornate
4	Small	Cork	France	Green	No	Ornate
5	Small	Screw	USA	Green	Yes	Simple
6	Small	Screw	France	Green	Yes	Simple
7	Large	Cork	USA	Green	No	Ornate
8	Small	Cork	France	Brown	No	Simple
9	Large	Cork	USA	Brown	No	Simple
10	Large	Screw	France	Green	Yes	Ornate
11	Small	Screw	USA	Brown	No	Ornate
12	Small	Screw	USA	Brown	Yes	Ornate

Results—Basic Data

Table 6.3 shows the basic array of bottle by content analysis of the label and by consumer ratings. As we can clearly see, the consumers differentiate among the bottles on a variety of characteristics, primarily those involving acceptance and image. From these studies, we find that consumers can differentiate among rose wine bottles in terms of sensory expectations (e.g. dry versus semi-sweet) even if the information does not clearly appear on the label. Thus, the initial learning to emerge from this exercise suggests that the consumers react to characteristics of the rose wine bottles (which ones, we as yet do not know) and, based upon these characteristics, form impressions of quality and expected sensory profile.

As part of the testing, the panelists had to estimate the appropriate price for the product. Note that as the acceptance of the product or the perceived quality increased, consumers feel that the wine will cost more.

Relating Content Analysis Of Rose Wine Bottles To Attribute Ratings

The previous section provided Burkhart with clear indications of discrimination among the different rose wine bottles, but it cannot indicate which elements of the bottles or labels generated the discrimination. In order to find out which bottle elements play the greatest role in differentiation, one has to relate the presence or absence of elements to attribute ratings. By doing so, it becomes possible to determine which elements generate consumer reactions. Furthermore, by knowing how bottle elements correspond to attribute ratings, Burkhart recognized that he could modify the label or the bottle to communicate desired perceptions. For example, if neck wrapping generated a high degree of perceived quality, then for the more expensive rose wines Burkhart could recommend that his suppliers provide neck wraps.

Concept Of Dummy Variable Regression Analysis (DVRA)

Table 6.3 shows the "anatomy" of each rose wine bottle, in terms of the presence versus absence of specific bottle elements, along with the attribute ratings. This section deals with developing a "model" or equation which relates the presence/absence of an element (e.g., neck wrapping) to attribute rating.

Researchers have developed procedures known as regression analysis to relate independent variables to a dependent variable. For instance, one might wish to relate income to a person's age and to the number of years of education. The regression equation appears as follows (Eq. 6.1):

TABLE 6.3
DATABASE FOR ROSE PACKAGE STUDY SHOWING ANATOMY OF BOTTLES (CONTENT ANALYSIS) AND CONSUMER ATTRIBUTE RATINGS

WINE CODE	CONTENT ANALYSIS OF BOTTLES					CONSUMER RATINGS				
	Cork Yes	USA Yes	Brown Yes	Neck Yes	Ornate	Purchase	Quality	Dry Flavor	Price Would Pay	Unique
1	0	1	1	1	1	39	48	74	3.92	41
2	1	0	0	0	0	32	51	63	3.43	29
3	1	0	1	0	0	37	59	76	4.21	37
4	1	1	1	1	0	48	68	84	4.78	56
5	0	0	1	0	1	31	32	53	2.09	37
6	0	1	1	0	1	46	56	78	4.65	39
7	1	0	1	1	0	42	62	65	4.57	38
8	1	1	0	1	1	57	58	87	4.98	42
9	1	0	0	1	1	42	52	71	4.32	46
10	0	1	1	0	0	36	38	63	2.87	39
11	0	0	0	1	0	41	44	68	3.78	25
12	0	0	0	0	0	31	28	52	1.99	26

Panelists used the 0-100 point scale for ratings. For price they provided a dollar and cents figure per bottle. For content analysis, 0 = No, 1 = Yes

Income = A + B (Age) + C (Years of Education) (6.1)

Let us recast the foregoing equation in terms of the current case history; attribute rating as a function of the presence/absence of specific elements of the rose bottle (Eq. 6.2):

Attribute Rating = A + B (Presence of Cork) + C (Presence of Neck Wrap) . . . (6.2)

The foregoing equation tries to relate the attribute rating (e.g., perceived high quality) to the presence of a cork, to the presence of a neck wrap, etc.

The independent variables for the regression equation constitute the characteristics of the bottle. Table 6.3 lists the characteristics (e.g., cork, neck wrap, green color). Note that a specific bottle either has or does not have the specific characteristic. If the rose bottle has the specific characteristic, then the independent variable for that characteristic assumes a value 1. On the other hand, if the rose bottle lacks that particular characteristic (e.g., the bottle has a metal cap and thus does not have a cork) then the characteristic assumes a value 0.

Given both the content analysis (which tells us which characteristic each bottle possesses) and the attribute rating (which tells us how consumers perceive the bottle), our next step consists of relating the independent variables to the dependent variable. We do so by the simple method of regression analysis. Regression analysis provides the researcher with a measure of the partwise contribution of each element (e.g., neck wrap) to each attribute. Table 6.4 provides the equations for this set of attributes.

Key Conclusions

The models shown in Table 6.4 help Burkhart and his research group to understand better how the physical variables generate consumer perceptions. Some key conclusions follow. Note that these conclusions help the marketer of rose wines understand what particular package characteristics generate consumer perceptions.

(1) The acceptance attributes vary with the characteristics of the rose bottle. In particular, having a cork rather than a cap generates a significant increase in the perceived quality of the wine. Furthermore, a neck wrap tends to increase perceived quality. The color of the bottle (brown versus green) shows little impact on purchase intent but does affect perceived quality.

(2) The sensory attribute (dryness) varies primarily with the type of closure (cork) and the country of origin (France).

(3) The proper price (which covaries with overall acceptance) also varies dramatically with the properties of the wine bottle. By changing from a

screw cap to a cork, one increases the perceived "fair price" of the wine by $1.11.

TABLE 6.4
PARAMETERS OF ADDITIVE MODELS RELATING CONSUMER RATINGS OF ROSE WINE BOTTLES TO PRESENCE/ABSENCE OF BOTTLE CHARACTERISTICS

	ATTRIBUTES				
	Purchase	Quality	Dry Flavor	Uniqueness	Unit Price ($)
Constant	31.6	31.8	55.5	23.6	2.41
BOTTLE ELEMENT					
Closure					
Screw	0	0	0	0	0
Cork	5.3	17.5	10.8	8.7	1.11
Origin					
France	0	0	0	0	0
USA	8.8	6.5	13.8	6.6	0.69
Bottle Color					
Green	0	0	0	0	0
Brown	−2.2	6.8	−0.3	6.9	0.22
Neck Wrap					
No	0	0	0	0	0
Yes	5.4	5.7	4.4	3.3	0.71
Label					
Plain	0	0	0	0	0
Ornate	2.2	−1.1	2.1	3.8	0.18
R Square	0.76	0.81	0.76	0.77	0.72

Constant = rating expected for a rose wine bottle having the following elements:
Closure—screw cap
Origin—France
Color—green
Neck—no wrap
Label—plain

In Summary

When consumers evaluate packages, they respond to a variety of cues. If the product tester or sensory analyst can perform a content analysis to determine the presence or absence of physical cues for each package, it becomes possible then to relate these cues to consumer attribute ratings. The resulting analysis generates a numerical measure, showing the partwise contribution of each package element to every attribute. The regression analysis procedure, a straightforward method, finds use here and the results allow for easy, straightforward interpretation.

SYSTEMATICALLY DEVELOPING PACKAGES TO COMMUNICATE SENSORY ATTRIBUTES

The previous case histories demonstrated a modest, rather than a dramatic relation between sensory characteristics and package. This section deals with developing a package which communicates specific sensory characteristics of the product.

A Line Of Mexican Sauces

The Drennen Corporation, headquartered in Arizona, manufactures a line of Mexican sauces. Until 1970 or so, Mexican cuisine confined itself to a limited region, principally in the southwest. In the mid to late 1970's, however, its popularity expanded and soon a variety of markets began to demand increased variety of Mexican products.

While reaping the benefit of this increased interest, Mary Drennen, president of the Drennen Corp., recognized that her company would have to expand its current line to satisfy the new wave of consumers. The Drennen Corp. manufactures and markets a hot picante sauce to satisfy the tastes of the "Tex-Mex" lovers in the Arizona market. However, market research analysis suggested that to most new consumers, unaccustomed to these hot sauces, the sauces would taste utterly too hot. Yet, the current package does not communicate the degree of spiciness, other than saying "hot".

An analysis of other packages for Mexican sauces revealed that they have a variety of different ways of communicating strength of heat. Some manufacturers used red predominantly on the label to denote "hot" and green to denote "mild". Other manufacturers used a thermometer scale, showing the continuum from hot to mild, and the position of the sauce on that continuum. Still, others relied on verbal communication, using descriptive phases.

In order to develop the best communications for the label, Mary Drennen contracted with a package design firm to develop a variety of alternative labels for her sauce products. The labels would systematically vary, in terms of the verbiage, the color of the words and the thermometer scale along with the size of the label. Table 6.5 shows the array of different labels created by the design firm for this study. Note that Table 6.5 shows a variety of different labels, targeting both at "hot" and at "mild" sauce users.

The use of systematically varied labels, rather than simply one or two "executions" differs from the traditional package development and evaluation sequence, which does not look for patterns among package elements.

TABLE 6.5
SYSTEMATIC VARIATIONS OF LABELS
FOR THE MEXICAN SAUCE PROJECT

Label	Label Color	Thermometer Level	Label Word	Label Shape
1	Red	None	Mild	A
2	Red	None	None	B
3	Red	None	Hot	B
4	Red	None	Very Hot	A
5	Red	Yes	Mild	A
6	Red	Yes	None	B
7	Red	Yes	Hot	B
8	Red	Yes	Very Hot	A
9	Green	None	None	B
10	Green	None	Mild	A
11	Green	None	Hot	A
12	Green	None	Very Hot	B
13	Green	Yes	None	B
14	Green	Yes	Mild	A
15	Green	Yes	Hot	A
16	Green	Yes	Very Hot	B

Label Color = predominant color of label.
Thermometer = the label has a thermometer scale showing the heat level.
Verbiage = the label prominently displays the heat level of the sauce.
Label Shape = A: a squarish shape, B: a rectangle.

Procedure

The procedure for this study followed the procedures thus far used in this book. The panelists, comprising of category users and interested nonusers (purchasers of Mexican sauces at least one per month, now or expected in the future) evaluated each of the test bottles, using a wide variety of attributes. During the introduction and prior to the actual evaluation, the panelists had a chance to evaluate a single sauce using the same characteristics. This introductory evaluation, prior to the actual evaluation of the bottle prototypes, provided Drennen with the opportunity to anchor the panelist's ratings in concrete experience.

Table 6.6 provides the average ratings for each of the bottles. Note the great deal of discrimination on the attributes, confirming the hypothesis that the change in the label can generate significant changes in the consumer's impression of the product. We also observe changes in the expected sensory characteristics of the sauce. The sensory changes show as much or even more variation versus the acceptance and image characteristics.

TABLE 6.6
CONSUMER RATINGS ASSIGNED TO
SYSTEMATICALLY VARIED SAUCE PACKAGES

Package	Purchase	Hotness	Good Taste	Mexican	Price Would Pay	Eye Catching
1	26	16	31	30	131	34
2	31	19	38	57	135	50
3	44	37	38	27	157	45
4	42	51	17	42	168	22
5	28	23	38	71	135	41
6	44	26	47	34	136	64
7	44	41	37	55	126	68
8	31	50	28	44	159	41
9	36	32	25	55	180	16
10	26	18	35	31	149	44
11	66	37	39	46	139	46
12	39	49	16	22	160	22
13	22	27	38	64	149	33
14	52	23	35	34	139	60
15	63	42	42	23	184	63
16	29	51	24	44	118	37

All scales in 0-100 format except price shown.
Price shown in actual cents that a panelist says she would pay for bottle of the sauce (e.g., 131 = $1.31).

Understanding What Each Element Brings To Every Attribute Rating

The systematic variation of elements for the bottle allows the marketer to clearly understand the marginal, or partwise contribution of these elements to attributes. Since the package designer independently varied the physical characteristics, according to a specific design, it becomes a straightforward matter to relate the presence or absence of each label element to every consumer rated attribute.

In order to develop a model, which summarizes how the variables generate perceptions, we first have to represent each label in terms of its "architecture" (namely, the presence/absence of particular elements). Table 6.7 shows the architecture. If a label has a "1" in the variable called "green" this means that the label has a predominantly green color, and therefore not a red color.

TABLE 6.7
BINARY CODING OF MEXICAN
SAUCE LABELS FOR ANALYSIS

Label	Label Color		Thermometer		Verbiage on Label				Label Shape	
	Green	Red	Yes	No	Very* Mild	Mild	Hot	Very Hot	Rectangle	Square
1	0	1	0	1	0	1	0	0	0	1
2	0	1	0	1	1	0	0	0	1	0
3	0	1	0	1	0	0	1	0	1	0
4	0	1	0	1	0	0	0	1	0	1
5	0	1	1	0	1	0	0	0	0	1
6	0	1	1	0	0	1	0	0	1	0
7	0	1	1	0	0	0	1	0	1	0
8	0	1	1	0	0	0	0	1	0	1
9	1	0	0	1	0	1	0	0	0	1
10	1	0	0	1	1	0	0	0	1	0
11	1	0	0	1	0	0	1	0	1	0
12	1	0	0	1	0	0	0	1	0	1
13	1	0	1	0	1	0	0	0	0	1
14	1	0	1	0	0	1	0	0	1	0
15	1	0	1	0	0	0	1	0	1	0
16	1	0	1	0	0	0	0	1	0	1

*Not stated on package (coded as none).

Developing The Model By Regression Analysis

We can develop the additive model by straightforward regression analysis, as we did previously. This time, each variable either assumes a value of 1 or a value of 0. We can then determine the "weight" or number of points brought by each variable, when it assumes the value 1 (namely, when it appears).

Table 6.8 shows the parameters of the model. The model acts as a shorthand summary. It shows, quite distinctly and clearly, what occurs in the attribute ratings when the package designer makes systematic variations in a label by changing the color, mentioning the "hotness", etc.

TABLE 6.8
PARAMETERS OF ADDITIVE MODEL FOR
MEXICAN SAUCE BOTTLES

	Purchase	Hotness	Good Taste	Mexican	Price Would Pay
Intercept*	25	25	33	59	154
Color					
Red	0	0	0	0	0
Green	5.4	2	-2.7	-5.3	9.1
Thermometer					
No	0	0	0	0	0
Yes	0.4	3	6.1	7.2	-9.3
Shape					
Round	0	0	0	0	0
Rectangle	10.3	-3	5.6	-16	-8.9
Heat Statement					
Very Mild	0	0	0	0	0
Mild	-.3	-6	-2.4	-11	11.5
Hot	15.8	14.8	-1.1	-6.6	5.9
Very Hot	7.1	22.8	-13	-22	-3.2
Multiple R	0.63	0.97	0.88	0.42	0.24

* = Expected rating for label with these properties:
Reference Label Color = Red
Thermometer = Not shown
Label Shape = Round
Heat Level = Not mentioned (very mild as a reference)

One element from each class must assume the reference value of 0. It does not matter which element takes on the zero reference value.

Utility Of The Model

Models relating independently varied characteristics (e.g., package variables) to attribute ratings provide the product tester, sensory analyst and marketer with a tool that has two purposes.

First, in terms of knowledge building, the model shows the interrelation between independent variables and consumer perceptions. Quite often, such knowledge accretes from many studies, conducted over the years, with different panelists, stimuli, and attributes. This knowledge represents an amalgam of observations, not necessarily pulled together into a coherent whole. In contrast, the model provides a coherency, based upon a database that possesses many key variables, analyzed by the same set of people, using the same scale and the same attributes.

Second in terms of engineering and optimizing, the model provides a utilitarian roadmap. All too often package designers, marketers, researchers and product sensory analysts work towards optimizing a product or package, using incomplete data. A package evaluation might consist of simply modifying one characteristic (e.g., neck wrapping), with a decision contingent upon the outcome of that limited test. The model allows the researcher and marketer to weigh the impact of many alternatives in order to make a decision.

AN OVERVIEW

This chapter has illustrated one method for the evaluation of packaging. The techniques described allow the product tester to understand the response to the package, much as one understands the response to a product.

One key additional variable brought into play here concerns the concept of content analysis and systematic design. By breaking down packaging into component variables, it becomes possible to determine how specific package variables generate consumer perceptions. Thus, rather than limiting oneself only to consumer reactions to the "entire package" or "gestalt" it now becomes possible to trace consumer reactions to package elements.

REFERENCES

MOSKOWITZ, H. R. 1981. Psychophysical approaches to package design and evaluation. In: *Handbook Of Package Design Research* pp. 505-534. (W. Stern, ed.) John Wiley, New York.

STERN, W. 1981. *Handbook Of Package Design Research.* John Wiley, New York.

CHAPTER 7

CONSUMER EVALUATION OF PRICE VARIABLES

BACKGROUND

Traditionally, product testers working in an R&D environment have shied away from "pricing" or other economic analyses of products, preferring instead to concentrate on the more formulation-related characteristics. On the other hand, marketers and marketing researchers, concerned with the performance of products in the background of daily life, pay attention to pricing variables as one element of the marketing mix.

This chapter concerns the evaluation of price as part of the testing procedure for products. It looks at pricing as one factor that influences purchase intent, and as a variable which can act as a surrogate measure of acceptance. The chapter concentrates on pricing evaluation within the confines of product and package testing.

ASKING QUESTIONS ABOUT PRICE

How does the researcher ask price-related questions? We respond to price variables in many different ways. For instance, we can volunteer a price for a particular stimulus. Or, someone can give us a price, to which we react. Or, we can react to a price range, either expressed in terms of numbers or in terms of qualitatively different labels (expensive, fair, cheap, etc.).

In product testing, the researcher also has a number of ways to present price questions. One way consists of presenting the panelist with a price. The panelist has to react by rating purchase intent, by saying something about the price (e.g., too high, too low, just right), etc. Another way of asking pricing questions consists of presenting the panelist with a set of price points or prices. The panelist then must select which particular price, from the set, comes closest to the "fair price" of the item. Most panelists have little or no trouble doing either task. Prototypical instructions for the task appear in Table 7.1.

TABLE 7.1
SAMPLE INSTRUCTIONS FOR RATING PRICE

SET 1— PANELIST ASKED TO PROVIDE PROPER PRICE:

After tasting this product, please write in the fair price that you think you would pay.

SET 2— PANELIST ASKED TO RATE PURCHASE INTENT AT VARIOUS PRICES:

Below you will see various prices for this product. For each price we want you to rate your purchase intent:

Your purchase interest if the item cost $0.79.
Your purchase interest if the item cost $0.99.
Your purchase interest if the item cost $1.09.
Your purchase interest if the item cost $1.29.
Your purchase interest if the item cost $1.39.

SET 3— PANELIST ASKED TO RATE PURCHASE INTENT IF THE ITEM COSTS MORE THAN THEIR REGULAR ITEM:

Please rate your purchase intent in this item if it costs 30 cents less than your regular—(item name).
Please rate your purchase intent in this item if it costs 20 cents more than your regular—(item name).

SET 4— PANELIST ASKED TO SELECT THE APPROPRIATE PRICE FOR THE ITEM

Please select which of the prices below comes closest to a "fair price."

A. $0.79
B. $0.99
C. $1.09
D. $1.29
E. $1.39

Types Of Analyses Involving Price Variables

This chapter deals with several different types of questions that the product tester and marketer can answer using price as a variable in product evaluation. The questions follow.

(1) Do consumers know the proper price for a product?

(2) How does purchase intent vary with price? How does purchase intent covary with both price and product acceptance?

(3) Can we develop a general quantitative expression interrelating product acceptance, stated item price, actual item fair price and product acceptance or product quality?

DO CONSUMERS KNOW THE PRICE OF A PRODUCT

Background

This section deals with the ability of consumers to estimate the price of a product. Can they do it? Does pricing act independently of product quality or product acceptance, or in fact, does the perceived fair price of an item actually correlate, in almost a perfect sense, with the perceived acceptance of the product?

CASE HISTORY—SNACK CHEESES

The Witt Corporation of Wisconsin manufactures and markets a line of snack cheeses which enjoy popularity in the midwestern states. Over the past four years, Richard Witt, president, has seen wide fluctuations in the cost of cheese. In the processed snack cheese business, this fluctuation translates to a variation of cents per pound of cheese, enough sometimes to severely impact profitability.

Richard Witt recognized that to insure stability and consumer loyalty he had to market his snack cheeses at a price that consumers would find attractive. A cheese selling for too high a price might not generate the necessary volume. A cheese selling for too low a price might generate some profits when the cheese costs reached their lower levels, but would lose money for the corporation when the cost of goods rose.

Test Design

The test design for the study appears in Table 7.2. Note that for this study, the panelists (all cheese purchasers and eaters) had to eat some of each sample of cheese and then select that price which they thought most appropriate for the product. The panelists evaluated the cheeses both blind (without benefit of identification) and branded (with the label, etc., but without the actual price).

Altogether, 150 consumers participated in this study. Since each panelist selected the one price for each cheese that they thought most appropriate, the data that we work with consists of the distribution of "appropriate prices" for each cheese. Table 7.3 shows the distribution, for each of the cheeses.

Key findings from this study include the following.

(1) Consumers have an idea of the fair price of a cheese product. Consumers do not simply put down the lowest price as a fair price.

TABLE 7.2
TEST DESIGN FOR CHEESE STUDY

STEP 1—	Panelist recruited for the study (qualified as cheese eaters.)
STEP 2—	Panelists oriented in evaluation by warmup exercise.
STEP 3—	Panelists rate first cheese, "blind" (without identification), scaling in on attributes. Sensory attributes (appearance, aroma, taste/flavor, texture). Liking attributes (overall, purchase intent, liking of sensory characteristics, such as liking of appearance, liking of aroma, etc.). Panelists select a "fair price" for a 1 pound piece of this cheese, if sold at their local supermarket. The prices appear on the questionnaire.
STEP 4—	Panelists rate remaining cheeses (4 in total) on attributes, following the approach of Step 3. They rate all cheese on a "blind basis", each panelists following a randomized order of products.
STEP 5—	Panelists follow the same sequence this time, however, rating the cheese on an identified basis (type of cheese, manufacturer, picture of cheese fully wrapped). They use the same scale and attributes.

(2) The distribution of fair prices varies, according to the acceptance of the cheese. Those cheeses achieving higher consumer acceptance also tend to command higher fair prices.

(3) We can relate the modal or typical price to product acceptance by means of a simple equation, which appears below. (The independent variable = product acceptance, as measured by overall liking, whereas the dependent variable = most representative fair price) (Eq. 7.1 and 7.2).

$$\text{Fair Price} = A + B\ (\text{Overall Liking}) \qquad (7.1)$$

$$\text{Fair Price} = 102 + 0.25\ (\text{Overall Liking}) \qquad (R^2 = 0.84) \qquad (7.2)$$

(4) The branding of a cheese tends to increase the perceived fair price for the cheese, although not to the same level for each cheese (Eq. 7.3).

$$\text{Fair Price} = 86.5 + 0.58\ (\text{Overall Liking}) \qquad (R^2 = 0.49) \qquad (7.3)$$

Overall, then, the cheese study suggests that consumers do have a fair price in mind for cheeses. Individuals differ from each other, but we can arrive at a single, or modal fair price. This fair price will change for the same cheese if we present the cheese "branded" instead of blind.

TABLE 7.3
RATING LIKING AND DISTRIBUTION OF FAIR PRICES FOR FOUR CHEESES

		PERCENT WHO FEEL THIS PRICE REPRSENTS A FAIR PRICE					
Cheese	Rated Liking	$0.79	$0.99	$1.09	$1.29	$1.39	Average Fair Price ($)
		Numbers Below Represent Percentages					
Blind							
A	35	16	21	32	17	14	1.097
B	42	13	15	27	31	14	1.14
C	51	8	19	32	28	13	1.142
D	58	5	17	30	40	8	1.162
Branded							
A	43	17	27	21	22	13	1.095
B	50	14	15	25	12	34	1.159
C	57	10	13	29	21	27	1.17
D	51	5	12	26	24	33	1.21

PRICE AND LIKING AS DETERMINANTS OF PURCHASE INTENT

The previous case history dealt with the most simplistic of cases; the panelist had to choose which of several prices best fit a specific product. For this next case history, we will evaluate price another way. The consumers will receive products with varying price levels. For each combination of product and price level, the consumer will rate purchase intent on a scale. We will focus our interest in the relation between purchase intent, and two independent variables; item acceptance (rated by the panelist) and price (provided by the marketer). In this way, we will have an opportunity to measure the relative impact of price versus acceptance (namely, quality) as joint determining factors of purchase intent.

CASE HISTORY—PREPARED STUFFINGS

The Rosen Corporation markets prepared stuffings for turkeys and chickens, under its own label, as well as co-packs for other companies. The prepared stuffing market has expanded in size due to the convenience of the product and the increased consumption of fowl and fish, in place of red meat. During this time, Ted Rosen, president, launched two very successful entries into the market and instructed his R&D product developers to produce three more flavor line extensions to round out the Rosen line.

In a convenience food market, consumers often spend a great deal more money than they ordinarily would because of the convenience involved. With a rapidly growing market, Rosen did not know exactly how best to price the product so that it would attract consumers. He recognized that the lower the price the greater volume he could expect but did not know the precise relation.

Test Design

In order to determine the relation between product cost, product acceptance and purchase intent, Rosen decided to run a simple experiment. In the experiment, he would present to panelists four different products, each priced at one of four different prices. This generated a total of 16 combinations. From these combinations, he could measure purchase intent for each combination and relate that to acceptance of the product and cost. This test design would allow Rosen and his research staff to factor out the contribution of price versus the contribution of product acceptance.

TABLE 7.4
RELATION BETWEEN LIKING OF TURKEY STUFFING, PRICE AT WHICH OFFERED, AND PURCHASE INTENT

PRODUCT	PRICE OF STUFFING/BOX				LIKING
	$1.59	$2.09	$2.49	$2.99	
A	31	29	22	19	41
B	45	36	31	22	46
C	51	42	27	24	56
D	62	43	31	26	63

Numbers in body of table reflect purchase intent (0 = definitely not buy, 100 = definitely buy)

Results

Table 7.4 shows the results of the study in terms of purchase intent ratings, overall acceptance and unit price of the stuffing products. As we can see, with increasing unit price, purchase intent ratings decrease, suggesting that consumers say they would reduce their interest in a stuffing product as the price increases. All well and good. However, can we develop a mathematical relation which quantifies how unit increases in price affect purchase intent?

In order to answer the question, let us develop a model or equation relating cost of the stuffing to purchase intent. Since we have four different stimuli (four flavors), we first develop four equations, one for each stuffing flavor. We can develop either a linear equation, as shown below (Eq. 7.4) or a power function equation (Eq. 7.5):

Linear Equation: Purchase Intent = A − B (Unit Price) (7.4)

(Interpretation: As the unit price increases 1 unit, the purchase intent rating changes by B units on the purchase intent scale.)

Power Function Equation: Purchase Intent = C (Unit Price)$^{-D}$ (7.5)

(Interpretation: If the exponent D equals 1, then a 1% increase in unit price changes purchase intent by 1% on the scale. If the exponent D exceeds 1, then a 1% increase in unit price generates more than a 1% decrease in purchase intent. Finally, if the exponent D drops below 1, then a 1% increase in unit price generates less than a 1% decrease in purchase intent.)

As Table 7.5 shows, the sign of the coefficient B in the linear equation, or the exponent D in the power function takes on a negative value. This confirms the intuitive observation that as price increases, tendency to purchase decreases. In general, we find the exponent D to exceed 1.0. This means that percent increases in the stated price of the item generate commensurately more drop in the purchase intent than we might expect. Consumers appear highly sensitive to the price of the item and the price can swing purchase intent fairly strongly.

Combining Price And Acceptance

Can we combine the data for price and acceptance, and determine how they trade off to generate purchase intent? To do so requires that we develop an equation which contains two independent variables; unit price and acceptance. In our study on prepared stuffings, we have a total of 16 observations or "cases", corresponding to the four flavors × four price

TABLE 7.5
(A) SIMPLE EQUATIONS RELATING PURCHASE INTENT TO PRICE

Product	Purchase = A + B (Price)	R^2	Price = C $(Price)^D$	R^2
A	46.4 – 9.25	0.94	47.6 – 0.82	0.91
B	72.8 – 17.34	0.98	77.6 – 1.09	0.95
C	83.3 – 20.66	0.93	95.9 – 1.28	0.93
D	100.1 – 26.03	0.93	119.1 – 1.42	0.99

(B) EQUATIONS JOINTLY RELATING PRICE AND LIKING TO PURCHASE INTENT

Purchase Intent = 43.7 + 0.61 (Liking) – 18.01 (Price)	$R^2 = 0.85$
Purchase Intent = 2.45 $(Liking)^{0.89}$ $(Price)^{-1.15}$	$R^2 = 0.91$

points. For each case we know the item price (Rosen's research director Lynn Hill set that price), as well as the average acceptance of the item (from the liking rating assigned to that item, independent of price) and the purchase intent rating assigned to the combination of item and price.

The next step consists of developing a model or equation, using the technique of multiple linear regression. To do so, let us consider two different types of equations (Eq. 7.6):

$$\text{Plane: Purchase Intent} = A + B\,(\text{Price}) + C\,(\text{Liking}) \qquad (7.6)$$

The planar or multiple linear equation above states that we determine purchase intent by weighting the price and the liking separately. The regression program computes the value of A (intercept, expected purchase intent at 0 price, 0 liking), the slope for price (B), and the slope for liking (C). The parameters appear in Table 7.5 and confirm that pricing plays a stronger role. We can also look at the power function equation (Eq. 7.7):

$$\text{Purchase Intent} = D\,(\text{Price})^E\,(\text{Liking})^F \qquad (7.7)$$

The power function equation represents a multiplicative expression. The same rules hold for the exponents here as held before; if the exponent (E) exceeds 1, then 1% increases in price or liking generate more than 1% changes in purchase intent. Conversely, if the exponent drops below 1, then 1% increases generate less than 1% changes in purchase intent.

To help interpret the magnitude of the slopes, Table 7.6 presents some linear and power function values and the interpretation. Note that as the exponent increases beyond 1, small changes in the independent variable (e.g., price) generate commensurately larger changes in the dependent variable (e.g., purchase intent).

TABLE 7.6
HOW PERCENT CHANGE IN UNIT PRICE OR ACCEPTANCE GENERATES PERCENTAGE CHANGES IN PURCHASE INTENT

Exponent	Percent Change in Price or in Acceptance			
	1	2	3	4
−1.5	−1.5	−2.9	−4.3	−5.7
−1.2	−1.2	−2.3	−3.5	−4.6
−0.9	−0.89	−1.8	−2.6	−3.5
−0.6	−0.60	−1.2	−1.8	−2.3
−0.3	−0.30	−0.59	−0.88	−1.2
0	0	0	0	0
0.3	0.299	0.596	0.891	1.18
0.6	0.599	1.20	1.79	2.38
0.9	0.900	1.80	2.70	3.59
1.2	1.20	2.40	3.61	4.82
1.5	1.50	3.01	4.53	6.06

Numbers in table represent percent change in purchase intent expected for a 1-4 percent increase in either price or acceptance. The magnitude of the change depends upon the exponent, shown at the left, and the percent increase in price (or acceptance) shown at the top.

Interpreting the Results

In product development and marketing quite often, the manufacturer

TABLE 7.7
DATABASE FOR FROZEN ENTREES OF DIFFERENT TYPES OFFERED AT VARIOUS PRICES

ENTREE	OFFERED UNIT PRICE	CONSUMER RATED FAIR PRICE	OFFERED PRICE/ FAIR PRICE × 100	PURCHASE INTENT AT OFFERED PRICE	ENTREE LIKING RATING
A	.79	.91	86	55	45
A	.89	.91	97	43	45
*A	.99	.91	108	40	45
A	1.09	.91	119	29	45
B	1.19	1.41	84	51	42
B	1.29	1.41	91	46	42
*B	1.49	1.41	105	31	42
B	1.69	1.41	119	27	42
C	2.19	2.05	106	51	55
*C	2.29	2.05	111	43	55
C	2.39	2.05	116	39	55
C	2.59	2.05	126	32	55
D	3.19	3.43	93	52	48
D	3.39	3.43	98	43	48
*D	3.59	3.43	104	41	48
D	3.79	3.43	110	33	48
E	3.89	3.91	99	43	46
*E	4.09	3.91	104	40	46
E	4.29	3.91	109	27	46
E	4.49	3.91	114	19	46
F	4.39	4.76	92	58	51
F	4.49	4.76	94	51	51
*F	4.59	4.76	96	42	51
F	4.79	4.76	100	31	51

A = Entree 1
B = Entree 2
C = Entree 3
D = Entree 4
E = Entree 5
F = Entree 6

*Price at which entree normally retails.

does not know the relation between perceived quality (acceptance), price and purchase intent. The data just discussed suggest that price plays an overwhelming role in generating purchase intent. Thus, from a strategic point of view, it appears best to concentrate on reducing price. The manufacturer might wish to increase product quality, but beyond a minimal level of quality it appears that price factors, not quality factors, operate to generate purchase.

EVALUATING PRICE, ACCEPTANCE, AND PURCHASE RELATIONS FOR PRODUCTS WHICH QUALITATIVELY VARY OVER A WIDE RANGE

The previous sections dealt with a limited array of products, representing small differences from one another. A continuing question in consumer goods concerns the existence of a general price—acceptance—purchase intent relation for items in the same general class which vary over a wide range of prices and which differ qualitatively from each other. For instance, frozen entrees constitute such a category. The entrees vary in type, acceptance and cost (from 59 cents at the low end to $4-5.00 for specialty items).

For products that vary over a wide range, both of price and acceptability (but which one might classify together), the price variation and the acceptance variation loom so large as to overshadow the simplistic relation shown in Table 7.7. However, we might uncover the underlying relation by the simple procedure of "normalizing" the price. The investigator can instruct panelists first to assign an estimate of the "fair price" of each entree. Afterwards, the panelists can rate purchase intent for each entree at several different price points around this fair price. By so doing, the researcher does not have to use the same price points for the various products (which may really differ dramatically from each other in actual dollar value).

The relation between purchase intent, acceptance, and price now becomes a relation between purchase intent, acceptance and "relative price". We define relative price as the quantity: price offered/fair price.

Table 7.8 shows the results of this exercise for a variety of entrees. Note that the entrees range in value over a span of several dollars, so that the normalization procedure effectively brings all of the entrees down to a common price range.

TABLE 7.8
RELATION BETWEEN PURCHASE INTENT, ENTREE ACCEPTANCE (LIKING), OFFERING PRICE, AND RATED "FAIR PRICE"

1. Relation Between Purchase and Both Offering Price and Liking—Without Taking Into Account "Fair Price"

Linear: Purchase Intent = 15.6 − 1.66 (Price of Offering) + 0.61 (Liking) $R^2 = 0.08$

Power: Purchase Intent = 9.89 (Price of Offering) $(\text{Liking})^{1.05}$ $R^2 = 0.12$

2. Relation Between Purchase Intent and Both Offering Price and Liking—After "Correcting" the Offering Price By the "Fair Price"

Linear: $\text{Purchase Intent} = 76.3 - 0.79 \left(\frac{\text{Price of Offering}}{\text{Fair Price}}\right) + 0.95\,(\text{Liking})$ $R^2 = 0.72$

Power: $\text{Purchase} = 5754 \left(\frac{\text{Price of Offering}}{\text{Fair Price}}\right)^{-2.35} \times (\text{Liking})^{1.57}$ $R^2 = 0.67$

Price of offering = price at which the manufacturer offers the item.

Fair price = panelist estimates of appropriate price for the item.

AN OVERVIEW

The evaluation of price variables complicates product testing. Most R&D product research deals with the acceptance of products without price or other marketing variables. However, in the real world of consumer behavior, price variables may equal or outweigh the effect of acceptance.

This chapter has illustrated some techniques by which the researcher can get a feeling about the relative importance of price versus acceptance. Typically, one will find that price does outweigh acceptance. This means that consumers pay more attention to price than to product quality, although in general the product quality has to exceed a certain lower threshold, below which no price reduction will suffice to induce purchase.

REFERENCES

GABOR, A. and GRANGER, C. W. J. 1964. Price sensitivity of the consumer. J. Advertising Res. *4,* 40-44.

GABOR, A. and GRANGER, C. W. J. 1964. On the price consciousness of consumers. Appl. Stat. *10,* 710-188.

GALANTER, E. 1962. The direct measurement of utility and subjective probability. Amer. J. Psychol. *75,* 208-220.

JACOBY, J., OLSON, J. C. and HADDOCK, R. A. 1971. Price, brand name, and product composition characteristics as determinants of perceived quality. J. Appl. Psychol. *55,* 570-579.

KAMEN, J. and TOMAN, R. J. 1970. Psychophysics of prices. J. Marketing Res. *7,* 27-35.

LEAVITT, H. 1954. A note on some experimental findings about the meaning of price. J. Business *27,* 205-210.

MCCONNELL, J. D. 1968. An experimental examination of the price-quality relationship. J. Business *41,* 439-444.

MCCONNELL, J. D. 1968. Effect of pricing on perceptions of product quality. J. Appl. Psychol. *52,* 331-334.

MONROE, K. B. 1973. Buyer's subjective perception of price. J. Marketing Res. *10,* 70-80.

MONROE, K. B. 1971. Psychophysics of price: A reappraisal. J. Marketing *8,* 248-251.

MONROE, K. B. and DELLA BITTA, A. J. 1978. Models for pricing decisions. J. Marketing Res. *15,* 417.

MOSKOWITZ, H. R. and RABINO, S. 1981. Price, quality and preference—implications for marketing strategy. Boston University School of Management, Working Paper Series, Boston, MA.

NEWMAN, D. and BECKNELL, J. 1970. The price-quality relationship as a tool in consumer research. Proceedings, 78th Annual Conference, American Psychological Association, 729-730.

PETERSON, R. 1970. The price-perceived quality relationship: Experimental evidence. J. Marketing Res. *7,* 525-528.

RIESZ, P. C. 1980. A major price-perceived quality study reexamined. J. Marketing Res. *17,* 259-262.

TULL, D., BORING, R. A. and GONSIOR, M. H. 1964. A note on the relationship of price and imputed quality. J. Business *37,* 186-191.

VALENZI, E. R. and ANDREWS, I. R. 1971. Effect of price information on product quality ratings. J. Appl. Psychol. *55,* 87-91.

CHAPTER 8

PRODUCT TESTING WITH CHILDREN

INTRODUCTION

A glance through the scientific literature on product testing will reveal that much of our knowledge of how to test products comes from experience and experiments using adults. Testing foods with children poses an entirely new set of problems, combining new food preferences with procedural difficulties due to problems with behavior and comprehension.

This chapter deals with the pragmatics of testing foods with children. It offers procedures which have worked in the past and which allow the researcher and product tester to secure useful data from children. The reader should keep in mind, however, that nothing succeeds like good practical experience with children. The product tester who proposes to work with children can follow the guidelines set up here. However, the tester should run a pilot study with children to flesh out some of the key points and to uncover hidden problems which always manage to emerge when children participate

SOME KEY ISSUES TO KEEP IN MIND FOR PRODUCT TESTING WITH CHILDREN

Sensory Development

Do children have the same sensory acuities as do adults? Quite often, one hears that children possess a different "sensory system" than do adults and, as a consequence, the children "taste foods differently." Basic research studies on the senses of vision and audition suggest that children react to tones and lights much as adults do and thus do not differ particularly from adults.

For the chemical senses, taste and smell, we do not know the answers with quite as much certainty. We do know that as people get older, their acuity diminishes. The threshold level or lowest concentration of a material needed to excite taste or smell sensations increases but the increases occur as we get older, starting at about forty or so. We cannot project the trend backwards to conclude that children, either at preschool or in school, possess greater acuity than do adolescents and young adults.

Problems With Language

Scales. Young children, especially those who have not had experience with arithmetic, have problems with the concept of magnitude or amount. Typically, to these children, the continuum of magnitude foreshortens itself into a small set of nodal points, such as "a little", a "moderate amount" (not a common point) and "a lot". Children can use line scales to denote "amount", but generally they place their markers on these scales at the extreme ends to denote their impressions of the product.

Attributes. Children also have problems understanding what attributes mean. Children can and do differentiate among colors but when it comes to flavors and tastes, the children may have difficulty. Quite often children confuse attributes such as tartness (sourness) and bitterness. For unusual sweeteners, children may confuse the sweet taste with off-tastes present and fail to differentiate the sweetness from the accompanying tastes.

Problems with the meaning of the attributes pose difficulties in testing children. Despite the interviewer's desire to explain the meaning of the attribute, quite often the children just simply do not catch on.

Field Dependence Versus Field Independence

Colors influence what we taste. Color a candy the wrong color and many people will not correctly identify the flavor. They will attend to the color. For children, field dependence (or dependence on the visual input) generally overrides the reaction to flavor and aroma. As a consequence, the child's reaction to the product may emerge most highly correlated to the visual characteristics, rather than derive from the actual flavor composition.

CASE HISTORY—CHOCOLATE BAR CANDY

The Kornheiser Candy Company manufactures chocolate bars. During the past several years, interest has grown in the development of a new candy bar for young children with specific health benefits associated with the candy. Alan Kornheiser, president, recommended that the company manufacture and market a bar containing chocolate and soy protein, along with vitamins and minerals. In effect, the chocolate bar would constitute a meal for a child. In particular, the use of a chocolate bar would appeal to children who like candies, and might be used as a nutritional supplement for problem eaters among the young children (ages 3-10).

R&D developed a set of 6 alternative formulations for the candy bars, comprising 3 varying ratios of chocolate and protein, along with two different surface textures; smooth and rough. These designs, presented schematically in Table 8.1, represented an array of sensorially different products, at least to the product developer and to the director of R&D at the Kornheiser Co. However, these people did not know whether or not children would accept the bars, and if indeed the products failed in acceptance tests, then how to change the characteristics to improve acceptance.

The marketing research director, Bert Krieger, recognized the need to test among the target audience, namely young children. Additionally, he recognized the difficulties which might ensue because these young children do not understand many attributes and may not understand the scale.

TABLE 8.1
SCHEMATIC FOR CHILDREN'S CANDY
COMPRISING DIFFERENT RATIOS OF CHOCOLATES TO
PROTEIN AND ONE OF TWO TEXTURES

Product	Chocolate/Protein	Texture
1	A	S
2	B	S
3	C	S
4	A	R
5	B	R
6	C	R

Code
A = 60% Chocolate
B = 70% Chocolate
C = 80% Chocolate

S = Smooth Texture
R = Rough Texture

Working With Young Children

Since part of the study involved young children (ages 5-7) who had not had experience with scaling, Krieger realized that the traditional approaches to sensory analysis of candies would not apply. The children could not use the conventional 0-100 point scale, nor even a fixed point scale comprising fewer categories. Rather, the children had to use a more visual type of scale with a limited number of attributes.

One attractive procedure for scaling consists of presenting children with a series of faces, denoting degree of liking or amount. Figure 1 shows the "facial hedonic" scale, that Krieger used for the study. Here, the children had to choose which of the nine different faces best represented how they felt about the candy that they had just tested. The facial hedonic scale does not necessarily provide a truly equal interval scale. The difference in liking from Snoopy 1 (least liked) to Snoopy 2 (next least liked), does not necessarily equal the difference in liking from Snoopy 8 to Snoopy 9 (most liked). Nonetheless, Krieger used the scale, recognizing that the children would have fewer problems with this type of scale than with the more conventional number scale.

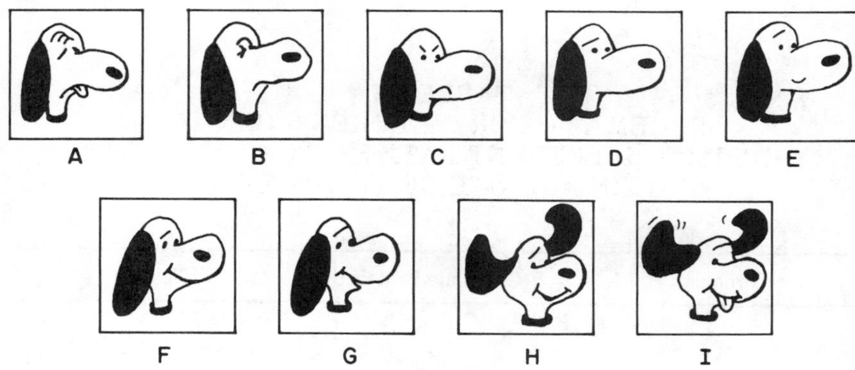

FIG. 8.1. FACIAL HEDONIC ("SNOOPY") SCALE.
The scale goes from A (representing dislike extremely) to "I" (like extremely). The 9 points on the scale correspond to 6, 17, 29, 42, 54, 64, 73, 82 and 90, respectively, on a 0-100 point scale. However, the child reacts to the face, not to the numerical equivalent.

Test Procedure

The sequence of activities for the chocolate bar test appears in Table 8.2. Note that for this test, with young children, each of the younger children works with one interviewer. In contrast, the techniques discussed previously which used a classroom type session, wherein each panelist worked alone and interacted with an interviewer only after completing a product evaluation.

Generally, young children (8 and below) have a hard time paying attention for long time periods. Hence, for the best results in an extended product test, the research director recognized that he had to provide both an adequate testing area and a waiting area, where the children could amuse themselves, by watching television or by coloring. This procedure generates good data because the children do the testing for only a limited time, after which they can relax in a play environment.

TABLE 8.2
SEQUENCE OF ACTIVITIES FOR CHILDREN'S EVALUATION OF CANDY BARS

STEP 1—	Child recruited by telephone, invited to participate for a 2 hour session.
STEP 2—	Mother/father brings the child to the test center. About 20 children participate in a single session.
STEP 3—	Children play in an assigned room, under supervision of an interviewer.
STEP 4—	When the child's turn comes up to evaluate the first product, an interviewer brings the child out of the room, and also picks up the proper product for that child, for that evaluation.
STEP 5—	The interviewer brings the child and the candy sample to another interviewer. The first interviewer then leaves the child with the second interviewer (questioner).
STEP 6—	The questioner shows the child the Snoopy faces, and explains the meaning of the scale (from love to hate).
STEP 7—	The questioner asks the child to look at the bar, and to point to the Snoopy face that best describes how the child feels about the way the bar looks.
STEP 8—	The questioner records the rating.
STEP 9—	The questioner repeats steps 7-8, for all attributes, for that product. In all cases, the child rates liking.
STEP 10—	The questioner then instructs another interviewer to return the child to the play area.

Note: The child takes a drink of water before evaluating each product.

At least 7 minutes elapse between evaluations of products. With a 2 hour session, this allows for at least 10 products that a child can rate, at a relaxed, comfortable pace.

Results—Discrimination And Scale Behavior

The initial analysis consisted first of an assessment of discrimination across products for the younger and the older children. Keep in mind that both the younger and the older children used a Snoopy or facial hedonic scale to evaluate overall liking. In addition, however, the older children worked with the conventional 0-100 scale for other attributes. Did the older children show more differences on the same (Snoopy) scale than the younger children? Table 8.3 shows the results of an analysis of variance with matched samples of younger versus older children, both groups using the Snoopy facial hedonic scale. From Table 8.3, we see that the younger children exhibited smaller differences in degree of liking than did the older children. This finding should not surprise anyone who has worked with children, because children seem to have a more polarized view of the hedonic world; they either like (love) or dislike (hate) things, rather than showing graded levels of acceptance. In contrast, the older children tend to show more gradations of acceptance. Table 8.4 shows the distribution of ratings and reveals that the younger children clustered their ratings at the top of the Snoopy scale.

TABLE 8.3
RELATIVE DISCRIMINATION ON ATTRIBUTES: COMPARISON OF YOUNG CHILDREN VS. OLDER CHILDREN USING ANALYSIS OF VARIANCE*

Liking Attribute Scale	Young Kids (Snoopy)	Older Kids (Snoopy)	Older Kids (0-100)
Appearance	2.2	3.7	5.1
Aroma	0.6	1.2	2.5
Taste/Flavor	1.7	2.2	3.5
Texture	1.8	2.6	3.6
Overall	1.1	2.8	3.7

Test Conditions:

15 Children per panel.
Each child rated every product once.
Each child rated all six test products (see Table 1).
The younger children used a Snoopy (facial hedonic) scale.
The older children used both a Snoopy scale and an anchored, 0-100 scale.

All values in the table represent F ratios (matched samples, products)

TABLE 8.4
DISTRIBUTION OF LIKING RATINGS
FOR CANDY BARS—ON SNOOPY SCALE
(LUMPING ALL SIX PRODUCTS TOGETHER)

	Snoopy	Older Children (8-12 Years Old	Younger Children (6-7 Years Old)
(Dislike)	1	32	15
	2	7	2
	3	7	2
	4	6	1
	5	2	4
	6	2	4
	7	11	10
	8	11	14
(Like)	9	22	48
Total:		100%	100%

Numbers in Table = Percentage of panelists selecting the Snoopy scale for their ratings.

GETTING MORE FROM THE DATA BY INTEGRATING THE DATA BASE

The previous sections concerned ratings of overall liking and attribute liking. We saw that the younger children tend to polarize their ratings. Can we develop a method by which to discover how and which specific attributes generate the acceptance, as rated by these younger children (or, conversely, by the older children)? We probably cannot use the ratings of attribute liking assigned by the younger children because they exhibit polarization and all attribute liking tend to correlate with the overall liking (halo effect). We might, however, use the attribute ratings assigned by older children (on the 0-100 point scale) to predict acceptance for younger children and for older children, respectively.

The approach used to relate liking ratings to attribute ratings appears schematically in Table 8.5. In essence, we allow the older children to perform two operations simultaneously. First, these older children act as objective registrators of perceived attribute intensity, by providing sensory profile ratings on the 0-100 scale. (For that matter, any other source of the sensory or formula profiles for the various products would do as well. Here, the older children act as convenient sources of this sensory information). Second, these older children provide liking ratings. Finally, the younger children provide liking ratings, using the Snoopy Scale (converted to an equivalent 0-100 scale).

Given two sources of information; first, a bank of sensory attribute ratings and, secondarily, a bank of liking ratings (from older and younger children, respectively), we can now interrelate these two sources of information, either by correlation analysis or by curve fitting.

TABLE 8.5
STEPS FOLLOWED TO INTEGRATE RATINGS OF YOUNGER AND OLDER CHILDREN

1. Instruct older children to rate each Snoopy face in terms of liking, on a 0-100 liking scale. This generates a numerical equivalent* for each point on the facial hedonic scale.

2. Convert each child's Snoopy rating to its equivalent 0-100 scale value, using the outcome of Step 1.

3. Average the ratings assigned by the children for each candy and for each attribute. This generates the child's numerical liking rating.

4. Relate older child or adult sensory ratings to the child's numerical liking rating. Use either linear or parabolic (quadratic) equations to relate sensory ratings to degree of liking.

*Average numerical equivalent of the Snoopy scale from adult and children's ratings equal the following:

Snoopy	Rating
1 (least liked)	6
2	17
3	29
4	42
5	54
6	64
7	73
8	82
9 (most liked)	90

TABLE 8.6
LINEAR CORRELATIONS BETWEEN SENSORY ATTRIBUTE RATINGS (ASSIGNED BY OLDER CHILDREN) AND LIKING RATINGS (ASSIGNED BY YOUNGER CHILDREN)

	Data Base Liking		Attribute Ratings (Older Child)					
Product	Younger Child	Older Child	Dark	Sweet	Bitter	Chocolate	Crunchy	Starchy
1	66	54	36	46	57	63	48	42
2	65	50	43	44	64	71	35	47
3	70	56	53	55	52	76	49	49
4	63	35	50	40	54	67	56	48
5	69	45	49	56	56	68	57	36
6	76	60	42	55	51	71	65	42
Darkness	−0.04	−0.40						
Sweetness	0.84	0.60						
Bitterness	−0.59	−0.19						
Chocolate Flavor	0.44	0.37						
Crunchiness	0.60	0.02						
Starchiness	−0.34	0.08						

Correlating Attribute Ratings And Liking

The first analysis consists of correlating attribute ratings (from the older children) with the facial hedonic, Snoopy ratings, assigned by both groups. Does there exist a linear relation? If we do find a significant linear trend (e.g., between liking and perceived sweetness) then we can conclude that liking covaries with the attribute. Of course we do not necessarily know the nature of this relation (e.g., does liking increase dramatically with changes in sweetness, or only slightly, albeit consistently, thus giving rise to a high correlation)?

Table 8.6 presents the data base of ratings and the correlations between the sensory attribute ratings from the older children, and the liking ratings, from the older and younger children, respectively. Note the emergence of significant correlations, exceeding 0.5, (in absolute value) meaning that there do exist some strong linear relations between attribute level and liking. Reiterating a previous point, however, we do not know the quantitative nature of the relation.

Developing Curves Relating Attribute Ratings And Liking

Scientific research tells us that as sensory attribute level (or formulation level) increases, liking changes. However, the relation may not follow a straight line and usually does not. Rather, in many cases the relation between liking (as the dependent variable) and sensory attribute level (as the independent variable) conforms to an inverted U-shaped curve, similar to that shown in Fig. 8.2. The curve may accentuate the upwards sloping portion, or the downwards sloping portion. The relation may evidence a fairly steep curve, meaning that liking varies quite dramatically with sensory attribute level. In contrast, quite often we may observe a fairly flat curve, still containing a noticeable peak in the midrange, but nonetheless without a sharp drop-off in acceptance above or below that peak. A key benefit of building these curves consists of the recognition that the curve actually describes the magnitude of liking, and how degree of liking changes in a quantitative manner with sensory level.

The equation that we fit to the data follows the general form of a parabola, containing linear (X) and quadratic (X^2) terms. We write the equation as follows (Eq.8.1):

$$\text{Liking (Snoopy)} = A + B\,(\text{Attribute}) + C\,(\text{Attribute}^2) \qquad (8.1)$$

The equation summarizes the relation between attribute level and liking. Usually, it provides a moderate, rather than a perfect fit to the data. Nonetheless, the equation allows the product developer a good first guess about the underlying relation between attribute level and liking. In that sense the function fitting method acts as a device to promote pattern recognition, which highlights and emphasizes latent, underlying patterns between liking and attribute level.

Parenthetically, in order to develop very good fitting parabolic relations between attribute level and liking, the product developer has to systematically vary one formula ingredient alone, over a wide range, and have panelists rate liking. Done properly that operation will generate accurate parabolic equations. The sweetness of sugar versus liking of sugar, for sugar solutions represents a good example. In real world applications, we must make do with qualitative variations of several different formula levels. The qualitative variations never provide the control of level and the range necessary to generate the perfect parabolic form. Thus, we rely upon regression analysis to uncover the general form. We use fitted equation values of liking versus the attribute level to understand better the likely relation between attribute level and acceptance.

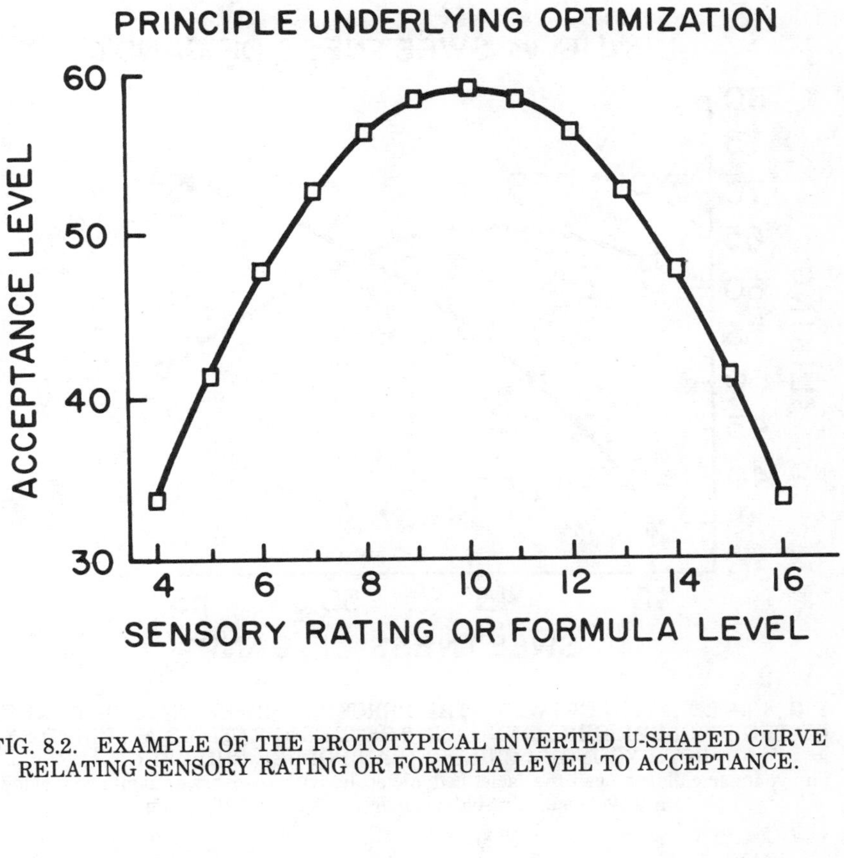

FIG. 8.2. EXAMPLE OF THE PROTOTYPICAL INVERTED U-SHAPED CURVE RELATING SENSORY RATING OR FORMULA LEVEL TO ACCEPTANCE.

Examples Of Curves

Figures 8.3 and 8.4 show some fitted curves relating liking ratings (older versus younger children) versus perceived sweetness (Fig. 8.3) and perceived crunchiness (Fig. 8.4). Note that the curves provide the marketer and product developer with an idea of how liking varies with sensory characteristics and the differences between younger and older children.

The curves provide the product developer with some additional key information, specifically the sensitivity to acceptance to sensory characteristics (illustrated by the shape of the liking curve) and the location of optimum points (peak levels of the curve). Finally, the curves provide an idea of the highest level of acceptance possible.

Sensitivity Of Liking To Sensory Attributes

Figure 8.3 shows that the younger and older children differ from each other. Keep in mind that the liking ratings come from both groups

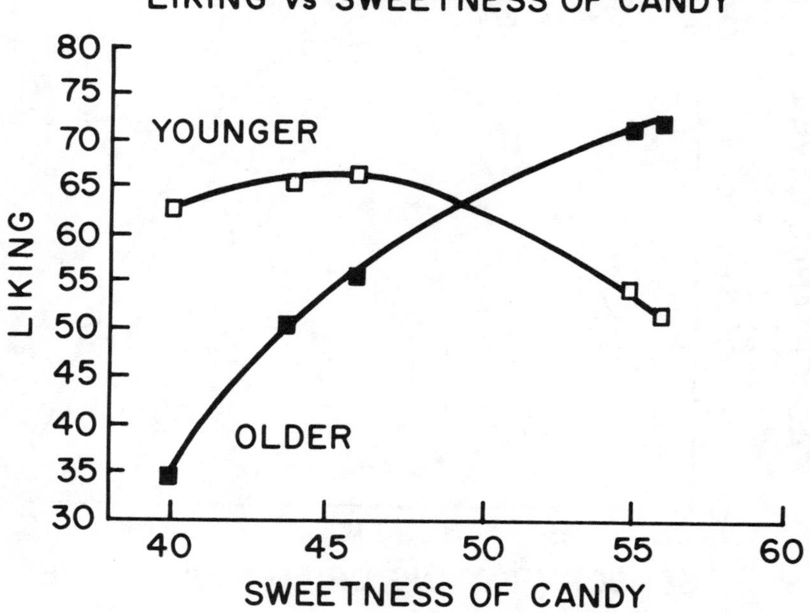

FIG. 8.3. RELATION BETWEEN THE PERCEIVED SWEETNESS OF CANDY (RATED BY OLDER CHILDREN), AND THE LIKING RATINGS ASSIGNED BY BOTH YOUNGER CHILDREN AND OLDER CHILDREN.
The younger children used the facial hedonic scale, with their assignments converted to a 0-100 scale. The older children used the 0-100 scale.

separately (Snoopy hedonic values), whereas the sensory attributes come from the older children's ratings. We find that younger children show less sensitivity to sweetness changes than do older children, but similar sensitivity to crunchiness.

Optimum Levels

The shapes of the curves in Fig. 8.3 and Fig. 8.4 differ, for older versus younger children. The older children tend to peak at a higher sweetness level, whereas the younger children peak at a middle to lower level, as if they do not want a product that has too intense a taste or texture. Qualitatively, this information provides R&D with an idea of how children react to changes in sensory characteristics, but does not yet provide clear cut direction for product improvement. The axes of the figures represent sensory characteristics, not formula variations. Hence the information thus far obtained can point the product developer to the proper target product and products around the target (namely, those that achieve the highest level), but will not provide the actual formulation.

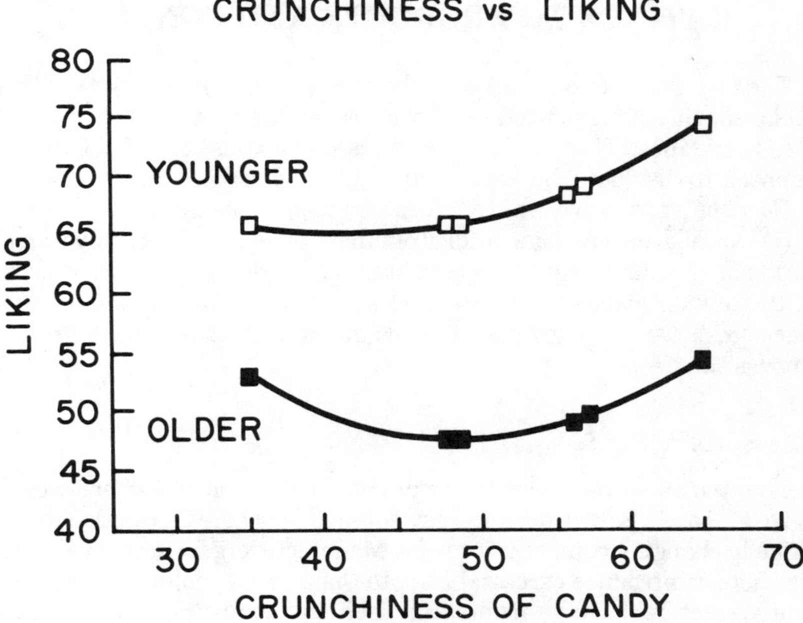

FIG. 8.4. RELATION BETWEEN THE CRUNCHINESS OF CANDY (RATED BY OLDER CHILDREN), AND THE LIKING RATINGS ASSIGNED BY BOTH OLDER CHILDREN AND YOUNGER CHILDREN.
As in Fig. 8.3, the younger children used the facial hedonic scale, whereas the older children used the 0-100 scale.

Using Other Sources Of Sensory Information

The previous section concentrated on children's reactions, using the ratings of older children on sensory attributes as the key independent variable. In actual practice, one needs to obtain a good measure of the independent variable. One need not use the children's ratings as the source of the sensory attributes. Rather, the children can simply rate overall liking and liking of the specific attributes, using whatever scale makes them feel most comfortable. The sensory scale can come from a number of other sources, including an in-house expert panel, or adult ratings of the same products. Since the approach develops relations between liking and sensory attributes, we search for the optimal sensory level and then refer back to the product that generates that optimal level. As long as the two panels (children, in-house expert or adult) evaluate the exact set of products, we can relate the children's liking rating to specific test products, and thus provide R&D with direction.

COMPARISON OF CHILDREN'S AND ADULTS RATINGS TO PRODUCTS AND CONCEPTS

The previous section dealt with the arrangement of testing facilities for children, the implementation of the test and the analysis of results for R&D guidance. This section continues our evaluation of children's responses to products, but also deals with packages.

For this section we want to focus on the following issues.

(1) Do children's ratings differ from those of adults, when they rate blind products (no identification) versus branded products (with identification)?

(2) How do children react to packages versus how do adults react to packages? Do both groups of consumers walk away with the same impressions?

The Specific Study

The study involved package and product evaluation of dry, presweetened cereals. The U.S. market for presweetened, dry cereals represents a continually changing competitive arena. Manufacturers from the major cereal marketers introduce cereals, promote them to the children by premiums and attractive package fronts and then induce awareness by television and print advertising. The cereals have a short life, sometimes just a few years. A longer term perspective will reveal that many cereals rely upon concepts from other food categories (e.g., chocolate-flavored cereals, cereals that resemble fruits).

CASE HISTORY—THE RILEY CEREAL COMPANY

Dan Riley, president of the Riley Cereal Company (division of a multinational corporation), introduced a line of successful children's cereals during the late 1960's. His string of successes continued unabated for 15 years, as his company grew. Starting in the south, he expanded his franchise, introducing new cereals, first in the southeast, then in the northeast and finally in the midwest and west.

During these formative years, other cereal manufacturers also grew, enjoying the same type of receptivity which greeted the Riley introductions. However, eventually, in the late 1970's, it seemed as if the cereal market had finally begun to saturate with the new entries. The return on investment for the new cereals began to shrink. Media costs (advertising on television) grew inordinately high and eventually profits began to shrink.

In early 1981, recognizing that the growth trend had slowed down, Dan Riley commissioned a consulting firm to do an exhaustive evaluation of the consumer market for dry, presweetened children's cereal to find out what particular characteristics of advertising, promotion, package and product provided the necessary "hot buttons" to increase consumer interest and maintain loyalty. This case history presents part of the results of that study, limiting itself to evaluation of products and package, by groups of children and teens and by adults (mothers).

Test Specifics

The test consisted of the evaluation of actual products and packages by three groups, each of 25 individuals; younger children (8-12), older teens (13-17), and adult women (mothers, but not of the children in the panel).

The stimuli comprised of eight different dry cereals, two unsweetened, and six presweetened, and representing different products currently on the market. The panelists tested each of the eight cereals first without benefit of brand and afterwards knowing the brand as presented by the label and the manufacturer, but without any graphics that one would ordinarily find on a box of dry cereal. The third portion of the test consisted of the evaluation of the package with many of the same attributes, but also with some additional attributes thrown in. Finally, the panelists answered questions about their food habits and preferences as well.

Comparison Of Ratings Of Cereal

Our analyses consist of a comparison of the ratings of the eight cereals,

TABLE 8.7
LIKING RATINGS ASSIGNED TO CEREALS AND PACKAGE FRONTS

		BLIND			PACKAGE FRONT			BRANDED		
Cereal	Type	Adult	Teen	Child	Adult	Teen	Child	Adult	Teen	Child
1	Unsweetened	45	40	41	42	51	43	51	36	56
2	Unsweetened	51	36	40	46	48	46	57	41	54
	Average	48	38	40	44	49	44	54	38	55
3	Presweet	36	39	48	42	46	68	29	41	68
4	Presweet	38	43	51	40	43	64	31	37	64
5	Presweet	40	46	56	28	41	59	29	41	64
6	Presweet	32	42	53	39	43	66	23	46	73
7	Presweet	31	37	51	35	46	62	23	42	59
8	Presweet	27	32	57	33	39	65	17	32	78
	Average	34	39	52	36	43	64	25	39	67

on both a blind and a branded basis for overall liking by the three groups of consumers. Do they all like the cereals to the same degree? Since all panelists used the same 0-100 scale, we can easily compare the average ratings assigned by the panelists, as well as assess the degree of significance in liking. Table 8.7 shows the ratings, by product, by age and by test condition (blind versus branded). We see immediately that the adults downrate the presweets, whereas the younger children uprate them. The children tend, in general, to assign higher ratings overall to all products on a blind basis, but nonetheless these young children do show substantially greater acceptability for the sweet cereals, relative to the unsweetened types.

We also see some interest effects due to branding. For one, adults and teens show different reactions than do children (Table 8.8). Adults show a loss in acceptance for presweetened cereals, wherein (as one might expect) children show a dramatic increase in acceptance when they know the cereal that they evaluate.

TABLE 8.8
BRANDING EFFECT—BY PANEL GROUP (CEREALS)

		Branded Rating—Blind Rating		
Cereal	Type	Adult	Teen	Child
1	Unsweetened	6	−4	15
2	Unsweetened	6	5	14
	Average	6	0	15
3	Presweet	− 7	2	20
4	Presweet	− 7	−6	13
5	Presweet	−11	−5	8
6	Presweet	− 9	4	20
7	Presweet	− 8	5	8
8	Presweet	−10	0	21
	Average	− 9	0	15

AN OVERVIEW

Research with children poses some of the most difficult problems in sensory analysis and product testing. Children have low attention spans and limited comprehension of the task, making matters difficult on the field end, where data collection occurs. At the analysis stage, things become even more difficult, as one tries to sort through the data to discover the underlying patterns.

As stated in the introduction to this chapter, no perfect method exists by which to evaluate children's reactions to products. Children polarize in hedonics, liking or disliking foods at either extreme of the scale. Yet, by combining chidren's hedonic ratings (e.g., via a facial hedonic scale) with attribute ratings obtained from adults (or older children or expert panels) it becomes possible to link children's acceptance reactions with a product's sensory characteristics. This chapter has illustrated one approach designed to generate that linkage and to use it to understand what characteristics make children accept products. It also has illustrated an approach to measuring children's (and adults') susceptibility to brand identification as that identification affects acceptability.

REFERENCES

CESARIO, D. A. 1981. Techniques of conducting package design research with children. In: *Handbook Of Package Design Research* (W. Stern, ed.) pp. 356-371. John Wiley, New York.

GOLDBERG, M. E., GORN, G. J. and GIBSON, W. 1978. TV messages for snack and breakfast foods: Do they influence children's preferences. J. Consumer Res. *5,* 73-81.

SECTION II.
MINING THE DATABASE FOR INSIGHTS

CHAPTER 9

DEVELOPING AND OPTIMIZING CONCEPTS FOR FOOD PRODUCTS

INTRODUCTION

This chapter deals with one of the earliest stages in product testing; concept development and optimization. All too often, the success of a food product depends as much upon the appeal of the concept as it does upon the acceptability of the food itself. The concept or positioning of the food intrigues the consumer and provides a means for enticing the consumer to try the food. Only with initial trial, in fact, can the manufacturer assure himself of repeat purchase. A ho-hum concept can detract from acceptance and reduce the opportunities for the product to attain success.

THE STAGES OF CONCEPT DEVELOPMENT AND OPTIMIZATION

Unlike product development, concept development and refinement (or optimization) often occurs outside the R&D laboratories. Typically, a marketing department with the help of an advertising agency develops a bank of early stage, prototype concepts, which they screen for promise. The winning concepts undergo further refinement until finally the marketer selects a limited number of the most promising concepts. These concepts constitute statements about the product against which product developers formulate a product.

Very Early Concept Generation

Very early in the development process, marketing develops rough concept statements. Generally, these represent little more than statements about products. Table 9.1 lists a few early stage concept statements. Note that the concepts really provide only a benefit or two, or a short description of the product without elaboration.

In today's competitive market, marketers have the opportunity to hire outside specialists or "boutiques" to provide a battery of these early concepts. Specialists abound whose job consists of running group sessions with consumers, in which the participants generate a multitude of product ideas. The specialist provides the proper environment to nourish the consumers' "creative juices". In these sessions, the consumers have the opportunity to discuss products and to offer their own ideas, without criticism and within a framework of positive feedback (no matter how bizarre the idea). After a number of these sessions, the moderator begins to perceive the pattern in the ideas offered, and can fine-tune some of the ideas, while trimming their number to a manageable few.

TABLE 9.1
THREE EXAMPLES OF SOME EARLY STAGE CONCEPTS

Cake Concept

New Dieter's Chocolate Swirl Cake
Half the calories
Same rich flavor
Easy to make

Bread Concept

Bran Wheat Bread With Raisins
Health and flavor in one package
Golden brown with delicious raisins
Available at $1.09 per package

Sausage Concept

Golden Farms All Beef Sausage
Bite size links, all beef sausage
Delicious flavors, regular and spicy
For children and adults
Available in your frozen food section

Promise Testing

During the early concept development stage, manufacturers like to get an idea of the opportunity or at least the acceptability of the concepts that consumers have generated. Some manufacturers and advertising agencies have instituted a technique they call "promise testing". Promise testing consists of nothing more than presenting the prototype concepts to consumers, to secure ratings of purchase intent, uniqueness and sometimes believability. For instance, consider the array of ratings for the ten concepts listed in Table 9.2. From the ratings (assigned by a group of 50 users of cake mixes), we can see that cake Concepts 5 and 10 have great promise and sufficient uniqueness to warrant further work.

In view of the roughness of the concepts tested at this early phase, most manufacturers do not take the results of promise testing too seriously. Rather, quite often the manufacturers use the results, as a simple screening device, to eliminate the worst concepts in the array and do not pay attention to improving the concepts which perform well. As a screening device, the promise testing procedure does an adequate job. The user should recognize that the concepts tested really represent "rough" statements about the product, prior to any creative embellishment.

TABLE 9.2
PROMISE TESTING RESULTS FOR TEN CAKE CONCEPTS

Concept	Statement	Purchase Intent	Uniqueness
1	Chocolate Swirl, fast bake	45	39
2	Honey almond fudge	56	59
3	Pineapple cheese cake	46	39
4	Summer fruit cake	34	60
5	Baba au Rhum cake	65	58
6	Apple cake with raisins	58	37
7	Orange bundt cake	41	47
8	Hungarian tort cake	51	63
9	Layered cookie cake	44	69
10	Linzer cake	65	72

Note: a description and picture of each cake accompanied the questionnaire. Panelists rated each cake on purchase intent and uniqueness.

CONCEPT EVALUATION AND OPTIMIZATION

This section deals with the evaluation and optimization of concepts. The optimization stage usually occurs early in the concept development cycle after the manufacturer has selected an ensemble of concepts with which to work. The optimization procedure determines what each and every element in the concept contributes to acceptance and communication. By these measurements, it becomes possible to discover what elements generate the highest acceptance for the concept and, if necessary, what the concept developer (marketer, advertising agency) should do to improve the concept. We will spend most of the chapter dealing with this approach.

CASE HISTORY—ADULT CEREALS

Adult, dry cereals represents a highly competitive product category. In contrast to children's presweetened cereals (in which products come and go with a tide-like regularity), the adult dry cereal market has relatively few entries. However, the competitiveness comes from the advertising spending levels and the efforts made to capture various positions in the mind of the consumer (e.g., health orientation versus flavor orientation versus convenience).

The Dropkin Corporation manufactures adult dry cereals. In its efforts to increase market share versus its giant competitors, it has had to rely upon marketing expertise and creative advertising, rather than upon sheer size and distribution capacity. Consequently, when the time came to develop a new adult-oriented cereal, combining a flavor and health story, the Dropkin Corp. turned to a marketing consulting group for help in concept development and positioning.

Initial Concept Test Results

A series of focus groups, conducted with adult consumers early in the development process, revealed interest in a cereal that would deliver both nutritional and flavor benefits. However, at the same time, the consumers who participated in these focus groups continued to insist that many of the in-market products "talked health" but few, if any, of the products actually looked like they would deliver the promised and desired health or nutrition benefits. Few of the health oriented products could support a health claim without the verbiage. Those cereals which did have health orientation and differed from the run of the mill dry cereals did so either because they had an unconventional appearance (e.g., a Swiss product, containing raisins) or because they resembled granola and had a sweet taste with coconut, dates and other assorted fruits.

In view of the necessity for remaining conventional, yet communicating the health and flavor benefits, the creative group hired by the Dropkin Corp. decided to investigate positionings based upon well-known ingredients and process characteristics. Thus, fiber, bran, fruit, multi-grain and other key elements came under consideration as specific product characteristics which could support the health positioning.

Concept Architecture

In the development of concepts, the marketer and product developer can increase the chances for success by systematically varying the concept elements within a specific structural framework or architecture. By representing each concept as a combination of structural elements, we can quantify the contribution of each structural element to acceptance and to the communication of flavor and health/nutrition. Furthermore, in developing the concept, we can provide alternatives or substitutes for each structural element of the concept. If the concept performs well except for one part, then we can quickly substitute a better performing element.

For adult oriented cereals, the creative group suggested that the concept should comprise three distinct and major structural elements; Authority (or reason to believe), Flavor Message and Health Message. By developing concepts comprising different elements, but all falling into the same framework, one could diagnose which part of the concept generated acceptance and which did not and, for the weak parts of the concept (e.g., weak health/nutrition message), substitute a better performing element(s), thus improving the concept.

Developing Elements For A Concept

As part of the development cycle, the creative group generated an array of concept elements for each part of the concept (authority, flavor message, health/nutrition message). These elements emerged from the creative group sessions. A staff analyst at the creative group worked on the elements, polishing and modifying them so that they would fit into the final concept architecture. Table 9.3 presents the alternative elements that one could use for each of the three components of the cereal concept.

With additional investigation into the needs and wants of adult cereal users, it soon became apparent that other concept elements would warrant inclusion into the cereal concept. Preparation specifics (e.g., stone ground) and price factors (e.g., 1 box for $1.89) merited inclusion, even though they did not specifically fall under one of the three architectural elements. Consequently, the creative director decided to develop concepts comprising two parts; first, the basic architecture (1 element from each of the following: authority, flavor and health/nutrition) and second, ancillary architecture, comprising up to 2 additional messages about the product and a price element. Table 9.4 shows the revised architecture of the concept.

TABLE 9.3
STRUCTURE OF ADULT ORIENTED CEREAL CONCEPTS
(VARIABLES, ELEMENTS)

Authority (3 Elements)

A. Dietitians and doctors recommend a good breakfast, with cereal and milk, for a good start to your day.

B. Scientific evidence shows that a good cereal in the morning makes your day go better.

C. Scientific tests show that those who have good breakfasts start the day off feeling better, and have a better day.

Flavor Message (5 Elements)

D. A great tasting cereal with the brand you need.

E. Sweet and crunchy with the flavor you love.

F. Comes in honey, graham and bran flavors.

G. Has stone ground bran for better taste and better health.

H. Low in salt, high in fiber.

Health/Nutrition (3 Elements)

I. Doctors and dietitians recommend bran for better health.

J. Doctors and dietitians recommend bran for better digestion, and better nutrition.

K. Our cereal provides the roughage you need, to keep you healthy. Doctors recommend roughage for better digestion and better nutrition.

Ancillary Elements (4 Elements)

L. Priced at only $1.89 per box.

M. Available in small packages for one breakfast servings.

N. Fresh packed, and sealed in foil to maintain the flavor and nutrition.

O. Have it for snacks, too.

Developing Prototype Concepts

In order to optimize the new cereal concept, the marketer wanted to determine which specific elements in the cereal concept generated the maximum purchase intent (namely, which concept elements worked and which did not). To do so required development of a series of test or prototype concepts. Each prototype concept comprised a set of concept elements; one element each from authority, flavor, health and price, and up to 2 additional elements from the miscellaneous group. Note also that some of the concepts lacked an authority message, others lacked a flavor message, etc. The absence of a specific concept element (e.g., no price mentioned, no authority mentioned) also constituted an option. In this way, one could quantify the partwise contribution of each element with the baseline represented by the entire absence of that element.

Test Concepts—Their Architecture

Given the set of elements and basic architecture, shown in Tables 9.3 and 9.4, and recognizing that one wanted a model showing what each element contributed, the creative director develop a set of 72 concepts. These concepts constitute various arrangements of the concept elements, with the property that for each architectural element (e.g., flavor message) either one or zero element appeared. The set of concepts represents a small fraction of the possible 1056 different concepts that one might create

TABLE 9.4
BASIC STRUCTURE OF THE ADULT CEREAL CONCEPT INTRODUCING "HEALTH" BRAND CEREAL, FROM RIGHTWAY INC.

Authority

One of the 3 authority elements present, or no element present.

Flavor Message

One of 5 flavor messages (from the set of 5), woven together in a sentence structure, or no element present.

Health/Nutrition Message

One of the 3 health/nutrition elements present, or no element present.

Ancillary Factors

Between 0 and 2 ancillary messages present (from the set of 4), woven together in a sentence structure.

from the set. Table 9.5 shows the composition of 5 different concepts developed by randomly selecting one (or none) element from each concept variable.

To the panelist involved in a concept evaluation and optimization test, the concepts presented do not necessarily appear to possess the structured order which actually underlies them. Most panelists in these studies recognize that the elements in the concepts repeat from concept to concept but have no idea about the underlying structure.

Running The Evaluation

The test design generated a total of 72 different concepts. To make matters easy in the field during data collection, the marketing research field director suggested that the panelists work with "booklets". Each booklet would contain 4 concepts in a specific order. For this study, covering a total of 72 concepts, the test generated a total of 18 booklets, each with 4 concepts. Additionally, the research director tested 4 competitors in concept form as benchmarks. Although the concepts appeared in a fixed order in the booklet, the panelists evaluated the booklets in a randomized order, unique for each panelist. This procedure randomizes the order of concepts, but not perfectly. Within the booklet, the order of concepts remains the same. However, the approach does insure sufficient randomization to reduce bias due to order.

TABLE 9.5
THE ANATOMY OF SYSTEMATICALLY VARIED CONCEPTS FOR ADULT CEREAL*

Concept	Authority			Flavor Message					Health			Other Message			
	A	B	C	D	E	F	G	H	I	J	K	L	M	N	O
1	1	0	0	1	0	0	0	0	0	0	0	1	0	1	0
2	0	1	0	0	0	1	0	0	1	0	0	0	1	0	0
3	1	0	0	0	1	0	0	0	0	0	1	0	0	0	0
4	0	0	1	0	0	0	0	1	0	1	0	0	0	1	1
72	1	0	0	0	0	0	0	0	1	0	0	0	1	0	0

*1 Denotes the presence of the element in the concept, and 0 denotes the absence of the element in the concept.

Data Analysis Of The Results—Full Panel

The initial data comprises a matrix of concepts by attribute ratings. Table 9.6 shows part of this relatively large matrix (7 attributes × 5 concepts). By itself, the raw data of the type in Table 9.6 provides the user with an idea of the relative acceptance and communication of complete concepts. In the matrix, we do have reference concepts, comprising the competitive products, reduced to concept statement. This allows the marketer an idea of the relative strengths and weaknesses of the competition, as well as determine which concepts from the test array look like they will achieve high consumer acceptance.

However, by itself, the data shown in Table 9.6 provide only the scores for actual concepts. They do not provide diagnoses why the concepts win or lose, and specifically, the contribution of each of the elements within the concept to acceptance and to the communication of attributes.

TABLE 9.6
EXAMPLE OF DATA (RATINGS) FROM CONSUMER FOR CONCEPTS

Concept	Purchase	Believe	Unique	Good Flavor	For Adult	Convenient	Nutritious
1	35	44	50	31	46	30	41
2	40	46	32	...	...	...	...
3	44	40	...	...	...	...	...
4	33	35	...	...	...	...	...
....	...	...	...	...	...	...	...
72	38	45	...	...	...	...	...

Numbers in table show average ratings on an anchored 0-100 scale.

Developing An Additive Model For Concept Elements

If we conceive of the matrix of concept elements (Table 9.5) and append to it the matrix of attribute ratings for each concept (Table 9.4), we will have the necessary data input for a regression model, or equation. The independent variables become the presence or absence of specific concept elements. The dependent variable becomes the attribute rating. The total number of observations or cases for the regression comes to 72, one case for each concept developed by systematic variations.

The results from the regression equation appear in Table 9.7. Note that these results pertain to the database generated from the average rating across all panelists.

Interpreting The Results

The additive model provides the marketer and market researcher with a simplified description of how components of a concept generate attribute ratings. For instance, let us consider purchase intent as the dependent variable.

(1) If we present the panelists only with the title of the new cereal but no additional information about the category or the specific product we expect to obtain the rating equal to the intercept, or a rating of 35, on purchase intent.

(2) Looking at the first set of variables in the concept, corresponding to authority, we can now ask the following question: How many points does each of these elements add to purchase intent? Table 9.7 shows the answer. Note that the contribution to purchase intent varies by element. The elements differ from each other. "Dietitians recommend . . . " generates the highest contribution (namely, 2.1 points).

(3) We can follow this line of reasoning, looking at each concept variable, and the elements contained within that concept variable. Thus, for the next concept variable, flavor, we have 5 different elements. The element sweet and crunchy shows the highest partwise contribution to purchase intent (4.3 points), and the element low in salt shows the least (namely, −1.1 points).

Although we systematically varied the concept elements and obtained the best fitting equation (or additive model), the question still remains as to how well the model fits the data. Does the additive model provide an adequate expression of how the elements combine with each other to generate purchase intent? In order to answer this question, we have to compute measures of goodness-of-fit, specifically the standard error of the regression and the multiple R squared value.

The Multiple R Squared Value

In regression analysis, we attempt to fit a dependent variable by one or more weighted independent variables. Once we have found the best fitting weight values (namely, those that minimize the sum of squares of the deviations between predicted ratings and actual ratings) we usually observe discrepancies. For each case or observation, we know the actual rating, as assigned by the panelist. From the model we also have the predicted rating, whose value we can compute, since we already know the values for the independent variable, for that particular case.

In our study, the panelists each evaluated a total of 72 different concepts systematically varied by design. This generates a total of 72 predicted ratings, using the additive model. We can correlate the actual rating and the predicted rating (using the model). The square of the correlation tells us the percentage variation in the dependent variable (e.g., purchase intent rating) that we can predict, knowing the independent variables and given the model. Obviously, the higher the correlation, the higher the prediction. The multiple R squared varies from a high of 1.0 (100% or all of the variability predicted) down to a low of 0 (or none of the variability predicted). For our data, we find that we can predict 74% variability, which represents almost ¾ of the variation in the ratings.

The Standard Error Of The Regression

The regression equation provides a prediction of the likely purchase intent rating that we would obtain for each combination of concept elements. Since the predictions do not necessarily agree perfectly with the actual observed values, we would like to know the "average" variability of prediction. The standard error of the regression provides us that measure. Suppose the value for purchase intent equals 2.35. If we repeat the measurements, then on the average we will predict the actual mean value for each concept that we originally obtained. However, the variability of the predictions does not guarantee that. Rather, we may expect to undershoot or overshoot. In fact, if we consider the difference between the predicted and obtained values, the average will equal 0, but the standard deviation will equal 2.35. This means that 68% of the time, we can predict the purchase intent rating with a value of ± 2.35. Most of the time (95%) we can predict within a range of approximately ± 2 standard errors, or ± 4.70 rating points.

Clearly, from the above discussion, the higher the standard error, the poorer the prediction, because the range around the predicted value become larger. The standard error of the regression depends upon two factors. First, as just noted, the standard error increases as the prediction becomes poorer. This occurs because of the unexplained variability of the data. Second, the higher the numbers for the dependent variable, the greater the standard error of the regression. By multiplying all of the dependent variables (observed purchase intent ratings) by 100, (so that now we have a 0-10,000 scale), we automatically multiply the standard error of regression by a factor of 100, making it 235, rather than 2.35.

TABLE 9.7
PARAMETERS OF ADDITIVE MODEL FOR CEREAL CONCEPTS

	Purchase	Believe	Unique	Good Flavor	For Adult	Convenient	Nutritious
Intercept	35	39	41	32	41	25	42
Authority							
A Dieticians Recommend	2.1	2.3	2.1	0.3	2.9	0.1	3.4
B Scientific Evidence	1.1	1.8	2.2	0.4	2.7	−0.3	4.1
C Scientific Tests	0.3	1.1	4.6	0.4	3.1	−0.1	3.9
Flavor Message							
D Great Tasting	0.1	0.2	0.2	7.1	2.1	0.2	0.2
E Sweet and Crunchy	4.3	1.1	−0.7	11.2	−3.2	0.4	0.3
F Comes in Honey	2.6	3.9	−0.2	8.6	1.2	0.9	0.7
G Stone Ground Bran	0.3	−4.2	2.9	2.1	4.6	0.1	1.9
H Low in Salt	−1.1	1.2	3.4	−4.7	3.2	−0.2	6.4

TABLE 9.7 (Continued)
PARAMETERS OF ADDITIVE MODEL FOR CEREAL CONCEPTS

	Purchase	Believe	Unique	Good Flavor	For Adult	Convenient	Nutritious
Health/Nutrition							
I For Better Health	0.2	3.1	0.3	0.2	1.9	0.2	4.9
J For Better Digestion	0.6	1.2	0.7	0.2	2.6	0.3	5.4
K Roughage	1.3	1.1	0.6	0.1	3.6	0.1	4.2
Ancillary Factors							
L Priced at $1.89	0.2	0.2	−0.1	−0.3	−0.3	0.7	−0.1
M Single Servings	1.5	1.3	3.6	0.1	−1.3	4.7	−0.3
N Fresh Packed/Foil	1.1	1.2	3.2	2.4	0.3	2.1	4.1
O For Snacks	0.2	−3.9	4.6	1.7	0.2	4.1	−0.2
Multiple R Squared	0.74	0.72	0.56	0.81	0.59	0.69	0.79
Standard Error	2.3	2.7	2.3	3.2	3.6	3.9	2.4

The Communication Profile

The equations presented in Table 9.7 allow the marketer to understand the likely profile of communications generated by selecting specific elements of the concept. For instance, we find that purchase intent increases most rapidly for specific elements such as sweet and crunchy. In contrast, believability increases more rapidly with other elements such as for better health, comes in honey flavor, etc.

The equations act as shorthand expressions to show concept elements generate ratings. They provide the marketer with a powerful tool for selecting elements which generate specific responses such as maximum acceptance.

Maximizing Purchase Intent By Selecting The Proper Concept Elements

The first exercise in restructuring a concept consists of maximizing acceptance. Table 9.8 presents the elements present in the current concept, prior to the study. Marketing had used this concept as its platform for the product. Note that with the aid of the additive model we can now determine what each of the concept elements "brings to the party". We find some concept elements bring very little and perhaps allow for substitutes which can improve acceptance.

By selecting the elements from Table 9.7 which generate the highest level of purchase intent, we can now improve the current concept, as Table 9.8 shows. The structure of the concept remains the same. We have altered the composition of the concepts by a simplistic replacement of the elements.

The next evaluation consists of estimating the concept signature or communication of attributes. Table 9.8 revealed that we can straightforwardly increase purchase intent. In which specific attributes of communication does this improvement reveal itself? Table 9.9 shows the likely attribute profile for the current concept and the expected profile for the optimized concept. We find an increase in the communication of good flavor, but no dramatic increase in any of the other concept elements. We conclude, therefore, that the improvement comes from an increase in the communication of flavor, a key reinforcing dimension for a food concept.

Alternative Or Fallback Concepts Which Satisfy Other Criteria

Just because we have an additive model that allows us to maximize purchase intent does not mean that the appropriate or optimal answer consists of picking those particular concept elements which separately

TABLE 9.8
COMPARISON OF CURRENT VS. OPTIMIZED CONCEPTS FOR CEREAL

Current Concept

Introduction—Introducing New Right Time Brand Cereal

Authority

Dietitians and doctors recommend a good breakfast with cereal and milk for a good start to your day.

Flavor

A great tasting cereal, with the bran you need.

Health/Nutrition

Doctors and dietitians recommend bran for better health.

Ancillary Factors

Priced at $1.89.
Available in small packages, for one breakfast serving.

Optimized Concept

Introduction—Introducing New Right Time Bran Cereal

Authority

Dietitians and doctors recommend a good breakfast with cereal and milk for a start to your day.

Flavor

Right Time Cereal is sweet and crunchy, with the flavor you love.

Health/Nutrition

Our cereal provides the roughage you need, to keep you healthy. Doctors recommend roughage for better digestion and better nutrition.

Ancillary Factors

Available in small packages, for one breakfast serving. Fresh packed, and sealed in foil too, to maintain flavor and nutrition.

Note: Consumers only saw the concept, not the architecture (spelled out here, in terms of authority, flavor, health/nutrition, and ancillary factors).

TABLE 9.9
EXPECTED PROFILE OF RATINGS FOR CONCEPTS

	Element	Purchase	Believe	Unique	Good Flavor	For Adult	Convenient	Nutritious
Strategy (Current)								
Intercept		35	39	41	32	41	25	42
Authority	(A)	2.1	2.3	2.1	0.3	2.9	0.1	3.4
Flavor	(D)	0.1	0.2	0.2	7.1	2.1	0.2	0.2
Health	(I)	0.2	3.1	0.3	0.2	1.9	0.2	4.9
Ancillary	(M)	0.2	0.2	−0.1	−0.3	−0.3	0.7	−0.1
Total		37.6	44.8	43.5	39.3	47.6	26.2	50.4
Strategy (High Purchase)								
Intercept		35	39	41	32	41	25	42
Authority	(A)	2.1	2.3	2.1	0.3	2.9	0.1	3.4
Flavor	(E)	4.3	1.1	−0.7	11.2	−3.2	0.4	0.3
Health	(K)	1.3	1.1	0.6	0.1	3.6	0.1	4.2
Ancillary	(M)	1.5	1.3	3.6	0.1	−1.3	4.7	−0.3
Total		44.2	44.8	46.6	44.6	43.0	30.3	49.6

TABLE 9.9 (Continued)
EXPECTED PROFILE OF RATINGS FOR CONCEPTS

	Element	Purchase	Believe	Unique	Good Flavor	For Adult	Convenient	Nutritious
Strategy (Good Flavor)								
Intercept		35	39	41	32	41	25	42
Authority	(C)	0.3	1.1	4.6	0.4	3.1	-0.1	3.9
Flavor	(E)	4.3	1.1	-0.7	11.2	-3.2	0.4	0.3
Health	(J)	0.6	1.2	0.7	0.2	2.6	0.3	5.4
Ancillary	(O)	1.1	1.2	3.2	2.4	0.3	2.1	4.1
Total		41.3	43.6	48.8	46.2	43.8	27.7	55.7
Strategy (Nutrition/Health)								
Intercept		35	39	41	32	41	25	42
Authority	(B)	1.1	1.8	2.2	0.4	2.7	-0.3	4.1
Flavor	(H)	-1.1	1.2	3.4	-4.7	3.2	-0.2	6.4
Health	(K)	1.3	1.1	0.6	0.1	3.6	0.1	4.2
Ancillary	(O)	1.1	1.2	3.2	2.4	0.3	2.1	4.1
Total		37.4	44.3	47.4	39.6	47.8	26.7	60.8

generate the highest purchase intent rating. From time to time, the marketer may wish to satisfy other goals such as maximizing purchase intent, while at the same time communicating specific benefits such as good flavor. Indeed, in many cases, the communication of flavor or convenience does not automatically generate the highest scoring concept. Yet, in the marketing flow, solid communication, a key point, in spite of potential (and generally small) losses in acceptance, may prove more attractive than selecting a general motherhood concept which generates high purchase intent, but for the wrong reasons (strategically).

Table 9.9 shows some alternative concepts, not necessarily equal to the optimal concept in terms of purchase intent, but nonetheless concepts that simultaneously achieve high purchase intent scores, and (most importantly), strongly communicate key benefits, such as flavor or nutrition/health.

SEGMENTING CONSUMERS BY THEIR RESPONSES TO CONCEPTS

The previous section dealt with aggregate data from the entire panel of consumers. However, we know from years of experience and from numerous studies that consumers differ among themselves in their susceptibility to different advertising messages. Some individuals tune into messages about health, others become entranced with messages having to do with flavor, whereas still other consumers perk up their ears if the advertisement or positioning deals with convenience.

To what extent does the aggregate model, developed above, represent the individuals in the population? Do there exist segments of individuals differentially tuned to the various elements of the concept, with these individuals generating unique, individual additive models, with parameters (or coefficients) different from those seen in Table 9.7?

To answer this question requires that we develop a method for grouping consumers showing similar patterns of responses to the concepts. One way of grouping, shown schematically in Table 9.10, consists of developing an additive model for each panelist. The numbers in the model represent the way that consumer looks at the various elements. For instance, consider Table 9.11 which shows three different individual models (hypothetical), one for an individual most attentive to flavor messages, one attentive to convenience messages (usage), and a third not particularly attentive to any one type of message.

If we can develop these models on an individual basis, and cluster individuals showing similar patterns of coefficients for the model, then we have a basis for dividing up the panel of consumers into segments with diverse susceptibilities to the concept elements. Furthermore, by clustering procedures, we can identify individuals showing quantitatively similar patterns and place them into one group. These individuals comprise one cluster or segment of the population. For a limited number of segments (e.g., 3), with each individual assigned to one and only one segment, we end up with clusters of individuals showing similar behavior within a cluster, and quite dissimilar behavior across clusters.

By following the analytic procedure (Table 9.10) the marketing research director developed the individual additive models, one per panelist, using the attribute of purchase intent as the dependent variable. The Clustering Procedure (known as the K Means Clustering Procedure) revealed the existence of three distinct clusters, based upon the individual additive models. The Clustering Procedure itself does not name the clusters, per se, but rather reveals the number of clusters, and which particular individuals fall into each cluster.

TABLE 9.10
STEPS INVOLVED IN SEGMENTING CONSUMERS ACCORDING TO CONCEPT RESPONSES

Step 1.	For each consumer, store his/her ratings of purchase intent for each concept evaluated.
Step 2.	Develop a multiple linear regression equation, relating the presence or absence of concept elements to that particular individual's ratings of purchase intent (or other criterion variable, such as liking).
Step 3.	Each individual generates a set of weighting factors, appropriate for his/her model.
Step 4.	Factor analyze the profile of weighting factors. Compute the factor loadings of each individual on the smaller set of dimensions which emerge from the factor analysis.
Step 5.	Cluster individuals together who show similar patterns of loadings on the basic dimensions, emerging from Step 4.
Step 6.	For each cluster (or segment) re-compute the additive model. Use the average rating of purchase intent for each concept as the dependent variable, and the concept design as the independent variable(s).
Step 7.	The result generates new models, one per segment, with individuals in the segments similar to each other in their responsivity to concept elements.

TABLE 9.11
ADDITIVE MODELS FOR PURCHASE INTENT: TOTAL VS. INDIVIDUAL SHOWING DIFFERENT NEEDS AND WANTS IN A CEREAL

		THREE INDIVIDUAL ORIENTATIONS		
	Total	Flavor	Health	Convenience
Intercept	35	43	36	40
Authority				
A Dietitians Recommend	2.1	0.6	5.6	0.3
B Scientific Evidence	1.1	0.5	6.1	0.2
C Scientific Tests	0.3	-0.1	3.9	0.6
Flavor Message				
D Great Tasting	0.1	4.1	1.8	2.1
E Sweet and Crunchy	4.3	3.9	2.1	3.2
F Comes in Honey	2.6	5.2	1.4	2.7
G Stone Ground Bran	0.3	-1.2	5.9	-0.4
H Low in Salt	-1.1	3.5	4.2	-1.4
Health/Nutrition				
I For Better Health	0.2	2.1	4.3	0.3
J For Better Digestion	0.6	1.2	4.1	0.5
K Roughage	1.3	-1.1	3.9	0.2
Ancillary Factors				
L Priced at $1.89	0.2	1.1	-0.1	-0.3
M Single Servings	1.5	0.9	3.6	7.1
N Fresh Packed/Foil	1.1	1.4	3.2	4.7
O For Snacks	0.2	2.2	4.6	6.2

Results-Clustering the Panel Into the Segments

Table 9.12 shows the additive models generated for each cluster. Looking at the table, we can label cluster 1 or segment 1 as "flavor seekers". These individuals pay a great deal of attention to flavor related elements. The remaining elements show very low additive constants, suggesting that for these particular individuals in the flavor seeker group the other elements of the concept do not act as significant attention getters, or as promoters of purchase intent.

The additive model in Table 9.12 for cluster or segment 2 suggests the name "nutrition oriented" or "health oriented". The panelists belonging in this second segment show the highest reactivity to attributes dealing with nutrition. In contrast, they like the flavor reinforcement messages, but not to the degree that consumers in the first segment do.

Finally, for the third cluster, we find these individuals tending to react very little to most of the elements in the concepts. They seem uninvolved with the product. No particular element "turns them on". Fortunately for the marketer, they constitute a relatively low proportion (18%) of the panel. We might wish to call these individuals the "uninvolved".

TABLE 9.12
ADDITIVE MODEL FOR CEREAL CONCEPTS, BASED UPON SEGMENTING CONSUMERS INTO THREE DISTINCT SEGMENTS

	Purchase (100%)	Flavor (52%)	Nutrition (30%)	Indifferent (18%)
	Percent of Panelists			
Intercept	35	40	36	29
Authority				
A Dietitians Recommend	2.1	-0.1	4.1	0.6
B Scientific Evidence	1.1	0.2	2.5	0.6
C Scientific Tests	0.3	0.2	3.3	-1.1
Flavor Message				
D Great Tasting	0.1	3.5	2.1	-0.3
E Sweet and Crunchy	4.3	5.9	0.6	-0.7
F Comes in Honey	2.6	4.7	0.2	2.1
G Stone Ground Bran	0.3	-0.6	0.8	0.2
H Low in Salt	-1.1	-1.4	1.9	-0.3
Health/Nutrition				
I For Better Health	0.2	0.5	1.3	-0.2
J For Better Digestion	0.6	0.2	2.3	0.4
K Roughage	1.3	0.4	3.6	0.8
Ancillary Factors				
L Priced at $1.89	0.2	.6	-0.7	0.7
M Single Servings	1.5	1.3	2.3	0.9
N Fresh Packed/Foil	1.1	1.2	0.5	0.6
O For Snacks	0.2	1.2	-0.3	-0.2
Multiple R Squared	0.74	0.66	0.69	0.44

Do More Segments Exist—And If So, How Many

Clustering procedures designed to uncover segments do not represent a 100% perfect method, which precisely defines the number of different types of individuals. Rather, the number of clusters of consumers uncovered depends upon the statistical criteria used to define a cluster, and the criterion invoked to stop the clustering process. For these data, we might easily have gone on to 4, 5 or more different clusters, and attempted to give each group a name. Why did we stop at 3?

For the K Means Clustering System, used here, we computed the distance between the coordinates associated with each person, and the centroid of the cluster to which he or she belonged. If we assume that all panelists fall into one large cluster, the sum of these distances (across panelists) maximizes. As we partition panelists into their appropriate clusters, the total variability diminishes, because although the people remain fixed in the coordinate space, the distance to the center point (centroid) of their cluster begins to drop. The smallest total distance (from each panelist to his/her centroid) occurs when each person constitutes a cluster, and thus the distance (or variability) of each person to his/her cluster becomes 0. Table 9.13 shows what occurs as we increase the number of clusters or segments. Note the initial rapid drop in variability, as we go from 1 to 2 to 3 clusters. As we continue, however, we find that each additional cluster generates a smaller decrement in variability. Indeed, after a while it looks like relatively little marginal improvement occurs as we add clusters. We select the number of clusters by looking at the drop in variability, and try to find that number of clusters at which we secure the greatest drop in variability per additional cluster, while substantially reducing total variability, and while maintaining a parsimonious number of clusters. Judgmentally, this might occur at two, three or four clusters. Beyond four, however, we can see relatively little improvement by reduction of variability.

Satisfying Different Segments

Having isolated individuals with divergent points of view, who seem susceptible to different messages, we face the problem of satisfying these individuals by correctly choosing elements in the concept. For instance, if we select elements to please the individuals in the flavor oriented segment, we do little to attract individuals in the health oriented segments. Do there exist any particular elements which appeal highly to both groups. For the present, we can forget about the consumers in the uninvolved segment, because we have found nothing which dramatically appeals to them.

TABLE 9.13
HOW INCREASING THE NUMBER OF CLUSTERS OR SEGMENTS REDUCES THE TOTAL VARIABILITY MEASURE OF THE DATA*

Number of Clusters	Relative Variability	Change in Total Squared Distances
1	100	—
2	68	32
3	47	53
4	40	60
5	35	65
6	32	68
7	29	71

*Defined as the total sum of squares of the difference between each person and the centroid of his/her cluster.

Table 9.12 shows the additive model for purchase intent. We find that if we select high performing elements for one segment, we do not maximize purchase intent for the other segment. Thus, we have to content ourselves with redefining the marketing goal. We may wish to satisfy both groups equally, or we may wish to optimize purchase intent for one group (e.g., flavor oriented), making sure not to "turn off" the other group.

Some alternative strategies appear in Table 9.14. Note the second strategy, to maximize purchase intent for the flavor oriented group. The appropriate selection of high performing concept elements generates a highly acceptable concept for these flavor oriented individuals, but does not do as well for the nutrition/health oriented. An alternative strategy, replacing some elements with others, drops down purchase intent slightly for the flavor oriented, but enhances it for the health oriented. We should opt for that strategy. The third and fourth columns show similar reasoning, this time initially focusing on maximizing purchase intent for the "health or nutrition oriented" segment. The initial choice of elements generates high purchase intent for that group, but has elements less than acceptable to the flavor oriented group. However, a small rearrangement of the elements (column 4) generates the necessary improvement, with no dramatic loss of acceptance to the health segment.

TABLE 9.14
COMPARISON OF FOUR STRATEGIES FOR SELECTING CEREAL CONCEPTS

	(1) Total	(2) Flavor	(3) Health 1	(4) Health 2
Intercept				
Authority				
A Dietitians Recommend	A		A	A or
B Scientific Evidence		B or		B
C Scientific Tests		C		
Flavor Message				
D Great Tasting			D	D
E Sweet and Crunchy	E	E or		
F Comes in Honey		F	or	
G Stone Ground Bran				
H Low in Salt			H	
Health/Nutrition				
I For Better Health		I		
J For Better Digestion				
K Roughage	K		K	K
Ancillary Factors				
L Priced at $1.89	M	M	M	M
M Single Servings		N		
N Fresh Packed/Foil		or		
O For Snacks		O		

Total= A concept strongly appealing to the average consumer.
Flavor= A concept strongly appealing to flavor seekers.
Health 1= A concept strongly appealing to health/nutrition seekers.
Health 2= A concept appealing to health/nutrition seekers, but also appeals to flavor oriented consumers.

Integrating Feasibility And Cost Into The Concept Optimization Approach

The previous sections have dealt almost exclusively with consumer based evaluations of concepts. We selected concept elements on the basis of their attractiveness to the consumer, in motivating stated purchase intent. Or, for other cases, we selected concept elements because they highlighted specific and desirable communication points.

Quite often marketers and marketing researchers ignore technical inputs to concept development. For instance, suppose the different concept elements carry with them various costs, timing, or feasibility values. The most attractive concept element may cost too much money. Despite its ability to enhance purchase intent to a significant degree (e.g., 6 points more than any other concept element), the cost may exceed that of any other element, by 50% or more. How can we factor in these external considerations of cost, timing and feasibility?

Let us pursue the additive model again, this time using cost, timing, or feasibility as the dependent variables. We must involve R&D and engineering in the evaluation of the separate concepts. For each test concept developed, we must obtain an estimate of total dollar cost for implementing that concept, as well as an estimate of time, and an estimate of feasibility (e.g., probability that one can actually deliver that concept). These represent subjective estimates, except perhaps in the case of cost where one might cost out each element in the concept. The key here consists of obtaining these cost, timing and feasibility values for each concept tested. Table 9.15 shows a partial list of these values for some of the concepts tested. Keep in mind that R&D must react to every concept, rather than each element separately.

The next step consists of developing models relating the presence or absence of each concept element to each of these three variables, respectively. Rather than using consumer ratings as the dependent variable, we now use R&D estimates. Table 9.16 shows the results, in terms of these equations, as well as the additive model for overall purchase intent (entire panel).

Given the models in Table 9.16, we now see that choosing the best performing elements may generate too much cost. We can reduce the cost of the product, by selecting alternative concept elements, generating almost as high purchase intent, but which cost less, or which have greater probability of succeeding. Table 9.17 lists some alternative concepts based upon consumer and R&D considerations.

AN OVERVIEW TO CONCEPT DEVELOPMENT AND OPTIMIZATION

Proper development of concepts remains a key area in product development, which occurs early in the process. Marketers have developed screening procedures for concepts, and the concepts that win in these screening tests then go (in a more refined form) to R&D for product development.

TABLE 9.15
ANATOMY OF CONCEPTS VS. R & D ESTIMATES OF COST, TIMING AND FEASIBILITY*

Concept	Authority			Flavor Message					Health			Other Message				R&D Ratings		
	A	B	C	D	E	F	G	H	I	J	K	L	M	N	O	Cost	Timing	Feasibility
1	1	0	0	1	0	0	0	0	0	0	0	1	0	1	0	36	38	34
2	0	1	0	0	0	1	0	0	1	0	0	0	1	0	0	32	32	46
3	1	0	0	0	1	0	0	0	0	0	1	0	0	0	0	24	34	41
4	0	0	1	0	0	0	0	1	0	1	0	0	0	1	1	39	47	29
72	1	0	0	0	0	0	0	0	1	0	0	0	1	0	0	31	26	45

1 denotes the presence of the element in the concept; and a
0 denotes the absence of the element in the concept.
*All based on a 0-100 scale:
0 = low cost, rapid timing, low feasibility
100 = high cost, slow timing, high feasibility

TABLE 9.16
COMPARISON OF ADDITIVE MODELS FOR CEREAL BASED ON CONSUMER RATINGS OF PURCHASE INTENT VS. R & D RATINGS*
OF THE SAME CONCEPTS ON THREE DIMENSIONS

	Consumer	R&D Ratings		
	Purchase	Cost Goods	Timing	Feasibility
Intercept	35	22	27	42
Authority				
A Dietitians Recommend	2.1	3.7	0.3	-0.6
B Scientific Evidence	1.1	4.2	5.7	-0.7
C Scientific Tests	0.3	3.3	5.8	-0.9
Flavor Message				
D Great Tasting	0.1	2.5	4.7	-0.8
E Sweet and Crunchy	4.3	0.2	6.2	-0.3
F Comes in Honey	2.6	3.1	1.9	-0.1
G Stone Ground Bran	0.3	6.4	5.4	-1.7
H Low in Salt	-1.1	3.5	7.2	-3.6
Health/Nutrition				
I For Better Health	0.2	0.2	0.1	0.2
J For Better Digestion	0.6	0.1	0.2	0.1
K Roughage	1.3	0.1	0.2	-0.2
Ancillary Factors				
L Priced at $1.89	0.2	0.1	0.3	0.3
M Single Servings	1.5	3.8	0.7	1.2
N Fresh Packed/Foil	1.1	6.2	3.6	-4.7
O For Snacks	0.2	2.7	0.4	-2.1
Multiple R Squared	0.74	0.67	0.81	0.88
Standard Error	2.3	2.1	2.6	1.9

*0-100 scale
Cost = relative cost of goods
Timing = relative timing to develop
Feasibility = relative cost of goods

TABLE 9.17
HOW MARKETING AND R & D USE THE ADDITIVE MODELS TO SELECT CONCEPTS

	ADDITIVE MODELS*				GOALS**		
		R&D					
	Consumer Purchase	Cost of Goods	Timing	Feasibility	Maximize Consumer Purchase	Rapid Development of Product	Least Cost of Goods
Intercept	35	22	27	42	X	X	X
Authority							
A Dietitians Recommend	2.1	3.7	0.3	−0.6	A	A	A
B Scientific Evidence	1.1	4.2	5.7	−0.7			
C Scientific Tests	0.3	3.3	5.8	−0.9			
Flavor Message							
D Great Tasting	0.1	2.5	4.7	−0.8			
E Sweet and Crunchy	4.3	0.2	6.2	−0.3	E		E
F Comes in Honey	2.6	3.1	1.9	−0.1		E	
G Stone Ground Bran	0.3	6.4	5.4	−1.7		or	
H Low in Salt	−1.1	3.5	7.2	−3.6		H	
Health/Nutrition							
I For Better Health	0.2	0.2	0.1	0.2			
J For Better Digestion	0.6	0.1	0.2	0.1			
K Roughage	1.3	0.1	0.2	−0.2	K	K	K

TABLE 9.17 (Continued)
HOW MARKETING AND R & D USE THE ADDITIVE MODELS TO SELECT CONCEPTS

	ADDITIVE MODELS*				GOALS**		
		R&D					
	Consumer Purchase	Cost of Goods	Timing	Feasibility	Maximize Consumer Purchase	Rapid Development of Product	Least Cost of Goods
Ancillary Factors							
L Priced at $1.89	0.2	0.1	0.3	0.3			L
M Single Servings	1.5	3.8	0.7	1.2	M	M	
N Fresh Packed/Foil	1.1	6.2	3.6	−4.7			
O For Snacks	0.2	2.7	0.4	−2.1			
Multiple R Squared	0.74	0.67	0.81	0.88			
Standard Error	2.3	2.1	2.6	1.9			

*Additive models from consumers and R & D:
Purchase Intent (Consumers)
Relative Cost of Goods
Relative Timing to Develop
Relative Cost of Goods

**Alternative concepts keeping R & D in the selection process

This chapter has presented a systematic approach to concept evaluation and optimization, that allows the marketer to learn about the concept. Given systematic variations of concepts, one can understand how specific concept elements generate attribute ratings and acceptance, and then select those elements in a concept which show the greatest promise for enhancing acceptance and/or attribute communication. One can also use the procedure to segment the consumer population into different groups of individuals, showing individualized patterns of attentiveness to concept elements.

In terms of R&D involvement, the evaluation of the cost, feasibility and timing of the concept, and its relation to concept elements provides the opportunity to select winning concepts that R&D can develop into products in a timely and cost effective fashion.

The concept evaluation phase has traditionally remained within the purview of marketing and marketing research, rather than in the domain of R&D product development. However, product developers must become involved with the procedures, the test, and the interpretation of results, because ultimately they have to create the product which the concept promises.

REFERENCES

CATTIN, P. and WITTINK, D. R. 1982. Commercial use of conjoint analysis: A survey. J. Marketing *46,* 44-53.

GREEN, P. E. 1984. Hybrid models for conjoint analysis: An expository review. J. Marketing Res. *21,* 155-169.

GREEN, P. E. and GOLDBERG, S. M. 1981. A general approach to product design optimization via conjoint analysis. J. Marketing *45,* 17-37.

GREEN, P. E. and SRINIVASAN, V. 1978. Conjoint analysis in consumer research: Issues and outlook. J. Consumer Res. *5,* 103-123.

JOHNSON, R. M. 1974. Trade-off analysis of consumer values. J. Marketing Res. *11,* 121-127.

MOSKOWITZ, H. R. and CHANDLER, J. W. 1978. Consumer perceptions, attitudes, and tradeoffs regarding flavor and other product characteristics. Food Technol. *322,* (Nov.), 34-37.

SHANTEAU, J. C. and ANDERSON, N. H. 1969. Test of a conflict model for preference judgment. J. Mathematical Psych. *6,* 312-325.

CHAPTER 10

SEGMENTING CONSUMERS BY SENSORY PREFERENCES AND LEVELS OF LIKING

INTRODUCTION

Everyday observation reveals that consumers exhibit different likes and dislikes. We like different foods, and even like the same food prepared in different ways. Marketers have realized that the consumer population divides itself into segments, whether based upon demographic variables (age, region), or based upon attitudinal variables (e.g., predisposition to eat certain foods, attitudes towards foods). Recently, however, marketers have begun to focus their interest on segmentation which occurs because of psychological differences among people (called psychographic segmentation), or flavor preference differences (called product response segmentation). This chapter deals with segmenting the consumer primarily by revealed taste preferences (product response segmentation).

VARIABILITY IN ACCEPTANCE AND THE EXISTENCE OF SEGMENTS

Practitioners who work with reasonably large samples of consumers quickly find that individuals differ among themselves more dramatically in terms of what they like or dislike, than they differ in their sensory perceptions. One can demonstrate this difference among consumers with a simple taste evaluation. Give 50 consumers two cups of regular coffee, one strong and the other weak. Ask the consumers to scale perceptual characteristics, including sensory attributes, and liking attributes, using a simple scale (e.g., 0-100) such as that shown in Table 10.1. Then, compute the average and the variability (e.g., standard error). The results, shown for two samples of coffee in Table 10.1 reveal that the consumers differentiate the coffees, both in terms of sensory attributes and in terms of liking. More striking differences among attributes appear when we compare the variability of the ratings for the coffee on sensory attributes (strength of flavor), versus the variability on the attribute of "liking of flavor". Furthermore, this increased variability of liking, or hedonic scores continues to emerge, even if we look at the difference between the two coffees, on a panelist by panelist basis, first computing the average differences between coffee A and coffee B, and then computing the standard error of that difference.

Often, scientific researchers "throw up their hands" at this seemingly exorbitant variability of liking. After all, they reason, the variability among individuals looms so large for liking ratings, and seems so much smaller for sensory ratings that it appears futile to work with the liking ratings. The increased variability signals cloudier, or muddier data, and promises fewer clear trends to discover. In contrast, for the more tractable sensory attributes, one generally discovers more well-behaved trends, without the ever present inter-panelist variability to cloud these trends, and mar their statistical significance.

TABLE 10.1
COMPARISON OF MEANS AND VARIABILITIES OF RATINGS ASSIGNED TO TWO COFFEES BY THE SAME GROUP OF PANELISTS

COFFEE A			COFFEE B		
Attribute	Mean Rating	Standard Error	Attribute	Mean Rating	Standard Error
Liking			**Liking**		
Total	38	3.8	Total	58	4.1
Appearance	39	3.4	Appearance	55	3.6
Flavor	31	4.2	Flavor	42	4.1
Sensory			**Sensory**		
Grainy	47	1.7	Grainy	51	1.7
Dark	61	1.9	Dark	42	1.8
Aroma	31	2.6	Aroma	47	2.8
Flavor	36	2.3	Flavor	37	2.4
Bitter	27	2.3	Bitter	19	2.2

Base Size = 100 panelists evaluating two regular roast coffees using a 0-100 fixed point scale.

GETTING A MORE PRAGMATIC PERSPECTIVE ON INDIVIDUAL VARIABILITY

Let us reconsider what the inter-panelist variability really means. In essence, it says that people differ from each other. Perhaps there exist clusters of individuals who resemble each other in terms of liking ratings, and do not resemble individuals lying in another cluster. In a previous chapter on concept development we saw inter-individual differences in acceptability of consumers for cereals, and a method for discovering clusters of like-behaving individuals. Does that general clustering approach work here?

Strategies For Better Understanding Variability And Segments

This chapter presents two different approaches to segmenting consumers into different groups.

(1) Clustering consumers by their responses to questions that deal with demographics.

(2) Clustering consumers into likers versus dislikers of specific foods in the test. Here we focus interest on responses to the test stimuli. Likers of the products tested fall into one group, and dislikers of the test stimuli fall into a second group.

(3) Clustering consumers into segments based upon how sensory attributes relate to liking. For instance, for coffee we may discover a segment of individuals whose liking rating increases as the perceived strength of the coffee increases. In contrast, we may find another group showing the opposite effect; their liking rating for the coffee decreases as the perceived strength of the coffee increases.

CASE HISTORY— THE GAUSS BEVERAGE COMPANY

Cal Gauss founded a carbonated beverage company in 1965, operating out of Minnesota. The Gauss Beverage Company began its existence by blending concentrates for a variety of upper midwest beverage companies, generally on the small scale (less than 50 million dollars per year). These small companies employed in-house flavorists who worked with Cal Gauss and with his product development team to develop and fine tune the beverages. Often, these beverages could compete in a saturated market because of their unusual flavors (tropical fruits, for instance). The small companies serviced by Cal Gauss managed over the years to find and occupy small and profitable niches in the ever expanded market.

In 1972 the management of the Gauss Beverage Company decided to venture into formulating, bottling and marketing tropical beverages under their proprietary labels. Management and marketing recognized that their seven years of experience had given them a clear understanding of consumer preferences, at least for the upper midwest market. They recognized that they would compete in a market against many of their former customers. In view of the high cost of entry, management decided to search for a flavor niche that needed filling. They wanted to know whether there did exist in the market a group of consumers who would respond positively to a new beverage, dissimilar to beverages currently on the market. The beverage had to fall in the category of fruit/tropical fruit, because in that area lay Cal Gauss' marketing and technical strengths.

Segmenting Consumers Into Preference Groups

The fruit beverage market does not enjoy the same cohesiveness as does the cola market. A lot of different types of flavors exist within the one major category, including orange, lemon-lime, as well as exotic flavors. The initial foray into this crowded market cannot encompass all of these different flavors at once, because of the expense of producing the different beverages, and the possibility that there exists only a relatively small number of consumers preferring each flavor of beverage.

Recognizing the "fractionated" nature of the beverage market means coming to terms with limiting one's scope and ambition. Gauss recognized that for optimum results he would have to develop a product, or small line of products, satisfying two constraints. (1) The product had to taste very good, so that once consumers purchased it, they would buy it again, on a frequent cycle, but without heavy spending for television, radio, or print advertisements (or in-store promotions) by Guass. All of these vehicles to promote consumption and repeat purchase cost money, well beyond the resources available to the Gauss Beverage Co. In essence, the product had to truly taste "good", and good enough to stand by itself in a crowded marketplace. (2) The product had to appeal to a sufficiently large number of people, namely the potential audience of consumers, or else no matter how good it tasted, too few people would ultimately purchase it.

These considerations, from the business point of view, reduced the number of alternative products considered by the marketing group. First, an evaluation of sales reports for the beverage category revealed that too few people drank the highly exotic, south sea island, tropical fruit beverages. Although the Gauss Beverage Co. had supplied tropical fruit flavors for its customers, the business opportunities available did not warrant going into competition with them. Quite obviously, the consumers did not drink enough of these tropical fruit-flavored beverages to sustain a new entry, or so the situation appeared from analyzing current market share reports.

Attention then turned to the big sellers; orange and lemon-lime. Orange seemed more promising than lemon-lime, because of the wide range of existing orange flavors. Marketing observed that over the past twenty years (starting in 1951), several dozen different orange carbonated beverages had appeared, enjoying various degrees of success and acceptance. It appeared as if the market could sustain a continued cycle of entry, trial, rejection, and then new entry. In contrast, for the exotic tropical fruit flavors it quickly became apparent that only a limited number of entries had appeared over 20 years, without the rapid change, suggesting that consumers likely to buy the exotic flavors did so, and when satisfied remained with the product.

The Final Marketing Decision Prior To Research

Based upon the foregoing train of reasoning, and backed up with current market share and volume estimates for the various beverages, the marketing group recommended work on orange flavored carbonated beverages as a likely area of entry. The beverages appealed both to children and to adults, and had a sufficiently large reservoir of potential consumers in the upper midwest market to warrant launching one (or even two) beverages. The Gauss Beverage Company possessed the technical expertise to blend the flavors to satisfy consumers, as well as having access to bottling lines.

Defining Consumer Taste Preferences For Orange Soda

The initial research step consists of defining what consumers want in an orange soda, and afterwards directing R&D to create that flavor experience. The initial research consists of focus group sessions. In these sessions, a group of consumers (limited to between 8 and 12 individuals) gathers for a 2 hour discussion, led by a moderator. The moderator begins the session ("warmup") by introducing himself/herself, and asking each participant to do likewise. Then, and following a basic outline for the discussion, the topics begin with general attitudes towards foods and carbonated beverages. As the session continues, the moderator skillfully leads the discussion into the area of carbonated orange beverages, probing consumers as to how they perceive the market of these beverages (e.g., how do they divide up these beverages, such as those for adults versus children, or other and more flavor oriented criteria). Finally, the discussion focuses on how consumers describe the orange beverages they drink now, the problems with these beverages, and how consumers describe the orange carbonated beverage they would like to have. During the discussion other topics emerge, such as reasons for drinking, price, availability, awareness of advertising and promotion, what works in advertising, etc.

The focus groups for the orange beverage quickly revealed the following key factors that dominated consumer perceptions:

(1) Most orange beverages seemed directed towards children, not towards adults.

(2) Orange beverages might appeal to adults, but needed a different type of flavor. Consumers could not accurately describe the sensory characteristics of this flavor system, but did say that it should definitely not appeal to children. It seemed as if, in the consumer's opinion, two beverages should exist; a children's beverage and an adult beverage.

(3) Consumer loyalty to beverages fluctuated as a function of price. When the price of the carbonated beverage increased, consumers switched, purchasing a national brand or house brand currently on sale.

(4) Consumers felt that orange sodas satiated them too quickly (in contrast to colas or to lemon-lime beverages). Some thought that the sugar level gave rise to the satiation, whereas others thought that the flavor quality itself (the "sticky sweet note") caused the satiation. No consumer realized that the sweetener level in orange beverages matched that of most colas.

(5) Consumers liked the idea of a diet orange soda, but felt that many of the diet orange sodas that they had purchased simply did not "taste good".

(6) The ideal orange soda had to have "real orange flavor". However, no one knew what that meant. The real flavor seemed another way of describing "natural" and "good tasting".

Overall, the group sessions, done in four markets, with two groups per market (87 people total, adults and teens) suggested the general conclusion that there exists a clear need for a tasty orange soda. The groups could not describe the sensory profile of the soda, nor reveal whether there exist different taste segments, but the groups did clearly reveal unsatisfied consumer needs (at least on an attitudinal basis).

Evaluating The Competitive Frame And Prototypes For Flavor Direction

Group sessions can provide only a limited amount of information, most of it attitudinal in nature. In order to fulfill the management directive (develop an orange product or line of products satisfying the consumer), one has to go out and do the experiment, make the measurements, and search for flavor preference segments. Only in this fashion can one uncover preference segments for the orange beverage, and then provide products optimally acceptable to those individuals.

Test Design

The marketing and R&D groups recognized that in order to answer the question they had to evaluate a wide range of formulations. Not knowing whether in fact there existed flavor preference segments, even among orange beverage consumers, they had to test a sufficiently large number of consumers. They could ask these consumers to describe the types of orange beverages that they liked. That attitudinal information might provide a key to flavor preferences. Presumably individuals who liked the sweeter, more candy flavored orange beverages would say so, whereas those preferring the bitter orange note would also say so. However, the marketing group did not know whether this attitudinal segmentation alone (by description of the self-designed optimal orange flavor for soda) would suffice to segment the consumer population in an accurate manner. During the course of the planning meetings the sensory analysis expert from R&D added that she felt consumers had such a poor vocabulary for flavor description that most of the consumers would have a difficult time verbalizing the sensory profile of orange.

As a consequence of these planning meetings, all of the involved groups in the task agreed to a specific test design that would accomplish the objectives. Basically, the consumers would do five things during the course of a two day test:

(1) Describe their food preferences

(2) Evaluate various orange beverages blind

(3) Profile their ideal orange beverage right after evaluating the blind products

(4) Evaluate 4 of the 6 different products on a labeled basis. The labels would involve descriptions of the beverage, along with the manufacturer. In phase 4, interest focused on the ability of a description on the label to influence ratings

(5) Rate a number of statements pertaining to attitudes towards foods, primarily directed at providing an idea of one's psychological orientation to foods and flavor.

Results—Average Ratings Of The Orange Beverages

The first analysis consists of determining the average ratings of the various orange beverages. Some of the results appear in Table 10.2, showing the ratings for liking and the ratings for some specific sensory characteristics, such as darkness of color, aroma intensity, sweetness, strength of orange flavor, type of orange flavor (whether more towards the type of flavor known as candy or more towards the type of flavor known as fruit-like).

As one can clearly see from Table 10.2, the consumers could easily distinguish the various orange beverages, both on sensory characteristics and on liking characteristics. We see a substantial range of acceptance, from a low of 43 (denoting modest acceptance) to a high of 71 (denoting a great deal of acceptance). Furthermore, we see moderately wide ranges of scores for the sensory attributes (15-20 points) confirming that the products selected for the test (4 commercial products, along with 2 specially developed prototypes) varied on a wide variety of dimensions.

TABLE 10.2
PROFILES OF CARBONATED ORANGE BEVERAGES ON ATTRIBUTES

	Orange Beverage Products						
	Ideal	A	B	C	D	E	F
Overall Liking	92	71	56	43	56	61	53
S.E.	1.2	3.6	3.5	3.4	3.7	3.2	3.1
Like Appearance	92	60	50	52	56	51	43
S.E.	1.2	3.1	3.2	2.9	3.1	3.2	2.8
Darkness	74	38	51	52	43	36	31
S.E.	1.8	1.6	1.5	1.6	1.4	1.5	1.5
Aroma Strength	80	43	44	48	47	41	28
S.E.	2.2	2.9	2.9	2.8	2.8	2.6	2.6
Sweetness	66	69	56	49	62	56	51
S.E.	2.1	2.7	2.5	2.1	2.4	2.4	2.2
Tartness	30	36	40	41	43	49	32
S.E.	1.9	2.1	2.3	2.1	2.2	2.1	1.9
Flavor Strength	72	72	66	57	63	63	55
S.E.	2.1	1.9	2.2	1.9	2.1	2.2	2.3
Type of Flavor	85	41	35	28	49	47	56
0=Candy	2.6	3.1	2.9	2.6	2.8	2.6	2.7
100=Fruit							

First Number=Mean
S.E.=Standard Error

Table 10.2 also shows the variability of the ratings. We see that the liking scales engender higher variability in ratings than do the sensory attribute scales. This simply means that individuals differ among each other more in what they like than in the sensory characteristics that they perceive. Ordinarily, this variability would simply measure differences among people. However, in view of our interest in segmenting consumers by taste preferences, this variability tells us that we may find individuals falling into different liking clusters. Indeed, the higher variability points to the probable existence of clusters. A lower variability would suggest greater homogeneity in the consumer population, at least in terms of taste, likes and dislikes.

Differences Among Consumers By Age

The first analysis in our segmentation of consumers consists of dividing the panel by age, into adults, teens and children. Table 10.3 shows the

TABLE 10.3
LIKING RATINGS ASSIGNED TO ORANGE BEVERAGES BY AGE GROUP AND THE SENSORY PROFILE OF EACH BEVERAGE

	Orange Beverage Products						
	Ideal	A	B	C	D	E	F
Liking Profiles							
Overall Liking	92	71	56	43	56	61	53
Adult (21+)	89	60	43	36	55	61	54
Teen (12-17)	91	73	58	48	63	59	54
Child (7-11)	96	80	67	45	50	63	51
Sensory Profiles							
Darkness	74	38	51	52	43	36	31
Aroma Strength	80	43	44	48	47	41	28
Sweetness	66	69	56	49	62	56	51
Tartness	30	36	40	41	43	49	32
Flavor Strength	72	72	66	57	63	63	55
Type of Flavor 0=Candy 100=Fruit	85	41	35	28	49	47	56

Note: Sensory profiles from total panel.
N=50 adults, 50 teens, 50 children.

ratings for the three groups. We see clearly that the groups do, in fact differ from each other albeit not dramatically. The adults tend to prefer the beverages having a tarter and less sweet taste, whereas the teens and children like the sweeter beverages. Despite the differences, the three groups do not seem radically different from each other. Their preference or acceptance differences for the beverages appear more a matter of degree in relative acceptance, rather than a polarization into distinct groups.

Marketing researchers who work with large samples of consumers often find that consumers in different age groups (as well as in different markets) show distinct differences in the products they like and dislike. Indeed segmentation of preference by age or market or product usage reflects the most straightforward analysis one can perform on the data. The researcher assumes that one can, in theory, account for acceptance differences by demographic differences, inherent in demographic, and brand usage data. Often, one finds these differences, but generally these differences do not emerge as dramatically related to liking, except perhaps in some unusual cases (e.g., Mexican food preferences, in Texas versus in California versus the rest of the U.S.).

Learning More About The Age Segments By Attributes Versus Liking

Table 10.3 simply revealed the existence of three different segments of consumers, differing by age, and exhibiting different degrees of liking. Before moving on to other methods of segmenting, let us look at the relation between attribute level and degree of liking, first for the entire panel, and then for the age segments (older, younger). The relation will help clarify the differences between the segments.

Researchers over the years have found that as a sensory attribute increases liking first increases, peaks, and then drops down. (We saw this relation explicated in greater detail in Chapter 1). Figure 10.1 shows the prototypical relation. We can fit a smooth curve to relations between an independent variable (e.g., sweetness of orange soda) and a dependent variable (e.g., liking of the beverage, overall). Generally, we will obtain a smooth function if we systematically vary one ingredient and measure liking. However, here, where we looked at the entire category of orange sodas, we could not systematically vary degree of sweetness, but had to content ourselves with having the consumer rate sweetness along with overall liking. By using fitted functions relating liking to attributes, we can discover the most probable underlying pattern between attribute level and liking. Despite the imperfect fit of the model or curve to the data, the results still instruct us. Furthermore, if we have two groups of consumers, we can develop the curves for each group separately, and compare them. The comparison will reveal to us whether these consumer segments react similarly or differently to attribute level, as it generates liking.

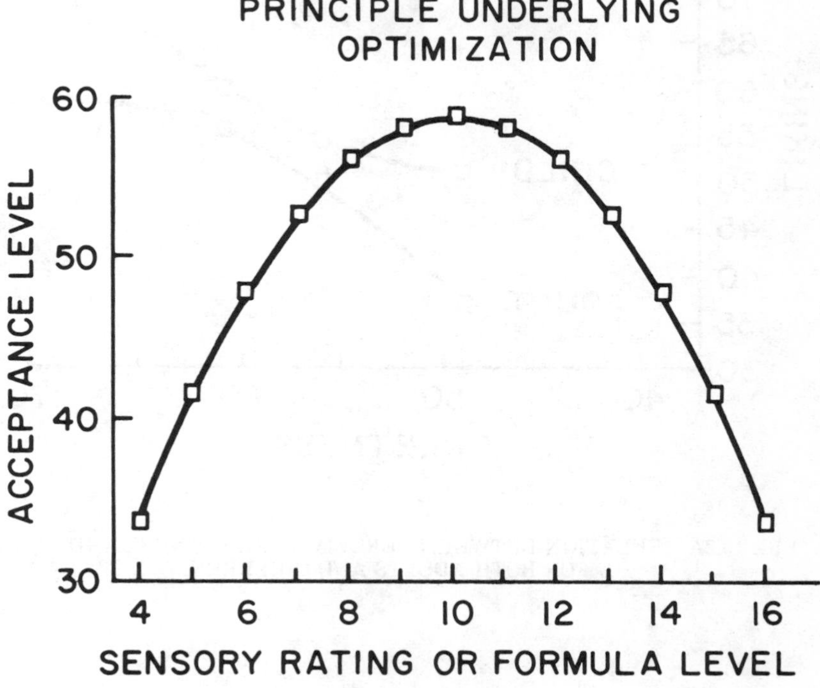

FIG. 10.1. PROTOTYPICAL, INVERTED U-SHAPED RELATION BETWEEN LIKING (ORDINATE) AND EITHER SENSORY ATTRIBUTE LEVEL OR FORMULATION LEVEL.
This curve represents the trend that one might find by evaluating the data from a group of consumers.

The value of the fitted curves becomes more apparent when we use it to compare two or more segments as children versus adults. In Fig. 10.2A, the independent variable, perceived sweetness, comes from the average ratings of the entire panel to the various prototypes (tested blind). We do this in order to make sure that the independent variable (a sensory attribute) stays constant, to facilitate comparison among two or more

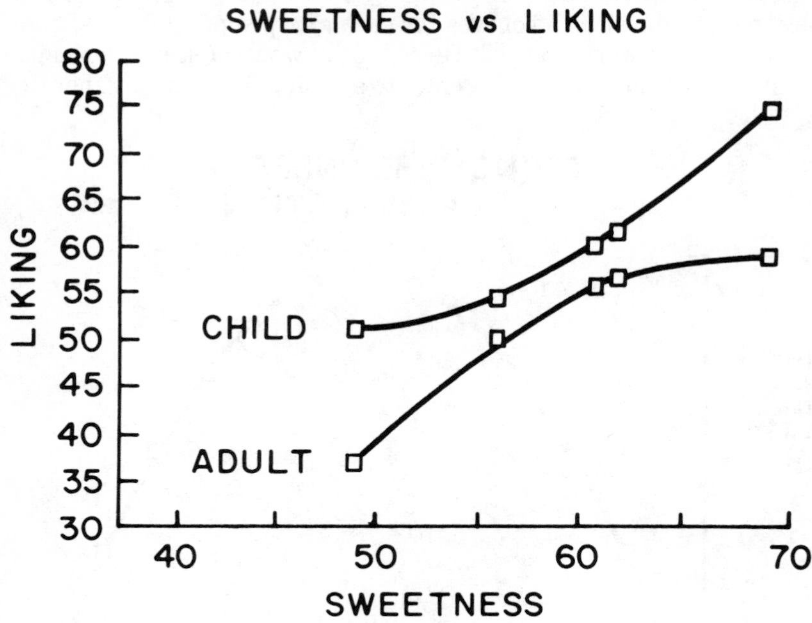

FIG. 10.2A. RELATION BETWEEN PERCEIVED SWEETNESS AND LIKING, FOR BOTH ADULTS AND CHILDREN.

groups. The dependent variable, overall liking, comes from each group separately. The liking ratings represent fitted values. Figure 10.2B shows the two curves, one for the adults and one for the children versus flavor type. Note the differences, with the adults showing an increased acceptance of fruitier flavor/tastes.

Segmenting On The Basis Of Attitudes

The next approach for segmenting consumers consists of looking at their attitudes, both in general, and towards foods and beverages in particular. Attitudinal segmentation consists of dividing people into clusters based upon their responses to questionnaires probing attitudes, rather than basing their clusters on where consumers live, their age, sex, etc.

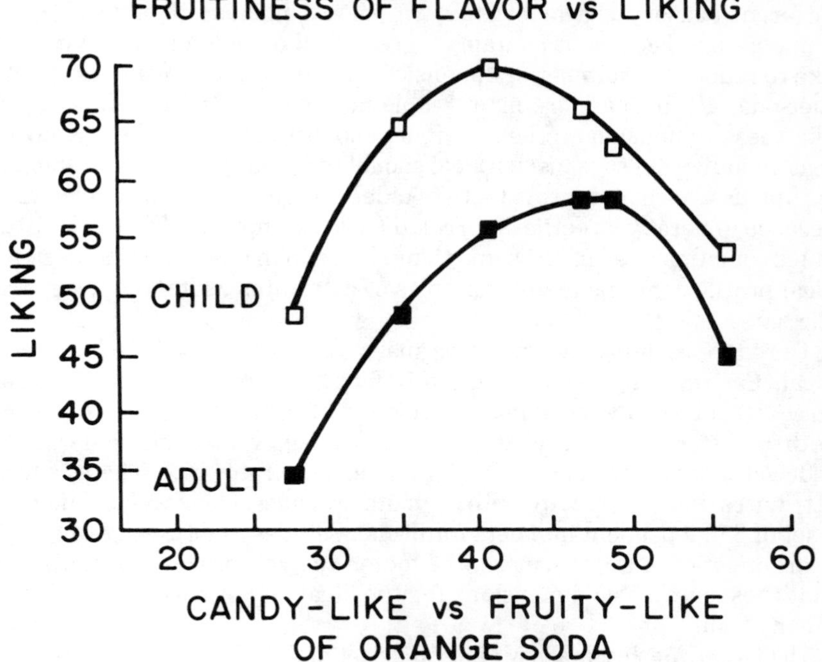

FIG. 10.2B. RELATION BETWEEN FLAVOR TYPE (CANDY VERSUS FRUITY) AND LIKING, FOR BOTH ADULTS AND CHILDREN.

In the study the panelists profiled the ideal beverage, which represents part of their attitudinal repertoire. A person's self-designed ideal beverage represents how the person feels about the beverage. It may, or may not have anything in common with what the consumer actually likes when he or she has a chance to drink the beverage.

The self-designed ideal for the beverage generated a sensory profile of the product that consumers felt that they would like to have. We looked at the profile of sensory attributes for the self-designed ideal (e.g., darkness, sweetness, tartness). These represent sensory, not liking characteristics. Do individuals fall into discrete clusters, based upon the self-designed ideal? If so, then can we uncover these clusters, and see how they differ in the actual response to beverages?

Although the panelists profiled their ideal orange soda on a variety of different sensory characteristics, we should not use their profile data immediately, because it contains a great deal of redundancy. We would like to reduce the number of dimensions on which the consumers profiled the soda, down to a more manageable number. Furthermore, we would like these dimensions to behave independently of each other. Knowing that an individual says his/her ideal should have a high sweetness and high syrupiness does not provide two independent pieces of information, because generally sweetness correlates with syrupiness. These two attributes sometimes tell us the same thing. More than likely, the self-designed ideal profile contains many examples of attributes which really describe the same thing.

To reduce redundancy, we factor analyze the ratings of the self-designed ideal. Factor analysis allows us to reduce the number of different sensory attributes to a more manageable set of basic attributes. We began with 6 different sensory attributes. The factor analysis generated a reduced set of 3 different attributes, as shown in Table 10.4. These reduced attributes do not correlate with each other. Thus each individual now has a set of 3 independent numbers for his/her self-designed ideal, rather than a larger set of 6. Furthermore, the factor analysis procedure guarantees that these new basic dimensions for the ideal do not correlate with each other at all.

The results of this analysis generate a set of data, consisting of 150 rows (one per panelist), and 3 columns (one per new, independent attribute, from the factor analysis). We can compare this data set to a geometrical space, with each panelist representing a point in the space, and each of the three independent attributes in Table 10.4. representing the coordinate in that space. The space has 3 dimensions, and we locate each person in the space by knowing his/her coordinates.

To find clusters of panelists we resort to conventional clustering procedures, such as the K Means Clustering Method. Briefly, we try to reduce the variability in the system (defined as the distance of each panelist to the cluster to which he/she belongs). The variability reaches its highest point when we consider all panelists to lie in one cluster, and compute the distances between each panelist and the center (centroid) of the cluster. As we divide individuals into smaller clusters, the big mass fractionates into smaller, and more cohesive clusters. The distances decrease between the points and the center of the cluster. The clustering procedure attempts to locate each person in one of a limited number of clusters in order to minimize the total distance from each person to his/her cluster.

The clustering procedure generated a total of 2 different segments. To find out what we should call these segments we need to return to the self-designed ideal profile for orange soda, and compute the profile assigned

TABLE 10.4
DATA MATRIX OF IDEAL RATINGS FOR ORANGE SODA—COMPARING RAW ATTRIBUTE RATINGS AND THE FACTOR SCORES FOR THE PANELISTS

	RAW ATTRIBUTE RATINGS FOR IDEAL						FACTOR ANALYSIS SCORES		
							Factor Scores		
Panelist	Darkness	Aroma Strength	Sweetness	Tartness	Flavor Strength	Candy, Fruit	A	B	C
1	82	68	58	45	88	90	.25	−.66	.61
2	76	74	77	33	61	81	.25	−.41	.79
3	81	89	68	21	79	95	.32	−.54	.75
4	68	81	71	8	61	72	.31	−.48	.78
150	62	73	69	38	59	67	.22	−.44	.72

The three factor scores represent the three independent variables which emerge from factor analysis of the profile of the Ideal Orange Soda. The subsequent clustering to find segments of similar consumers based upon the self-designed ideal uses the factor scores for the panelists, not the original or raw scores.

by each segment. The total profile and the profiles assigned by the two segments appear in Table 10.5. We can call the first segment the "sweet lovers", and the second segment the "tart, fruit/flavor" seekers.

Despite the fact that we can cluster the panelists by their self-designed ideal, we still do not know whether the clustering generates different ratings of liking. Indeed, we ought to inquire as to whether the differences that we find among panelists on the self-designed ideal represent large differences or small differences when we look at how the groups rate the actual products. Quite often individuals seem different on an attitudinal basis, but appear more similar than expected when it comes to actual behavior. Fortunately, we have the ratings assigned by these consumers to the actual beverages. The ratings appear in Table 10.5, and show somewhat larger differences from cluster (or segment) to cluster than we saw when we segmented by age (a demographic variable). Thus, attitudinal segmentation separates individuals more than does demographic segmentation, at least for orange beverages.

Our next analysis concerns the relation between attitudinal segments, sensory attributes, and overall liking. This time we perform the same analysis as we did previously; namely, we relate overall liking to sweetness, fitting a curve to the data, and looking at the smoothed function. Figure 10.3 shows the results, and reveals that the groups differ, rather dramatically. The low sweetness segment that we inferred from the self-designed ideal shows the maximum liking at the low sweetness level. In contrast, the high sweetness segment shows the highest liking at the high sweetness level. The groups do differ, both attitudinally and behaviorally. Even more important, however, we find that the attitudes do predict behavior.

Our final segmentation analysis looks at the relation between attribute level and liking, on a panelist by panelist basis, and then tried to find clusters of panelists who exhibit similar patterns of relations (between attribute level and liking).

Recall the prototype relation between attribute level and degree of liking, which follows an inverted U-shaped curve and which emerges if we explore a sufficiently wide range of levels of the independent variable. Although we tend to find this inverted U-shaped curve, on an individual basis we may find all sorts of curves, including linear upwards sloping (so that increases in the attribute level generate increases in liking, with evidence of a peak level, or perhaps even without evidence of a point of diminishing returns). Another individual might generate a clear downwards sloping curve, suggesting that liking drops down in a consistent, systematic matter with increasing attribute level. Finally, individuals may exhibit steep or flat inverted U or conventional U-shaped curves.

If we develop the curve relating an attribute level to liking, using a

TABLE 10.5
LIKING RATINGS BY ATTITUDINAL SEGMENTS (FROM IDEAL) AND TOTAL PANEL PROFILE

	Orange Beverage Products								
Like Ratings for Sensory Segments	Ideal	A	B	C	D	E	F		
Overall Liking	92	71	56	43	56	61	53		
Segment 1	94	82	65	60	72	65	55		
Segment 2	90	54	42	16	31	55	50		
Sensory Ratings from Total Panel								Ideal Segment 1	Ideal Segment 2
Darkness	74	38	51	52	43	36	31	72	76
Aroma Strength	80	43	44	48	47	41	28	82	78
Sweetness	66	69	56	49	62	56	51	71	62
Tartness	30	36	40	41	43	49	32	26	34
Flavor Strength	72	72	66	57	63	63	55	74	70
Type of Flavor	85	41	35	28	49	47	56	83	87

Tentative Labels
Segment 1 = Sweet Lovers = 41%
Segment 2 = Tart, Fruit Flavor Lovers = 59%

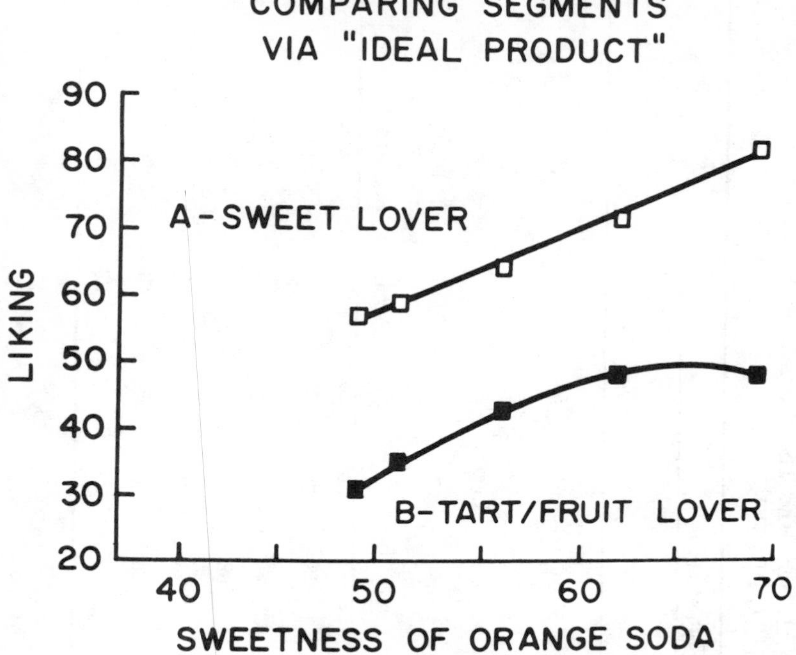

FIG. 10.3. COMPARISON OF TWO TYPES OF CURVES RELATING SWEETNESS TO LIKING.

These curves come from the segmentation of consumers on the basis of attitudes (namely, clustering consumers based upon their self-defined ideal orange beverage). Note the greater difference in pattern relating sweetness to liking for these segments, versus segmentation of the consumer panel by age (adult versus teen versus child).

quadratic equation [Liking = A + B (Attribute) + C (Attribute^2)], we can compare individuals in several ways. The easiest way, and the one chosen here, consists of determining the attribute level for each individual at which overall liking reaches its peak point. Figure 10.4 compares two individuals. It shows how liking varies with attribute level for panelist A, and panelist B, respectively. Then it shows the attribute level at which panelist A's liking ratings reach their highest point and similarly for panelist B. Keep in mind the following.

(1) The sensory attribute level, acting as the independent variable, comes from the total panel. With a panelist evaluating 6 products on an attribute (e.g., sweetness), and with a base of 150 panelists, we end up with 6 levels of sweetness, each the average from 150 individuals.

(2) The liking rating comes from each individual panelist.

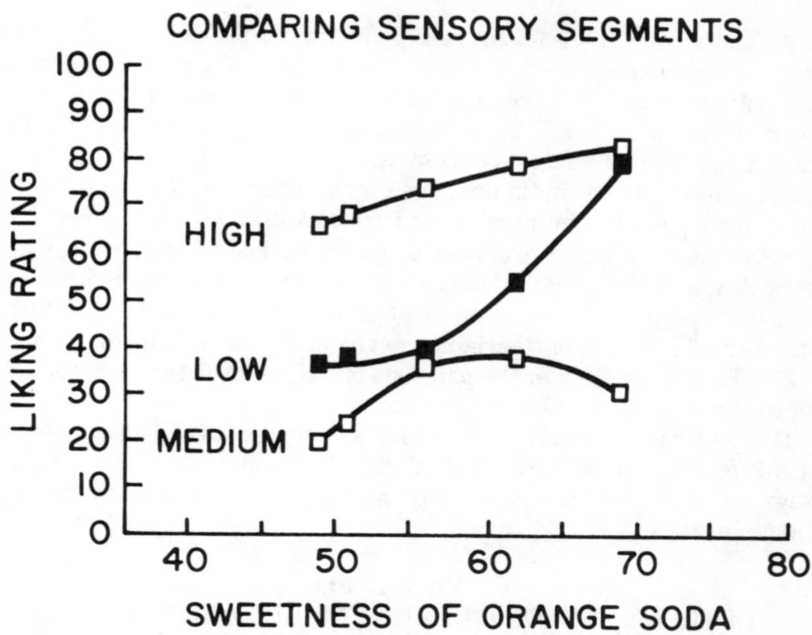

FIG. 10.4. COMPARISON OF SENSORY SEGMENTS FOR ORANGE BEVERAGE, OBTAINED BY SEGMENTING CONSUMERS ON THE BASIS OF HOW SENSORY ATTRIBUTES GENERATE LIKING RATING.
Note the extreme differences between the segments, greater than the differences obtained by segmenting either according to demographics, or according to the self defined ideal product.

(3) The quadratic or parabolic equation allows, but does not force, liking to achieve an optimum level in the middle range. Liking might just as easily achieve its optimal level at the upper or lower extreme. A linear equation would never allow the researcher to discover an optimal level in the mid-range of the independent variable.

(4) We evaluate the curve for each panelist, on an individual-by-individual basis, to discover where liking reaches its highest point. Each individual will have one attribute level at which liking maximizes.

(5) We then go to the ordinate, or the value of the attribute, and find what attribute level gave rise to the highest acceptance level.

(6) We perform this analysis for each panelist on a variety of different sensory attributes.

(7) The resulting database looks similar to that shown in Table 10.6. For 150 panelists, evaluating liking and 6 attributes, we have a matrix of 150 (panelists)×6 (optimal levels, one per attribute)

(8) The optimal levels for the sensory attributes probably contains a great deal of redundancy. Recall that for the ratings of the ideal, we reduced the actual number of attributes from 6 down to 3, by factor analysis, and then clustered on the 3, independent (orthogonal) attributes. We follow the same procedure here. We factor analyze the 6 variables (each variable corresponding to the optimum level for the attribute). The factor analysis procedure reduces the number of variables or attributes, down from 6 (containing correlated variables), to a more manageable number, with the property that the new variables do not correlate with each other at all.

(9) We compute the factor score of each individual, on the new, reduced number of independent variables developed from factor analysis.

(10) Finally, we cluster the panelists on the reduced set of factor scores, to determine the number of segments.

(11) The result of steps 1-10 consists of segments of individuals showing different optimal levels of attributes. Individuals clustered in the same segment show a similar pattern of optimal levels, and thus similar acceptance profiles.

TABLE 10.6
OPTIMAL SENSORY LEVELS OF SIX ATTRIBUTES OF ORANGE SODA ON A PANELIST BY PANELIST BASIS

SENSORY PROFILES	PANELIST NUMBER				
	1	2	3	4	150
Darkness	52	52	52	39	33
Aroma Strength	47	46	45	35	28
Sweetness	51	60	50	49	62
Tartness	49	45	40	36	41
Flavor Strength	57	65	70	65	58
Type of Flavor 0=Candy, 100=Fruit	28	33	42	45	45

Numbers in table show attribute level (within range tested) at which panelist's liking rating reaches its optimal level.

Results

The results of the analysis generated 3 segments, as shown in Table 10.7, which provides the profile of the optimum product, for the total panel, and for each of the three segments. Note that in Table 10.7 we have computed the average optimal level for each attribute, for each segment.

We can name the three segments as follows:

Segment A (53%) = High sweet lover
Segment B (28%) = Medium sweet lover
Segment C (19%) = Low sweet, high impact.

TABLE 10.7
OPTIMAL SENSORY LEVELS OF SIX ATTRIBUTES OF ORANGE SODA FOR THE THREE SEGMENTS UNCOVERED BY PRODUCT RESPONSE SEGMENTATION

	Sensory Segment		
	A	B	C
Darkness	39	42	45
Aroma Strength	33	37	45
Sweetness	63	58	54
Tartness	37	40	44
Flavor Strength	58	61	67
Type of Flavor (0 = Candy, 100 = Fruit)	32	41	43

Segment A (53% of the Consumers) = High Sweet, Candy Seekers
Segment B (28% of the Consumers) = Medium Sweet
Segment C (19% of the Consumers) = Low Sweetness, High Impact

Since these segments differ in the actual taste preferences, we expect them to generate quite different patterns of acceptance for the actual beverages. Table 10.8 shows their ratings of liking, for all of the beverages. Note the wide variations in acceptance, even wider in some instances than the differences among segments for a product obtained when we segmented the panelists on the basis of the self-designed ideal. The sensory, or product response segmentation clearly breaks apart individuals into dramatically different groups.

Relating Attribute Level To Liking—For The Sensory Segment

Our last analysis for this segment consists of fitting curves relating attribute level to liking. Figure 10.4 shows these curves for the three segments. We see immediately that the sweetness versus liking curve differs dramatically among the three segments, as it should. We selected the segments in terms of different patterns of liking versus sensory attributes, and attempted to maximize the difference in liking versus attributes, across the segments.

TABLE 10.8
LIKING RATINGS OF SENSORY SEGMENTS
AND TOTAL PANEL PROFILE

	ORANGE BEVERAGE PRODUCTS					
	A	B	C	D	E	F
Liking Ratings for Sensory Segments						
Overall Liking	71	56	43	56	61	53
Sensory A High Sweet	83	71	63	80	74	74
Sensory B Medium Sweet	86	43	14	29	55	21
Sensory C Low Sweet	32	39	32	35	41	43
Sensory Ratings from Total Panel						
Darkness	38	51	52	43	36	31
Aroma Strength	43	44	48	47	41	28
Sweetness	69	56	49	62	56	51
Tartness	36	40	41	43	49	32
Flavor of Strength	72	66	57	63	63	55
Type of Flavor 0=Candy, 100=Fruit	41	35	28	49	47	56

Composition Of The Segments

By themselves, the segments only tell us that in the population we can find "different types of people". From a product development point of view, we can determine the sensory characteristics appealing to each segment, and formulate products accordingly. From a marketing point of view, however, we need to answer the following questions.

(1) What type of people does each segment comprise?

(2) How do these consumers react to the in-market products?

(3) Do these consumers drink a lot of orange soda, or just a little? Even if we could develop a product which would satisfy a segment, this segment may consume too little soda to warrant attention, or the segment may comprise too few individuals.

Table 10.9 shows the composition of the segments, following the two ways of segmenting the consumers (namely, by the self-designed ideal versus by responses to products). In general, the consumers preferring the sweet products tend to come from the younger group of panelists, whereas those preferring the less sweet, tarter, stronger orange flavored products tend to come from the older group. In terms of level of liking, the older consumers like the product less than do the younger consumers. We find more younger panelists falling into the segments of individuals who truly love the beverage (at least by their ratings).

TABLE 10.9
COMPOSITION OF THE CONSUMER PANEL, TOTAL AND BY SEGMENT

		Attitudinal Segmentation From Ideal		Product Response Segmentation From Actual Liking Ratings Versus Sensory Attribute Profile		
Base	Total Panel	Sweet Taste Lover (1)	Tart Fruit Lover (2)	High Sweet Candy (A)	Medium Sweet (B)	Low Sweet High Impact (C)
Base	100%	47%	53%	53%	28%	19%
Age						
12-17	33	[63]	21	[22	18	12
18-24	32	17	18	31	[30	25
23-34	15	10	[26	38]	36]	[35
35-49	20	10	35]	9	16	28]
Total %	100	100	100	100	100	100
Frequency of Consumption						
1/Week	16	21	33	10	20	31
2-4/Week	21	12	41	11	16	19
5-6/Week	25	15	12	15	21	17
1/Day	19	37	8	16	24	16
2/Day	10	10	4	30	12	12
3+/Day	9	5	2	18	7	5
Total %	100	100	100	100	100	100

Table 10.9 also shows the frequency of consumption of various types of beverages, and lists some key observations. We find that the various segments represent different types of behaviors when it comes to orange beverage.

Further Analysis Of The Segments

The next analysis will concern only the segmentation of consumers by product response. Our interest now focuses on the promise or opportunity if the Gauss Beverage Co. develops a product for each of the three segments. For which segment(s) should the product developer target a product?

Let us first look at how the segments rated competitor products. Table 10.10 shows the ratings of the different blind competitor products, on a segment by segment basis. We see here that the segments differ in their reactions to the products, both in terms of level of absolute acceptance, and in the ranking of the different products. We conclude that the greatest opportunities, thus far, may lie with segment A (high sweet).

TABLE 10.10
LIKING RATINGS FOR ORANGE BEVERAGE—BLIND AND BRANDED BY TOTAL PANEL AND BY SENSORY (PRODUCT RESPONSE) SEGMENT

	Total		Segment A High Sweet		Segment B Medium Sweet		Segment C Low Sweet	
Product	Blind	Branded	Blind	Branded	Blind	Branded	Blind	Branded
A	71	N.A.	83	N.A.	86	N.A.	32	N.A.
B	56	N.A.	71	N.A.	43	N.A.	39	N.A.
C*	43	56	63	76	14	36	32	59
D*	56	53	80	85	29	31	35	48
E*	61	64	74	79	55	58	41	54
F*	53	57	74	77	21	38	43	66
Average Liking Rating*	53	57	72	79	29	40	37	56

A, B = R&D Prototypes
C, D, E, F = In-market orange sodas purchased by marketing and tested (both blind and branded)

*Only in-market products (C, D, E, F) used for this computation.

Let us now look at the ratings of the branded product. Segment A likes R&D prototypes as much or more than it likes the competition's. Segment B looks promising as well. Recall that the panelists had an opportunity to rate the branded products, for a number of competitors. We find the following trends, based upon a comparison of the blind versus the branded ratings.

(1) A branding effect does exist.

(2) Generally, however, we find a relatively small brand effect, usually in the positive direction.

(3) Among the three segments we find differences in the brand effect (defined as branded-blind rating).

(4) The most promising segments A (high sweet) and B (medium sweet) show a modest, rather than a strong sensitivity to brand. When the panelists in these segments discovered the brand names of the orange sodas, they increased their ratings, but only slightly.

SETTING NEW TARGETS FOR PRODUCT DEVELOPMENT FROM SEGMENTATION DATA: THE INSTANT COFFEE STUDY REVISITED

Background

The previous sections of this chapter have shown how to segment consumers on the basis of sensory preferences as well as on the basis of attitudes (via the self-designed ideal product). This section deals with the utilization of segmentation results to define targets for product development.

Revisiting The Instant Coffee Study

In a previous chapter (2) we saw the results of an audit of instant coffees. In that study, the panelists had an opportunity to evaluate a total of thirteen different coffees, blind and branded. The study results, analyzed further, using the product-response (sensory) segmentation methods discussed in this chapter, generated two clearly different segments of consumers. One segment, comprising approximately 40% of the population, consisted of consumers who behaviorally liked the milder impact coffees. The other segment, comprising the remaining 60% of the consumers, comprised individuals who behaviorally liked the stronger impact coffees. When asked to rate their self-designed ideal, both consumer segments said that they wanted coffees with low bitterness, high flavor intensity, etc.

Relating Attribute Level To Liking On A Segment By Segment Basis

After uncovering the segments, and identifying the consumers falling into each segment, the next step consisted of relating attribute ratings to liking, for each segment separately. How do these segments differ from each other? The clustering procedures suggested quite dramatic differences. Do these individuals evidence different patterns relating sensory attribute ratings of instant coffee to liking?

The appropriate analysis consisted of developing simple parabolic regression equations relating sensory attribute level (average from the entire panel) to liking (average from the panelists within a segment).

Figure 10.5 shows the curves for liking of appearance versus perceived darkness of grains, for the two segments (labeled mild and strong). Note that as the granules appear darker (in the cup, prior to adding water) both segments of consumers say that they like the appearance even more.

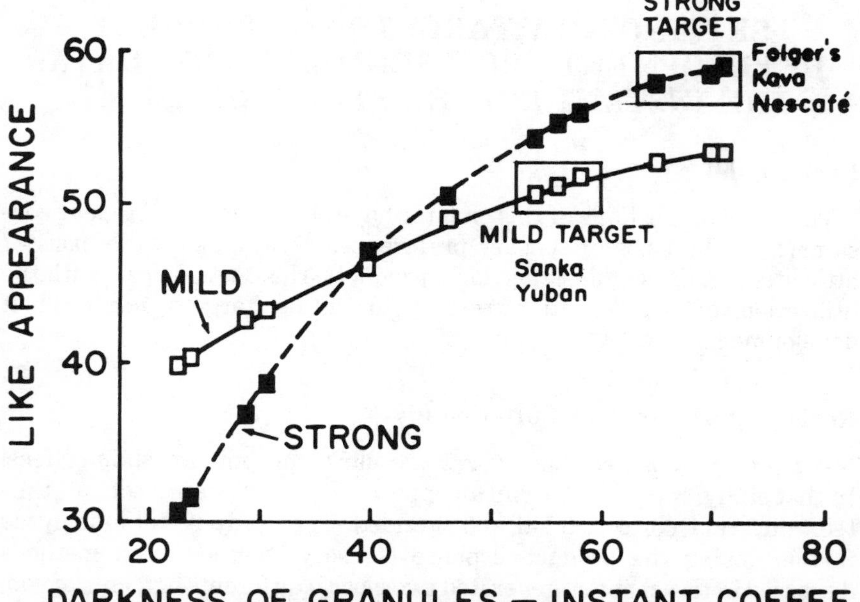

FIG. 10.5. COMPARISON OF TWO SEGMENTS WITH DIFFERENT PREFERENCES.

The strong segment likes the appearance of instant coffee (dry) much more as the granules get darker. The mild segment also likes the coffees when darker, but they seem less sensitive to color, as it increases acceptance.

However, the strong segment shows greater sensitivity, because liking of appearance increases more rapidly, and to a higher level. Furthermore, it becomes possible to target product development efforts, for a product that will appeal either to one segment, or to both segments. In Fig. 10.5, the appropriate targets for the strong segment include a darkness similar to that presented by Folger's, Kava, or Nescafe. In contrast, the mild segment (which also likes darker appearing granules) should have as a target slightly, but not very much lighter grains, such as the color of Sanka or Yuban.

Following the same analysis, this time for purchase intent versus perceived bitterness, we see dramatically different patterns. The strong segment likes coffees with increasingly bitter taste, but eventually rejects coffees having too bitter a taste. In contrast, the mild segment finds coffees increasingly unacceptable as the bitterness increases.

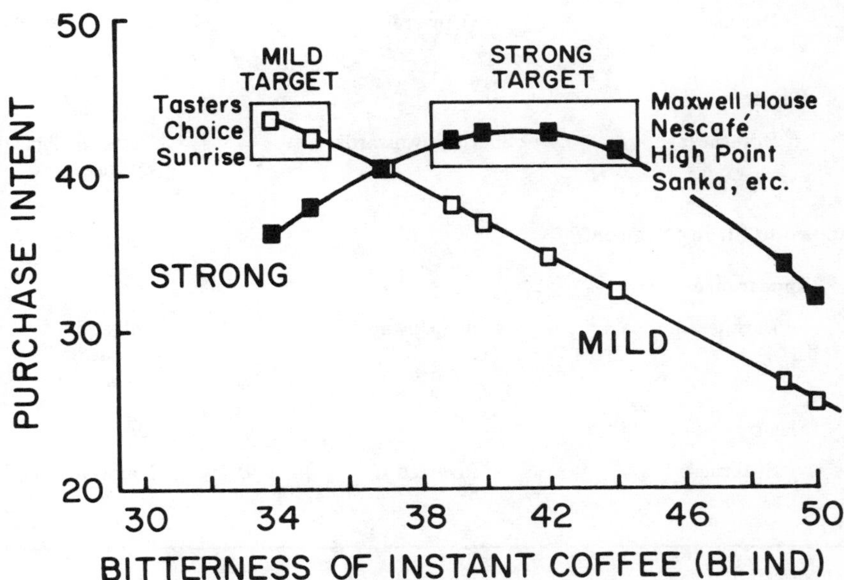

FIG. 10.6. COMPARISON OF THE SAME TWO SEGMENTS OF COFFEE—STRONG VERSUS MILD.
The strong segment likes the product more as the coffee tastes more bitter, until the bitterness reaches an optimum, beyond which acceptance decreases. In contrast, for the mild segment acceptance decreases as the coffee tastes more bitter.

Since the relation between acceptance and sensory characteristic involves actual products, it becomes a straightforward task to determine the pattern relating liking to sensory attribute, estimate where the relation reaches its maximum, and select representative products as targets for further product development. Table 10.11 shows such a prescription, based upon the coffee data.

TABLE 10.11
COFFEE STUDY
SETTING DEVELOPMENT TARGETS BASED ON
PRODUCT RESPONSE SEGMENTATION

DIMENSION/ATTRIBUTE	PATTERN	TARGET
Appeal to Mild Segment		
Appearance		
Darkness	Upwards	Sanka Yuban
Flavor		
Bitterness	Sharp Downwards	Taster's Choice Sunrise
Appeal to Strong Segment		
Appearance		
Darkness	Sharp Upwards	Folger's Nescafe Kava
Flavor		
Bitterness	Inverted U	Maxwell House Nescafe High Point

AN OVERVIEW

Segmentation as a strategy for marketing has become increasingly popular over the past twenty years. Marketers recognize that they no longer market to one cohesive group of consumers. Individuals differ from each other, in psychological, demographic, and taste-preference characteristics.

Traditionally, product developers have not participated in the segmentation, but rather marketing has dictated the profile of products that they believe will satisfy a specific segment. Usually marketing researchers uncover these segments by clustering individuals with similar attitudes, and behaviors in a category. This chapter introduces a method of segmenting by sensory preferences, and level of acceptance. The differences among consumers in terms of acceptance of different products becomes clear, and dramatic when we segment individuals by taste preferences. The product developer no longer has to worry that perhaps the segments uncovered by differentiating people according to attitudes have little or nothing to do with taste preferences. Here we segment on the basis of actual responses to products. Hence, when product developers now work with directionality provided by the segmentation, they work with true, enhanced differences in product acceptance. The products which appeal to the different segments must, necessarily, differ substantially from each other, and represent quite different sensory profiles, targeted at quite different consumer segments.

REFERENCES

ARNOLD, S. J. 1979. A test for clusters. J. Marketing Res. *16,* 545-551.

HEMPENIUS, W. L., LISKA, B. J. and HARRINGTON, R. B. 1969. Selected factors affecting consumer detection and preferences of flavor levels in sour cream. J. Dairy Sci. *52,* 594-597.

MOSKOWITZ, H. R. 1972. Subjective ideals and sensory optimization in evaluating perceptual dimensions in food. J. Appl. Psych. *56,* 60-66.

MOSKOWITZ, H. R., STANLEY, D. W. and CHANDLER, J. W. 1977. The eclipse method: Optimizing product formulation through a consumer generated ideal sensory profile. Canad. Inst. Food Sci. *10,* 161-168.

CHAPTER 11

RELATING EXPERT AND CONSUMER RATINGS TO DEVELOP AN INTEGRATED DATABASE

INTRODUCTION

Product testers and sensory analysts can use a variety of different panels. Traditionally, many sensory analysts have preferred to use expert panels. These panels comprise a limited number of individuals, possessing varied amounts of experience and expertise, whether in overall evaluation or in specific food categories.

Marketing researchers work virtually 100% with consumers, seeking consumer impressions of products, sensory reactions, directions for product improvement, and finally overall acceptance. In contrast, the sensory analyst who works with an expert panel uses the panel to replace an instrument. The panel acts as an objective registrator of the characteristics of a product. The panelists first undergo training to participate in such a panel. The panelists develop their objectivity and repertoire of response for the panel over time, and with feedback from the panel leader.

Corporate archives containing data from product tests will inevitably emerge with two different sets of results, one from marketing research and one from R&D (who often use the expert panels). Sometimes these results agree with each other when both panelists (consumer, expert) test the same product. Often they disagree, and point to different directions.

How do we relate consumer data to the assessments performed by expert panelists? Should we simply correlate expert ratings with the consumer ratings looking for points of agreement or disagreement? Or, can we develop a method to predict consumer data from expert panel data, perhaps after performing a transformation on the expert's ratings? This chapter deals with the interrelation among experts and consumers in product testing.

THE EXPERT PANEL—PEOPLE, TECHNIQUES, MEASUREMENTS

Expert panels come in all sizes and shapes. At the product development stage, many R&D groups develop their own expert panels by selecting participants who have had several years of experience with the product. Although the participants in the panel may not have received formal training in describing the sensory nuances of products, their experience has taught them what the different characteristics mean, what sensory characteristics the "gold standard" or reference product possesses, and what deviations may occur from that gold standard for various batch runs.

On the other end of the experience spectrum, we have expert panels comprising individuals who undergo an intensive training to evaluate a specific product or class of products. The training may last a few hours, a few weeks, or a few months. These individuals do not spend years with the product, absorbing the characteristics and honing perception by osmosis. Rather, they consciously work at evaluating the product in question, usually participating with a group of other individuals also selected. The panel exists for a specific purpose; to profile a specific product, in a limited time frame. The orientation to the product for these individuals constitutes a more formalized approach. This second type of expert panel comprises a task force, selected for sensory analysis.

Expert panelists work with one or another method of descriptive analysis. Panelists evaluate the product on a variety of attributes, agreed-upon ahead of time by the panel members. Each panel member evaluates the product on this list of characteristics, to generate a product "signature". Consumers may perform the same types of evaluation as well, but with a number of points of difference.

(1) The expert panelists do not rate degree of liking. The consumers do. The expert panelists confine themselves strictly to the evaluation of nonevaluative sensory characteristics. Ideally, they replace a "machine". Their ratings must demonstrate a high degree of reliability from session to session.

(2) The experts use a bank of attributes whose meaning they agree upon and define prior to the evaluation. All participants in the expert panel should use the same definition of the attributes. In contrast, consumers have different definitions of the same attributes.

(3) The experts may evaluate the same product several times to provide replicate judgments. In contrast, the consumer panelists usually evaluate each product only one time. The expert panel boosts sample size by obtaining replicate ratings from the same people, whereas the consumer panel boosts up the base size by adding more people.

(4) The expert may use either simple scales (0-9, 0-100), or more complex scales such as a line scale, anchored at both ends or a modified category, fixed point scale, such as shown in Table 11.1, and which is used by Arthur D. Little Inc. for their Flavor Profile technique.

(5) The expert panel often evaluates products on a host of attributes which may not mean much to the consumer. The expert panel looks for certain nuances in product appearance, aroma, flavor/taste, and texture. Consumers can and do pick up sensory nuances but lack the language to describe them. The expert panel possesses the language to describe these characteristics, and indeed quite often the panelists spend a great deal of time developing the language to pick up these subtle sensory characteristics.

(6) The consumer data lends itself to the large scale statistics. The expert panel data generally does not, because the panel may comprise as few as 6 individuals.

(7) The expert panel represents a substantial corporate investment. It demands many dozens of hours to become proficient once learning profile characteristics. This demands loyalty and persistence on the part of the participants, because the training and evaluations take time. In contrast, the consumer panel occurs only once for a particular product, and costs a great deal less money. Experts come from employees, whereas consumer panels usually (but not always) comprise individuals from the outside, consumer population.

TABLE 11.1
THE INTENSITY SCALE FOR
THE FLAVOR PROFILE PROCEDURE

SCALE VALUE	DESCRIPTION
0	Not Present
) (	Threshold
1	Weak
2	Moderate
3	Strong

Source: Caul (1957)

Problems Involved With Correlating Experts and Consumers

Traditionally, one thinks of research with experts or with consumers as providing a single, seamless web of information about a product. The ratings assigned by consumers should (but do not always) agree with the ratings assigned by experts. Differences found by experts should (but do not always) emerge as consumer perceivable differences.

Informal observation of sensory analysis laboratories will quickly dispel this idealization, and reveal that consumer panels and experts do not necessarily agree with each other. Consumers use a rougher, less detailed language to describe their perceptions. A consumer likes or does not like a food product. Only afterwards, and under specific instructions, will a consumer profile his or her sensory reactions. In contrast, an expert panelist who has undergone training in descriptive analysis knows how to talk about the product, what the different terms mean, and how to evaluate the order of appearance of the sensory characteristics after chewing and eating. These attributes may elude the average consumer, who often cannot even define the terms used by experts.

HOW TO BRING CONSUMERS AND EXPERTS TOGETHER

The remaining portion of this chapter deals with techniques to bring together consumer and expert panel data. For the most part, the techniques we discuss utilize various types of data analysis, rather than procedures. Consumers do not, will not, and probably cannot speak the language of experts. Nonetheless, this should not stop us from attempting to predict consumer ratings from the ratings assigned by expert panelists, even if both groups use entirely different scales.

A CASE HISTORY—QUALITY CHOCOLATE FLAVORS

The Wilkins Chocolate Company manufactures and markets several lines of high quality chocolates. Originally an English-Italian concern, the company became multinational in the early 1970's under the leadership of Leah Wilkins, the founder. During the period of rapid expansion, the procedures used for evaluating product quality and characteristics changed. Originally, Leah Wilkins herself tasted all of the chocolates. Generally, she could accurately select the best products for the consumer. However, with the expansion of the market into North America, and with the growth of the business by a factor of six over a four year period, it soon became clear that the company needed two things; a panel of experts who could replace Leah Wilkins (now busy with administration and running a multimillion dollar business), and a consumer testing system. Furthermore, in light of the quality image of the chocolates the marketers needed to walk the fine line between acceptance as a mass product, and perceived quality, which many consumers in the mass market would not necessarily find the most acceptable. Consumers preferred the sweet, lower quality chocolates, but these did not accord with the Wilkins image.

The Expert Panel

The first panel developed consisted of ten experts. The individuals participating in the panel came from the chocolate industry, but did not participate in product development. Rather, these individuals comprised secretaries, telephone operators, and product people, who had worked with Wilkins for at least two years, who showed a great deal of interest in the products produced, and who would remain with the company for the foreseeable future. The experts did not generally purchase high quality chocolates in stores, since they received virtually an unlimited supply at work. They did prefer these higher quality chocolates to the mass marketed ones, however.

Training The Expert Panel

Training an expert panel entails a set of steps, listed below.

(1) Introduction to the product. All participants in the expert panel had had experience with the chocolates, but none had undergone a systematized introduction to a wide variety of different chocolates. The introduction consisted of a lecture about chocolates, their history, the flavor nuances, and some concepts about the elements which constitutes high quality. In the first phase, these introductory lectures served to place all of the participants in the expert panel on an equal footing, in terms of background. During the introduction, the panelists had an opportunity to sample the different chocolates so that they could experience first hand the characteristics emphasized by the lecturers.

(2) Learning attributes and a reference scale. The expert panelists then proceeded to learn different terms which describe chocolate flavor. During this step the panelists again participated in a series of lectures, where they learned about the product and its characteristics from other experts. In the second phase, they had a chance to taste various chocolates, modified either by processing or by formulation to change the sensory attributes. This phase anchored the attributes, and the scale (a 1-5 scale).

(3) Development of additional terms. The final part of the orientation consisted of an active evaluation of a variety of chocolates, both those manufactured by Wilkins and by competitors. Here, the panelists used their knowledge in a more active fashion. First, they profiled their sensory impressions of the various chocolates on the attributes that they had learned. They did this exercise several times, looking at their answers and discussing their impressions among themselves as a group, until all panelists felt that they clearly understood the characteristics. Parenthetically, the agreement among members of the panel represents a key characteristic of an expert panel. For the basic sensory analysis of simple attributes the panelists should agree among themselves. Practice and discussion of results, over an extended period, will bring all of the panelists into line, so that they will end up using the scale in a consistent, reliable, and uniform fashion, from panelist to panelist, replicate to replicate.

The Chocolate Evaluation Study—Experts' Results

The expert panelists evaluated 9 samples of chocolate (A-I) purchased from leading competitors, both in Europe and in the U.S. Prior to the actual evaluations, the experts developed their lexicon of attributes, basing the lexicon on a list of terms previously developed for sensory evaluation research, and based upon discussions. Table 11.2 lists the attributes selected by the experts to represent their impressions of the various chocolates.

The expert panel evaluations required about two weeks to complete. The panel met for approximately 90 minutes, a total of four times. During the test sessions the panelists inspected the chocolates, tasted them, and then rated each chocolate on the set of attributes. Each panelist tasted every chocolate twice, in a rotated order. After evaluating the chocolates, at the end of a session, the panelists discussed their impressions with each other. This discussion helped to focus attention on the key attributes.

Table 11.2 presents the ratings assigned by the expert panel of 10 individuals (2 replicates per product). Note that the panelists perceived a wide number of differences among the products. Of particular interest note the evaluation of attributes both initially, and after 30 seconds. Such evaluations of the sensory impressions over time helps to uncover specific sensory problems which might emerge during the course of eating. A cursory taste and a quick evaluation might possibly miss those problems.

By itself, the information contained in Table 11.2 tells us nothing about consumer reactions to the chocolates. Instead, it provides a signature of the 9 chocolates, based upon the expert's impression. We do not know whether the expert's rating of characteristics agrees with the ratings assigned by consumers, or whether the sensory attributes evaluated by the experts suffice to predict consumer acceptance.

TABLE 11.2
RESULTS OF EXPERT PANEL EVALUATION OF NINE CHOCOLATES

ATTRIBUTE	CHOCOLATE SAMPLES								
	A	B	C	D	E	F	G	H	I
Appearance									
Darkness	2.4	2.9	3.3	3.6	3.9	4.1	4.1	4.3	4.6
Mottle	1.1	1.8	1.5	2.1	1.9	2.3	1.7	2.2	1.9
Shiny	3.4	3.6	2.1	3.8	3.6	2.1	1.4	3.9	3.2
Size (Area)	3.6	3.7	3.9	3.2	2.7	3.4	3.5	2.9	4.1
Thickness	2.1	2.6	2.4	2.2	2.6	2.1	1.8	2.5	2.1
Aroma									
Strength	1.9	2.2	2.3	1.9	3.1	2.4	2.6	1.9	2.4
Chocolate	2.3	2.6	2.1	2.4	2.7	2.2	2.1	2.6	3.1
Vanilla	1.6	1.2	1.1	1.2	2.8	1.1	1.4	1.6	2.9
Fruity/Not Citrus	1.1	1.2	1.1	1.1	1.2	1.1	1.9	1.1	2.5
Fruity/Citrus	2.1	1.1	1.3	1.4	1.1	1.7	1.2	1.1	1.3
Taste: Initial									
Strength	2.4	2.7	3.1	2.6	3.9	3.1	3.7	2.7	3.9
Chocolate	3.2	3.6	3.1	3.6	3.9	3.1	3.4	4.1	4.7
Vanilla	1.9	1.6	1.5	1.6	3.1	1.6	1.9	1.9	3.6
Bitter	1.3	1.3	1.4	1.3	0.9	1.3	1.1	1.1	0.6
Almond	2.1	1.6	1.2	1.6	2.6	2.4	2.1	2.1	3.5
Milky	1.8	1.9	1.8	1.8	2.6	1.7	2.1	1.9	2.6
Taste: after 30 sec									
Strength	2.6	3.2	3.5	3.1	4.2	3.6	4.1	3.2	4.6
Chocolate	3.1	3.8	4.1	3.6	4.6	4.1	4.3	4.1	4.6
Vanilla	2.7	2.3	2.3	2.4	4.1	2.3	2.8	2.6	4.1
Bitter	1.2	1.2	1.3	1.2	0.9	1.2	1.1	1.1	0.8
Burnt	0.9	0.9	1.1	0.9	0.7	0.9	0.8	0.8	0.6
Texture: Initial									
Surface Hardness	2.6	2.7	3.1	2.4	3.2	2.5	2.5	2.2	2.7
Fattiness	2.6	2.7	3.1	2.4	3.5	2.6	2.4	2.1	2.5
Adhesiveness	2.1	2.5	2.3	2.4	2.6	2.1	2.4	2.3	2.5
Mouth Coating	1.8	1.9	2.3	1.5	2.6	1.7	1.9	1.3	1.9
Texture: after 30 sec									
Fattiness	2.2	2.1	3.1	3.2	3.9	3.3	2.9	3.1	2.9
Adhesiveness	1.3	1.4	1.4	1.4	1.5	1.3	1.4	1.5	1.5
Mouth Coating	2.9	3.3	4.3	2.1	4.2	2.4	3.1	1.6	2.9
Rate of Melting	2.5	2.3	3.9	4.1	4.3	4.1	3.6	3.8	3.2

Panelists Used a 0-5 Scale with:
0 = Not Present
5 = Extremely Intense

TABLE 11.3
RESULTS OF CONSUMER RATINGS OF
THE SAME NINE CHOCOLATES

	CHOCOLATE SAMPLE								
ATTRIBUTE	A	B	C	D	E	F	G	H	I
Appearance									
Liking	39	43	58	58	61	61	62	68	69
Darkness	41	46	53	58	59	60	68	76	79
Shiny	31	33	21	34	32	19	12	40	31
Size (Area)	37	38	40	31	25	35	37	26	42
Thickness	26	32	31	31	35	31	26	35	26
Aroma									
Liking	31	42	33	35	58	37	38	39	49
Strength	31	36	38	31	58	41	46	32	41
Chocolate	41	52	38	46	55	39	34	57	71
Taste									
Liking	57	71	65	69	82	61	79	76	84
Strength	46	51	57	46	61	53	65	51	63
Chocolate	46	54	44	56	63	46	53	67	79
Bitter	15	16	18	14	10	14	12	14	7
Milky	34	36	34	35	41	29	40	34	46
Taste—After 30 Sec.									
Liking	54	68	67	65	78	64	81	79	81
Texture									
Liking	25	22	46	49	58	53	47	43	36
Hardness	56	59	68	54	69	56	59	49	58
Mouth Coating	17	19	21	12	23	15	17	15	17
Rate of Melting	15	12	29	35	41	37	28	31	19
Overall									
High Quality	45	49	56	59	64	58	63	61	64
Caloric	68	78	71	71	75	61	61	74	79
For Special Occasion	51	56	64	68	72	66	71	71	75
Overall Liking	55	63	69	77	79	75	82	79	79
Purchase Intent	48	59	61	73	71	71	77	72	75

Consumer Panelists Used An Anchored 0-100 Point Scale

Consumer Panel Ratings

The second stage of this project consisted of ratings assigned by a group of 50 consumer panelists. Consumers do not possess as extensive and refined a language to describe their perceptions, but nonetheless consumers can and do rate the simpler sensory characteristics (e.g., bitterness, sweetness, chocolate flavor, hardness, melt in mouth). The consumers rated their impressions of the same set of chocolates. Each consumer panelist evaluated all of the 9 products, on a rotated basis, during a 3-hour test session. The consumers rated each chocolate sample on a set of consumer-relevant attributes shown in Table 11.3. Note that the consumers used a variety of descriptor terms to rate the sensory characteristics of the chocolate samples. In addition, however, the consumers rated acceptance and image characteristics (e.g., perceived quality, caloric density). The consumers used a 0-100 point anchored scale. The expert panelists used a 0-5 point scale.

Relating Experts And Consumers—Similar Attributes

The first analysis consists of relating the expert and the consumer ratings of similar attributes. For instance, both panels rated perceived chocolate flavor. Do these attribute ratings agree with each other? Can we develop a relation between the expert panelist rating and the consumer panelist rating of the same attributes. Does this relation follow a straight line? If so, does the slope of the line equal 1.0, meaning that the two panels perceive equal differences among the products?

To answer these questions, we can develop a regression equation (straight line) relating consumer ratings (as the dependent variable) versus expert panel ratings (as the independent variable). The correlation between the two sets of ratings tells us how closely the two data sets agree with each other.

This first analysis appears in Table 11.4, which shows the results for the common attributes. In general, when consumers and experts rate the same attributes, their ratings agree with each other, but not perfectly. If an expert perceives a chocolate to possess a very high level of a characteristic, more than likely the consumer will perceive the same high intensity, and similarly for samples possessing a very low level of an attribute. In the middle range the ranking of chocolates on attributes may not agree from expert panelist to consumer panelist.

To answer the second question (regarding similarity of ratings between consumers and experts), we have to look at the slope of the line relating the two ratings. If the line has a slope of 20, we conclude that both groups perceive equal differences among the samples, because the 0-5 expert scale should match the 0-100 consumer scale. If the line has a slope lower than 20, this suggests that the experts perceive larger differences than the consumers do. If the line has a slope exceeding 20, this suggests that the experts perceive smaller differences than the consumers do. Table 4 suggests that the consumers perceive smaller differences among the products than experts do, since most of the lines have slopes lower than 20. The experts and consumers tend to agree with each other in terms of the relative degree of an attribute present in chocolate. However, the experts perceive the chocolates as more different from each other.

Areas of Disagreement

For some attributes, specifically those involving unusual flavor or texture characteristics (e.g., milky, mouth coatings), the experts and the consumers do not agree with each other (Table 11.4). Their ratings do not correlate with each other or at least not highly. For these specific attributes consumers probably do not perceive too many differences among the samples, because they do not know what exactly to look for. In contrast, experts do know what to look for, and their ratings reflect the differences.

TABLE 11.4
EQUATIONS RELATING CONSUMER RATINGS TO EXPERT PANEL RATINGS

Attribute	Consumer Rating = Constant	+ B (Expert Rating)	R^2
Darkness	−2.81	17.0	0.90
Shiny	−0.76	9.6	0.96
Size	−10.3	13.0	0.97
Thick	5.4	11.0	0.70
Aroma Strength	−11.1	21.9	0.99
Chocolate Aroma	38.6	35.3	0.97
Taste Intensity	18.6	11.6	0.90
Chocolate Taste/Flavor	−22.0	21.6	0.97
Milky	9.9	13.1	0.83
Hardness	7.4	19.3	0.94
Mouth Coating	2.7	7.8	0.84
Rate of Melting In Mouth	−20.7	13.6	0.94

Using Experts To Predict Consumer Acceptance

Expert panelists act as objective evaluators of a product, and generally do not assign ratings of acceptance. However, one can use their sensory attribute ratings as independent variables, from which to predict overall consumer acceptance.

In this study, we can correlate the ratings of experts with consumer ratings acceptance. The simplest procedure consists of linear correlations between expert attribute ratings and consumer acceptance. This procedure assumes that there exists a straight line relation between what the consumer likes, and the sensory attribute(s) that the expert perceives. Table 11.5 shows this analysis. We find a few attributes (e.g., darkness) assigned by experts which directly correlate with consumer acceptance.

From time to time researchers in the food industry use multiple linear regression to relate expert panel ratings of attributes to consumer accept-

TABLE 11.5
LINEAR RELATIONS BETWEEN SENSORY ATTRIBUTES RATED BY EXPERTS AND CONSUMER LIKING RATINGS

Consumer Rating	=	A	+	B (Expert Rating)	R^2
		(A) APPEARANCE			
Like Appearance	=	6.4	+	13.8 (Darkness)	0.93
Like Appearance	=	63.5	−	1.9 (Shine)	0.03
Like Appearance	=	72.7	−	4.4 (Size)	0.04
Like Appearance	=	67.9	−	4.5 (Thick)	0.01
		(B) AROMA			
Like Aroma	=	2.7	+	16.3 (Aroma Strength)	0.57
Like Aroma	=	−5.3	+	18.5 (Chocolate Aroma)	0.51
		(C) TASTE/FLAVOR			
Like Taste	=	33.7	+	12.1 (Flavor, Time 0)	0.55
Like Taste	=	19.8	+	14.2 (Chocolate, Time 0)	0.64
Like Taste	=	25.0	+	23.0 (Milky Flavor)	0.71
		(D) TEXTURE			
Like Texture	=	24.2	+	6.7 (Texture, Time 0)	0.03
Like Texture	=	28.3	+	7.3 (Coating, Time 0)	0.05
Like Texture	=	−16.6	+	16.6 (Melts, Time 0)	0.96

ance, rather than correlating each attribute rated by an expert to consumer liking. We can perform the same statistical analysis here, provided that the sensory attributes used by the experts do not correlate with each other. Table 11.6 shows a reduced number of uncorrelated attributes (from experts) emerging from factor analysis (to reduce redundancy), and the results of linear regression. The independent variables for linear regression consist of the ratings assigned by the experts, but the dependent variable consists of the average rating assigned by the consumer, for degree of liking.

TABLE 11.6
RELATION BETWEEN SEVERAL SENSORY ATTRIBUTES BY EXPERTS AND CONSUMER LIKING RATINGS

(A) UNCORRELATED ATTRIBUTES FROM FACTOR ANALYSIS

Thick
Dark
Size
Milky (Time 0)
Hard (Time 0)

(B) EQUATIONS RELATING CONSUMER ATTRIBUTE LIKING TO THE FIVE UNCORRELATED ATTRIBUTES EVALUATED BY EXPERTS

	Consumer Liking Ratings				
Expert Attributes	Like Appearance	Like Aroma	Like Taste	Like Texture	Like Overall
Constant	−3.9	−16.4	14.6	49.9	51.7
Thick	0.9	8.1*	6.9	−18.9	−5.0
Dark	15.7**	1.5	3.9	15.2**	11.5**
Size	−0.6	−2.9	0.6	−18.1	−5.4*
Milky	−5.4	18.9**	21.6**	−23.2**	−1.6
Hard	5.5	1.8	−7.2	34.1**	4.7
Multiple R2	0.95	0.93	0.86	0.96	0.91

*Significant (T Value Exceeds 1.0)
**Highly Significant (T Value Exceeds 2.0)

Nonlinear Relations

The previous section stressed linear relations. However, we know from research in sensory science that the relation between sensory characteristics and acceptance does not usually follow a straight line, but rather forms a parabola, with a peak in the mid-range. If so, then the previous section may mislead the product developer, because it bases itself upon linear relations.

We can develop the nonlinear, parabolic relations between expert panel rating and consumer acceptance, using standard regression procedures. Again, we relate consumer acceptance to expert panelist rating by means of a simple equation, easily solved on a computer by the multiple regression procedure (Eq. 11.1):

$$\text{Consumer Liking} = A + B\ (\text{Expert Rating}) + C\ (\text{Expert Rating}^2) \qquad 11.1$$

The foregoing equation allows consumer acceptance to peak in a mid-range of attribute level, with the attribute level (independent variable) assigned by the expert.

Following this procedure, the marketing director solved the equations for a number of attributes. The equations, and the point at which they optimize and target products generating the optimal level appear in Table 11.7.

TABLE 11.7
PARABOLIC CURVES AND OPTIMAL LEVELS FOR SENSORY ATTRIBUTES (RATED BY EXPERTS) VERSUS CONSUMER LIKE RATINGS

Liking =	A +	B (Attribute) +	C (Attribute)^2	R^2
Like Appearance	−20	29.6 (Darkness)	−2.25 (Darkness)^2	0.94
Like Appearance	71	−7.4 (Thickness)	0.64 (Thickness)^2	0.01
Like Appearance	352	−171.8 (Size)	24.73 (Size)^2	0.26
Like Taste	−211	245.2 (Milky)	−50.79 (Milky)^2	0.84
Like Texture	535	−371.8 (Hardness)	69.22 (Hardness)^2	0.35

Attribute	Optimal Sensory Level	Target Product Closest to That Level
Darkness	4.1—4.6	F, G, H, I
Thickness	1.8—2.6	All Products Viable
Size	2.7 or 4.1	E or I
Milky Taste (Time 0)	2.2—2.6	E, G, I
Hardness	2.2 or 3.1	H or C

Table 11.7 provides a roadmap for product developers to aid ongoing development. The expert panelist can evaluate the sensory characteristics of new, prototype chocolates, using the same scale and attributes as he/she used to profile the base set. For each new product, one can estimate the likely consumer acceptance rating, using the equations in Table 11.7.

Using Several Attributes As Predictors Of Consumer Acceptance

Using one attribute alone as rated by an expert to predict consumer acceptance does not generate the best predictive system. We would like to use a number of attributes. However, the problem can become severe because we have to use linear terms and quadratic terms, and possibly interaction terms among attributes to predict consumer acceptance. If the consumers profile the chocolate on 6 attributes, this generates a potential of 6 (linear) terms, 6 quadratic terms and $6 \times 5/2$ or 15 interaction terms. Yet, we know that we cannot use one term alone, or even that term and its square (to generate a parabola). We must use more terms to insure adequate prediction.

One way of using a number of terms consists first of factor analyzing the terms, as we did in Table 11.6 to reduce the redundancy. Two attributes recommend themselves: darkness and milkiness.

The second step consists of developing an equation using the linear and square terms of these attributes, without either the cross or interaction terms. Table 11.8 shows the set of equations. We then eliminate insignificant terms, by removing those predictor terms whose absolute T values fail to reach 1.0, and then recompute the parameters of the equation. We end up with a predictor equation having the following properties:

(1) The predictor terms (attribute ratings by an expert panel) form a parsimonious set, uncorrelated with each other

(2) We use linear and quadratic terms, where relevant, to predict consumer acceptance

(3) We use only significant terms (in a statistical sense).

The final equation in Table 11.8 (Eq. 11.6) allows us to estimate the likely consumer reaction to different sensory profiles of quality chocolates, as rated by experts. Keep in mind that we cannot optimize quality or acceptance, since we do not know the physical formulations. However, we can estimate the likely consumer reactions to chocolates of this type, given the profiles assigned by the expert panel.

Sensitivity Analysis Of Consumer Acceptance To Attributes

Our final analysis consists of measuring the sensitivity of consumer acceptance to attributes rated by the expert. Equation 6 of Table 11.8

provides a shorthand description of how attributes profiled by experts correspond to consumer acceptance. Furthermore, the model allows us to answer "what if" questions.

One question to answer concerns the sensitivity of consumer likings, darkness and milkiness. Using the experts as objective evaluators, do we expect to see dramatic changes in consumer acceptance of these quality products, if the expert finds the darkness to decrease, or the milkiness to become increasingly noticeable, etc.?

TABLE 11.8
ALTERNATIVE EQUATIONS RELATING OVERALL LIKING (RATED BY CONSUMERS) TO MILKINESS AND DARKNESS (RATED BY EXPERTS)

Equation	Constant	Milky	$Milky^2$	Dark	$Dark^2$	Milky X Dark	Multiple R^2
1	48.8	12.0*	——	——	——	——	0.21
2	-28.1	84.3	-16.5	——	——	——	0.22
3	51.1	——	——	——	——	2.9	0.60
4	-97.5	67.8*	——	42.3**	——	-16.2*	0.91
5	-157.1	-127.8*	-14.9*	39.9**	——	-14.9*	0.92
6 (Final)	-43.9	——	——	54.9**	-6.5**	0.71*	0.95

*Coefficient achieves a T value exceeding 1 (in absolute terms)
**Coefficient achieves a T value exceeding 2 (in absolute terms)

To answer this question we have listed out the trends, in terms of expected consumer acceptance, for changes in the darkness and milkiness ratings assigned by an expert panel. We have kept milkiness constant at one of four levels, and let darkness increase and then computed the likely consumer rating of overall liking. These trends appear in Table 11.9. They suggest a high sensitivity to perceived darkness at low milkiness levels, but much less consumer sensitivity of acceptance to darkness at high milkiness levels.

TABLE 11.9
EXPECTED RATINGS OF CONSUMER LIKING OF CHOCOLATE FOR SAMPLES OF CHOCOLATE ACHIEVING SPECIFIC SCORES BY AN EXPERT PANEL

OPTION	EXPERT RATING		CONSUMER RATING
	Dark	Milky	Liking
1	2	1.5	36
2	2.5	1.5	44
3	3	1.5	53
4	3.5	1.5	62
5	4	1.5	71
6	4.5	1.5	80
7	2	2	58
8	2.5	2	64
9	3	2	69
10	3.5	2	74
11	4	2	79
12	4.5	2	84
13	2	2.5	74
14	2.5	2.5	75
15	3	2.5	76
16	3.5	2.5	78
17	4	2.5	79
18	4.5	2.5	80
19	2	3	82
20	2.5	3	79
21	3	3	77
22	3.5	3	74
23	4	3	72
24	4.5	3	70

AN OVERVIEW

Traditional uses of expert panelists have involved the development of profiles to guide product developers, or profiles which act as guides in quality control. This chapter provides a different way of looking at expert panelists, namely as instruments, whose readings one can relate to consumer ratings. The correlation, by means of equations and models, allows the product developer to understand the likely consumer reaction, either in terms of sensory perception or in terms of acceptance, which will ensue once the expert panelist notices a difference between products.

Given this relation between consumers and expert panelists, the expert panel, an in-house group, can now become more active in directing product developers. Once we establish a link between the experts and the consumers, the experts can clearly point the way towards profiles that correlate most highly with consumer acceptance.

REFERENCES

BLOM, G. 1955. How many taste testers? Wallerstein Laboratories Communications *18,* 173-178.

BRUVOLD, W. H. 1970. Laboratory panel estimation of consumer assessments of taste and flavor. J. Appl. Psych. *54,* 326-330.

CALVIN, L. D. and SATHER, L. A. 1959. A comparison of student preference panels with a household consumer panel. Food Technol. *13,* 469-472.

CARDELLO, A. V., MALLER, O., KAPSALIS, J. G., SEGARS, R. A., SAWYER, F. M., MURPHY, C. and MOSKOWITZ, H. R. 1982. Perception of texture by trained and consumer panelists. J. Food Sci. *47,* 1186-1197.

CAUL, J. F. 1957. Profile method of flavor analysis in *Advances in Food Research.* pp. 1-40.

CIVILLE, G. V. and SZCZESNIAK, A. S. 1973. Guidelines to training a texture profile panel. J. Texture Stud. *4,* 204-223.

CONGER, S. S. and ZOOK, K. 1968. Laboratory preferences and acceptance panels: A case in point. Food Technol. *22,* 189-192.

DETHMERS,A. E. 1968. Experienced vs. inexperienced judges for preference testing. Food Prod. Dev. *2,* 22-23.

GACULA, M. C., PARKER, L. A., KUBALA, J. J. and REAUME, J. 1974. Data analysis: A variable sequential test for selection of sensory panels. J. Food Sci. *39,* 61-63.

HARDING, P. L. and WADLEY, F. M. 1948. Teen-age students versus adults as taste judges of temple oranges. Food Res. *13,* 6-10.

KRAMER, AC. Y. 1955. A method of choosing judges for a sensory experiment. Food Res. *20,* 492-496.

LOMBARDI, G. J. 1951. The sequential selection of judges for organoleptic testing. M.S. Thesis, Virginia Polytechnic Institute & State University, Blacksburg, Virginia.

MURPHY, E. F., CLARK, B. S. and BERGLUND, R. M. 1958. A consumer survey versus panel testing for acceptance evaluation of Maine sardines. Food Technol. *12,* 222-226.

OUGH, C. S. and AMERINE, M. A. 1967. Rose wine colour preferences and preference stability by an experienced and inexperienced panel. J. Food Sci. *32,* 706-711.

PANGBORN, R. M., SIMONE, M. J., LEONARD, S. J. and GARNATZ, G. 1958. Comparison of mass panel and household consumer responses to canned cling peaches. Food Technol. *12,* 693-698.

SATHER, L. A. 1968. Methodology studies with laboratory and home preference panels. Food Technol. *22,* 188-189.

SATHER, L. A., CALVIN, L. D. and LIMING, N. E. 1965. Relation of preference panel and trained panel scores on sterile milk concentrates. J. Dairy Sci. *48,* 877-880.

SATHER, L. A., CALVIN, L. and TAMSMA, A. 1963. Relation of preference panel and trained panel scores on dry whole milk. J. Dairy Sci. *46,* 1054-1058.

WEISS, J. J. 1981. Selection of sensory judges. J. Food Quality *4,* 55-63.

SECTION III.
Using the Data for Technical and Marketing Guidance

CHAPTER 12

SCREENING MANY SUBMISSIONS OR NEW INGREDIENTS

INTRODUCTION

Food product developers and marketers maintain a continuing interest in ingredients, for a number of reasons. First, cost plays an important role. If one can use a substitute ingredient to replace an expensive one, the difference drops to the bottom line and increases profitability. As long as the consumer cannot notice the difference, this substitution should not impact the long term viability of the product. Second, tastes change. New ingredients bring in new sensory characteristics, and perhaps some that will enhance consumer acceptance. Thus, the intelligent marketer and product developer always looks for new ingredients. Finally, these new ingredients may possess a unique functionality in terms of promoting storage stability, keeping the product fresher, allowing the product to perform better during the heating or preparation cycle, etc.

How can a product developer or a marketer test many alternatives to generate a product having greater flavor, or a yogurt or other sweet dairy product with even one flavor, (e.g., orange)? One may have dozens of submissions from which to choose, created by the flavor houses, and presented to the food technologist. Which flavor seems best, and at what concentration in the final product? Another difficulty may stem from the desire to improve a product by changing the spice system. Which of many spice systems should one use? The problem becomes even more complicated, because now we deal with qualitative variations, and many different themes, rather than with different "executions" or varieties of a single flavor.

This chapter presents three case histories; one dealing with the selection of a specific type of spice for a relaunch of a food product. The second deals with the evaluation of many ingredients in a soup and the third pertains with evaluations of different flavor levels for ice cream.

SELECTING THE RIGHT SPICE FOR A NEW SAUSAGE

The Scott Sausage Company manufactures a line of pure beef sausages. Over the past three years, its president, Robert Scott, invested heavily in new plant equipment to modernize the company, which he had inherited from his father, the founder. At the same time, the market for beef sausage underwent a rapid change. New entries, with novel flavor notes, coupled with intensive promotion and couponing made the category more competitive, and less profitable.

Scott, a marketer and a successful entrepreneur in his business recognized two needs; first, to improve distribution and recognition of his line of sausages, and second, the need for new products with new flavors to appeal to segments currently using competitors.

The initial foray into product development generated a variety of alternative products. Michelle Gutworth, his product development expert, realized the need to create a wide spectrum of alternative meat flavorings, not just small modifications of the current line. To accomplish this objective she invited flavor experts from a number of supply houses to a meeting, at which she described the Scott program of new product development. During the meeting, she requested ideas as to flavors, and invited submissions of new flavoring concepts. She also graciously offered the product development laboratories at her company as a resource. She assigned a technician to the project, with the responsibility of evaluating the new submissions, and incorporating these spice/flavoring submissions into the current emulsion used for the all-beef sausage.

Evaluating Alternative Submissions

One has little problem evaluating one to three submissions for spices. Panelists can evaluate these submissions in a straightforward test. How can one evaluate a more extensive battery of submissions? Furthermore, which submission should one choose; one that scores highest in acceptance at a fixed concentration, one that shows least sensitivity to changes in spice level (allowing substantial costs reductions), or one which comes closest, in profile and sensory quality, to the current in-market product?

Gutworth recognized the need to evaluate the sausage spice systems at several levels, to insure that she would not miss a promising system because of concentration (namely, the spice system would have scored better had it appeared at a higher or lower concentration). Furthermore, evaluation of the same spice system at several levels would allow her to determine the sensitivity of the flavor perception to spice level.

Test Design

The first test consisted of an evaluation of three spice submissions, each at two levels, designed to represent intense versus mild. The suppliers recommended levels for the submissions, and Gutworth's technician developed the prototypes accordingly.

In view of the marketing goal, to create an improved all-beef sausage to appeal to both current users and nonusers, marketing recommended that the screening test include users and aware nonusers, who expressed favorable attitudes towards an all-beef sausage. By including these two groups, one could then select that particular spice submission which showed the greatest promise. Furthermore, since Gutworth included the spices at two clearly different levels (perceptibly so to the consumer) one could also assess the general reaction of the consumers to high versus low sausage flavorings.

Table 12.1 shows the results of the study, in terms of acceptance, perceived flavor, and quality, as rated by the total panel, and by the two subgroups. Note that in many of these developmental studies, where R&D focuses interest on ingredients, one needs only a limited number of panel participants, properly screened, to participate. In this study, a total of 60 panelists participated, 30 from each group. All panelists evaluated every one of the 3 submissions, at both high and low levels, in a randomized order.

Results

Looking at Table 12.1 we see the following pattern emerging, which helps with the decision about the spices.

(1) Current all-beef sausage consumers assign the products higher liking ratings than do the aware nontriers (Part A). This should come as no surprise. Marketing researchers often find that users assign products higher ratings than do nonusers.

(2) The panelists perceived some differences among the submissions, in terms of acceptance and spiciness. Level of spice, rather than type, generated the differences in perceived spiciness.

(3) Although R&D attempted to match the spices at the high and low level (on a perceptual basis), the high and low levels from a single spice blend did not generate exactly equal differences from one spice blend to another.

(4) We can develop a straight line relation between spice level and perceived spiciness. By so doing, it becomes possible to ascertain how perceived spiciness increases with physical level. Table 12.1 (Part B) shows these six functions, and suggests that the spices do not generate parallel

TABLE 12.1
DATABASE FOR SPICED MEAT SUBMISSIONS THREE SPICE SUPPLIERS (A, B, C) INCORPORATED AT TWO LEVELS IN FINAL PRODUCT

A. DATABASE

	FORMULA		LIKING RATING			ATTRIBUTE				
Product	Spice Type	Usage Level	Total Panel	Current User	Aware Nontrier	Spicy Flavor	Quality	Unit Cost	Cost Slope*	Spiciness Slope
1	A	H (2X)	40	46	34	65	58	1.2	6.7	4
2	A	L (X)	31	34	28	61	46	0.6		
3	B	H (2X)	50	58	42	68	46	3	10.7	16
4	B	L (X)	56	48	64	52	31	1.5		
5	C	H (2X)	38	42	34	69	39	2.6	7.7	10
6	C	L (X)	39	41	37	59	45	1.3		

*Defined as $\left(\frac{\text{(Spiciness of High Level—Spiciness of Low Level)}}{\text{Cost of High Level—Cost of Low Level}}\right)$

B. EQUATIONS RELATING PERCEIVED SPICINESS TO COST AND LEVEL OF INCLUSION

Submission	Spiciness	= M	+B (Cost/Unit)
A		57	6.7
B		36	10.7
C		49	7.7

Submission	Spiciness	= M	+B (Level of Inclusion)
A		57	4
B		36	16
C		49	10

C. LEVELS AT WHICH EACH SUBMISSION REACHES THE SAME PERCEIVED SPICINESS

TARGET	SUBMISSION A		SUBMISSION B		SUBMISSION C	
SPICINESS	Level	Cost	Level	Cost	Level	Cost
60	0.75	0.4505	1.5	2.243	1.1	1.430
65	2	1.201	1.81	2.710	1.6	2.081
70	3.25	1.952	2.13	3.178	2.1	2.731

relations between perceived spiciness and physical spice level, since the slopes differ.

(5) R&D looked at the relative cost to achieve a given level of spiciness. The spices varied in cost, as quoted by the salesman from the spice supplier. Looking at Table 12.1 (Part A), we see a range in cost/lb of almost 3:1. However, we cannot go by this unit alone, because product developers can incorporate the spices at different levels. Thus, to equate spice submissions on a price basis, one first has to determine a level of perceived spice flavor, equal across three spice submissions. Then, one has to determine the concentration for each spice needed to achieve that perceived level, and finally compute the unit costs. These appear in Table 12.1. Spice submission A recommends itself as the least expensive option to achieve an adequate spice perception; however it does not necessarily achieve the highest acceptance.

(6) Integrating all of the above information, it appears best to incorporate spice submission A into the sausage. It provides an adequate (but not optimal) level of acceptance. Submission A represents the least expensive submission to achieve the target level of spice flavor.

One should keep in mind that this initial screening of alternative submissions provides a very rudimentary procedure, but one used throughout the entire food industry for screening purposes. Quite often, R&D does not vary the level of the submission at all, but simply takes the submission as provided by the supplier, incorporates it into the product at the recommended level, and makes an informal judgment. Product developers can use judgment, or run small church panels. This author recommends the use of consumers, representing the target audience, along with the evaluation of the submission at several concentrations to insure a fair evaluation of the submission at different sensory and cost levels.

SCREENING DESIGNS FOR MULTIPLE INGREDIENTS IN ONE PRODUCT

Background

Our second case history concerns the selection of the most appropriate ingredients for a product. Whereas the previous case history concerned the selection of a single spice, we now turn our attention to a full product, where we have the option of incorporating one or several new ingredients to generate a modified taste impression.

CASE HISTORY—THE KERCHEVAL FINE FOODS COMPANY

Ron Kercheval, founder of Kercheval Fine Food Products (abbreviated henceforth as KFF) in Oregon, has developed a line of high quality soups, appealing to the specialty foods market. Many of his soups comprise unique ingredients, or blends. Founded in 1980, KFF began by supplying imported soups and high quality gourmet foods in stores on the west coast. Over a rapid, two year expansion, however, the company developed a line of exotic soups, using fine seafood ingredients.

Early in 1984, Kercheval recognized the need for a spicy soup based on red snapper. The soup (red snapper soup) did not yet exist in the markets served by KFF. No one at KFF knew precisely what the soup should taste like. However, focus group sessions with a number of consumers who purchase and consume fine or gourmet soups quickly revealed interest in a spicy, thick soup. Other than that, no one knew whether the soup should contain potatoes, vegetables, specific spices, pieces of fish, etc.

A systematic exploration of the large number of potential ingredients that one might put into the red snapper soup could takes months, or years of effort, with a large expenditure of money, and possibly little or no return on the invested dollars and time. At the same time, however, the opportunity window seemed sufficiently large to warrant some type of quantitative research, beyond the group sessions. After having attended four focus group sessions, Kercheval soon realized that these discussions could provide R&D with qualitative direction about consumer desires, but could not direct them any further. He found that focus groups generated many hypotheses and insights, but the groups did not converge to a single direction for R&D.

Many marketers and product developers face problems similar to those that Kercheval faced. A new or relaunched product can have a variety of nuances developed for it, as long as one selects the appropriate ingredients or process variables. For a limited number, say two to four ingredients, it makes sense to explore the alternatives in a systematic fashion, varying the concentration of each option and measuring consumer reactions to the new product prototype. Indeed, statistically, with a limited number of ingredient alternatives it becomes feasible to evaluate the various formula variables in different combinations with each other. (We shall deal with that issue later on, in the chapter devoted to product optimization.)

Statisticians have recognized the need to develop efficient methods for screening many alternatives. They have developed procedures known as screening designs, which designate certain combinations of variables. Each variable assumes the value "1" if present in the prototype, or "0" if absent.

One popular approach, known as the Plackett-Burman screening design, appears schematically in Table 12.2. The table lists 12 alternative combinations that R&D has to develop, incorporating the new ingredients or processes in a specified manner. The design allows the investigator to measure the contribution of each new ingredient or variable. We have to limit the variation of the ingredient to one level only (present at that level or absent). The design limits the amount of information that one can obtain about the ingredient. The design allows the product developer to uncover the major effect of adding the ingredient.

Kercheval's R&D director developed a list of six different formula variables that one might use for the snapper soup. This included 2 different types of vegetables, 2 types of spices, a new starch and a new additive to enhance visual appeal. Table 12.2 shows the design. Note that the screening design required a total of 12 plant runs, to generate the various prototypes.

TABLE 12.2
SCHEMATIC FOR PLACKETT-BURMAN SCREENING DESIGN PRESENCE/ABSENCE OF SIX INGREDIENTS IN SNAPPER SOUP

	INGREDIENTS FOR SNAPPER SOUP					
PRODUCT	A	B	C	D	E	F
1	1	1	0	1	1	1
2	1	0	1	1	1	0
3	0	1	1	1	0	0
4	1	1	1	0	0	0
5	1	1	0	0	0	1
6	1	0	0	0	1	0
7	0	0	0	1	0	1
8	0	0	1	0	1	1
9	0	1	0	1	1	0
10	1	0	1	1	0	1
11	0	1	1	0	1	1
12	0	0	0	0	0	0

0 = Ingredient absent from the soup
1 = Ingredient present in the soup
A = Vegetable A
B = Vegetable B
C = Spice C
D = Spice D
E = Starch
F = Visual additive for eye appeal

Field Implementation

Working with soups in the field or experimental portion raises a number of difficulties not encountered with many other products. First, one must serve the soup freshly prepared, and have it evaluated with no more than a 3-4 minute wait between end of preparation and serving. Otherwise, the soup may get cold, with the aroma decreasing, and the flavor impact changing. Second, in most test facilities one cannot easily prepare all the 12 soups simultaneously, to have them available for the panelist. Rather, one has to test the soup in "blocks". At any one time, the interviewer or the kitchen staff can prepare only four soups, falling into one single block. The soups (12 kinds) generate 3 such blocks. With several groups, one can rotate the order of the blocks, on a group by group basis, and always rotate the four soups within the block. This blocking procedure allows a more efficient field execution because at any one time the preparation demands attention to four soups only, not to twelve.

The study proceeded, with a panel of 40 consumers of gourmet soups. Due to the unusual nature of the soup (red snapper soup representing an unusually exotic product), the screening criterion changed. The panelists who participated in the Kercheval study had to have incomes above $30,000 (per family), and had to have purchased and eaten a gourmet soup in the past two months. The interviewers responsible for the recruiting followed the screener shown in Table 12.3, which allowed them to identify the target consumers fairly quickly. Note the stringent criteria for a panelist to qualify. By requiring the panelist to have personally bought and consumed one of the more exotic soups, Kercheval insured that the panelists participating in the study would validly represent the actual consumer who would eventually purchase the soup.

TABLE 12.3
EXAMPLE OF SCREENER USED TO FIND QUALIFYING PANELISTS FOR SOUP STUDY

Hello, I am calling on behalf of ___________, a nationally known market research company. May I talk to you for a few minutes.

Which of the following foods do you/have you eaten in the past month?

Waffles ___________
Cola Beverages ___________
Croissants ___________
Soups ___________ (if no, terminate)
Canned meats ___________

TABLE 12.3 (Continued)

Let's talk a little about soups.

Which types of soups have you eaten?

Which types of soups have you yourself purchased?

(INTERVIEWER, CHECK ALLOWABLE LIST OF SOUPS. IF THE RESPONDENT MENTIONS NONE OF THE SOUPS ON THE LIST, THEN TERMINATE)

I'd like to ask you the next questions just for classification purposes:

Your age:

( ) 18-24
( ) 25-34
( ) 35-49
( ) 49+

Your employment:

( ) Employed full time
( ) Employed part time (20 hours or less)
( ) Not employed

Your approximate family income:

( ) 15,000 or less (TERMINATE)
( ) 15,0001-29,999 (TERMINATE)
( ) 30,000-45,000
( ) ABOVE 45,000

I would like to invite you to participate in a test on soups, on ___________, May _______, at ___________, from 6:00 PM to 10:00 PM. We will pay you ___________ for participating.

Respondent Yes ( ), No ( )

Interviewer

Name ________________________________

Date ________________

Time _________

Results

The results of the study generate a matrix of products by attributes, part of which appears in Table 12.4. Note that the panelists can and do perceive differences among the various samples. However, a simple inspection of Table 12.4 does not reveal the extent to which each of the 6 different ingredients impacts on every sensory attribute, and on acceptance. In order to measure the impact quantitatively, we use the analytic procedure for screening designs shown in Table 12.5 (example, spiciness).

TABLE 12.4
CONSUMER RATINGS OF FISH SOUP ON ATTRIBUTES

Product	Overall Liking	Difficult to Prepare	Spiciness	Fishy Flavor
1	46	32	38	51
2	31	46	61	42
3	67	36	37	57
4	36	57	46	31
5	17	29	47	43
6	37	36	31	48
7	18	27	38	51
8	38	31	48	49
9	57	37	35	31
10	61	69	69	42
11	42	43	39	59
12	57	58	52	31

A = Vegetable A
B = Vegetable B
C = Spice C
D = Spice D
E = Starch
F = Visual additive for appearance

Table 12.6 shows the effect of each ingredient. Note that the higher the effect, the more impact the ingredient possesses.

We can now see clearly what each of the 6 different ingredients generates in terms of sensory characteristics and in terms of acceptance. From this table, Kercheval could then determine the proper ingredients for the red snapper soup. That determination, however, remains a matter of judgment. The statistical analysis can only act as a guide, and as a source of information for decision making. It can never substitute for the deci-

TABLE 12.5
WORKSHEET FOR SCREENING DESIGN TO SHOW MAJOR EFFECTS

	Formula Variables (A-F)							Additional Columns Required by the Analysis					Average Consumer Attribute Rating
Product	Mean	A	B	C	D	E	F	G	H	I	J	K	Spiciness
1	1	1	1	0	1	1	1	0	0	0	1	0	38
2	1	1	0	1	1	1	0	0	0	1	0	1	61
3	1	0	1	1	1	0	0	0	1	0	1	1	37
4	1	1	1	1	0	0	0	1	0	1	1	0	46
5	1	1	1	0	0	0	1	0	1	1	0	1	47
6	1	1	0	0	0	1	0	1	1	0	1	1	31
7	1	0	0	0	1	0	1	1	0	1	1	1	68
8	1	0	0	1	0	1	1	0	1	1	1	0	48
9	1	0	1	0	1	1	0	1	1	1	0	0	35
10	1	1	0	1	1	0	1	1	1	0	0	0	69
11	1	0	1	1	0	1	1	1	0	0	0	1	39
12	1	0	0	0	0	0	0	0	0	0	0	0	52
Note:	Assigned Factor Effects							Unassigned Effects					
Sum/1**	571	292	242	300	308	252	309	288	267	305	268	283	
Sum/0	0	279	329	271	263	319	262	283	304	266	303	288	
Total	571	571	571	571	571	571	571	571	571	571	571	571	
Diff. 1-0	571	13	−87	29	45	−67	47	5	−37	39	−35	−5	
Effect ECT	47.6	2.17	-15.0 *	4.83	7.5	-11.0	7.83	0.833	-6.2	6.5	-5.8	-0.83	

Significant*

COMPUTATION OF STANDARD ERROR

	G	H	I	J	K
A Square of Effect	0.694	38.0	42.3	34.0	0.694
B Total the Squares	116.0				
C Divide by the Number of Values	23.1				
D Compute the Square Root	4.81				
E This Number = Standard Error = D	4.81				
F Multiply by Confidence Range (2.57 = Value for 95%)	2.57 × 4.81 = 12.4				
G An Effect Exceeding F = Significant at the 95% Confidence Level	12.4				

(One can reduce the criterion of F to obtain more significant effects.)

**Sum/1 defined by adding up all ratings of "spiciness" for products having 1's
Sum/0 defined by adding up all ratings of "spiciness" for products having 0's.

sion making process, because it simply yields numbers. The marketer and marketing researcher, as well as the product developer must use those numbers (quantitative inputs) to make their decision (a qualitative decision, namely, yes/no or go/no go).

TABLE 12.6
THE IMPACT OF EACH INGREDIENT ON ATTRIBUTE RATINGS*

Ingredient	Overall Liking	Difficult to Prepare	Spiciness	Fishy Flavor
A	−0.75	0.73	0.45	−0.54
B	0.34	−0.65	[−3.11]	0.23
C	0.64	1.25	[1.00	0.64
D	0.79	−0.14	1.55]	0.46
E	−0.07	[−1.01]	[−2.29]	0.64
F	−0.98	−0.77	[1.84	1.41]

A = Vegetable A
B = Vegetable B
C = Spice C
D = Spice D
E = Starch
F = Visual additive for appearance

Table 12.5 provides the computational approach used to develop these numbers

*Results from the analysis of the screening design

IMPROVING THE COMMUNICATION BETWEEN FLAVOR HOUSES, CUSTOMERS AND CONSUMERS

Flavor and fragrance suppliers work under a great deal of pressure. Customers, food companies, call upon their suppliers to provide flavors for specific target groups. Often the flavor houses receive short marketing or R&D briefs describing the new flavor or array of flavors (e.g., a set of flavors for yogurts, appealing to children, and comprising strawberry, pina colada, and blueberry). In reaction to this request, the flavorist creates the flavor, puts into the customer's base (unflavored yogurt), modifies the flavor, and then submits it to the customer for further testing.

In the best of all worlds, one's flavor submission should pass acceptance and stability tests. Many submissions fail on one or both counts. The ultimate consumer may not like the product flavored with the submission. Or, as happens quite often, the flavor proves unstable, and/or incompatible with the base. Over a period of time the flavor may degrade. What seemed like a perfectly good flavor to start with turns to an unacceptable flavor after a month or two in storage.

We cannot predict stability in storage. However, we can discuss the reasons why so many submissions prove unacceptable. In the main, the flavorist has to satisfy so many customers that he or she has little time to perfect and test each submission prior to submitting it to the customer. Furthermore, quite often the customer calls the flavor house and request a flavor, without asking the flavorist or the technical applications group to put the flavor into the base. Rather, the customer (usually R&D at a food manufacturer) takes the liquid flavor, screens it, and then if R&D likes the flavor, a technician goes to work putting the flavor up in a base for further work. Consequently, many submissions fail on the first screening.

Through many years of experience, the author has found that one key way of increasing the odds for a successful submission consists of "doing one's homework". R&D and marketing at a food company have the task of generating a product that will equal or beat competition on a blind test basis. The flavor (or other ingredient) represents one of the tools by which they have to accomplish the task. A simple submission of a bottle of flavor for an end use, or even the flavor put into the product for testing (e.g., the strawberry flavor incorporated into the customer's yogurt base) does not really help the R&D or marketer accomplish the true, underlying objective of "beating the competition". The R&D product developer and marketer still have to screen the submission, compare it to competition, and evaluate it in terms of cost. Generally, they receive one-half to several dozen submissions, and pay relatively little attention to each submission. It should come as no surprise that the odds of a successful submission drop below 10%. A flavor house must make many submissions to stay in business, in light of the low probability of success.

Measuring The Competitive Frame Along With The Submission

One way of improving one's service to the customer consists of evaluating one's submission in a test, versus the key competitors. A small panel of consumers (not more than 25), who evaluate the submission on a blind basis, and rate it on attributes, can also provide data on the competition as well. The results of the panel generate a data sheet, similar to that shown in Table 12.7.

Despite the fact that inevitably the R&D product developer and the market researcher will retest the submission if it looks promising, the

TABLE 12.7
EXAMPLE OF A SUBMISSION SHEET
COMPANY SUBMITTING: World Flavors Inc.
CUSTOMER: Children's Cereal Inc.
DATE: June 2, 1984
PRODUCT: Peanut Butter Kid's Cereal (Customer Provided Unflavored Product)
PANEL: 27 Adults (Consumers, Mothers With Children)

	Submission Levels			Competitors—Same Flavor*			
	1.5	2	2.5	A	B	C	D
Color							
Darkness	26	34	39	43	29	36	38
Aroma							
Strength	31	36	39	32	30	39	44
Taste/Flavor							
Sweetness	67	64	62	59	53	69	61
Peanut Butter	29	36	42	32	27	43	48
Nutty	17	18	23	16	12	19	25
Estery/Fruity	36	42	46	35	31	39	46
Texture/Mouthfeel							
Hardness	41	43	43	42	47	41	39
Crunchiness	63	64	64	63	61	66	59
Overall							
Purchase	43	46	46	46	39	38	47
Liking	51	55	53	53	46	44	54
Child would like	47	49	54	53	51	48	58
Quality	39	43	42	42	31	43	46
Artificial (0) vs natural (100)	61	60	53	42	46	41	32
Cost of Flavor	1.5	2.0	2.5	N.A.	N.A.	N.A.	N.A.

inclusion of the consumer ratings along with one's submission gives the customer a feeling of how well the submission performs. If the submission performs well in this early stage consumer evaluation, more than likely the R&D group will seriously consider it, even if the flavor evaluator does not feel particularly positive about the submission from his or her informal evaluation. Furthermore, if the submission looks like it will perform poorly, this information has value for the creative flavorist who made the submission. Either the flavorist can modify the submission, if time and potential financial promise merit the modification, or the flavor house can drop the submission, because the flavor will probably not perform well. Finally, one should never overlook the opportunity to develop a data base comprising one's creations and the competition. This data base can help the flavorist improve the quality of his/her creations, by indicating early which creations consumers find acceptable and which they do not. The key requirement is that the flavor house have an applications department, where they can put the flavor into the customer's base, or at least a neutral, representative base, for consumer evaluation.

EVALUATING FLAVOR SUBMISSIONS FOR COST EFFECTIVENESS

We close this chapter with an evaluation of the cost effectiveness of flavor submission. Our first case history, about sausage spices, dealt in part with the cost of the submission. This section continues with that topic, dealing with two issues; the evaluation of different submissions at a variety of concentrations for cost reductions, and for economic evaluation (namely, which submission looks like a better buy).

In the typical product development cycle, the developer has so much work to finish that he/she has little opportunity to systematically explore flavor submissions at different levels. Once one makes the decision about the specific flavor, then the product developer looks for the best level to use. The concentrations of the flavor will vary depending upon the specific submission, the product, etc. Afterwards, the product developer will consider the cost of the flavor to see whether indeed the product can sustain the cost of the particular flavor chosen. If it can, then all is well and good. If it turns out that the flavor costs too much for the product, then either the developer tries to reduce the concentration, or begins to look for another flavor.

CASE HISTORY—PEACH YOGURT FLAVOR

Linda Barbely owns a small dairy company in the southwest, which she founded in 1968. Since that time, she has developed a variety of successful products, including a line of flavored yogurts. Recently, she decided to increase the depth of the line by adding to it a number of new flavors, including peach. The yogurt had to have natural flavorings, so Barbely called four suppliers to submit their best peach flavors for yogurt.

Typically, one might solicit a flavor at the proper inclusion level. Barbely recognized that no one really knew the proper level for peach yogurt flavor, so she provided each of the four suppliers with a sufficient amount of her unflavored base to create prototypes incorporating five concentrations of flavored yogurt.

Upon receipt of the 4 sets of 5 levels each, one set from each of the 4 suppliers, she submitted the yogurts to consumer test, using a small church panel in the Phoenix area, which had been used several times previously for screening. The panelists in the test consisted of flavored yogurt consumers, who during the screening phase, expressed positive reactions to the idea of a peach flavored yogurt. The panelists did not know whose product they would test, nor did they realize that they would evaluate various concentrations of different submissions.

During the actual test, each individual from a panel of 60 evaluated a total of 10 of the 20 yogurts, scaling each one on a variety of characteristics, including flavor intensity, aroma intensity, naturalness, and, of course, overall acceptance.

The results from the early phase screening appear in Table 12.8. Note that although the four suppliers provided a range of 5 levels each, the perceived range of peach flavor differs. Specifically, supplier A's range seems the most limited, whereas supplier C's range seems the largest. We do not know, however, whether the differences in the range result from differences in the ratio of concentrations used, or functional differences among the various submissions.

The next analysis consists of finding a winning submission. The overall acceptance values point to the high concentrations of all submissions as the most highly acceptable. Note also that ratings of the competitive frame appears in Table 12.8 which provides an anchor. The highest concentrations of suppliers B and C appear most promising.

Can We Reduce The Concentration And Save Money On The Flavor

Traditionally, the product developer might stop at this point, after having selected a winning submission. However, Barbely recognized that she might not have to use the highest concentration, which costs the most money. Rather, she could relate cost and peach flavor to concentration, develop a smooth curve for the two winning submissions, and then decide the concentration which she would most like to use.

TABLE 12.8
COMPARISON OF FOUR PEACH FLAVOR SUBMISSIONS FOR YOGURT, AT FIVE LEVELS OF INCLUSION

Level	Inclusion Concentration					Range of Ratings
	100	90	80	70	60	
Flavor Strength						
A	52	47	44	41	39	13
B	61	53	47	44	43	18
C	56	53	51	48	33	23
D	58	54	50	47	44	14
X	66	——	——	——	——	——
Y	57	——	——	——	——	——
Z	53	——	——	——	——	——
Liking						
A	71	61	55	50	46	25
B	69	58	54	49	47	22
C	65	61	57	53	50	15
D	71	71	66	63	57	14
X	61	——	——	——	——	——
Y	74	——	——	——	——	——
Z	69	——	——	——	——	——

Cost of Goods

	Unit Cost	Total Cost of Inclusion				
A	1.7	170	153	136	119	102
B	1.5	150	135	120	105	90
C	1.3	130	117	104	91	78
D	1.1	110	99	88	77	66

A—D = Submissions of various suppliers for peach flavor in yogurt
X—Z = Three in-market competitors

Figure 12.1 shows how cost varies with perceived flavor for the two peach flavors. We see here a very important difference between the submissions B and C. On an absolute numerical basis, flavor house B's submission at the highest concentration wins (Table 12.8). However, note the difference between the two flavors. Per unit dollars spent, to achieve moderate perceived flavor, submission C generates more perceived flavor. Only at the high peach flavor levels does submission B look as promising.

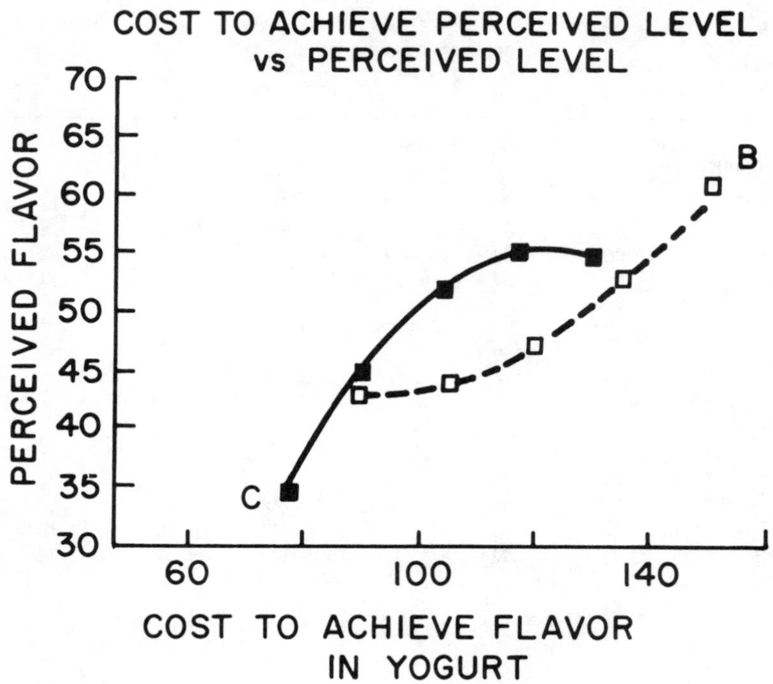

FIG. 12.1. RELATION BETWEEN COST TO ACHIEVE A SPECIFIC FLAVOR INTENSITY IN YOGURT (ABSCISSA) AND THE PERCEIVED FLAVOR (ORDINATE).

The graph compares two submissions: C and B. Note that within the middle cost range, the same cost of goods generates stronger flavor intensity using submission C. However, submission C becomes less cost effective at higher flavor levels, and indeed beyond a certain flavor level (55) no concentration of submission C will provide the desired perception.

AN OVERVIEW

This chapter has dealt with the evaluation of various submissions and new ingredients for food. The key to success, from the developer's point of view, consists in a disciplined evaluation of the alternatives. Where possible, one might wish to evaluate the submission at several concentrations, to assess effectiveness versus concentration and stability. Often, such systematic testing goes against the traditional method, consisting of a rudimentary (but educated) evaluation of a single level of the submission.

For multiple ingredients, other procedures recommend themselves, specifically experimental designs known as "screening designs." Rather than evaluating each ingredient or component singly, holding all others constant, the screening designs allow the product developer to evaluate mixtures of components, which more accurately resemble the complexities found in real foods.

REFERENCE

PLACKETT, R.L. and BURMAN, J.D. 1946. The design of optimum multifactorial experiments. Bio metrika *33,* 305-325.

CHAPTER 13

OPTIMIZING PRODUCTS FOR ACCEPTANCE, COST AND STABILITY

INTRODUCTION

During the past five years, product marketers and developers have increasingly realized the need to accelerate the process of development. With increasing competition comes the need to take advantage of all resources. Time to develop products, and the back-and-forth testing cycle, so common in traditional development and research, becomes a luxury one can ill afford. Marketers accelerate schedules to take advantage of market opportunities. Product developers react to the resulting time pressures, and accelerate the development of products.

If one polls the staff of product development groups, one will quickly discover that the development cycle consists of many starts and stops. Usually, the product developer responds to several different pressures, from various sources in the corporation. As a consequence, the sequence of development lacks the smoothness and direction that it could otherwise have. Product developers often have to "throw together" a prototype for a test in order to meet a schedule. Any learning which occurs, and which could become useful later, occurs by happenstance. The individual product developer does benefit by many of his/her false starts and small failures, prior to developing a winning prototype. More often than not, however, this learning, so valuable for future work, occurs in a haphazard, idiosyncratic and uncontrolled fashion. The product developer actually doing the formulation benefits from the experience, but the experience and learning does not become institutionalized, available readily to others who may have to continue the project later.

Experimental Designs And Learning

Statisticians recognize the utility of systematically exploring variables. They have developed a branch of statistics known as "experimental design." The techniques allow researchers to create different combinations of variables in such a way that the investigator can discover how these variables act singly and in concert to generate a response (the dependent variable). Rather than creating thousands of test prototypes, to insure that one has taken into account interactions among the variables, the statistician lays out a limited and feasible number of combinations which will accomplish the same objective.

In many product development situations, R&D has already explored a variety of ingredients, and has rejected some, while accepting others. Furthermore, the issue often becomes one of determining the best or optimum combination of this limited set of ingredients. Product developers and marketers alike know that even with a limited number of ingredients, one can substantially modify acceptance and sensory characteristics simply by varying the ratios among the ingredients, and their absolute level in the particular product. Given this situation, with a limited number of ingredients, the method of statistical design recommends itself as an efficient procedure to explore a wide variety of combinations. From the data, one can determine how formula variables generate perceptions, change acceptance, and affect the cost of goods. Thus, the product developer has a chance to learn about the product, as well as fine-tune it.

CASE HISTORY—SPICY PASTA SAUCES

Pasta consumption in the U.S. has grown very quickly over the past ten years. With this growth has come a proliferation of pasta sauces offered by major manufacturers. A quick glance down the grocery aisles will reveal a wide selection of pasta sauces, beginning with the simple tomato sauces, then going to meat, then to rich/zesty sauces, and finally to ethnic sauces. As competition increased in the sauce market, the manufacturers had to develop different types of sauces to capture new niches. One could not maintain one's growth and profit margins by offering a single, unflavored sauce, or even a short line consisting of simple tomato sauce, mushroom based sauce, and meat base sauce.

Jerry Freeman of Freeman Foods Inc. founded his company in the early 1970's with a small line of pasta sauces for the midwest U.S. Freeman Foods typified the small U.S. food company, catering to a limited market and producing the finest product available. However, over time, competition began to erode Freeman's share, especially in the Michigan/Wisconsin/Illinois market and in the Dallas area where Freeman Foods enjoyed its greatest strength. Responding to this competition, Freeman decided to develop a line of pasta sauces with new flavorings, and target this line at potential customers who currently purchased competitive products.

The first stage in Freeman's marketing plans called for evaluation of the existing (in-market) pasta sauces along with prototypes to determine what flavors consumers liked. From small scale studies with church panels it appeared that consumers might find a sharper tomato sauce flavor acceptable, if Freeman could provide the right spice blend, color, and texture. At the project inception, the Freeman line consisted of simple pasta sauces (tomato, mushroom, meat), but marketing quickly realized the need for the spicier alternatives that departed from the more traditional bland flavors.

Early Stage Flavor Screening—First Research Steps

The initial foray into developing the spice line consisted of an evaluation of the competitive frame of spiced pasta sauces to determine consumer likes and dislikes. Beginning with a set of focus groups, Freeman's research director, Trudy Peeps, quickly determined that consumers had a relatively poor, undeveloped language to describe spices and flavor nuances. The consumers knew what they liked and disliked, but had difficulty describing the types of positively accepted spices that they perceived in various pasta sauce products.

The second step consisted of a small, formalized screening of a variety of in-market pasta sauces, along with several submissions. Trudy recognized that tastes differ across the U.S. For this initial evaluation, therefore, she chose two markets; Dallas, a home territory of Freeman foods, and suburban New York City, a highly competitive market, but a promising one.

The screening consisted of small panels of 50 consumers in each market, all adult women, who during a telephone screening interview satisfied the two basic criteria to qualify for inclusion. First, the women had to have prepared and eaten pasta sauces at least three times in the past two months. Second, they had to express high positive interest in a spicy pasta sauce. The research director definitely wanted consumers who showed interest in the potential Freeman entry, and wanted to screen out those particular individuals who stuck with "middle of the road", bland pasta sauces. These individuals by their very responses to the screening questionnaire (Table 13.1) would probably never purchase spicy pasta sauces, even though these consumers may account for much of the volume of regular pasta sauce.

Table 13.2 shows the results by total panel and by market for overall liking and perceived spiciness of the sauce. Note that we do find several highly performing pasta sauces including competitors, and submissions. These pasta sauces do not necessarily outperform the bland flavors (Table 13.2), but come close in overall acceptability. Parenthetically, we do not

TABLE 13.1
EXAMPLE OF A SCREENING QUESTIONNAIRE FOR PASTA SAUCE

Hello, my name is ___________, from the Attitude Group, Inc., a nationally known market research company. May I talk to you for a few minutes about some products?

1. Which of these products have you prepared and eaten in the past two months (earlier from scratch or from a package)?

   Lasagna
   Fried Rice (Chinese)
   Pasta (Spaghetti) Sauce (IF NO, TERMINATE)

2. Of the following three pasta sauces, which one would you like the best? Which one would you like second best?

   Regular Pasta Sauce
   Pasta Sauce With Mushrooms
   Highly Spiced Pasta Sauce (IF NOT 1ST OR 2ND, TERMINATE)

I would like to invite you to participate in a tasting of some pasta sauces at ___________, on June 17, 1984. We will pay you $35.00 to participate for a four hour session.

Yes ___________ No___________

---

necessarily expect the highly spiced products to meet the overall acceptance achieved by the blander products. Highly spiced products tend to polarize consumers. Some consumers like them; others dislike them. Yet, consumers, whether they like or dislike these spicy pasta sauces, accept many of the blander tomato based products which have low spice flavor (spiciness = 50 or less).

Prior to selecting a pasta sauce spice system with which to proceed, the research director also looked at the distribution of liking ratings for the winning sauces, to assess the degree of polarization. As one might expect, the sauces did polarize. The winning entry (D in Table 13.2) showed the lowest level of polarization, but nonetheless did antagonize a small number of consumers (16%).

Experimental Designs To Optimize The Pasta Sauce

After selecting the prototype for further work, R&D and marketing met to decide next steps. All participants at the meeting recognized the need

TABLE 13.2
RATINGS OF EIGHT PASTA SAUCES ON SPICINESS AND LIKING (SCREENING PHASE PRIOR TO OPTIMIZATION)

Product	Spiciness	Liking Ratings (0-100)			Polarization (Percent)	
		Total	N.Y.	Dallas	% Love	% Hate
A (Test)	67	49	58	40	31	35
B (Comp)	64	52	45	59	24	31
C (Comp)	61	56	46	66	23	21
D (Test)	50	58	52	64	18	16
E (Comp)	50	52	48	56	18	26
F (Comp)	48	43	50	36	15	27
G (Test)	46	51	56	46	18	25
H (Comp)	42	43	48	38	15	29

Polarization defined as the proportion of panelists rating the sample at the extreme
love: rating of 75 or more on the 0-100 scale
hate: rating of 25 or less on the 0-100 scale

Comp = Competitor

Test = Test Formula

to improve the product and gain acceptance. They recognized that they would have to fine-tune the spice level and the consistency, and possibly they might have to add in meat or mushrooms. Consumers at the focus group felt strongly that the addition of visible solids such as meat or mushrooms would substantially increase acceptance, and would add perceived value to the new sauce entry.

Based upon the results of the study, the R&D director, Bob Flynn, suggested development of a Mexican spiced pasta sauce, with a noticeable (but not overwhelming) chili note. Furthermore, he suggested the addition of a constant amount of meat, and systematic variations in thickness (via a thickening agent) and variations in spice composition. The pasta sauce would then take on some of the characteristics of a chili sauce, but without the overwhelming chili flavor. Research on consumer usage patterns revealed that many consumers use pasta sauce as an ingredient for other products. This information suggested to the marketers that a mild chili based sauce might find other uses as well, besides simply as a topping for pasta.

To create alternative product formulations requires a systematic variation of five ingredients (thickener, salt (or sodium chloride), pepper, oregano, and onions). Furthermore, one should not limit oneself to a narrow formulation range, but rather explore a wide range. Thus, for one ingredient, it pays to create several distinctly different levels of formulation, to explore the wide range. However, for 5 ingredients which vary simultaneously, how does one go about creating a manageable array? One might systematically vary only one of the five formula variables, (e.g., thickener), holding the other four constant. This would generate a base product and 16 additional variations (3 levels each of thickener, salt, pepper, chili, and onion, respectively). However, that strategy would fail to uncover synergisms or interactions among the formula variables. Another solution, albeit an expensive one, consists of creating all 729 combinations (3 × 3 × 3× 3 × 3) embodying each of the three levels of the formula variables combined with each other. Only in the most simple of cases, with a limited number of variables would this procedure work.

One standard way of reducing the number of variants to test consists of arraying the formulations in a fractional factorial design. The design allows the product developer to test some, but not all of the combinations. The design minimizes the number of alternatives needed for development and testing.

One particularly popular design for product optimization, known as the central composite design, appears schematically in Table 13.3. It allows the researcher to test either 3 or 5 levels of each variable. Note that with the design it becomes possible to measure pairwise interactions among variables (but not three-way or higher interactions), as well as nonlinearities in a variable. These two properties become especially valuable in the evaluation of foods. We know that as the concentration of an ingredient increases acceptance first increases, peaks, and then drops down. Given this general pattern, we need an experimental design that can explore a sufficiently wide range of ingredients, and can detect the curvilinearity. Had we limited our evaluation to two levels of each variable, we never could establish a curvilinear relation with an optimum, or peak point in the middle.

Specific Design For The Pasta Sauce

After various discussions, R&D and marketing research decided to use the central composite design for 5 variables. At this point they decided upon the schematic array, but did not yet know the actual concentrations of the three ingredients. Bob Flynn at R&D suggested that his staff ex-

TABLE 13.3
TEST DESIGN FOR THE PASTA SAUCES

Product Code	Thickener	Salt	Pepper Level	Onion Level	Chili Level
1	H	H	H	H	H
2	H	H	H	L	L
3	H	H	L	H	L
4	H	H	L	L	H
5	H	L	H	H	L
6	H	L	H	L	H
7	H	L	L	H	H
8	H	L	L	L	L
9	L	H	H	H	L
10	L	H	H	L	H
11	L	H	L	H	H
12	L	H	L	L	L
13	L	L	H	H	H
14	L	L	H	L	L
15	L	L	L	H	L
16	L	L	L	L	H
17	+A	M	M	M	M
18	−A	M	M	M	M
19	M	+A	M	M	M
20	M	−A	M	M	M
21	M	M	+	M	M
22	M	M	−A	M	M
23	M	M	M	+A	M
24	M	M	M	−A	M
25	M	M	M	M	+A
26	M	M	M	M	−A
27	M	M	M	M	M
28	M	M	L	M	ML
29	M	M	M	M	ML
30	+A	+A	H	+A	H
31	H	H	+A	+A	+A
32	M	+A	M	M	ML
33	M	M	H	+A	H
34	M	M	M	H	H
35	M	M	M	+A	ML
36	M	M	−A	−A	ML
37	M	L	−A	−A	ML
L +A	8.3	3.2	3.0	3.6	2.5
E H	7.3	2.5	2.3	2.5	1.75
V M	6.3	1.9	1.5	1.0	1.0
E L	5.3	1.0	0.75	0.5	1.0
L −A	5.3	0.5	0	0	0.5
S					

Products 1-27 come from the Experimental Design and the remaining 10 represent probes.

plore the ranges of the individual ingredients, and submit the extremes to an evaluation before proceeding. All participants in the project wanted to insure that the prototypes would taste noticeably different from each other. Parenthetically, quite often, product developers who use experimental designs to systematically vary ingredients fail to make the most of the product array. They limit the range of the ingredients to a narrow spread. For the pasta sauces, R&D wanted to insure that the sauce blends ranged from noticeably spicy to hardly spicy at all. They recognized that some of the products might not taste particularly good, but they avoided the ever-present temptation of eliminating those poor performers and only going forward with good products for the test. Proper use of the experimental design procedure requires the evaluation of a wide range of ingredients, and the consumer evaluation of all of the prototypes dictated by the design, not just those which one feels will win in an acceptance sense.

After several weeks of product development, and evaluation of the ranges of the components, R&D finally presented marketing with its recommended ranges for the components. Using the schematic shown in Table 13.3, R&D developed three products in the grid: HHHHH (all highs), MMMMM (all medium), and LLLLL (all lows). An informal "cutting" or evaluation of these products at R&D quickly revealed the differences among the products. All tasted reasonably acceptable, but quite different from one another, in spice, in appearance, in texture, etc.

Table 13.3 presents the final experimental design, including the schematic (at the top), and the actual concentrations (on the bottom), corresponding to each level. In addition to the basic set of 27 formulations called for, R&D wanted to explore an additional 10 products within the same framework. These also appear in Table 13.3 in a separate section. Thus, the total number of prototypes came to 37 (27 from the design plus 10 additional equal 37.)

Parenthetically, when first presented with the concept of an experimental design, and the need to create a systematically varied group of prototypes, many product developers balk. They feel that this systematic variation demands too much time and costs too much money, and the outcome does not "pay out." On the other hand, in the usual sequence of product development the developer will undoubtedly create a large number of prototypes, often unsystematically. Just as much labor, if not more, goes into the development of these prototypes, which do not vary according to a design. If the product developer succeeds in generating a good product, all is well and good. If he/she does not, then the developer has to return to the drawing board to create more prototypes. Experimental design allows the developer to learn about the ingredients, and to project a direction for future work, if the products fail to meet acceptance standards.

Specifics Of The Test

For this optimization study both marketing and R&D recognized that the consumers would have to use the product at home, both in pasta, and as an ingredient in other foods. With 37 prototypes each panelist could test only a limited number. Based upon the timing constraints (marketing needed data 2 months from the beginning of the study), Trudy suggested that each panelist use only four of the 37 prototypes. Freeman suggested that the study include three competitors as well as benchmarks. The panelists would test each of the four "blind". They would test the competitors' samples repackaged in the same type of bottles that contained the prototypes.

Table 13.4 lists the specifics of the home use test. Note that with each panelist only testing four samples, and with the requirement of at least 30 ratings per product, the test required a total of 300 panelists. The marketing research director suggested that they divide the test into four markets, to represent the various regions of interest. This division into

TABLE 13.4
SEQUENCE OF ACTIVITIES FOR HOME USE TEST OF SPICY PASTA SAUCE

1. Panelist telephoned, qualified, invited to participate.
2. Panelist shows up at test site to learn about test.
3. Panelist goes through orientation evaluation of 1 product on attributes.
4. Panelist receives first product to evaluate at home, with instructions regarding:

   Preparation
   Evaluation
   When to Return to Pick Up Next Product

5. Panelist returns with completed questionnaire and receives next product.
6. Panelist follows steps 4-5 until she has tested all four products.
7. All 40 products assigned to panelists in randomized blocks of 4.
8. Panelist returns for final time, fills out a questionnaire probing attitude and usage, family size, cooking patterns, etc.
9. Panelist paid and dismissed.

four markets meant that each market would comprise a total of 75 panelists, and would generate only 7-8 ratings per prototype. However, in light of the developmental nature of this study, and in view of the fact that these 37 variations would generate a functional relation, the limited number of ratings for each prototype appeared adequate. Indeed, the study aimed at relating formula variations to acceptance, and developed the pattern of ratings. Thus, the precision in the study came from the full set of 40 (37 test, 3 commercial) prototypes integrated into a model, not from the precision of measuring acceptance of one product alone. Ordinarily, when marketing research or R&D wants to evaluate a single product, they may use panels of 50 and upwards, to achieve the necessary precision of measurement. However, here, we gain that precision because we develop an equation, based upon all the 37 experimental points.

Results—Do Panelists Discriminate Among The Prototypes

Before proceeding with any higher level analysis, the prudent researcher looks for validity. Simply stated, did the panelists differentiate among the products which R&D systematically varied? Table 13.5 shows part of the data matrix, which indicates that panelists do discriminate across the products, since their ratings differ from product to product. However, do their ratings track the actual formulations?

A key analysis to measure validity consists of correlating the formula variables with the sensory characteristics. Keep in mind that the correlation coefficient varies from a high of +1 (meaning a perfect linear relation between formulation and rating), down through 0 (denoting no relation), and further down to −1 (meaning a perfect inverse relation). Although the "true" or underlying relation might not follow a straight line, nonetheless the linear relation as indexed by the correlation coefficient provides a useful measure. We should see moderate to high positive correlations between formulation variables and sensory ratings. However, these generally do not equal 1.0, because of interactions among ingredients when they generate perceptions.

Table 13.6 shows the correlations, and reveals that the five formula variables do correlate with the sensory attributes, as we would expect. Since we compute the correlation coefficient across all 37 systematically varied products, we take into account all of the prototypes, not just the three which happen to have only one physical variable changing.

Building Product Models—Sensory Attributes

The first level of modeling consists of developing an equation relating

TABLE 13.5
DATABASE OF CONSUMER RATINGS FOR SPICY PASTA SAUCE (FULL PANEL)

Product	OVERALL Like	OVERALL Buy	Flavor	Chili	Onion	Salty	Spicy	Sharp	Hot	Pepper	After Taste	Off Taste	Consis-tency	Thick-ness
1	47	42	60	52	49	43	57	59	40	43	52	43	50	55
2	45	37	61	50	44	46	51	56	41	43	46	44	49	54
3	46	40	50	43	39	34	38	40	23	24	38	34	31	39
4	43	33	59	54	42	43	50	53	32	36	50	46	46	53
5	32	23	49	41	37	33	41	42	29	33	45	46	36	48
6	41	33	54	46	40	34	47	51	37	42	43	42	43	51
7	39	31	50	42	35	33	39	42	27	30	39	41	37	47
8	33	23	45	42	32	29	33	40	21	25	42	45	36	48
9	44	37	53	46	44	40	48	49	35	39	52	44	43	49
10	48	42	54	48	44	40	47	48	33	40	46	42	40	46
11	54	47	62	56	50	49	52	54	34	39	46	39	46	50
12	48	39	47	43	36	40	38	42	22	25	37	37	34	41
13	38	28	48	44	41	33	43	44	36	37	45	47	38	44
14	30	21	38	35	26	23	29	30	21	27	35	42	27	34
15	38	28	39	33	32	27	30	34	17	25	32	40	29	39
16	33	23	36	34	28	26	30	32	19	24	35	35	28	37
17	49	38	62	51	44	44	52	57	40	40	50	43	53	64
18	46	39	50	42	38	35	39	38	26	30	39	37	34	45
19	45	38	62	47	44	51	51	53	35	36	45	41	46	52
20	22	15	31	27	21	20	21	24	14	17	31	41	22	33
21	36	28	52	43	40	32	48	50	41	44	52	48	41	44
22	49	40	54	50	40	38	42	45	26	31	40	36	43	51
23	49	41	54	48	40	36	44	47	31	36	44	33	40	46
24	46	38	50	46	40	34	42	44	31	33	44	35	40	47
25	49	42	53	52	37	35	39	44	27	31	39	35	37	44
26	42	33	54	47	42	41	43	47	31	35	47	45	43	51
27	52	39	48	43	33	29	37	38	23	26	37	30	31	35
28	43	35	46	43	32	31	39	39	26	31	34	37	35	40
29	49	40	57	52	43	39	50	48	39	41	46	39	42	44
30	47	43	75	62	66	56	69	72	55	56	63	51	60	61
31	48	40	64	54	51	46	60	59	48	50	53	47	50	56
32	53	47	61	53	44	42	53	53	36	41	45	39	46	52
33	46	37	53	45	38	34	44	44	37	39	46	40	38	40
34	51	44	55	48	42	37	46	45	35	37	42	35	39	43
35	52	43	57	49	45	40	47	48	33	34	43	36	40	45
36	44	35	42	41	32	30	34	34	21	24	33	34	29	36
37	31	20	28	30	22	23	21	21	15	18	25	33	20	30

sensory characteristics to formulations. We could use a simple equation, written as follows (example, spiciness) (Eq. 13.1):

$$\text{Spiciness} = A + B\ (\text{Onion Level}) \tag{13.1}$$

This equation states that perceived thickness varies linearly with the onion level. The equation assumes that only the actual onion level impacts and affects perceived spiciness.

TABLE 13.6
VALIDITY ANALYSIS—CORRELATIONS OF FORMULA LEVELS WITH ATTRIBUTES

	FORMULA LEVELS				
ATTRIBUTES	THICKENER	SALT	PEPPER	CHILI	ONION
Overall Flavor Strength	0.53	0.76	0.42	0.32	0.41
Chili Flavor	0.45	0.74	0.29	0.40	0.33
Onion Flavor	0.44	0.73	0.44	0.33	0.50
Saltiness	0.40	0.84	0.29	0.25	0.33
Spiciness	0.49	0.75	0.52	0.37	0.43
Sharpness	0.54	0.72	0.49	0.34	0.39
Hotness	0.48	0.60	0.67	0.39	0.43
Peppery Flavor	0.42	0.58	0.69	0.41	0.43
Off Taste	0.37	0.09	0.63	0.20	0.19
Aftertaste	0.49	0.59	0.64	0.32	0.44
Consistency	0.56	0.67	0.45	0.28	0.33
Thickness	0.63	0.54	0.37	0.21	0.25

As simple and tractable as the equation seems, and as much as we would like to have such an equation, in reality things get more complicated. First, other variables, such as amount of meat influence thickness. We could modify the equation somewhat to accommodate other variables as well (Eq. 13.2):

$$\begin{aligned}\text{Spiciness} = A &+ B\ (\text{Thickener Level}) + C\ (\text{Salt Level}) \\ &+ D\ (\text{Pepper Level}) + E\ (\text{Oregano Level}) \\ &+ F\ (\text{Onion Level})\end{aligned} \tag{13.2}$$

The foregoing Eq. 13.2 states that perceived spiciness increases linearly with the five formula variables. The formula variables do not interact with each other. Furthermore, unit increases in the formula levels have the same effect, no matter at what level they begin. For instance, a 1-unit increase in thickener level increases perceived spiciness by B units, no matter whether we start from 0 thickener level, or from a very high thickener level.

Nonlinear Functions—Without Versus With Interactions

The foregoing equations assumed rather simplistic relations between formula ingredients and sensory attribute ratings. Had R&D simply varied one formula level, holding all others constant, perhaps the linear equation might work and represent the data. However, in actuality we find all sorts of nonlinearities, and interactions occurring. The nonlinear equations, which can deal with these interactions, become much more appropriate.

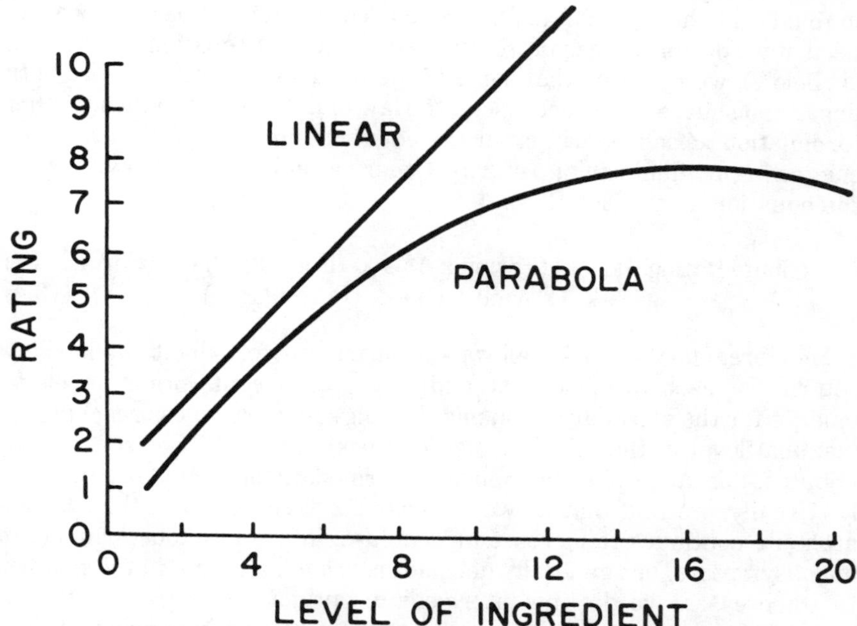

FIG. 13.1. COMPARISON OF A LINEAR AND NONLINEAR (PARABOLIC) FUNCTION RELATING INGREDIENT LEVEL TO RATING (×.1).
The ingredient level varies between 0 and 20. Note that with a parabolic function we see a diminishing returns of rating. As the formula level increases equal increments generate lesser increases in ratings.

Occasionally, we observe a simple relation, such as that shown in Fig. 13.1. As the formula level increases, the sensory attribute increases, but an a slower rate. We see evidence for an asymptote, and diminishing returns. Clearly, the relation does not obey a straight line. Although we probably do not (and in reality never will) know the "true" or underlying relation betwen formula level and sensory attribute, we can still "model" the pattern. We can use a variation of linear regression, containing linear and square terms (Eq. 13.3).

$$\text{Attribute Level} = k_0 + k_1\,(\text{Formula Level}) + k_2\,(\text{Formula Level}^2) \quad (13.3)$$

The foregoing equation uses the formula level and its square. If C has a negative value, but B has a positive value, this means that eventually we reach a point of diminishing returns. As the formula level increases, eventually the increase in perceived attribute level slows down.

We could model our five formula ingredients using the linear and square terms. The model, shown below, allows the sensory attribute to increase, at first rapidly, and then more slowly, with increasing formula levels. Keep in mind that the equation might prove adequate for the pasta sauce. Indeed, if we perform the appropriate statistics and fit equations to the data (as below), we may find that some of the formula variables require both linear and square terms because of the law of diminishing returns. Other formulation variables may enter the equation simply with linear terms, suggesting no diminishing returns. Other variables may not even enter the equation at all (Eq. 13.4):

$$\text{Attribute Rating} = k_0 + k_1\,(\text{Formula A}^2) + k_2\,(\text{Formula B}) + k_3\,(\text{Formula B}^2) + k_4\,(\text{Formula C}) + k_5\,(\text{Formula C}^2) \ldots . \quad (13.4)$$

The foregoing Eq. 13.4 allows the attribute to exhibit diminishing returns for each formula level, and may even permit optimal levels to emerge for the attribute in the middle range (e.g., spiciness reaching its maximal level in the middle range of thickener level). For sensory attributes, this latter phenomenon (an intermediate optimum) occurs rarely. Usually, we find that as we increase the formula level, the sensory attribute continues to increase or decrease, in a continuous manner. It may asymptote, but generally does not reach a maximum in the middle. In some cases, we do find intermediate optima. Saccharin sweetness reaches its maximum in the middle range of saccharin concentrations, primarily because as saccharin concentration increases, a bitter taste emerges which increases rapidly at higher concentrations and masks the sweetness. However, for most flavors and additives, we do not observe this behavior at least at the ranges where product developers would use them.

The final type of model one might use allows interactions to occur between variables. We know that ingredients do interact with each other. The flavor of a fruit comes from the subtle interaction of the chemicals in the fruit, not from one chemical alone. The interaction can become exceptionally complicated, and require years to unravel, even for a simple food. On the other hand, statistically, we can model the interactions, by adding interaction terms to the equation. Two types of terms appear below.

(1) Cross Product Terms (A × B). Here the ingredient levels multiply each other.

(2) Ratio Terms (A/B). Here the sensory rating varies as a function of the ratio of the ingredients (as well as the ingredients themselves).

To model the interactions, we develop these interaction terms, and use them as predictors, along with the linear and quadratic terms.

Stepwise Multiple Regression

Today, with the advent of microcomputers modeling has become a straightforward procedure, accessible to all who use regression packages. Regression analysis consists of a set of statistical routines to fit the coefficients of an equation. The procedures calculate that set of coefficients for the equation having the following property. The sum of squares of the differences between the actual ratings (observed in the test), and the predicted ratings (from the model) reaches its lowest level. By adjusting the coefficients, one can develop different models. Each model generates a set of predictions of the actual ratings. Only one set of coefficients generates a set of predictions satisfying the property of "minimum sum of squares" of predicted minus obtained values. Geometrically, the regression model generates a line if we relate the attribute rating to a single formulation (Fig. 13.1).

If we relate the attribute rating to the linear and square values of the formulation, we generate a parabola, shown in Fig. 13.1. If we relate the attribute rating to the linear values of two formula ingredients, we generate a plane, as shown in Fig. 13.2. Note that for three or more independent variables, we generate a "hyperplane", simple logically to the plane seen in Fig. 13.2, but in more dimensions.

Finally, if we relate the attribute rating to the linear and quadratic values (and to interactions, where appropriate), we generate a surface, as seen in Fig. 13.3.

Fitting The Current Data—Example Using Spiciness

To better understand the modeling process, let us fit the data for perceived spiciness, assigned by the entire panel, using first the linear, then the multiple-linear equations, and finally the nonlinear equations.

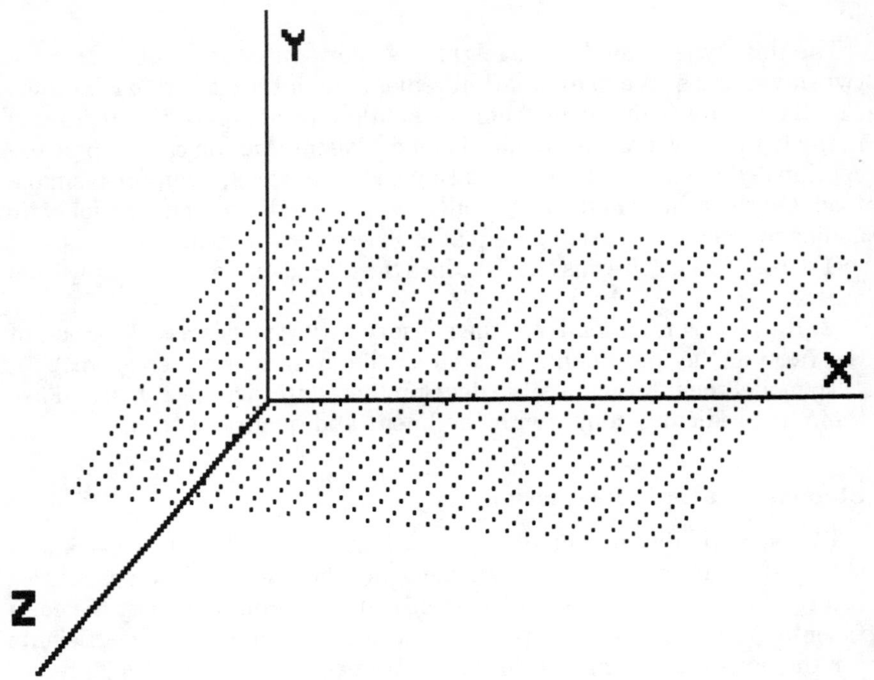

FIG. 13.2. EXAMPLE OF A PLANE RELATING THREE VARIABLES: INGREDIENTS X AND Z VERSUS ATTRIBUTE RATING Y.
Note that unit increases in X anywhere along the range generate the same increase in Y. The same goes for ingredient Z. The optimum values of X and Z lie at the extremes.

Table 13.7 shows how we build an equation, first using linear terms then interaction terms. We do not need to use square terms, because there does not exist the diminishing returns behavior within the range tested. Furthermore, the interaction terms take care of much of the nonlinearity of the relation between spiciness and formulations.

How Well Does An Equation Fit The Data

In our development of a model, we assume that the model represents the actual data but in a simplified, short-hand fashion. All measurements have error associated with it. Sensory ratings generate error, and thus we should not expect the equation (a model) to fit the data perfectly. Indeed, if the equation fits the data perfectly, this suggests that we may have used too many predictor terms. We should develop an equation having as few terms as possible, with all the terms statistically significant (namely, not due to chance), and with the equation accounting for as much

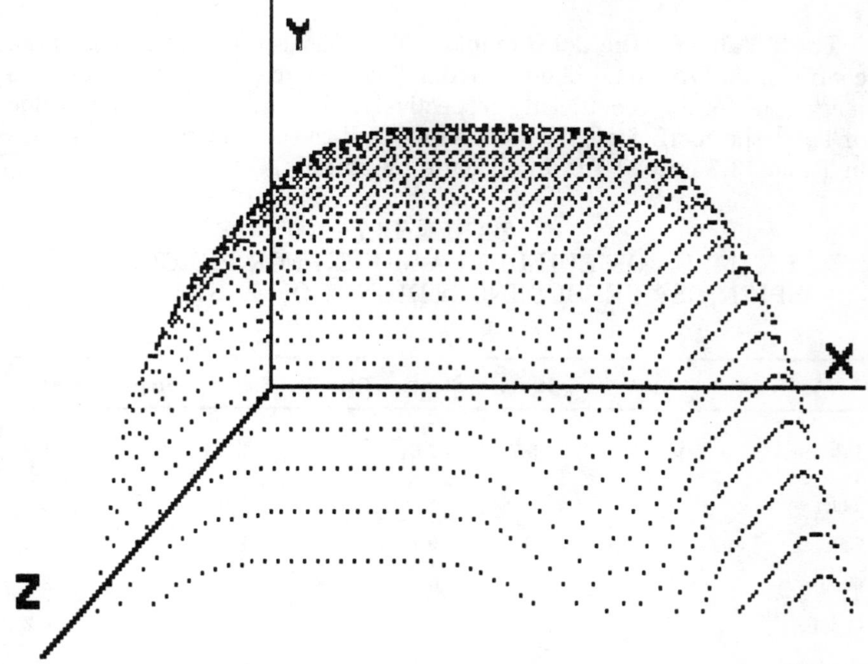

FIG. 13.3. EXAMPLE OF A SURFACE RELATING THREE VARIABLES: INGREDIENTS X AND Z VERSUS ATTRIBUTE RATING Y.
Note the existence of an optimum point (or region). The optimum values of X and Z lie in the middle range of the values, not at the extremes.

variability as possible. On the other hand, we should not use terms in the equation which increase the accuracy of prediction, if the terms do not reach statistical significance. We should aim for parsimony in the model, and not include every possible predictor.

In Table 13.7, note that we have used three different measures of goodness of fit.

The Multiple R-Square. This tells us the proportion of variability in the dependent variable explained by the independent variable. Normally the higher the multiple R-square, the better the model.

The F Ratio. A measure of variability explained by the model, divided by variability unexplained by the model. Again, the higher the better. However, the F ratio will actually decline from its maximum value if we continue to add in extraneous terms which increase the multple R-square (but only slightly).

The T Value for the Coefficients. This tells us the significance of the coefficients. We would like to have a T value exceeding 1.0 in absolute magnitude for each coefficient, respectively. The higher the absolute value of T, for the coefficient, the more significant the coefficient. All T values in Table 13.7 exceed 1.0 (in absolute magnitude).

TABLE 13.7
EXAMPLE OF BUILDING A MODEL FOR PERCEIVED SPICINESS VERSUS INGREDIENTS OF PASTA SAUCE

	Step 1	Step 2	Step 3	Step 4	Step 5	Step 6
Intercept	5.7	−2.6	−7.4	−5.8	0.11	−15.8
Thickener	5.8	4.3	3.9	3.6	2.3	4.6
Salt	0	9.7	9.4	9.1	8.7	9.0
Chili	0	0	5.8	4.7	3.3	3.9
Onion	0	0	0	1.8	1.1	10.2
Pepper	0	0	0	0	0	0
Thick X Pepper	0	0	0	0	0.6	0.6
Thick X Onion	0	0	0	0	0	−1.4
R^2	0.24	0.68	0.74	0.78	0.84	0.86
F Ratio	10.9	34.7	31.6	28.1	33.6	31.6

All terms in the equations have absolute values of T exceeding 1.0, meaning that these coefficients achieve statistical significance.
Thick means thickener.

Can We Fit All Sensory Attributes Equally Well

Does the modeling we perform on the attributes generate the same goodness of fit for each attribute? Those practitioners experienced in product testing of foods will probably know that we can fit some sensory attributes better than others. In particular, we can usually develop very parsimonious, statistically significant models relating appearance characteristics (darkness) and some texture characteristics (e.g., thickness) to formula variables. When it comes to sensory taste and aroma characteristics, generally we can generate very good fitting models for sweetness, tartness (sourness), and saltiness, but relatively poor models for bitterness and offtaste. For spice characteristics generally we develop a range from fair to very good models. The underlying reason may refer back to the "immediacy" of the sense impression. We have little problem recognizing differences in thickness (viscosity), sweetness, saltiness, or darkness of color. We may have more problems recognizing and scaling perceived offtaste, because the sense impression seems more subtle, and more fleeting (See Models, Table 13.8).

TABLE 13.8
EQUATIONS RELATING FORMULA VARIABLES TO SENSORY ATTRIBUTES

Terms	Flavor	Chili	Onion	Salty	Spicy	Sharp	Hot	Consis-tency	Pepper	Thick-ness	Off Taste	After-Taste
INT	−11.5	−4.2	14.8	9.3	−15.8	−16.0	2.8	−22.3	10.1	−3.0	20.5	−8.5
A	5.3	3.8	——	——	4.6	3.9	——	6.3	——	5.7	2.4	4.5
B	9.0	9.4	7.2	8.9	9.0	8.7	——	6.9	5.4	4.8	−2.9	3.4
C	——	——	−5.9	−11.1	——	−9.3	——	——	−9.2	−8.3	9.0	8.3
D	3.7	5.0	2.4	6.1	3.9	3.8	5.6	2.4	3.3	——	——	8.9
E	12.8	9.2	3.4	8.0	10.2	15.0	5.5	12.8	8.1	14.1	——	4.8
A^2	——	——	——	——	——	——	——	——	——	——	——	——
B^2	——	——	——	——	——	——	——	——	——	——	——	——
C^2	——	——	——	——	——	——	——	——	——	——	——	——
D^2	——	——	——	——	——	——	——	——	——	——	——	——
E^2	——	——	——	——	——	——	——	——	——	——	——	——
AB	——	——	——	——	——	——	0.9	——	——	——	——	——
AC	0.6	0.5	1.4	2.4	0.6	2.2	1.5	0.4	2.3	1.6	——	——
AD	——	——	——	——	——	——	——	——	——	——	——	——
AE	−1.5	−1.3	——	−1.1	−1.4	−2.0	−1.1	−1.9	−1.2	−2.2	−0.6	−1.3
BC	——	−1.5	——	——	——	——	——	——	——	——	——	——
BD	——	——	——	——	——	——	——	——	——	——	2.0	——
BE	——	——	——	——	——	——	——	——	——	——	——	1.0
CD	——	——	——	−2.4	——	——	−3.3	——	——	——	−4.3	−4.7
CE	1.4	——	−1.0	——	——	−1.0	——	——	——	——	——	1.5
DE	——	——	——	——	——	——	1.9	——	——	——	2.6	——
R^2	0.88	0.80	0.80	0.84	0.86	0.86	0.84	0.78	0.81	0.68	0.54	0.82
F Ratio	31.7	16.7	19.9	21.2	31.6	20.9	22.1	17.8	21.8	10.8	4.9	13.8

Terms = terms in the equation
INT = Intercept
A = Thickener
B = Salt
C = Pepper
D = Chili
E = Onion

Using The Models

The models developed above for spiciness and the other sensory characteristics provide a roadmap between formula variables and sensory ratings. For instance, given the specific ingredients formation, it becomes a straightforward matter to substitute the formulation into the array of equations, and generate a predicted sensory profile. This seems unnecessary, at first glance, because we have the actual ratings for the products. However, the ability to predict the likely sensory rating from an equation becomes extremely important in two instances.

(1) When we want to interpolate, to find out the estimated sensory profile for a combination of ingredients not directly tested, but still lying within the range of formulation levels tested.

(2) When we want to use the sensory profile as a constraint. We may wish to explore alternative formulations which satisfy certain criteria (e.g., maximize acceptance), but insure that we never generate a product with an inadmissable sensory profile. We need the roadmap relating formulations to ratings, and we cannot work with the actual numbers themselves. We cannot interpolate using the raw data.

Developing Models For Liking

We can develop models for liking using the same approach that we used to develop the models for sensory characteristics. Generally, if we systematically vary the formulations and extend the ingredients over a sufficiently wide range, we will generate an array of products whose optimally acceptable formulation lies somewhere in the mid-range, rather than at the upper or lower extreme. In general, we need the linear and the quadratic terms for the equations, and occasionally the cross terms. Keep in mind that for sensory equations, we usually use the linear and the interaction terms, and secondarily use the quadratic terms (Table 13.9).

Developing Models For The Different Markets And Age Groups

Marketing researchers know that "tastes" differ, often by age, and occasionally by market, and by product usage history. Thus, the overall models that we developed for acceptance for the panel as a whole may not apply to specific subgroups. We can break out the ratings of acceptance (purchase intent), for each subgroup separately, and develop a model for that subgroup. In this analysis, we will develop models for the ages (adult, teen), and for the four markets. Although each subgroup has fewer panelists, and thus fewer observations per product, keep in mind that when modeling ratings, we can achieve a significantly greater stability in the results. We use all of the 37 points (test formulations) to generate the model, not just one point. Thus, despite the reduced base size (which in turn makes the measurement of each point that much less precise) we still achieve a great deal of precision because we look for the pattern or trend of the data, not for the absolute value of each data point alone (Table 13.9).

TABLE 13.9
LIKING MODELS FOR PASTA SAUCE

		By Market				By Age			
	Total	N.Y.	Chicago	Dallas	L.A.	25-34	35-44	45-54	45+
Intercept	6.7	60.6	14.7	11.9	0	-2.5	-13.3	-9.4	2.7
A	—	-24.2	—	—	—	-.4	—	4.0	2.4
B	39.4	53.6	37.5	30.0	32.4	33.1	52.2	40.4	44.3
C	-8.3	—	-23.7	-7.7	—	-2.1	—	-13.6	-15.7
D	—	12.6	8.2	-23.4	14.6	17.7	8.9	—	-5.0
E	3.5	—	4.8	15.5	3.4	4.5	—	6.7	—
A^2	—	2.3	-0.8	—	—	—	—	—	—
B^2	-5.4	-7.3	-6.5	-4.1	-4.4	-4.7	-6.0	-5.5	-6.7
C^2	-2.4	-2.6	—	-2.7	-2.1	-3.1	-3.5	—	—
D^2	—	—	—	—	-7.4	-5.9	—	—	—
E^2	—	—	—	—	—	—	—	—	—
AB	-1.2	-2.7	1.2	—	-1.0	—	-1.8	-2.5	-2.4
AC	1.4	—	5.5	—	—	—	1.8	2.1	1.9
AD	—	—	—	3.5	—	—	—	—	—
AE	—	—	—	-2.0	—	—	—	-1.3	—
BC	—	3.9	-4.5	—	-2.2	—	-3.1	—	—
BD	-3.2	-5.2	-6.3	-4.0	—	-3.6	-7.7	—	—
BE	—	—	—	—	—	-1.9	2.2	2.5	2.2
CD	5.5	—	—	10.9	7.2	6.9	4.8	1.3	4.1
CE	-1.5	—	-2.1	-1.5	-1.2	—	-1.9	-1.4	-2.2
DE	—	—	—	—	—	—	—	—	—
R^2	0.91	0.66	0.89	0.86	0.78	0.80	0.84	0.73	0.82
F Ratio	23.7	5.8	19.2	14.4	9.4	9.1	12.2	6.1	11.6

A = Thickener
B = Salt
C = Pepper
D = Chili
E = Onion

Other Models—Cost Of Goods, Stability

So far, we have dealt with consumer inputs. Each of the formulations in the study has associated with it "objective" physical parameters, such as the total cost of goods, and the stability. It does marketing and R&D little good to develop a product if the cost of the product exceeds the level at which the product can return a profit. Thus, in any optimization study, we should insure that the cost of goods remains within specified bounds, and certainly lower than an upper cutoff level. In addition, the pasta sauces may show varying degrees of shelf stability. When developing the product, the prudent R&D developer or marketer should obtain measures of storage stability whenever possible (or at least estimate them). In this way, it becomes possible to optimize acceptance, but insure that the product remains shelf stable.

Table 13.10 shows additional equations pertaining to current unit cost, and to R&D estimates of storage stability. These equations usually require only linear terms.

TABLE 13.10
LINEAR EQUATIONS RELATING PASTA SAUCE INGREDIENTS TO COST AND STABILITY*

	COST OF GOODS	STORAGE STABILITY*
Intercept	––	11.09
A = Thickener	1.50	2.97
B = Salt	0.10	−0.09
C = Pepper	0.29	0.05
D = Chili	0.90	−1.67
E = Onion	2.70	−2.35
R^2	0.99	0.88

*Estimated by R & D

Optimizing Acceptance—The Simplest Case

The first optimization consists of trying to achieve the highest level of acceptance (purchase intent). As we modify the formula variables to maximize acceptance, we have to remain within the formulation boundaries. We cannot exceed the limits of the formulations tested, because we have no data in that region.

To optimize a function demands some type of systematic search among the formula ingredients. If we evaluate all combinations, or at least many combinations, we can optimize acceptance, because we need keep only that combination as the tentative optimum, until we evaluate yet another combination which scores higher in acceptance. Statisticians call this the "brute force" method of optimization. One simply divides each variable into a set number of discrete points (e.g., 10), and evaluates every combination of the points. For five variables, such as we have here for our pasta sauce, this would generate 10,000 combinations for evaluation ($10^5 = 100{,}000$), not an unreasonable number for the inexpensive computing power available in micro and mainframe computers. One should never discount the power of brute force techniques, especially with inexpensive computation, and enough time.

Hill Climbing Methods

Another method of optimizing, which generates answers faster, consists of "hill climbing". Figure 13.3 shows a typical surface (in idealized form), relating two variables to acceptance. The surface represents a hill. Suppose now, we randomly assign 5 points to this hill. Each point has an X coordinate (ingredient A), and a Z coordinate (ingredient B). We know that for every value of X and Z within the range tested, we can estimate the value of Y, the dependent variable. Thus, for each of the 5 points that we randomly threw on the mountain, we have a value of Y (e.g., expected liking).

The next step consists of discovering which of the 5 Y values (expected liking ratings) achieves the lowest value. One of the five will achieve the lowest value, even if its liking rating differs only marginally (e.g., by 0.0001) from the next lowest value achieved by another point. The hill climbing procedure tries to veer away from this point, because this point presumably represents a region at which acceptance decreases. Instead, we want to move the array of points in the opposite direction, which shows higher acceptance ratings.

To move the array of 5 points, we look now at the four highest points. They have a centroid, or average value of X, and average value of Z. We wish to move in a direction opposite the lowest point. To do this, draw a line between the centroid just computed (namely, the centroid of the 4 higher points), and the fifth point (namely, the lowest point). Figure 13.4 shows an illustration. The line provides the direction. We want to jump over the centroid point, as shown in Fig. 13.4.

This operation uncovers a new fifth point, lying on the other side of the centroid, away from the lowest scoring point, and presumably in the region where acceptance increases. In a sense, the optimizing algorithm "seeks" the regions at which acceptance grows, and actively avoids remaining in the region of low acceptance. The procedure stops when one can no longer improve acceptance by jumping over the centroid, away from a low scoring point.

For the simple optimization, the only constraint placed on the hill climbing algorithm consists of the requirement that every ingredient level (here X and Z) remain within bounds. If, perchance, during the jump the new values of X or Z exceed the bounds, one simply has to adjust the values of X and Z so they lie just within the limits allowed.

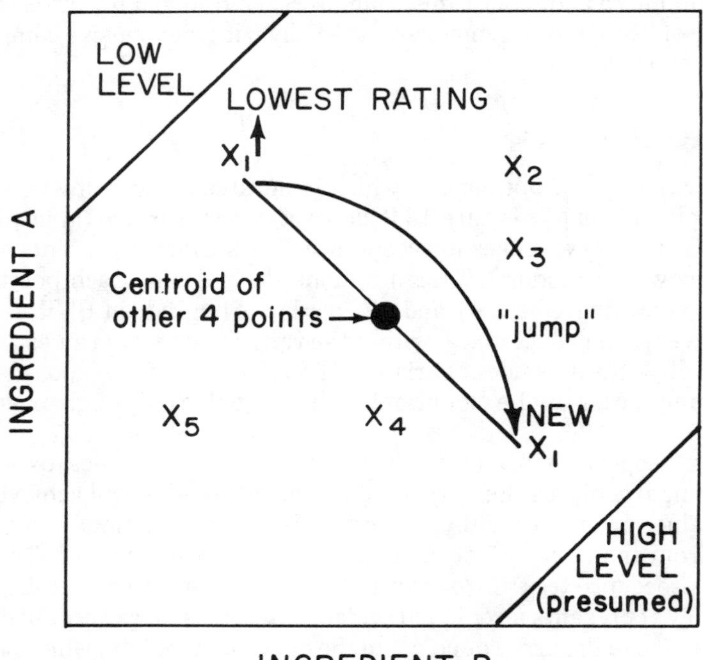

FIG. 13.4. EXAMPLE OF THE HILL CLIMBING ALGORITHM.
The figure shows 5 points. Points X2-X5 achieve higher ratings (according to the model) than does point X1. Therefore, move X1 away from its current position (in the region of low level) towards the high level region. To do so, compute the centroid of the points X2-X5. Jump over that centroid, away from X1 (the low region), in the direction of the high region.

Results—Simple Optimization

The results from the first, or simplest, optimization appear in Table 13.11. Table 13.11 presents a sequence of "steps" followed by the optimizer, as it climbs the acceptance hill. The optimizer used overall liking as the dependent variable. At each step, it attempted to improve acceptance, by the hill climbing method. Table 13.11 shows how the improvements start off with relatively large jumps in acceptance, and then slow down as the optimization technique reaches the peak of the hill. As one might expect, the closer one comes to the overall top of the hill (namely, the optimum product), the less room one will find to improve acceptance. Eventually, no movement will generate any increased acceptance. At that point, we have reached the top of the hill.

TABLE 13.11
SEQUENCE OF ITERATIONS TO OPTIMIZE ACCEPTANCE (LIKING)

	ITERATION NUMBER						
	1	2	3	4	5	6	7
Formulations							
Thickener (A)	6.08	5.31	5.79	5.59	5.30	5.45	5.45
Salt (B)	2.00	2.58	2.81	2.34	2.50	3.20	2.38
Pepper (C)	0.14	0.00	2.33	1.58	0.35	0.36	0.00
Chili (D)	1.75	1.31	2.50	2.41	1.00	1.00	1.00
Onion (E)	1.07	2.96	3.60	3.29	2.00	3.17	3.17
Consumer Ratings							
Liking	43	49	51	54	55	57	58
Flavor Strength	50	49	88	75	55	67	57
Chili Flavor	48	48	60	56	49	58	51
Onion Flavor	37	40	50	46	42	51	45
Saltiness	39	42	48	45	42	50	43
Spiciness	39	40	62	53	42	51	43
Pepperiness	28	30	47	41	31	37	31
Objective Measures							
Cost of Goods	14	12	22	20	18	18	18
Stability	22	21	14	15	15	16	16

All formulations and cost in relative units.

Computing The Profile Of The Optimum Product

Recall that the equations act as guides, or roadmaps. Given a specific formulation, one can rapidly estimate the likely response profile that panelists would assign to the product. In particular, we developed equations to relate sensory characteristics and formula variables (Table 13.8), as well as other equations relating acceptance measures to formulations (Table 13.9) and to cost of goods and stability (Table 13.10).

Given these equations, we can substitute the values for the optimum product and estimate the likely consumer reaction to the product. Keep in mind that the equations do not fit the data perfectly, and so our estimates come with errors of prediction. Nonetheless, they do allow us an idea of the likely sensory and acceptance ratings. Table 13.11 also shows the profile.

Overall Optimal Products Versus Local Maxima

Figure 13.3 illustrated the typical (smooth) surface that one might find which describes how acceptance varies with formula levels. In reality, when one works with equations, especially equations containing three way interactions ($A \times B \times C$ as predictors), one may generate surfaces having peaks and valleys scattered throughout. If the surface has a number of such peaks and valleys, the optimizer might get stuck going up one hill. It will reach the top of that hill and stop. However, the top corresponds only to that particular hill (called the local maximum), and not to the overall highest point, which may exist on another hill. The optimizer might never discover that highest hill, because it succeeded in climbing the lower hill. To avoid local maxima, one should begin the hill climbing routine at several different starting points. If each starting point ends with the same optimum, one can feel sure of having avoided local optima. Otherwise, one should continue to run the optimizer, until one point consistently comes up as the highest. Other local maxima or optima may appear, but if one point continues to emerge with the highest acceptance, we can feel sure that this represents the true, global optimum.

Sensitivity Analysis Around The Optimum

Table 13.11 presented the optimum, and the likely response profile of sensory and acceptance characteristics associated with that optimum. We have no feeling or idea about the nature of the surface. One straightforward analytical method for better understanding the surface consists of running a sensitivity analysis. To do so requires that we begin by holding four of the five formulation variables constant, at some fixed level. Then, one need only vary the fifth ingredient, in fixed steps, over the range that it would ordinarily take on in the experimental design. For each point one can estimate the likely response profile. This procedure, shown in Table 13.12 for the five ingredients, gives the researcher a pretty clear idea of

TABLE 13.12
SENSITIVITY OF PASTA SAUCE ATTRIBUTES TO FORMULATIONS

	THICKENER				SALT				PEPPER				CHILI				ONION			
	A	B	C	D	A	B	C	D	A	B	C	D	A	B	C	D	A	B	C	D
Formulations																				
Thickener (A)	[5.30	5.97	6.63	7.30]	5.45	5.45	5.45	5.45	5.45	5.45	5.45	5.45	5.45	5.45	5.45	5.45	5.45	5.45	5.45	5.45
Salt (B)	2.38	2.38	2.38	2.38	[1.00	1.73	2.47	3.20]	2.38	2.38	2.38	2.38	2.38	2.38	2.38	2.38	2.38	2.38	2.38	2.38
Pepper (C)	0.36	0.36	0.36	0.36	0.36	0.36	0.36	0.36	[0.00	1.00	2.00	3.00]	0.36	0.36	0.36	0.36	0.36	0.36	0.36	0.36
Chili (D)	1.00	1.00	1.00	1.00	1.00	1.00	1.00	1.00	1.00	1.00	1.00	1.00	[1.00	1.50	2.00	2.00]	1.00	1.00	1.00	1.00
Onion (E)	3.17	3.17	3.17	3.17	3.17	3.17	3.17	3.17	3.17	3.17	3.17	3.17	3.17	3.17	3.17	3.17	[0.00	1.20	2.40	3.60]
Consumer Ratings																				
Liking	58	56	55	53	42	53	58	57	58	56	48	36	58	55	52	49	48	52	55	59
Flavor Strength	60	60	61	61	48	54	61	67	57	65	73	80	60	62	64	66	44	50	56	62
Chili Flavor	50	50	50	50	38	45	51	58	51	50	49	48	50	53	55	58	44	46	49	51
Onion Flavor	45	45	45	46	35	40	45	51	45	44	42	41	45	46	47	48	35	39	42	46
Saltiness	43	41	40	38	31	37	44	50	43	43	42	42	43	45	48	51	36	39	41	44
Spiciness	44	44	44	45	31	38	45	51	43	46	49	53	44	46	48	50	36	39	42	45
Pepperiness	33	31	29	27	25	29	33	37	31	35	38	41	32	34	36	38	27	29	31	33
Objective Measures																				
Cost of Goods	18	19	20	21	18	18	18	18	18	18	18	19	18	18	19	17	9	13	17	17
Stability	16	18	20	22	17	17	16	16	16	17	17	18	16	15	15	14	24	21	18	15

All formulations and cost in relative units.

Each ingredient (e.g., thickener) varied across 4 levels (e.g., 5.30 to 7.30), with the remaining four formula variables held constant.

the likely reaction to deviations away from the optimum, for a specific formula variable.

Optimizing With Restricted Formula Boundaries

Suppose we wish to narrow the allowable range of the formulations. The original experimental design permitted us to assess a wide formulation range. However, for some reason we may wish to constrain the range. In fact, we may constrain the range in such a way that the optimum we discovered in Table 13.11 lies outside the allowable boundary. This type of problem often occurs in product development research.

Table 13.13 shows the likely optimum, and the estimated profile for the product, given a restricted range for the five, with the optimum previously

TABLE 13.13
COMPARISON OF TWO OPTIMA—WITHIN WIDE LIMITS VS. NARROW LIMITS

	A	B	C	E	F	G
	WIDE LIMITS			NARROW LIMITS		
	Low Limit	High Limit	Optimum	Low Limit	High Limit	Optimum
Formulations						
Thickener (A)	5.30	7.30	5.45	5.30	7.00	5.30
Salt (B)	1.00	3.20	2.38	1.00	2.00	2.00
Pepper (C)	0.00	3.00	0.00	0.00	2.50	1.34
Chili (D)	1.00	2.50	1.00	1.00	2.20	2.19
Onion (E)	0.00	3.60	3.17	0.00	3.00	3.00
Consumer Ratings						
Liking			58			52
Flavor Strength			57			67
Chili Flavor			51			52
Onion Flavor			45			43
Saltiness			43			42
Spiciness			43			47
Pepperiness			31			37
Objective Measures						
Cost of Goods			18			19
Stability			16			16

All formulations and cost in relative units.

discovered definitely lying outside the range (for salt and for onion). Note that the new optimum "bumps up" against the limits. The optimizer keeps trying to go in the direction of the overall optimum product, but cannot go beyond the allowed limits. Nonetheless, it does emerge with the best product, lying within the new constraints, and provides the likely profile of that product. In research and development programs which do not use systematically varied formulations and modeling, the change in the formulation limits often demands an entirely new piece of research to evaluate new prototypes. In contrast, the experimental design and modeling provides us with the roadmap. We merely need to change the limits, and recompute the optimum. The data base remains the same, and the original data maintains its integrity. We simply interrogate the database and the model with a slightly modified range of allowable variation.

Optimizing Acceptance For Two Subgroups Simultaneously

The previous sections dealt with the simplistic optimization of acceptance for one subgroup. Suppose, now, we wish to optimize the acceptability of pasta sauces for two entirely different segments; the spice lovers and the mild lovers, as uncovered by a sensory segmentation (Table 13.14). How can we develop a product that will satisfy both groups? Or, if no product exists, can we demonstrate that fact?

If we consult the expected liking ratings for the various subgroups, corresponding to the overall optimum product, we find that by and large the overall optimum satisfies both groups (Table 13.15). If we attempt to optimize acceptance for the first subgroup (spice lovers), we can improve the product for that group, but we dramatically decrease acceptance for the second segment (mild lovers). Table 13.15 shows the two separate optima, one for each segment, and the expected acceptance rating for the other segment.

An alternative approach consists of optimizing the acceptance rating assigned by one segment, but at the same time insuring that the acceptance rating for the "optimum product", assigned by the other group, does not fall below a certain minimum cutoff. Table 13.15 shows how one can generate a set of different optimum products, for the first sensory segment (spice lovers), while at the same time insuring a minimum acceptance level for the other segment (mild lovers). Note that as we reduce the constraint (namely, as we lower the minimum acceptance level allowed for segment 2) we increase the acceptance for the first segment. The two segments clearly like different products. Satisfying both at the same time generates a compromise product, optimum for neither group. Satisfying one group fails to satisfy the other. One can trade off acceptance by one group, to achieve acceptance by the other.

TABLE 13.14
LIKING EQUATIONS FOR TWO SENSORY SEGMENTS—
HIGH SPICE LOVER VS. MILD LOVER

	HIGH SPICE	MILD SPICE
Intercept	-4.2	-32.3
A		42.8
B	26.5	-27.1
C	-10.1	-11.5
D	12.7	
E	6.4	
A^2		-3.9
B^2	-2.9	
C^2	-1.5	
D^2		-9.9
E^2	1.5	-2.0
AB		
AC	2.4	
AD		
AE	-1.3	2.1
BC		
BD	-4.4	15.9
BE		
CD		6.2
CE	-1.2	
DE		-6.2
R^2	0.86	0.71
F Ratio	14.1	6.5

A = Thickener
B = Salt
C = Pepper
D = Chili
E = Onion
A sensory segmentation revealed other, much smaller segments beside these two.

Sensory Attributes As Constraints

From time to time, product developers want to construct a product which achieves two objectives simultaneously. First, they want the product to score high in terms of acceptance, to insure positive consumer response. Second, they want the sensory characteristics of the product to differ from other products on the market. The optimum product may

TABLE 13.15
OPTIMIZING LIKING OF PASTA SAUCE FOR TWO SENSORY SEGMENTS

	Total Group	Maximize High Spice Lovers	Maximize Mild Lovers	Optimizing High Spice With Mild Liking Exceeding 40	55
Formulations					
Thickener (A)	5.45	7.30	5.30	6.18	6.74
Salt (B)	2.38	3.20	1.00	3.19	3.20
Pepper (C)	0.00	1.11	0.00	0.00	0.57
Chili (D)	1.00	1.00	1.00	1.31	2.00
Onion (E)	3.17	3.60	1.25	3.36	0.03
Consumer Ratings					
Liking	[58]	51	36	52	37
Flavor Strength	57	77	35	67	63
Chili Flavor	51	56	33	60	61
Onion Flavor	45	53	29	52	45
Saltiness	43	48	27	50	50
Spiciness	43	55	25	52	54
Pepperiness	37	37	21	34	38
Objective Measures					
Cost of Goods	18	22	12	20	12
Stability	16	22	22	19	27
Segments/Liking					
High Spice Liker	57	[59]	29	[59	51]
Mild Liker	43	39	[67]	[40	55]

All formulations and cost in relative units.

or may not achieve both objectives. Indeed, quite often consumers like the products currently on the market, so that the optimization procedure generates a clone of existing products. When this occurs (and it does, more often than not) we generate a me-too product.

Suppose, however, we put an additional constraint on the optimization system. Keep in mind that the relation between acceptance and formulation characteristics looks like a surface. The top of that surface may generate a product similar to those already on the market. However, one can move away from the optimum, descending a little on the hill (namely, decreasing overall acceptance), in order to find a region whose formulations generate a qualitatively dissimilar and possibly novel sensory profile. The optimization technology permits that tradeoff. If we use the sensory characteristics as constraints, we optimize acceptance, while at the same time setting limits on the sensory profile that we will allow. No matter how good the optimum product performs in acceptance; if it does not satisfy the sensory constraints, we will not accept the solution.

In theory, the approach seems eminently reasonable. We have equations which relate formulations to sensory attributes. For every optimization step, we can estimate the sensory profile and accept or reject the solution. In practice, things become a little more complicated. Sometimes

TABLE 13.16
OPTIMIZING OVERALL LIKING—SUBJECT TO SENSORY ATTRIBUTES AS CONSTRAINTS

	OVERALL OPTIMUM	FLAVOR STRENGTH LEVEL AS CONSTRAINT			
		30	40	60	75
Formulations					
Thickener (A)	5.45	5.3	5.7	6.9	7.0
Salt (B)	2.38	1.0	1.9	1.9	3.1
Pepper (C)	0.00	0.0	0.2	1.4	1.0
Chili (D)	1.00	0.5	0.6	1.5	1.2
Onion (E)	3.17	0.0	0.2	1.5	3.6
Consumer Ratings					
Liking	58	33	47	48	52
Flavor Strength	57	[27	40	60	75]
Chili Flavor	51	28	39	48	57
Onion Flavor	45	23	31	40	53
Saltiness	43	21	31	38	48
Spiciness	43	20	31	45	54
Pepperiness	37	17	24	34	36
Objective Measures					
Cost of Goods	18	9	10	16	22
Stability	16	26	26	25	21
Subgroups					
High Spice Liker	57	24	39	45	57
Mild Liker	43	63	47	49	33

Note: All formulations and cost in relative units.

within the entire range of formulations, only a very few formulations can satisfy the sensory constraints. We may encounter exceptional difficulty finding that limited range of formulations which generates a desired sensory profile. Other times, the sensory constraints may generate incompatible answers. For instance, for the optimization of our pasta sauces, we may want a product having a very low perceived flavor intensity, along with a clearly noticeable spiciness.

If we limit ourselves to optimizing acceptance, subject to one sensory constraint, we will generally have little or no problem finding an array of products which satisfy that constraint. Table 13.16 shows some examples of alternative formulations which satisfy upper and low constraints on sensory characteristics (flavor intensity acting as a constraint at one of four levels).

R&D Parameters As Constraints

Each of the formulations developed and tested in this study has associated with it cost of goods, and estimated storage stability. These objective parameters, provided by R&D, can themselves act as constraints. For instance Table 13.10 allows us to estimate cost and stability for each alternative formulation that we generate through the optimization procedure. We can also optimize acceptance subject to constraints on cost, or stability, since we have these parameters represented by equations (Table 13.10).

Table 13.17 shows what might occur if we optimize acceptance, but continue to reduce the allowable cost of goods. At first, the optimum product costs less than the upper limit on cost, so we have no conflict. As we decrease the allowable cost, we begin to reduce the formula concentrations at a different rate for each ingredient. Since we modify the formulation, we also change acceptance, continually lowering it.

In traditional product development work, where R&D had to cost-reduce a product, the back and forth testing might require weeks, or months to accomplish as R&D first develops a product, sends it out to test, and then reads the results. Generally, cost reduction requires a number of iterations to insure that the consumers still accept the product. With the modeling technology, and with the integrated database, it now becomes possible to calculate the best performing product formulation, at a specific cost of goods. Since the approach generates an estimate of consumer acceptance, the product developer or marketer can estimate the viability of that cost-reduced product as a replacement for the current formulation.

Storage stability represents another R&D measure. By developing the relation between estimated stability and formulation ingredients, it becomes possible to calculate an array of products fabricated to achieve increasing levels of stability. One can also clearly see the relation between stability and acceptance. If they both move in the same direction, all is well and good. However, if they move in opposite directions (namely, as acceptance increases, estimated stability decreases), it then becomes possible to optimize acceptance, subject to a minimum stability value. Table 13.17 also illustrates some of these alternative formulations.

TABLE 13.17
OPTIMIZING LIKING UNDER SPECIFIED COST CONSTRAINTS AND STABILITY CONSTRAINTS

	No Constraint	Cost Less Than				Stability Greater Than	
		16	14	12	10	19	21
Formulations							
Thickener (A)	5.45	5.39	5.31	5.37	5.30	7.30	7.30
Salt (B)	2.38	2.27	2.82	2.59	2.75	2.10	2.48
Pepper (C)	0.00	2.31	0.00	0.00	0.00	2.14	0.63
Chili (D)	1.00	2.50	1.00	1.21	1.00	2.50	1.01
Onion (E)	3.17	1.61	1.73	0.95	0.00	3.60	3.49
Consumer Ratings							
Liking	58	53	53	49	48	54	54
Flavor Strength	57	67	54	49	45	82	66
Chili Flavor	51	52	51	49	47	56	51
Onion Flavor	45	43	43	40	37	50	47
Saltiness	43	38	44	42	40	44	40
Spiciness	43	51	43	40	37	56	47
Pepperiness	37	41	32	30	29	44	29
Objective Measures							
Cost of Goods	18	16	14	12	9	24	22
Stability	16	18	19	21	23	19	21

All formulations and cost in relative units.

AN OVERVIEW

Product modeling and optimization provide a unique opportunity for product developers and marketers. As this chapter has shown, one can accomplish a great deal by systematically varying the formulations, and submitting them to test. First, one learns about the relation between formulation and rating. This information helps build a fund of knowledge which leads, long term, to more efficient development. Second, one can rapidly decide on the best product, and get good direction, even though the test may not have directly included that product. Even if the optimum lies outside the range of ingredients tested the optimization technique can still help by pointing to the direction in a quantitative fashion. Finally, the product model and optimization procedure act dynamically, to answer "what if" questions. Traditionally, questions regarding cost reduction, satisfying two groups simultaneously, or developing products to satisfy specific sensory profiles required guesswork. With the product optimization approach, one can reduce the guesswork and obtain more definitive direction. R&D still has to create and formulate, but now the modeling gives them a better map to the consumer.

REFERENCES

BENDNARCYZK, A.A. and KRAMER, A. 1971. Practical approach to flavor development. Food Technol. *25,* 1098-1102, 1106-1107.

BOX, G. E. P. and HUNTER, J. S. 1957. Multifactor experimental designs for exploring response surfaces. Annals of Mathematical Stat. *28,* 95-242.

CORNELL, J. A. 1981. *Experiments With Mixtures.* John Wiley Interscience, New York.

CORNELL, J. A. and KNAPP, F. W. 1972. Sensory evaluation using composite complete-incomplete block designs. J. Food Sci. *37,* 876-882.

DUNN, G. and EVERITT, B. S. 1982. *An Introduction to Mathematical Taxonomy.* Cambridge University Press, Cambridge.

GORDON, J. 1965. Evaluation of sugar-acid-sweetness relationships in orange juice by a response surface approach. J. Food Sci. *30,* 903-907.

HARE, L. B. 1974. Mixture designs applied to food formulation. Food Technol. *28,* 50-62.

HARE, L. B. 1974. Design for mixture experiments involving process variables. Technometrics *21,* 159-173.

KISSELL, L. T. 1967. Optimization of white layer cake formulation by a multiple-factor experimental design. Cereal Chem. *44,* 253-268.

KISSELL, L. T. and MARSHALL, B. D. 1962. Multi-factor responses of cake quality to basic ingredient ratios. Cereal Chem. *39,* 16-30.

MARQUARDT, R. A., PEARSON, A. M., LARZELERE, H. E. and GREIG, W. S. 1963. Use of the balanced lattice design in determining consumer preferences for ham containing 16 difference combinations of salt and sugar. J. Food Sci. *28,* 421-424.

MOSKOWITZ, H. R. 1984. Sensory analysis, product modeling, and product optimization. In: *Analysis Of Foods And Beverages: Modern Techniques* (G. Charalambous, ed.), pp. 14-68, Academic Press, New York.

MOSKOWITZ, H. R. 1984. Optimizing consumer acceptance and perceived product quality. In: *Objective Methods In Food Quality Assessment.* (J. Kapsalis, ed.) CRC Uniscience Series. In Press.

MOSKOWITZ, H. R. and RABINO, S. 1983. Alternative strategies for product optimization. In: *Advances In Strategic Management* (R. Lamb, ed.) pp. 99-124. Greenwich, JAI Press.

MOSKOWITZ, H. R. and WEHRLY, T. 1972. Economic applications of sweetness scales. J. Food Sci. *37,* 411-415.

MYERS, R. H. 1971. *Response Surface Methodology.* Allyn and Bacon, Boston, MA.

RABINO, S. and MOSKOWITZ, H.R. 1982. Optimizing the product developing process using psychophysical scaling. J. Business Res. *10,* 295-308.

RABINO, S. and MOSKOWITZ, H. R. 1980. Optimizing the product development process: Strategical implications for new entrants. Sloan Management Review, Spring, 45-51.

CHAPTER 14

DEVELOPING PRODUCTS FROM CONCEPTS

INTRODUCTION

Product developers use concepts as broad based guidelines from which to develop products. In the typical scheme of product development, R&D receives a concept (either fully elaborated or simply a concept statement). From this concept they develop prototypes which marketing research and consumer testing evaluate for acceptance and for "fit to the concept." During the development cycle, the product developer may fabricate a number of alternative prototypes which hopefully deliver what the concept promises.

If we survey corporate product development "systems" which span the range from concept development to prototype development, a singular fact quickly becomes apparent, namely we do not find a straightforward method for translating concepts (promises on a piece of paper) to prototypes that deliver the promise. We rely upon the creative ingenuity of the product developer. For products demanding unique functional benefits of an objective nature (e.g., cooks faster), R&D knows whether or not they can deliver a product which fulfills the concept. For other products, having less objective or concrete, testable characteristics embodied in the concept, the task becomes more complicated. One has to engineer sensory responses to the product so that they support what the concept promises. Usually this promise takes the form of emotional benefits, harder to quantify and difficult to measure vis-à-vis the product which presumably delivers it.

This chapter presents two methods by which one can develop products which deliver what a concept promises:

(A) **Simple Maps.** Evaluation of many competitors, and the development of simple relations between sensory characteristics and concept promises.

(B) **Profile Matching.** Evaluation of systematically varied products, and the development of models relating formulations to concept promise elements. This involves the adjustment of a product formula to generate both acceptance and to deliver the attributes that the concept connotes.

SIMPLE MAPS

Simple maps refer to a straightforward process. Panelists evaluate a variety of products (in-market competitors, prototypes specifically developed) on a variety of characteristics. Some characteristics deal with the sensory properties of the product. Others deal with emotional or image characteristics, similar to those evoked by the concept (e.g., nutritious). The mapping procedure relates the image attribute to the sensory attributes. By building the map, at some point we discern which particular sensory attributes relate to the concept, and drive the perception of the product as delivering the intangible image and emotional benefits. The technique, as outlined below, builds a roadmap for product developers. It indicates specific, target products which act as reference points for product development. However, it does not and cannot provide direction in terms of formulation.

CASE HISTORY—WILSON'S FANCY ICE CREAM

Marj Wilson, president of a small dairy company in the Pacific northwest, manufactures high quality ice creams and markets her products to a small base of customers in the Washington and Oregon markets.

Wilson's ice creams possess all natural ingredients. One can characterize her line of flavors as having more cream, density and fruits in the finished product, compared to most competitors. The ice creams sell well, even though they cost more than the mass marketed competitors. Her products have increased their shelf space at retail, because of the overwhelmingly enthusiastic reception they receive when each new flavor rolls out.

Marketing research uncovered consumer interest in a line of European, unusually flavored ice cream. One flavor in particular, a brandy liqueur-flavored ice cream, had scored well in concept research conducted two years before. However, at that time, management concentrated on the introduction of a line of berry-flavored ice creams, and put the idea of brandy (and other liqueur-flavored ice creams) on the "back burner", for later consideration and introduction to the market. Two years later, an opportunity emerged for introducing the brandy liqueur-flavored ice cream.

Test Design

To develop the new brandy liqueur ice cream required the evaluation of a variety of alternative products, to see how well each delivered against the concept. In an initial foray to answer this problem, Marj suggested that the R&D director develop a variety of alternative flavors. For each flavor, she planned to have consumers evaluate the degree to which they liked the ice cream, and the degree to which the ice cream prototype fit the concept. During the planning phases, it soon became apparent that the ice cream required more than simply flavor variations. The density, types of inclusions (e.g., fruits), type of color, etc., could vary. Each different formulation represented yet another option to fit the highly promising brandy liqueur ice cream.

For the actual test, R&D produced 11 different ice cream samples, varying qualitatively in a variety of physical characteristics. They also purchased an in-market product as a benchmark. The panelists read the ice cream concept. Then, for each product, the panelists profiled the product on a variety of sensory characteristics (including strength of flavor, hardness, amount of inclusions, etc.). They also rated degree of liking as one key overall attribute, and degree to which the product delivered what the concept promised. Finally they rated their expectations of the concepts using the same attributes and scale. Table 14.1 provides some of the results from the panel of 60 consumers. Note that all consumers in the study participated after passing a screening interview, during which the interviewer made sure that the panelist purchases and consumes high quality premium ice creams. This screening insures that only qualified individuals participate in the panel.

First Level Analysis—Do the Products Fit the Concept

The first level of analysis consists of assessing the degree to which the various ice cream prototypes fit the concept. As noted in Table 14.1, product 5 represented an in-market brandy ice cream. Thus, in looking at the results of the ratings, we should keep in mind that we have an actual product, tested blind, which can serve as a reference standard. If the absolute magnitude of the scores for "fits the concept" seem low, this may result from a response bias to underrate the prototypes as fulfilling the concept, rather than from real product defects.

Table 14.1 reveals that the panelists rate all the prototypes as fitting the concept poorly. We deduce from this that panelists show a response bias, since even the actual in-market representative of this brandy ice cream category scores low. However, on a relative basis and based on direct ratings of fit, we find that product 1 achieves the best fit to the concept of a brandy liqueur ice cream.

TABLE 14.1
RATING OF 12 BRANDY LIQUEUR ICE CREAMS AND CONCEPT ON ATTRIBUTES

ATTRIBUTE	CONCEPT EXPECTATION	ICE CREAM PROTOTYPES											
		1	2	3	4	5*	6	7	8	9	10	11	12
Overall													
Like Overall	91	63	62	61	61	60	58	55	55	53	52	52	46
Purchase Intent	91	53	51	44	45	48	44	41	40	39	40	38	35
Fit to Concept													
Overall	N.A.	49	46	45	45	45	45	39	41	33	42	34	32
Appearance	N.A.	59	62	53	54	48	61	47	50	52	56	52	52
Flavor	N.A.	65	60	60	58	59	55	52	54	50	52	51	48
Texture	N.A.	61	58	58	56	58	53	53	55	46	50	48	45
Sensory													
Appearance													
Smoothness	61	56	59	60	60	53	55	57	52	46	53	55	47
Amount of Ingredients	58	66	57	64	52	74	50	53	60	65	73	60	61
Flavor													
Brandy Flavor	61	57	56	56	54	57	54	53	53	49	53	49	48
Sweetness	64	49	48	52	44	48	48	49	44	48	46	46	48
Texture													
Hardness	55	48	50	42	42	59	48	56	55	48	58	47	57
Creaminess	62	72	70	66	62	76	60	53	65	65	78	64	64
Image													
High Quality	91	66	64	60	60	65	61	57	57	55	59	54	53
Unique	92	59	52	54	50	59	43	45	50	47	51	51	54
Value	79	65	54	51	55	58	49	47	49	43	50	45	39
Filling	88	75	68	71	66	75	63	64	70	62	71	63	64
Heaviness	72	58	57	53	53	62	49	56	51	57	66	60	61

Procedure:

1. Read concept about the brandy liqueur ice cream.
2. Rate ice creams on all attributes.
   Each panelist rates 6 of 12 ice creams (randomly selected from the 12).
3. Rate concept as if it represented another ice cream prototype.

*In-market brandy liqueur ice cream.
N.A. = Not Asked.

A simplistic analysis, such as the one just illustrated above, can help the marketer and product developer sort through a variety of alternative executions of an early stage product designed to fit the concept. It does not yet provide the necessary learning which can help refine the development process. For that learning, we need to know which particular characteristics of the prototypes generated the fit to the concept.

Developing Simple Relations Between Attributes And Concept Fit

We know from the previous discussions in other chapters on acceptance that as a sensory characteristic (or formulation variable) increases, acceptance first increases, then peaks, and then drops down. R&D can use this information to discover the sensory attribute level corresponding to the maximum degree of liking. It then becomes a matter of formulating products which generate this sensory characteristic. That decision we must leave to the ingenuity of the product developer, since the relations we derive consist of consumer sensory reactions on the one hand, and consumer acceptance reactions on the other.

In a similar fashion, we can evaluate the relation between sensory characteristics (as the independent variable) versus rated fit to the concept (as the dependent variable). Does there exist a relation at all? If so, what does the relation look like? Does fit to a concept peak in the middle level of a sensory continuum (e.g., creaminess)? Does it peak at either end?

Developing Simple Models For Fit To Concept

In order to learn more about how sensory attributes generate fits to concepts, we develop simple models. As a sensory attribute increases, we determine the degree to which the rating of fits-the-concept changes. We look for that sensory level at which fit to the concept reaches its highest point. Furthermore, we look for the underlying pattern. We may find that as the attribute changes, perceived fit to the concept may vary dramatically. This finding suggests that the concept generates specific expections regarding that sensory attribute level. In contrast, we may find that the rating does not change at all. This second observation suggests that the concept generates no expectations regarding the sensory attribute level.

Table 14.2 lists the steps involved in developing the relation. Note that we use fitted functions, rather than the original data. By using the fitted data, we generate a smooth curve relating sensory attribute level to appropriateness for the concept. Thus, we use the regression model as a pattern recognition device, to help us better understand how sensory attributes correspond to expectations generated by the concept.

TABLE 14.2
SEQUENCE OF ANALYTIC STEPS TO DEVELOP SIMPLE RELATIONS BETWEEN SENSORY ATTRIBUTE LEVELS AND FIT OF ATTRIBUTE TO A CONCEPT STATEMENT

1. Consider each attribute, one at a time.
2. For a specific attribute (e.g., brandy flavor) develop a curve relating attribute level and attribute level squared, to the rating of "fits the concept."
3. As the dependent variable, choose the appropriate sense dimension:

   Example—for brandy flavor, this implies "fit of the attribute to the flavor expectation of the concept"

4. The equation should read like as follows:

   Rating of Fit to Concept = A + B (Attribute) + C (Attribute^2)

5. Compute the expected rating, for each prototype, using equation 4.
6. Plot out the smoothed or fitted relation between attribute level and fit to the concept from step 5.
7. Locate the maximum point on that curve—this corresponds to the sensory level at which the fit to the concept reaches its highest level (within the range of attribute levels tested).
8. Determine which prototype generates that level, and use that prototype as a reference for reformulation.

Figures 14.1 through 3 show some of the fitted relations between attribute level and fit to the concept. Table 14.3 summarizes the relations and also indicates which products should act as targets. Note that by providing R&D with target products, embodying the proper sensory characteristics, we end up making the product development job easier. Since we did not systematically vary the components of the different ice cream prototypes, we cannot provide formulation direction, although we can provide guidance, by pointing to specific products as targets for product development.

FITTING PRODUCTS TO CONCEPTS BY EXPERIMENTAL DESIGN AND MODELING

Background

The previous case history showed how to accelerate development by us-

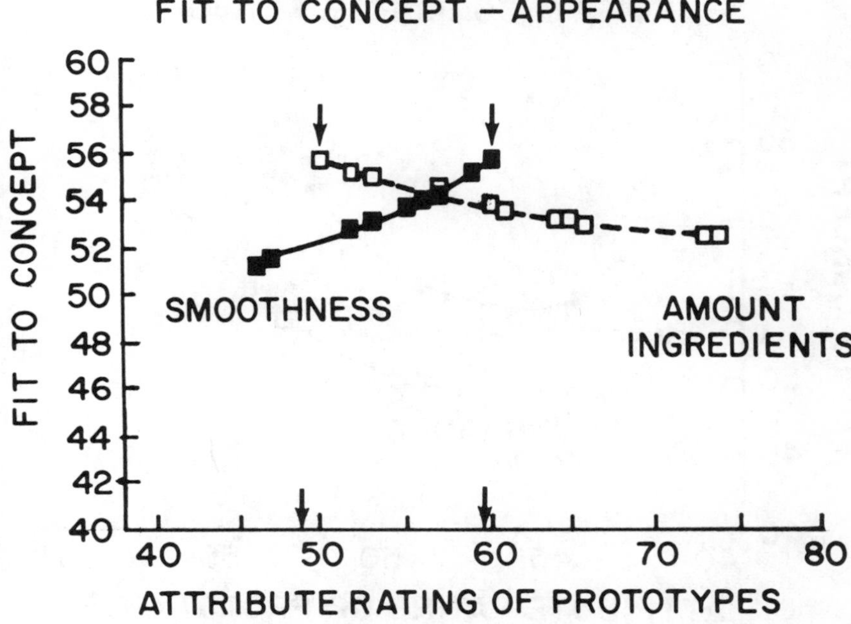

FIG. 14.1. FITTED RELATION BETWEEN APPEARANCE ATTRIBUTES (SMOOTHNESS, AMOUNT OF INGREDIENTS; ABSCISSA) AND RATED FIT OF THE APPEARANCE OF THE PROTOTYPES TO THE CONCEPT (ORDINATE). The vertical arrows denote the point at which the rated fit to the concept for appearance reaches its maximum level. From the attribute ratings one can then find the specific prototypes generating this highest fit.

ing panelists to perform two activities in the same session; evaluate the sensory attributes of the product, and then evaluate fit-to-the-concept. Unfortunately, without systematic formula variation, the product developer does not know what specific formula modifications to make, in order to improve the product so that it accords with the concept.

We saw previously in the chapter on optimization how by systematic formula variations the product developer could quickly decide on the most acceptable formulation, subject to cost or sensory constraints. Can we adapt the technology so that we modify the formulation of a product in such a way that it delivers what the concept promises?

Modifying The Optimization Hill Climbing Routine

When we optimize products we climb a hill, figuratively. At each stage,

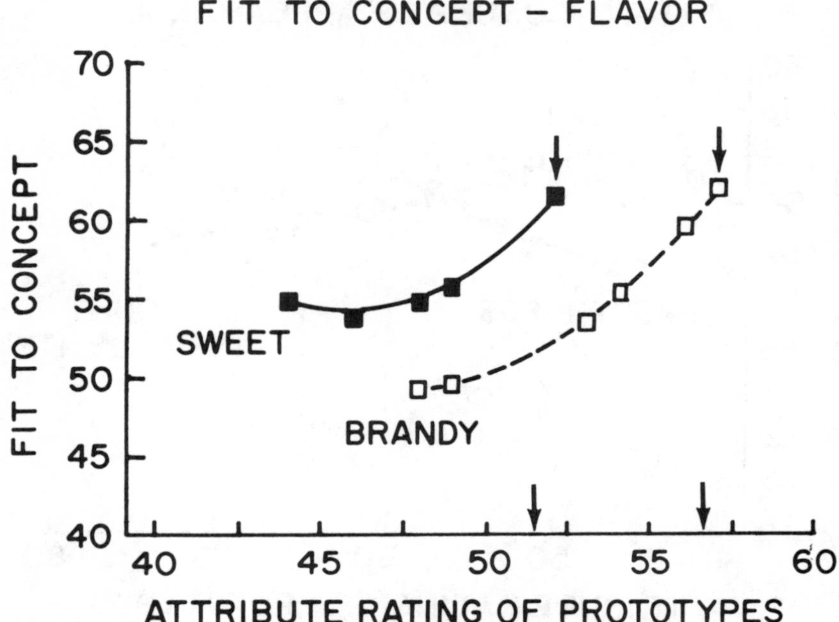

FIG. 14.2. FITTED RELATION BETWEEN FLAVOR ATTRIBUTES (SWEETNESS, BRANDY FLAVOR) AND RATED FIT OF THE FLAVOR PERCEPTION TO THE CONCEPT.
The same conventions hold as in Fig. 14.1.

we try to find that formulation which generates improved acceptance. We try to go as high as possible on the hill, and at the top we find the optimum product.

Let us modify this approach somewhat, and recast it in terms of optimizing the fit or closeness of a product sensory (or image) profile to a predesigned concept profile. Each product generates a response profile from consumers. The consumers may assign sensory ratings, liking ratings, or image ratings. Furthermore, since we know the formula variations, we can develop ad hoc, descriptive models, relating formula variations (and nonlinearities, interactions) to attribute ratings. Indeed, we can model any type of consumer rating provided, as long as we know the formulations of the products, and as long as these formulations vary according to a systematic design.

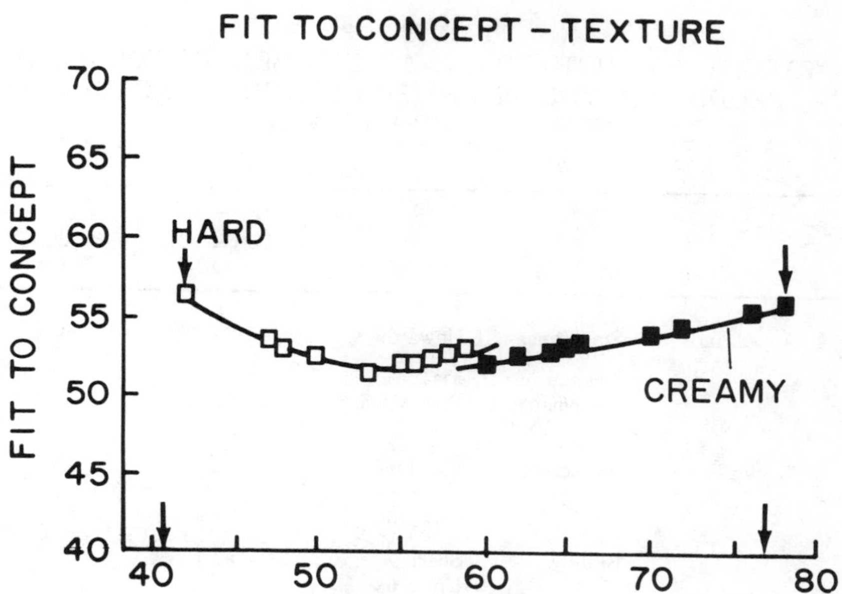

FIG. 14.3. FITTED RELATION BETWEEN TEXTURE ATTRIBUTES (HARDNESS, CREAMINESS) AND THE RATED FIT OF THE TEXTURE PERCEPTION TO THE CONCEPT.
The same conventions hold as in Fig. 14.1.

CASE HISTORY—CHARLOTTE'S CREAM LIQUEURS

Charlotte Campbell founded a small distilled spirits house in the late 1950's. Her main products included a line of fine quality liqueurs, of different flavors. These competed against other liqueurs at the high end of the price range. Many of her consumers perceived a common flavor "signature" in her offerings, unique to her products. Although consumers could not identify the specific notes, they could often distinguish between one of her products and an array of competitors, even on a blind basis. (Similarly, tobacco product developers often can recognize the prototypes from a single company, even though these prototypes represent cigarettes of different tar levels and flavor qualities. The formulator leaves a

TABLE 14.3
TARGET PRODUCTS TO ACT AS REFERENCES FOR R & D PRODUCT DEVELOPMENT FOR BRANDY ICE CREAM CONCEPT PRODUCT MATCH

	Sense Category	Attribute	Pattern	Optimum Perceived Level*	Product Target
A	Appearance	Smoothness	Upwards	60	2, 3, 4
		Amount of Ingredients	Flat Downwards	50	6, 7, 10
B	Taste/Flavor	Sweetness	Flat then Sharp Upwards	52	3
		Brandy	Sharp Upwards	57	5
C	Texture	Hardness	Downwards then Flat	40	3, 4
		Creaminess	Modest Upwards	70-80	1, 2, 5, 10

*Defined as that sensory level at which we see the highest expected rating of "attribute level fits the expectation generated by the concept"

signature or subtle imprint on the product, which carries over from one creation to the next).

In the early 1980's, the market for cream liqueurs expanded dramatically in the U.S. Charlotte Campbell recognized the emerging popularity of this drink category. After attending a number of focus groups conducted across the U.S., with current users of cream liqueurs as participants she put together an aggressive marketing plan to enter the category with her own product. Part of the plan included generating a product which had a distinctive character. The product had to clearly belong to the cream liqueur category, but had to possess the elegance which had come to symbolize the Campbell line.

Concept Formulation

In order to enter the competitive cream liqueur category, Campbell realized that first she had to develop a positioning and a concept. Part of the development process consisted of a search for a unique positioning. After extensive work, with a variety of moderators and focus groups, along with two consultants specializing in new products, she developed her positioning. The positioning consisted of a statement about the "flavor of old Europe, in a drink as modern as today." Along with this positioning (which connoted elegance and robustness at the same time), she commissioned a package designer to create a package for the new launch (Table 14.4).

TABLE 14.4
CONCEPT FOR CHARLOTTE CAMPBELL'S
NEW LIQUEUR PRODUCT

Introducing Charlotte's European Blend Cream Liqueur

Campbell's, one of America's finest distilleries, proudly brings you Charlotte's own EUROPEAN BLEND CREAM LIQUEUR. Combining the freshness of pure cream with a select assortment of European spices, this Cream Liqueur promises you joy in tasting.

Sip European Blend Cream Liqueur, enjoy its aroma, its flavor, and creamy smoothness. Use it like you would any fine liqueur. Enjoy it with friends, and after meals. Light in taste, just thick enough to savor but yet mild and rich to delight even the most discerning palate.

Product Development Guidance And Fitting The Product To The Concept

Our interest in Campbell's product comes from the product side. What sensory characteristics should the new product have, to deliver this unique taste of Europe? Clearly, the concept itself does not promise anything about taste or flavor, nor about color. Yet, the discussions in the focus group continued to generate expectations about the flavor and color. For one, consumers thought that the liqueur would have a mild sweet, rather than a cloying sweet taste. Many expected that the product would have a strong aroma and a creamy/smooth texture.

In the previous sections of this chapter we saw how consumers could evaluate various alternatives, and rate the degree of appropriateness to the concept. However, can we apply the response surface procedures so useful for optimizing a product, to the present case, where we want to match a concept profile?

Experimental Design

In order to use the product modelling, and response surface procedures, we have to develop alternative prototypes whose formulations systematically vary. For the cream liqueurs, we systematically vary the elements in such a way as to create alternative product formulations, differing level of spice blend added aromatic note, sweetener level and alcohol level. By so doing, we generate prototypes varying in the degree to which each fulfills what the concept promises. As a result, we can then adjust the formulations so that the expected ratings assigned to the prototypes match, as closely as possible, the profile of attributes promised by the concept.

For this study, Charlotte Campbell hired a professional blender, with twenty five years of experience in the liqueur blending business. The expert recommended the blend of three levels each of a spice blend (A), aromatic flavoring (B), sweetener (C) and alcohol level (D) (Table 14.5).

Test Procedures With Alcoholic Beverages

Testing alcoholic beverages requires different procedures from testing regular foods. Consumers cannot evaluate the 17 alternative prototypes like they can for snack chips. Indeed, in the most optimistic of cases they can test perhaps four or five alternatives, especially if they have to drink the prototype in order to get an impression of the mouthfeel, and impact at the back of the throat.

In this particular project, Campbell and her research manager decided to test each prototype, using at most 25 consumer ratings per prototype, in view of the developmental nature of the project. Furthermore, she contracted with a local volunteer group, to participate for three evenings. Each panelist would test 3 prototypes each evening, generating a total of 9 ratings per panelist. In total, she needed 25 × 17 or approximately 425 panelist ratings for the entire set. With each panelist rating 9 prototypes over three sessions, this required a total of 48 panelists.

The panelists who participated expressed interest in the category. All had had some experience with cream liqueurs, owing to the growing popularity of the category over the past two years. They constituted the most likely consumers. In order to minimize the total cost of the project at the "field end" (namely, involving panelists), the research director made a large donation to the volunteer social organization and paid a smaller incentive to the individual participants.

Questionnaire

The questionnaire for this study concentrated on three major topics:

(1) Sensory attributes
(2) Liking attributes
(3) Image attributes (e.g. smooth).

Researchers working with alcoholic beverages soon realize that much of consumer's reactions to the beverages comes by way of complex, image reactions (namely, such as high quality, or appropriate for important social occasions). The sensory and acceptance characteristics do have meaning, but the image characteristics outweigh them. Here we concentrate as much as possible on the sensory characteristics to provide R&D direction.

TABLE 14.5
EXPERIMENTAL DESIGN FOR CHARLOTTE'S CREAM LIQUEUR

	A	B	C	D
	Spice Blend	Aromatic Note	Sweetener Level	Alcohol Level
Product				
1	H	H	L	H
2	H	H	L	L
3	H	L	H	L
4	H	L	L	H
5	L	H	H	L
6	L	H	L	H
7	L	L	H	H
8	L	L	L	L
9	H	M	M	M
10	L	M	M	M
11	M	H	M	M
12	M	L	M	M
13	M	M	H	M
14	M	M	L	M
15	M	M	M	H
16	M	M	M	L
17	M	M	M	M
Levels				
L	9.5	0	1.5	13
M	11.0	2.5	2.5	15
H	13.0	5.0	3.5	16.5

*Relative levels shown

Initial Data Analysis

Table 14.6 shows the ratings assigned by the panelists to the 17 prototypes. Note the large differences across prototypes in sensory characteristics, and the differences among the prototypes for the attribute of fits-the-concept (from a low of 24 to a high of 78). The variation in sensory characteristics coupled with the variation in ratings of appropriateness suggests a possible link between formulations, sensory attributes and appropriateness ratings. This linkage allows us to vary the formulations to generate an optimum fit to the concept.

In addition, Table 14.6 (bottom) shows the expected profile of the concept, assigned by the panelists, after they had finished rating the products. Thus, we know what the concept promises on the attributes as well as what the prototypes deliver. Can we adjust the formulation to generate a sensory profile for the prototypes as similar as possible to the sensory profile suggested by the concept?

Developing The Product Model

As we saw in the previous chapter on optimization, we can develop straightforward models relating formula variations to attributes, whether these constitute sensory characteristics, acceptance characteristics, or more complex "image" characteristics. The modeling procedure relates independent formula variables to attributes, using linear, square and cross term values.

Table 14.7 shows the resulting models developed for the liqueurs. Note again that the only terms appearing in the equations comprise those whose T values exceeded 1.0 in absolute magnitude.

Maximizing Rated Fit-To-The-Concept

Our first exercise with the model consists of adjusting the formulations for the liqueur in order to maximize perceived fit-to-the-concept, (Table 14.8, column 2).

Although the panelists directly rated fit-of-product-to-the-concept, in the same session they also estimated the profile of the concept, using the same attributes and scale that they had used to profile the actual products. If, now, we adjust the product formulation to generate a prototype which delivers this desired profile (as connoted by the concept), do we still maintain a high level of acceptance? Or, will we find a dramatic loss of acceptance, if we deliver a product which matches the concept?

The procedure for adjusting the formulations to generate a profile matching (or as close as possible to) a target appears in detail in Table 14.9.

TABLE 14.6
DATABASE OF RATINGS—FOR CHARLOTTE'S LIQUEUR

	FORMULATION				ATTRIBUTE RATINGS								
Sample	Spice A	Aromatic Note B	Sweetener Level C	Alcohol Level D	Liking	Sweetness	Light Flavor	Creamy	Smooth	Thickness	Aroma Intensity	Fits the Concept	Sweet/Spicy
1	13	5	1.5	16.5	64	45	32	34	62	68	79	62	29
2	13	5	1.5	13	40	45	33	32	61	79	80	50	25
3	13	0	3.5	13	71	46	41	22	82	87	89	48	28
4	13	0	1.5	16.5	72	32	36	26	70	76	83	53	21
5	9.5	5	3.5	13	16	58	25	62	41	68	81	20	32
6	9.5	5	1.5	16.5	40	41	36	28	67	81	90	53	26
7	9.5	0	3.5	16.5	34	38	29	40	62	63	76	68	28
8	9.5	0	1.5	13	31	41	24	34	38	55	78	24	27
9	13	2.5	2.5	15	57	46	30	35	53	66	77	60	31
10	9.5	2.5	2.5	15	14	46	27	47	49	66	79	42	28
11	11	5	2.5	15	18	47	21	36	38	55	63	29	24
12	11	0	2.5	15	29	40	27	37	47	63	74	44	27
13	11	2.5	3.5	15	31	58	25	48	55	71	81	46	29
14	11	2.5	1.5	15	79	47	35	30	71	76	84	78	25
15	11	2.5	2.5	16.5	53	49	32	25	59	72	82	61	24
16	11	2.5	2.5	13	58	51	26	48	49	77	89	61	29
17	11	2.5	2.5	15	31	48	30	45	67	72	81	55	24
Concept Profile					—	45	50	60	80	62	78	—	60
Standard Error of Mean					—	3.1	3.5	2.9	3.1	2.9	2.9	—	3.0

*Only test prototypes shown

TABLE 14.7
PARAMETERS OF PRODUCT MODELS RELATING
CREAM LIQUEUR ATTRIBUTES
TO FORMULA VARIABLES

	Liking	Sweetness	Light Flavor	Creamy	Smooth	Thick-ness	Aroma Intensity	Fit Concept	Sweet/ Spicy
Intercept	452	−2.9	−882	1459	−634	−364	529	3165	1076
A	——	——	——	-127.32	51.69	62.08	1.21	-336.55	-117.11
A^2	-4.08	——	——	——	——	——	——	——	0.86
B	111.37	-8.89	-40.58	102.49	——	——	20.33	272.61	58.56
B^2	-2.89	-0.96	-0.46	-0.75	-1.44	-1.62	-1.61	-3.03	-0.18
C	-171.22	——	100.38	-93.80	——	78.71	——	-309.49	-76.70
C^2	18.95	3.10	3.13	——	13.04	-4.29	4.28	6.56	——
D	-49.55	7.89	57.06	-88.08	50.89	——	62.63	-162.83	-50.22
D^2	——	——	0.83	-2.12	——	1.90	2.19	——	——
AB	-2.11	1.06	2.67	-6.03	0.45	0.35	-0.82	——	0.26
AC	8.90	1.29	——	-5.55	——	-1.57	——	30.18	8.41
AD	5.34	-0.37	-5.27	10.18	-3.39	-3.93	——	17.76	5.14
BC	-11.89	1.64	4.88	-12.51	——	1.35	-1.65	-26.41	-5.86
BD	-3.15	——	——	——	——	——	——	-13.09	-3.07
CD	——	-1.92	-8.81	12.80	-4.59	-6.06	-1.36	——	——
F Ratio	5.8	16.0	10.1	9.4	8.8	14.5	10.7	8.3	4.6
R^2	0.93	0.95	0.96	0.95	0.87	0.96	0.93	0.92	0.91
Standard Error of Regression	9.0	2.1	1.9	4.5	5.9	3.7	2.5	6.5	1.5

Adjusting The Formulation To Match The Liqueur Concept Profile

The optimization method, adapted to fit a profile, generated a series of alternative formulations, the closest of which appears in Table 14.8 (column 3).

TABLE 14.8
FITTING A PROFILE BY SYSTEMATIC ADJUSTMENT OF INGREDIENTS

	Concept Promise (Direct Rating)	Maximizing Rated Fit to Concept (Direct Rating)	Fit the Concept Profile	Fit Concept (Liking = 1 Attribute)	Fit Concept Profile (Liking Equal to All Other Attributes Combined)
Formulation					
Spice Blend	—	9.5	9.5	12.8	10.4
Aromatic Note	—	4.4	1.7	0.8	4.3
Sweetener	—	1.5	2.2	3.5	1.5
Alcohol Level	—	13.0	13.4	14.8	13.4
Attributes					
Liking	—	99	30	89	92
Fits Concept	—	[240]*	80	[147]	[186]*
Sweetener	45	77	46	48	41
Light Flavor	50	[-20]*	20	12	10
Creamy	60	135*	60	61	61
Smooth	80	33	43	67	67
Thick	62	48	63	62	62
Aroma Strength	78	92	81	82	82
Sweet Spicy	60	77	38	52	52

*Rating lies beyond bounds tested.

Although we can generate a product which comes close to the desired profile, generally we can never achieve a perfect, 100% congruence because of several factors:

(1) The panelists specify a full profile as the target or goal. Satisfying one attribute by adjusting the formula may make it impossible to satisfy another attribute.

(2) The models do not fit the data perfectly, but provide only a best guess. As a consequence, the final formulation, even if it fits the goal 100%, has error associated with it. Although the model may show a perfect fit, still in reality discrepancies will occur between expected and obtained attribute values.

TABLE 14.9
ALGORITHM TO GENERATE A PRODUCT FORMULATION WHOSE PROFILE LIES AS CLOSE AS POSSIBLE TO A PREDESIGNATED GOAL PROFILE

Step 1. Develop equations relating formula variables to attributes (1 equation for each attribute). The equations may have linear, quadratic and cross terms.

Step 2. Select five points at random, each lying within formulation limits (upper and lower constraints).

Step 3. For each point, calculate its expected attribute profile, using the equations developed in Step 1.

Step 4. Calculate the distance between each of the five points (respectively), and the goal profile. Each attribute can have equal weight in calculating the distance, or one can weigh the attributes differentially. (More important attributes have higher weights.)

Step 5. Determine which of the 5 points generates the largest "distance" between its profile and the goal profile. Call this the "poorest fitting point."

Step 6. Calculate the centroid of the remaining 4 points.

Step 7. Draw a line between the poorest fitting point (from Step 5) and the centroid.

Step 8. "Reflect the poorest point" onto the other side of the centroid, in each dimension using the value 1.2. To make the "reflection" calculate the coordinates of the centroid, and of the poorest point. Assume that the centroid has coordinates (30, 20) for two dimensions, whereas the poorest point has coordinates (10, 14). The distance on X between the centroid (30) and the poorest point (10) equals $(30-10=20)$. Increase that value by a factor of 1.2, or $(20\times1.2=24)$. The new value of X equals 30 (centroid) + 24 (reflection distance) or 54.

Step 9. Follow Steps 8-9 for each coordinate at a time, to obtain new coordinate.

Step 10. For each new coordinate, check that the coordinate values lie within predesignated constraints. If not, and the coordinates lie outside the limit, bring them inside the limit a distance 0.001.

Step 11. This operation generates a new set of points—4 remaining the same, and a fifth which presumably lies closer to the goal profile than it did before.

Step 12. Repeat the steps, until no additional improvement appears in the closeness of fit, by reflecting the point.

Table 14.8 provides an estimate of the attribute profile associated with the various products. Note that the acceptance of this fitted formulation does not match the high level of acceptance achieved when we optimized the single attribute of fit-to-concept (Table 14.8). In general, when panelists provide a profile of a concept, a product satisfying that profile may not achieve optimal acceptance. Quite simply, there exists a discrepancy between what people say they want in a product and what they like most.

If we look more closely at the profiles of the products in Table 14.8, highest fit-to-concept versus delivering the concept attributes, we find the following:

(1) Consumers say they want a really light flavor (desired level = 50). Behaviorally, however, the much heavier flavor appears more appropriate.

(2) Consumers say they want a moderate creaminess (60 in Table 14.8). Behaviorally, when we maximize rated overall fit-to-concept, we find a substantially higher creaminess (135 in Table 14.8).

Researchers and product developers who work with new products recognize the difficulty in generating products which differ from those currently in the market and yet which achieve high acceptance. We know, for instance, that most salted snack foods have a great deal of salt, and owe much of their acceptance to the intense salt taste, which can broaden and enhance other flavor notes. On a concept or purely attitude basis, however, consumers want no or low salt products and a mild tasting product. Direct taste tests quickly reveal that despite the high level of concept acceptance achieved by these low salt snacks, nonetheless a product that delivers against the concept promise will lose acceptance. For high quality cream liqueurs in this case history, we see the same type of dissonance factor operating. Consumers say they want light and moderate creams but find the product delivering those attribute levels generate lower ratings (namely, overall liking and overall fit-to-the-concept).

A Compromise Product—Maximizing Liking and Delivering The Concept Profile

In many cases a marketer or product developer cannot simply make do with the product that generates the highest level of acceptance. Rather, the product must have certain sensory (or physical) characteristics in order to differentiate it from the other competitors, even at the risk of a slightly lower overall acceptance. The present case history shows two alternative products; one which maximizes the rated overall fit-to-concept (Table 14.8, column 2) and the other which maximizes the delivery of a specific attribute profile (Table 14.8, column 3). Can we develop an intermediate product, which has a sufficiently high level of acceptance, but still delivers a product with an attribute profile similar to that communicated by a concept?

To answer this question, let us go back to the optimizing approach used to fit a predesignated concept (Table 14.9). The technique adjusts the formulations in a goal seeking manner. Each new formulation generates a profile and the technique computes the geometric distance between the goal profile (namely, concept generated expectations) and the profile achieved by the test formulation. The search for new and improved formulations continues, as the algorithm attempts to minimize the distance between the two profiles (concept/promise versus prototype/delivery).

One way of achieving an acceptable product consists of making overall liking or purchase intent an integral part of the process. By setting up a high level of liking as a goal (along with sensory profile) one can incorporate acceptance into the distance measure. Furthermore, by making the desired acceptance level very high, one can make acceptance a key factor when fitting a profile.

A second way, compatible with the technique, consists of weighting the different attributes. Until now, the computer algorithm simply tallied up the distances between the two profiles, assigning each distance a weight of 1.0. However, one can assign the distances various weights, with the higher weights pushing the alogrithm to satisfy that attribute first. Thus, by incorporating acceptance into the picture as a goal (with high levels of acceptance as the target), and by weighting the attributes differentially, it becomes possible to develop a compromise product. The product will achieve higher acceptance, because acceptance acts as one of the goals and has a high weight attached to it. (Thus, the algorithm will try to maximize acceptance, because it wants to minimize the distance between product acceptance of the prototype and high goal acceptance promised by the concept). Secondly, because other attributes act as goals, and one can weight these attributes appropriately, the algorithm will "trade-off" some acceptance, to fulfill the alternative goal of fitting the desired sensory profile. In sum, the technique will try to accomplish both goals simultaneously; maximizing acceptance, and delivering a designated profile.

Table 14.8 shows two examples of this compromise, where we have set overall acceptance (purchase intent) of the product as a goal, along with several attributes as promised by the product (columns 4 and 5). Note that by adjusting the weights of the various attributes we can generate a variety of different solutions or prototypes, delivering different levels of acceptance, and different image and sensory characteristics. The exact solution, which alternative or prototype to choose, remains a marketing issue. To what degree does one want to sacrifice overall acceptance to generate a unique product that fulfills the concept?

AN OVERVIEW

Fitting products to concepts constitutes an important area of product development and product testing. The concept gives the product a purpose for existing. The concept creates expectations about the product in the mind of the consumer, whether these expectations take on concrete characteristics or just generalized image impressions.

The traditional methods for fitting a product to a concept consist of asking a consumer to rate the degree of fit between one concept and one product. This chapter has shown two additional methods, simple curves and response surface modeling. These methods provide both insight, and a variety of alternatives to the product developer, rather than providing a single reading (degree of fit).

The reader should bear in mind that quite often consumers really do not know what to expect about a product, based upon reading the concept. Our case history with liqueur revealed that fit-to-the-concept corresponded to degree of liking.

Finally, one should keep in mind that concepts often promise unique product characteristics. A product delivering these unique characteristics may not generate the desired consumer acceptance. It becomes, therefore, a matter of compromise, to generate a product that delivers sufficient uniqueness to support the marketing platform, but maintains enough similarity to products currently on the market to provide sufficient consumer acceptance approbation.

CHAPTER 15

CREATING PANELS FOR PRODUCT DEVELOPMENT AND QUALITY CONTROL: EFFICIENT PROCEDURES AND EXAMPLES

INTRODUCTION

With the growing importance of consumer research in product development and quality control, manufacturers have begun to look for efficient ways to develop panels, for both product development and quality control. In the traditional-minded companies, R&D group leaders and vice presidents have sought to develop and maintain in-house panels, comprising a few experts. These panels generally deal with a limited set of product categories, which they evaluate intensively over an extended period of time. During the course of this period, panelists spend a great deal of time working on the actual paneling or evaluation of the products, in order to guide product development and/or quality control.

This chapter deals with the development of panels, comprising consumers, who can act as guides in the development process, or in the quality control process. Because the approach deals with consumers, instead of in-house experts, it differs from the traditional methods used by many practitioners in sensory analysis. However, over a period of years, the author has seen a number of companies switch from using in-house experts to consumers because of financial considerations and because of the greater flexibility and productivity of paid consumers over in-house experts.

Consumers Versus Experts

Consumer panels differ from expert panels and both serve different purposes. Table 15.1 contrasts these two uses. Expert panels find their greatest use early in the development cycle. Although many practitioners develop formalized procedures for getting expert data and processing it,

TABLE 15.1
COMPARISON OF EXPERT VS. CONSUMER PANELS FOR PRODUCT RESEARCH

Panel Size

Expert: 4-10

Consumer: 25-50

Employment

Expert: Often in-house employees.

Consumer: Often local residents (generally non-employees, but sometimes companies use employees for broad scale testing).

Period of Training

Expert: Usually weeks to months.

Consumer: Little if any (except for familiarization).

Period of Participation

Expert: Weeks to years.

Consumer: Generally once for a particular project.

Specific Sensory Acuity

Expert: Often measured at start of study, sometimes a key qualifier.

Consumer: Rarely measured, not usually of interest.

Category Usage and Purchase Behavior

Expert: May or may not use product at home.

Consumer: Generally a category user, qualified on basis of usage.

Remuneration

Expert: Rare, participation a function of social and corporate dynamics.

Consumer: Frequent, participated motivated by remuneration.

Ability to Focus on Task

Expert: High, interrupted quite often by conflicting corporate responsibility.

Consumer: High, because of payment, low if not paid.

Actual Cost Per Hour for Participation

Expert: Real overhead ($30-$60 per hour) and opportunity cost for interrupted work. Out of pocket costs do not show up on "bottom line," but real costs definitely exist.

Consumer: Approximately $10/hour plus recruitment costs. Initially, appears expensive, but actually costs less in real dollars (factoring in overhead, etc.).

just as many use the experts on a "catch as catch can" basis, to provide judgment about prototypes during the initial development stages. Thus, these experts represent a resource, for feedback, not necessarily used in the manner intended. The sheer pressure of development work, and the conflicts in the allocation of time between panel work and other job related duties eventually wreak havoc even on the most enthusiastic and disciplined evaluation team. The work still gets done, but the original timing and disciplined evaluation by a group turns into an evaluation by qualified individuals at various times in a day. The panel turns into a collection of individuals, not a coherent group working together.

With the growing sophistication of product developers, and the increasing interest of marketing researchers in the early stage development process, we have seen the emergence of consumer panels for early stage guidance. These panels replace the more traditional expert panels. By using consumer panelists, paid for their participation and drawn from the local community, the product developer can tailor a panel to specific needs, and work with the panelists over an extended period of time, intensively if required. Money motivates people, and the opportunity to earn $10 or more per hour to participate suffices to entice many people to participate.

This chapter presents an approach, wherein the panels developed comprised consumers, rather than in-house experts, but where the consumers participated for an extended period, rather than just for one session alone. Thus, the case histories provide an amalgamation of procedures used by traditional sensory analysts who work with expert panels chosen from in-house workers, along with procedures developed by marketing researchers who generally confine their interest to consumers for a limited period of time.

Product Development Guidance—The Scott Cake Company

Don Scott founded a small, regional cake manufacturing company in 1963, in Maine. Over a period of 12 years the company grew at approximately 20% per year, blossoming into a well-known and highly respected New England company. Don Scott began by operating the company as a one-man show. Eventually, however, the pressures to manage a growing company led to the formalization of R&D and marketing, and eventually to an increased R&D function in the development of new products.

Don Scott's extensive experience with baked goods led him to recommend a panel for the ongoing direction of R&D. He recognized that the panel would have to represent the tastes of the consumers who purchase his cake products. He also recognized the possibility that by using the same panelists over and over he might develop a nonrepresentative group of self-taught experts, who would reject new products to which they had not become accustomed.

After a great deal of investigation into current procedures, Scott suggested that his R&D group develop a panel of consumers in their local market (a suburb of Portland, Maine). These consumers would comprise housewives and working men who purchase and consume Scott's cakes. None of the panel would come from either employees, or immediate relatives of employees. Furthermore, the panelists would participate in the guidance panel over an extended period (2 years or more) but not more frequently than once very two months. In this way, Scott and his R&D director could assure continuity of the panel and could train the panelists, when necessary, for specific projects.

A key benefit of Scott's overall plan, often not immediately apparent but very critical, consists of the relative availability of panel participants. In a manufacturing plant, panelists can participate only if their participation takes precedence over other activities. After a while, availability becomes a problem. With consumers in the local area, availability never becomes a problem. Scott's R&D director realized that she could recruit 50 or more individuals to participate. Each panel might comprise 15 individuals out of these 50, a proportion that guaranteed a full quota for each panel meeting.

Developing The Panel For Cake Testing

The mechanics of developing Scott's panel proceeded fairly smoothly and rather rapidly. Once R&D received the necessary funding to recruit individuals and pay them, the R&D director appointed a panel leader. The panel leader, chosen from the R&D group, had had some experience with product testing and sensory evaluation. She put an advertisement in the local paper, soliciting participants. A total of 80 people answered the advertisement. From the 80, 12 did not qualify, because they did not consume cakes, or they did not have the time available. Of the remaining 68, most responded that they would enjoy participating in the panel.

As preparation for the panel, the panel leader scheduled short interviews (20 minutes each), with groups of 8 individuals. During the short interviews, the panel leader and her two assistants enlarged on the purpose of the test. Each potential participant filled out a questionnaire about food likes and dislikes, purchase and consumption history, etc. This information constituted background information about the panelist.

Screening For Acuity And For Taste Preferences

Traditionally, one reads about expert panelists whose participants undergo screening to assure taste and smell acuity. Quite often these screening tests do not represent the ultimate task that the panelists will have to perform in the study. The screening tests may thus lack validity.

The R&D director developed a set of tasks representing the type of evaluations that the panelists would eventually perform. The screening tasks required the panelist to rate the perceived intensity of various prototypes on appearance, aroma, taste/flavor, and texture dimensions. The stimuli comprised cakes, systematically varied in physical composition to generate a noticeable range of each sensory characteristic. The panelists evaluated samples in each set (namely, appearance set, aroma set), rating perceived intensity on a 0-100 point scale. Then, the panel leader correlated each panelist's rating of perceived intensity with the physical concentration. Panelists qualified if their ratings of perceived intensity correlated reasonably well with the physical variable (Table 15.2).

Based upon these screening criteria, approximately ⅔ of the panelists appeared able to discriminate. Of course, the R&D director set a relatively lenient criterion (namely, the correlation between physical variation and attribute rating had to exceed 0.7). The physical stimuli within a set (e.g., texture set) differed sufficiently, so that a side-by-side comparison of adjacent levels of a product would clearly reveal the differences. The panelists did not have to pass an esoteric screening test, therefore. Rather, they simply had to prove their ability to "track" the physical levels of a stimulus. Scott's interest in developing the panel lay in guidance provided by the panel for making relatively large changes in physical formulations, not in a panelist's ability to pick up minor differences between products.

In terms of general approaches to panel development, the foregoing procedure differs somewhat from the standard methods, which rely upon ability to discriminate small differences. This author believes that discrimination ability, tested with products varying ever so slightly from each other, does not help product developers, who have to make large scale modifications. Practitioners who screen panelists on ability to discriminate, or to detect very low levels of stimuli may mistake sensory acuity with ability to perceive important product differences. The panel developed by Scott and his R&D director comprised individuals who could clearly pick up differences among products varying in meaningful ways. Note also that a vast majority of panelists (66%) passed the screening test. These panelists possessed normal acuity and sensitivity, and most importantly, could accurately rate changes in products varied in ingredients.

Developing A Language For The Guidance Panel

At the inception of the program, the R&D director recognized that the panel would have to evaluate a large number of cakes, and provide development guidance. Hence, the panelists had to share a common language and scale. Early in the program, when the panelists met in small groups of 10 to discuss their impressions of products, most of the panelists used a limited number of terms to describe their perceptions of the various

TABLE 15.2
SCREENING STIMULI USED TO ESTABLISH PANELIST DISCRIMINATION ABILITY

Appearance Set

4 angel food cakes, systematically varied in the amount of added food dye (0, 2, 4, 6 relative units of dye).

Aroma Set

4 angel food cakes, systematically varied in the amount of orange flavoring added (0, 3, 10, 30 relative units added of flavoring).

Taste Set

4 angel food cakes, systematically varied in the amount of sweetener (sucrose) added to the mix (1, 2, 4, 8 relative units).

Texture Set

4 angel food cakes, systematically varied in the level of emulsifier added (to make the product softer). (0, 2, 4, 6 relative units).

Panelist Task

For each test set, the panelist had to rate perceived intensity of the appropriate attribute, e.g., for texture the panelist had to rate each product on softness, with the highest softness possible equalling 100, and the lowest softness possible equalling 0. Within that 0-100 range the panelist had to rate each of the 4 products, but did not have to use the entire range.

cakes. Many terms belonged correctly to sensory characteristics (e.g., sweetness, sponginess, softness, fruit flavors, sweet aroma). At the same time, other words continued to emerge, drawn more from the world of advertising than from actual product evaluation. Terms such as richness, filling, natural, heavy, etc., continued to reappear from session to session. These terms did not refer to sensory characteristics, but to overall impressions. The panelists did agree amongst themselves as to the meaning of the words, but could not pin down the meaning to actual sensory impressions.

Developing Terminology

To develop a set of terms for the cakes, the panel leader first conducted discussion sessions. From these sessions she quickly narrowed down the terms to a few dozen. Some of the terms in Table 15.3 have a shared meaning among consumers (e.g., sweetness). Others, such as off-taste, need explanation. Still others, such as adhesiveness (sticks to the tongue, the teeth, etc.) required more detailed explanation. During the two initial training sessions (held at the start of the project), the panelists soon learned the meaning of each term, and some reference standards which illustrated high versus low levels of the attribute.

In order to finalize the attributes, the panel leader selected the 10 most important attributes (based upon the consumer's own opinions), and set these up as references, along with three examples, which would serve as high, medium, and low levels of the attributes. The full set of references come to 30 (10 attributes × 3 levels = 30). Each panelist had an opportunity to learn these standards over a two-week period, by coming into the R&D facility, at his or her leisure, and practicing with the standards. The stimuli for the standards comprised actual products, readily available on the market for texture and appearance, and some specially made chemicals at various dilutions for aroma. For taste evaluations of cake, R&D developed specific products, incorporating key ingredients at various concentrations, to illustrate sensory gradations.

Results From The Early Stage Training

The training or more properly orientation and familiarization sessions lasted two weeks (three sessions, two hours per session). During this time the panelists had an opportunity to become familiar with the standards, and the scale. Although at first the panelists experienced difficulty with assigning absolute values on the 0-100 point scale to match the references, they quickly learned how to do so. At the end of the two-week period, and after having spent 5-6 hours total, the panelists understood the scale and the reference standards. In effect, they "locked in" on reference points for specific attributes.

Using The Panel To Guide Research & Development

The panel saw its greatest use in the early stages of product development, even prior to a consumer panel test with a local church group. As the product developer produced new prototypes, the panel leader assembled a group of participants for a two hour test. During this test, the panelists evaluated the current products under development, along with competitors. They profiled the existing products, the competitor products, and the point (on the scales) that they thought the prototypes should

TABLE 15.3
TERMS USED TO DESCRIBE CAKES—FROM FOCUS GROUPS

Appearance Terms

Grainy
Dark
Light
Large
Fluffy
Mottled
Smooth on Top
Fine Texture
Dense
White
Creamy
Depth of Color

Aroma Terms

Fresh Baked
Strong
Sweet
Orangy
Warm

Taste/Flavor Terms

Sweet
Fruity
Citrus
Orangy
Lemony
Flat Taste
Vanilla Taste
Sweet Sticky Taste
Harsh Taste
Strong Taste

Texture Terms

Soft
Hard
Spongy
Chewy
Melts in Mouth
Springy
Doughy
Grainy
Smooth

TABLE 15.3 (Continued)
TERMS USED TO DESCRIBE CAKES—FROM FOCUS GROUPS

Texture Terms
Crispy
Tears Apart in Mouth
Sticks to Teeth
Fluffy
Image/Acceptance
Liking
High Quality
Fresh Baked
Home Made
Store Bought
Stale
Unique

achieve, based upon reading a concept statement about the product. This information about desired scale values, along with reference standards helped the product developer pinpoint problem areas and deficits.

How Does This Expertized Panel Differ From a Consumer Panel

The approach outlined above appears similar to what we have discussed previously for consumer panels. The exceptions consist of the repeated use of a single group of individuals and their training to profile a product in terms of level of attributes. In consumer research thus far, we have had panelists profiling existing and competitor products, but not generally used their input in terms of "desired level" as a key to product development (except for product-concept matching).

The panelists in this study do represent experts. At the same time, we clearly see that the panelists represent consumers in the community, who use the product, rather than convenience samples of panelists chosen from the plant or the office. In a sense we have created a new type of panelist; an "expertized" consumer. The panelist participates for a relatively extended period of time (perhaps 1-2 months), and may participate for 8-12 sessions. However, the panelist does not necessarily participate in other panels, nor does he or she act as a generalist, able to profile and direct other product categories. Rather, panelists come together as a task force to accomplish a limited product development objective. Participants in the panel still represent consumers, but this time a slightly more educated group (in terms of descriptive analysis). During the short two-week orientation they have learned the language for describing the particular product, and subsequently they provide clearer direction. They describe and guide product developers to produce a product that these panel participants like. In effect, the panel comprises a group of consumers who have enhanced their communication abilities.

DEVELOPING A PANEL FOR QUALITY CONTROL

The previous sections dealt with consumer "expertized" panels, devoted to specific products, and coming together as a task force. Expert panels have other uses, with quality control constituting a prime example. One can monitor day-to-day production of products using instruments, but quite often the defects which emerge do not register on a screen or a physical detector. It takes the eyes, nose and mouth of a consumer to recognize that somehow this batch differs from the products previously developed.

Quality control requires panelists who know the product well, and who can spot deviations from the norm. These panelists can undergo extensive training to become true experts. On the other hand, the panel can be comprised of consumers who provide repeated evaluations over a period of time, with their intitial evaluations constituting the norm for the product. The former method which required intensive orientation and training, has met with a great deal of favor in many companies, because it insures ongoing sameness of products. However, the panelists do not represent consumers, and the differences that they perceive from batch to batch may not reflect consumer perceptible differences. In contrast, the latter group, comprising consumers who test the same batch over a period of time, better simulates consumer reactions because the panelists do not undergo detailed training. Instead, the consumer panelists provide an ongoing measurement of the product.

This chapter presents a case history using the latter, consumer-oriented panel, as an alternative to experts.

The Light Cigarette Smoker Panel

Kohl Cigarette Company, Inc., manufactures a full line of cigarettes, ranging from full tar/flavor, down to ultra lights. Recently, it has begun a program of quality control in its light cigarettes (low tar), based upon complaints it received from loyal customers around the country. Several of its batches went out of spec, leading to dissatisfaction and potential loss of business from consumers who had become used to, and expected certain characteristics. Many complained of an unusual flavor while others complained of harshness greater than what normally existed in their regular smoke.

Carl Kohl, president of Kohl Cigarette Company, chaired a meeting with the aim of developing a group devoted to quality control. At this meeting, R&D, marketing and production discussed alternative methods for insuring quality control. The production group had already instituted a small, informal quality control panel, comprising individuals who had spent years in the tobacco business, primarily at the Kohl Cigarette Company and who knew the products intimately. Many of the production people knew the cigarette business quite well, and could recognize product defects almost immediately. Quite a number could even identify the type of defect and the probable source because of their detailed knowledge. This production group constituted a valuable resource in the quality control program, that Carl Kohl recognized as invaluable for the effort.

During the meeting, marketing lobbied for the use of a consumer panel to assure quality. The director of marketing, along with one of the marketing research managers, brought up the point that they had to link the in-depth knowledge of the production group with consumer perceptions. Many subtle distinctions that the product group felt to constitute departures from the product might actually elude consumers. In other cases, the research manager noted, consumer tastes might change. New cigarettes demanded a taste panel devoted to those particular cigarettes. The production people, with their grounding in years of work at Kohl Cigarette could not easily "shift gears" to work on quality control of a variety of cigarettes, especially the new ones that marketing had recently introduced.

Developing The Consumer Panel

After the discussion, the group decided to develop a consumer based quality control panel. The panel would constitute 100 smokers, based across the United States, all of whom smoked the particular brand (Kohl Preludes), a light cigarette in the low tar range. A marketing service group under contract to Kohl Cigarette Company developed the panel, which comprised 50 individuals in 3 cities. Although the original specifications called for 100 panelists, the marketing research group recognized the need for a larger panel, because of the inevitable attrition. Panelists would leave the group, either from loss of interest, or because they moved out of the city, making it difficult to keep in contact with the testing program.

A panel of consumers in three separate markets provides the Kohl Cigarette Company with a unique opportunity to sample the honest reactions of consumers in different parts of the country (east, midwest, west). In contrast, the traditional quality control panel so often used by manufacturers comprises consumers or experts in one market, generally in fact who work at one location (namely, the plant site). Although both types of panels have merit, the geographically dispersed panel allows a truer reading of consumer reactions. One need not worry about personal biases as much when working with a dispersed panel. In contrast, in-house panels, at the plant site or at the R&D facility, fall prey to biases. Participants try to second guess the test to find things wrong, so that they achieve an additional measure of stature. A dispersed panel, most of whom do not know each other, reduces much of this bias and provides for better answers.

A Double Panel

In view of the merits and deficits inherent both in in-house and external panels, the marketing research director, Meg Campbell, decided to develop a double panel, comprising in-house experts and external consumers. The double panel worked as follows.

(1) The in-house experts would sample each day's run for the cigarette, evaluating the cigarette on a variety of attributes. The in-house experts developed their own vocabulary and set of standards. They spent two weeks developing the criteria, since most needed only a short time to "come up to speed." The six individuals which constituted the panel all had had previous experience in the evaluation of cigarettes, each having worked at Kohl Cigarettes for at least five years. Additionally and importantly, each participant in the panel actually smoked the low tar entry on a regular basis, independent of participating on the panel, and prior to participating.

(2) If the in-house panel (base of six panelists) noticed a discrepancy between the day's production and their mental concept of the gold standard for the product, they would report the discrepancy on a form, shown in Table 15.4. Panelists smoked at least three cigarettes per day of the batch and recorded their impressions in the form shown. The panelists did not meet as a group to discuss their impressions, but rather evaluated the production run at their convenience during the day.

(3) If 2 of the 6 in-house panelists noticed a discrepancy that they considered important, then the quality control manager met with the panel members to determine the specific nature of the departure from specification. Meetings with the in-house panelists also occurred at random intervals as well, in order to insure that panelists would report their impressions honestly. Quite often, if panel participants do not like meetings because it interferes with their work, they will refrain from reporting pro-

TABLE 15.4
EXAMPLE OF FORM USED BY EXPERT PANELISTS AT THE KOHL COMPANY FOR THE EVALUATION OF DAILY PRODUCTION OF LIGHT CIGARETTES

Expert Panelist Name_________________Date____________Batch Number____________

Using the 0-5 rating scale, please rate this batch:

A. Flavor intensity upon first smoking __________

B. Mouth full of smoke __________

C. Impact/scratch at back of throat __________

D. Full flavored impression __________

E. Flavor intensity after ½ cigarette finished __________

F. Overall difference from reference (0 = identical) __________

G. Comments: __________

____

____

____

duction discrepancies, in order to not attend a panel meeting. By holding meetings at random intervals even when all production falls into specification, the quality control manager and the panel leader dissociate the meetings from the actual discovery of out-of-spec products.

(4) After the meeting, if the panel still agreed that the production batch fell out-of-spec, and seriously so, the quality assurance manager would then submit the product for testing, to the panel distributed in the three markets. Panelists in each market would receive a phone call, instructing them to expect the product in the mail. The panelists would receive the product, along with instructions about rating the product. Each panelist had a chance to evaluate one full package of current product (known to fall in-spec) and the test product (suspected of falling out-of-spec). The panelists would rate each package of cigarettes separately on a battery of attributes, and would not know which package corresponded to the product in question. Table 15.5 shows the questionnaire filled out by the consumer quality control panelists.

TABLE 15.5
EXAMPLE OF FORM USED BY CONSUMER PANELISTS OUTSIDE THE KOHL COMPANY FOR THE QUALITY CONTROL EVALUATION OF PROBLEM BATCHES OF LIGHT CIGARETTES

Panelist Name ______________________ Date ____________

ID	Please write in your 3 digit ID number
PRODUCT	Please write in the number 923
CD	Please write in the number "2"

PLEASE SMOKE THE PACK OF THE FIRST CIGARETTE, 103, AND RATE THESE CHARACTERISTICS:

Cigarette 103

A. How strong does the cigarette taste (0 = weak, 100 = strong).

B. How much of a mouthful of smoke do you get from this cigarette:
(0 = a little, 100 = a lot)

C. How much of a "hit" or impact do you get at the back of your mouth:
(0 = a little, 100 = a lot)

D. How full flavored does this cigarette taste:
(0 = flavor washed out, 100 = full flavored)

E. How much do you like this cigarette:
(0 = hate, 100 = love)

F. Where does this cigarette fall relative to your current brand:
(0 = very similar to my current brand, 100 = very different)

NOW, PLEASE SMOKE THE PACK OF THE SECOND CIGARETTE, 467, AND RATE THESE CHARACTERISTICS:

Cigarette 467

G. How strong does the cigarette taste:
(0 = weak, 100 = strong)

H. How much of a mouthful of smoke do you get from this cigarette:
(0 = a little, 100 = a lot)

I. How much of a "hit" or impact do you get at the back of your mouth:
(0 = a little, 100 = a lot)

J. How full flavored does this cigarette taste:
(0 = flavor washed out, 100 = full flavored)

K. How much do you like this cigarette:
(0 = hate, 100 = love)

L. Where does this cigarette fall relative to your current brand:
(0 = very similar, 100 = very different)

(5) After filling out the questionnaire, the panelists mailed their answer forms back to a central receiving office. They used mark sense cards (Fig. 15.1). Mark sense cards, whose circles the panelists darken after they assign their ratings, allows the quality control group to process the data quite rapidly, and perform statistical tests on the results, virtually overnight, even from a panel of hundreds of individuals. Within 7 days of discovery of a major problem (according to the in-house group) the Kohl Cigarette Company could thus obtain definitive consumer feedback from a reasonably sized panel of 150 individuals, approximately 50 in each of 3 cities.

(6) The reader should keep in mind that the two stage quality control system does not always use both stages. Only when the in-house experts feel that the product has substantially departed from specifications do they call in the confirmatory consumer quality control panel. In this way, it becomes possible to check the results of the in-house panel. Production does not depend upon a small group of individuals for the final say. Rather, the in-house panel, always available for evaluation and continually testing production runs, raises a red flag. The validation of that flag and warning comes from a separate, confirmatory panel of smokers, chosen from the actual consumer population, not from the local R&D production group.

AN OVERVIEW

This chapter discussed two types of panels; consumer panels geared to product development, and hybrid expert/consumer panels geared for quality control. As sensory analysis, product testing and quality control find increasing use in industry, management has become more aware of the need to integrate panel data into the processes of development and quality assurance. The traditional panel methods, using in-house experts, continues to find acceptance. However, an increasing number of manufacturers report difficulties with the panel, including unduly high cost to train participants, and panel burnout. After a few months, panel members stop participating with the same eagerness with which they began.

Consumer-oriented panels, even for early stage development and for quality control, reduce some of the problem associated with panel burnout. Consumers provide a never-ending, renewable resource of participants. Monetary remuneration insures the continued participation and in the end dramatically lowers the cost of the people, in real dollars. This author advocates using consumers, and training them, if necessary, as panel members. The productivity in panel information should increase substantially, and the problems in assembling and maintaining the panel should decrease commensurately, by using consumers, either in place of in-house experts (albeit with the necessary training) or in conjunction with the in-house expert, to reduce the panel workload.

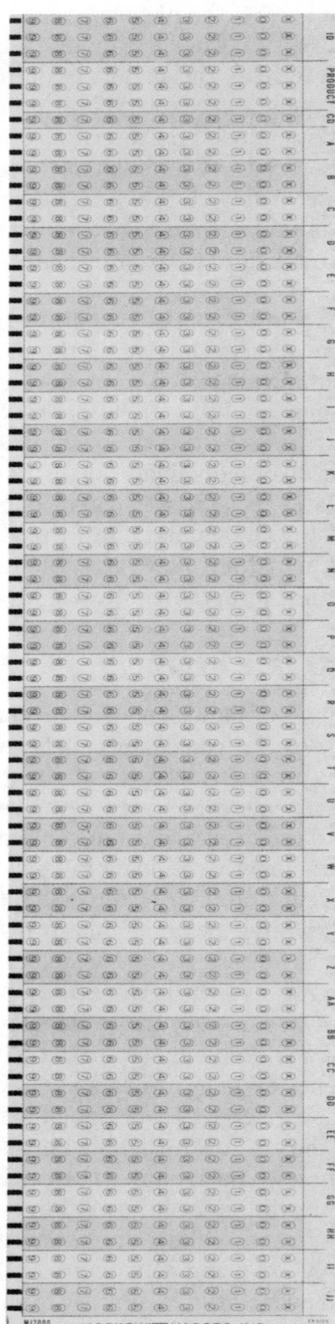

FIG. 15.1. EXAMPLE OF A MARK SENSE CARD, USED BY PANELISTS TO RECORD THEIR IMPRESSIONS OF THE CIGARETTES.

After writing in their ratings, they darken in the circles, so that a scanner can read the cards. Note that all numbers must have two digits. To record a 100, the panelist darkens in the two x's at the top of the columns of circles.

REFERENCES

BRANDT, D. A. 1964. Quality control in the distilled spirits industry. Lab. Practice *13,* 717-719.

CHARM, S. E., LEARSON, R. J., RONSIVALLI, L. J. and SCHWARTZ, M. 1972. Organoleptic technique predicts refrigeration shelf life of fish. Food Technol. *26,* 65-68.

COLSON, T. J. and BASSETTE, R. 1962. Consumer and taste panel evaluations of some methods for controlling feed flavors in milk. J. Dairy Sci. *45,* 182-186.

DRITSCHEL, M. E. 1970. How to evaluate margarine quality. Food Engin. *42,* 90-93.

HARRIES, J. M. 1960. The quality control of food by sensory assessment. In: *The Quality Control of Foods.* S.C.I. Monograph, 8, 128-137.

HENING, J. C. 1949. Operation of a routine testing group in a small laboratory. Sci. Monthly *69,* 130.

KIRKPATRICK, M. E., LAMB, J. C., DAWSON, E. H. and EISEN, I. N. 1957. Selection of a taste panel for evaluating the quality of processed milk. In: Methodology Of Sensory Testing, IFT SYMPOSIUM, Pittsburgh, Food Technology, 11, Supplement, 3-8.

LIMING, N. 1966. Consistency of a trained taste panel to test off-flavor of milk sample. J. Dairy Sci. *49,* 628-630.

MARCUSE, S. 1947. Applying control chart methods to taste testing. Food Industries *19,* 316-318.

MARCUSE, S. 1945. An application of the control chart method to the testing and marketing of foods. Amer. Statistical Assoc. *40,* 214-222.

MARTIN, S. L. 1973. Selection and training of judges. Food Technol. *22,* 22, 24, 26.

MEURSING, E. 1969. Quality control of cocoa powder: Methods for analyzing 7 properties. Manufacturing Confectioner *49,* 43-47.

MILLER, P. G., NAIR, J. H. and HARRIMAN, A. J. 1955. A household and laboratory type of panel for testing consumer preference. Food Technol. *9,* 445-449.

PARSON, W. A. 1971. Organoleptic assessment as a quality control medium. Food Industry In South Africa *24,* 5-11.

STEWART, R. A. 1971. Sensory evaluation and quality assurance, Food Technol. *25,* 401-404.

TOMPKINS, R. G. 1949. Organoleptic tests in the food industry. II. The use of a "tasting panel" for assessing the culinary quality of dried vegetables. Chemistry And Industry *11,* 167-168.

ZURCHER, C. 1971. Training tasters to recognize flavour faults in beers. Wallerstein Laboratories Communications *34,* 119-200.

CHAPTER 16

CATEGORY APPRAISAL OF FOODS USING CONSUMER EVALUATIONS

INTRODUCTION

This chapter deals with the evaluation of entire categories of food products. It looks at methods by which a marketer or product tester can assess the competitive frame of products tested several ways (e.g., blind, without identification; branded, with identification, image, such as by print advertisement or package alone, without benefit of product).

Quite often marketers and management want to evaluate entire categories of products, rather than focusing attention on one or two entries in the market. A company may wish to enter a new category, but before doing so may want to know the strengths or weaknesses of the competition. In other cases the company may wish to acquire a new subsidiary. The profit and loss (P&L) statements going back over the years provide one indication of financial health. Market share information, from such auditing services as Nielsen, provide another. A category appraisal, evaluating consumer reactions to actual products, provides a third bank of information that may actually indicate problems that the Nielsen and accounting data do not.

CASE HISTORY—MEXICAN FOODS

Background

The Admiral Foods Company grosses approximately 2.1 billion dollars in food sales each year, but under a variety of subsidiary names. Barbara Harris, president of the company and chief executive officer, developed her company by acquisitions. In each acquisition, she and her financial and marketing groups attempted to find companies with a strong product line. Through the resources of Admiral Foods, the management team then infused a broader vision into the company. Sometimes they took local products, and through marketing skill alone they brought the lines into national distribution. With her staff of skilled R&D product developers, Harris also refined the products to appeal to a broader base of consumers. Other times she instructed R&D to tailor the products so that the taste appealed to segments of consumers in other markets.

An analysis of secondary sources of information revealed that the Mexican food category showed great promise. Consumption of Mexican foods, at restaurants and now in the home, continued to grow at an accelerating rate across the U.S. The category appeared to hold great promise for Admiral Foods because of the potential of a national line of products. Admiral Foods already had developed lines of sauces (not Mexican) and frozen foods (primarily entrees), so it did possess both the requisite technical and marketing expertise in two key categories appropriate for Mexican foods (namely, hot sauces and frozen entrees).

The Key Business Issues Underlying The Audit Of Mexican Food

(1) Should The Admiral Foods Company get into the Mexican food business?

(2) If yes, what opportunities present themselves in terms of specific products?

(3) If yes, what specifically should The Admiral Foods Company do to help insure a successful entry?

Developing The Research Questions For The Category Appraisal

The foregoing Questions 1 through 3 concerned general business issues. This section lays out the research issues that one can answer, using consumer inputs.

(1) How do existing products fare in this category, according to consumer ratings of acceptance? Do consumers perceive wide ranges in acceptability from product to product (either of the same type, from different manufacturers, or of different types, from one or several manufacturers)?

(2) What drives acceptance; raw product performance on a blind basis, or branding, due to identification of the product and the manufacturer?

(3) What messages do the various products send in terms of advertising? Furthermore, to what aspects of the advertisements do consumers attend? Can we uncover consumer "hot buttons" or specific messages which enhance acceptance, and thus enhance the likelihood of a product success?

(4) Can we uncover segments of consumers? Refining this question further, can we discover segments of consumers showing different taste preferences? Or, consumers showing different sensitivities to advertising messages (e.g., health oriented versus convenience oriented). What products appeal to these segments?

(5) If we uncover segments, can we discover segments possessing a sizeable number of consumers (opportunity), with few products currently in the segment? If so, we may enter that segment more easily.

(6) What should R&D do to enter the segment, in terms of modifying existing products to appeal to the segment?

(7) What should marketing and advertising do to better communicate key elements that will excite the potential consumer?

The Mexican Food Market (Frozen Entrees)—Background Information

Using secondary data sources, the marketing research director, Marten Lenrow, and the director of marketing, Don Passaglia, compiled information about the Mexican food category, pertaining specifically to frozen entrees. They discovered, from attitude and usage studies, and from menu census data, that the market segments in a variety of ways, such as by eating occasion (snack versus meal), type of food (entree versus side dish), frequency of consumption (everyday versus ceremonial/entertainment), flavor type (hot versus mild), and market (northeast versus west versus Tex/Mex). Quite often the information available from the secondary sources consists of aggregate consumer behavior. No one knew from the data thus far collected whether consumers liked the types of entrees they purchased and ate, whether the consumers wanted new types of entrees, and what specifically about the Mexican food category they liked or disliked, respectively.

Focusing Attention On Wrapped Entrees In The Frozen Food Compartment

Admiral Foods had developed a large business in frozen foods and had the technology and distribution to support a line of frozen entrees. The recognition by the marketing manager, Passaglia, and by the marketing researcher, Lenrow, that consumers continued to increase their consumption of Mexican food focused increased attention on the opportunities available in this market. At a strategy meeting, the directors of the corporation decided to explore the opportunities further, concentrating on wrapped entree items (frozen enchiladas, burritos, tacos). Based upon several focus groups in various parts of the company, the directors quickly learned that these frozen entrees provided several key benefits.

(1) The frozen entree connoted value added, because frozen foods in general held great appeal to the middle and upper income housewife. Frozen connoted quality and freshness. The Admiral Foods Company prided itself on its quality image, so that the line of frozen Mexican entrees fitted right in with the corporate strategy and long term goals.

(2) Demographically, an increasing number of women work. Frozen entrees have the added value of convenience, along with quality, a characteristic appealing to the working woman.

(3) Visibility of the items stood out as a benefit, because the line comprised entrees. This visibility would enhance sales, and pay back the cost of development, advertising and promotion. Traditionally, The Admiral Foods Company spent a great deal of its revenue on advertising and promotion. Analysis after analysis pointed to the need for Admiral Foods to invest in products with visibility to justify these expenditures.

THE CATEGORY AUDIT—RESEARCH PROCEDURE

This section deals with the actual research performed by the marketing research group at Admiral Foods to answer the questions posed above.

Research Method

Further analysis of secondary data sources revealed approximately twenty products current in market, which comprised most of the frozen entrees having any substantial volume. The products, manufactured by a total of six companies, represented different enchiladas, burritos, and tacos. They varied in the type of filling (cheese, meat), in heat (some promised a hot product, others a more moderate product), and in the type of wrapping (hard versus soft).

Attitude and usage information about Mexican foods suggested a wide target audience, comprising men and women of all ages. For the particular research project, the marketing research director opted to include women ages 18-55 in the sample, half of whom did not work and half of whom did work. Quite often one settles for convenience samples, e.g., groups of individuals who can participate because they have a lot of free time during the day. Here, the nature of the product (a frozen entree, amenable to quick reheating) dictated that working women should participate, even though they do not constitute a so-called convenience sample. The marketing director recognized that the frozen entree might appeal to this group, because they could prepare it quickly after work.

In a printed manual, the Admiral Foods Company had set forth its research guidelines (specifics) regarding markets in which to test. Recognizing the need to have a more representative sample, the marketing research director suggested that they conduct the evaluations in three cities, representing a geographical spread; New York City, Omaha and Los Angeles.

Category appraisals demand a great deal from the consumers. The panelists have to evaluate products on a blind basis and on a branded basis, as well as rating their reactions to print advertisements and test concepts. Finally, the panelists have to fill out an attitude and usage questionnaire. These activities require more than a single day, but rather demand two days of participation, with approximately four hours each day. Table 16.1 presents the activities followed each day, and the approximate time required to perform these activities. Note that the sessions do not add to 240 minutes, or four hours. Inevitably, some panelists take longer to finish parts of the evaluation than do others. This asynchrony on the part of the panelists requires some slack time to insure that the sessions finish on or before the time promised to the panelists. Otherwise, the panelists become irritable and do not want to continue to participate.

Results—Performance Of The Products On A Blind Basis

The first analysis has as a goal to evaluate the performance of the 20 products on a blind basis. Table 16.2 shows some of the results, in terms of overall liking on a 0-100 scale. Table 16.2 shows the data broken down by different types of products (e.g., tacos, burritos, enchiladas), rated on overall liking by the total panel (all three markets combined), and by panelists in the three markets separately.

The key learning which emerged for Admiral Foods from this part of the study consists of the following.

(1) The acceptance of wrapped entrees varies considerably. On the average (pooling all markets together), enchiladas score higher than burritos, which score higher than tacos.

(2) Within a subcategory (e.g., tacos), consumers see different ranges of variation. Enchiladas, for example, show a higher range of variation in acceptance than do the tacos. We do not know whether tacos constitute more of a commodity item, as compared to enchiladas.

(3) Consumers in the various markets differ from each other. For instance, if we average the ratings assigned by the panelists across all the products they tried, we find that consumers in Los Angeles show the highest average liking rating, whereas consumers in Omaha show the lowest ratings. Does this represent true, or intrinsic differences among consumers as they respond to Mexican entrees? Or, as one might

TABLE 16.1
DESIGN OF CATEGORY APPRAISAL STUDY—
MEXICAN FOODS PRE-RECRUIT PANELISTS (TOTAL OF 102, 3 MARKETS, CATEGORY USERS)

Day 1	
Orient panelists in scaling to insure comprehension	20 Minutes
Panelist fills out attitude and usage questionnaire	30 Minutes
Panelist rates a random of 10 of 20 products blind	150 Minutes
9-10 minutes between samples	
For each product, data checked for consistency and correctness	
Day 2	
Panelist rates one product blind on attributes	15 Minutes
Panelist profiles 10 products branded	150 Minutes
Panelist profiles existing print ads on attributes	60 Minutes
Panelist paid and dismissed	

hypothesize, consumers in one market tend to up-rate products, whereas consumers in another market tend to down-rate products. We cannot answer this question from the current study. However, if the difference recurs, one way of answering the question consists of having consumers rate two or three other products (not Mexican foods) in the test, to measure their performance (e.g., chicken soup, cake). These products should not differ as dramatically from market to market as do the more ethnic Mexican food products.

(4) Manufacturers differ in the level of consumers acceptance of the products that they market (Table 16.3). We can average the products by manufacturer (not shown). Even though the manufacturers put out different items in their line, nonetheless we can obtain some idea of the average acceptance that they provide in their products. Manufacturer M (a volume leader in the category) actually delivers a poor set of entrees, based upon blind product acceptance. Manufacturers H and I (which have a broad line of entrees, but relatively little total volume) actually market the best tasting products.

(5) Flavor varieties differ in acceptance, with meat products gaining higher acceptance than cheese based products. (Data not shown for this break).

TABLE 16.2
PART OF DATABASE FOR MEXICAN FOODS
RATINGS OF PURCHASE INTENT ON A 0-100 SCALE

	Total	New York	Omaha	Los Angeles
Overall Average	47	44	42	55
Tacos				
Range (High-Low)	25	28	31	16
Average	41	46	33	45
A	54	60	50	53
B	37	48	19	44
C	39	35	41	42
Etcetera	...			
Burritos				
Range (High-Low)	30		Etcetera	
Average	47			
M	61			
N	43			
O	30			
Etcetera	...			
Enchiladas				
Range (High-Low)	36			
Average	53			
S	28			
T	66			
U	61			
Etcetera	...			

How Do The Branded Products Perform

The previous section revealed substantial differences among products on a blind basis. Do we find the same range of acceptance difference when we identify the product as to type and manufacturer? To do this part of the evaluation correctly, at the field site the panelists must see the actual product package, with all of the information available (e.g., manufacturer, type of product, picture of product, and price of the product).

Table 16.3 shows how the various products perform on a blind versus branded basis, as well as (on average) how do the various manufacturers and product types perform. The key differences which emerge from the

TABLE 16.3
COMPARISON OF BLIND AND BRANDED RATINGS FOR MEXICAN FROZEN ENTREE CATEGORY DATA FROM TOTAL PANEL

Product	Manufacturer	Blind	Branded	Brand Effect
Tacos				
A	H	54	56	2
B	I	37	52	15
C	J	39	57	18
D	K	38	43	5
E	L	38	44	6
F	M	40	48	8
Average		41	50	9
Burritos				
M	H	61	64	3
N	I	43	66	23
O	J	30	48	18
P	K	38	41	3
Q	L	52	48	−4
R	M	58	62	4
Average		47	54	7
Enchiladas				
S	H	28	35	7
T	I	66	73	7
U	J	61	71	10
V	K	29	34	5
W	L	29	34	5
X	M	32	37	5
Y	M	21	29	8
Average		38	44	6
By Manufacturer				
	H	48	52	+ 4
	I	49	64	+15
	J	43	59	+16
	K	35	39	+ 4
	L	40	42	+ 2
	M	35	44	+ 9

blind versus branded comparisons consists of changes due to manufacturer, more than changes due to product type (tacos versus burritos versus enchiladas, respectively). As Table 16.3 shows, manufacturers I and J exhibit very large brand values. When consumers find out the manufacturer, the ratings of acceptance jump. In contrast, manufacturer L, with a high volume, does not necessarily enjoy great brand value. To some extent, manufacturer L may enjoy the large market share because of price and distribution factors, not because of image and acceptance factors.

Relation Between Promotion & Advertising, and Product Ratings

The category appraisal provides marketers with an idea of how various factors affect consumer acceptance. Blinded product acceptance depends upon a combination of R&D expertise and the panelist's innate reaction to the category (predisposition to accept or reject products). Branded product acceptance calls into play other factors, including advertising, promotion and product uniqueness. The difference between blind and branded acceptance thus mirrors the impact of advertising and promotion.

In many categories, marketers can obtain measures of competitive advertising dollars, competitive "share of voice" (defined as the relative amount of advertising exposure in the category enjoyed by a particular brand or line), and promotion dollars. Often these represent estimates of expenditures, obtained by advertising agencies from their knowledge of media expenditures, or by marketing groups, from their knowledge of promotion activities in the category.

The Admiral Foods Company has a fully staffed department of marketing and marketing research professionals, with the job of evaluating competition. These professionals use a variety of sources, including Nielsen audit ratings, SAMI numbers (for warehouse shipments), and evaluations of promotion activities in newspapers via such companies as Majers. All in all, the marketing group developed a set of representative numbers, to assess level of spending, in advertising, (TV, radio, and print broken down separately), and promotion activity. The markets for the analysis differed, but we will consider simply national results, for simplicity. The analysis performed below lends itself to a market-by-market study.

The Data Base Used For Evaluating Advertising And Promotion

Table 16.4 presents part of the data base used for the evaluation of promotion and advertising on consumer reactions. Note the elements, including consumer ratings of each product (blind, branded, difference), estimated spending on different advertising media, estimated promotion activity, and share information.

TABLE 16.4
DATABASE FOR MEXICAN FOODS

Product	Manufacturer	CONSUMER ACCEPTANCE RATINGS			MARKETING VARIABLES			
		Blind	Branded	Difference	Estimated Share*	Promotion Spending**	Advertising Print**	Advertising Television**
Tacos								
A	H	54	56	2	19	500	161	591
B	I	37	52	15	21	622	217	636
C	J	39	57	18	10	745	129	653
D	K	38	43	5	30	362	158	454
E	L	38	44	6	11	724	161	668
F	M	40	48	8	9	749	105	629
Burritos								
M	H	61	64	3	19	500	161	591
N	I	43	66	23	21	622	217	636
O	J	30	48	18	10	745	129	653
P	K	38	41	3	30	362	158	454
Q	L	52	48	−4	11	724	161	668
R	M	58	62	4	9	749	105	629

TABLE 16.4 (Continued)
DATABASE FOR MEXICAN FOODS

Product	Manufacturer	CONSUMER ACCEPTANCE RATINGS			MARKETING VARIABLES			
		Blind	Branded	Difference	Estimated Share*	Promotion Spending**	Advertising Print**	Advertising Television**
Enchiladas								
S	H	28	35	7	19	500	161	591
T	I	66	73	7	21	622	217	636
U	J	61	71	10	10	745	129	653
V	K	29	34	5	30	362	158	454
W	L	29	34	5	11	724	161	668
X	M	32	37	5	9	749	105	629
Y	M	37	29	6	9	749	105	629

*Share numbers shown in terms of manufacturer. Breakout not available for product X manufacturer.

**In dollars.

Note: Data shown only for the three markets used for test (this caveat applies to both the consumer acceptance ratings and the marketing variables).

Although the data from Table 16.4 neither covers the entire U.S., nor represents all the products in the market, it can provide a company like Admiral Foods with indications about which particular characteristics drive consumer acceptance, market share, etc. Does advertising show the greatest correlation with share, and warehouse shipments (namely, volume)? Or, does promotion show a greater impact?

Results Of The Analysis

The analysis consisted of correlating variables with each other, and then running simple linear regressions. The marketing analysis looked at the relation between share in the market (Nielsen), and both product acceptance factors (blind, branded), and both promotion and advertising and then advertising and promotion (weighted separately). The results appear in Table 16.5. Note that advertising and promotion shows a greater impact than does basic product acceptance as a predictor of brand share. As many marketers know, promotions increase awareness and traffic, because they provide consumers with the product at a lower price. However, over a longer period, it requires advertising to instill a specific message, which creates added value to the product, over and above the actual product itself. Advertising hammers home the message, whereas promotion gets the consumer to try the product, because of a cost reduction, or other tangible benefit (e.g., a free gift accompanying the product, or sent to the consumer with a proof of purchase). Both advertising and promotion outweigh basic consumer acceptance of the product by taste.

Key Trends

A summary of the learning obtained by relating consumer perceptions of the product to exogenous marketing variables (advertising, promotion), revealed the following:

(1) Brand value—clearly different from one manufacturer to another.

(2) Effect of advertising versus promotion—both appear more effective than product acceptance as predictors of success in the market. Unit dollars spent in TV generate more brand share than unit dollars spent on print advertising. Both forms of advertising show greater effectiveness than the same dollar expenditure in promotion.

(3) Manufacturers H and I show the highest acceptance on a blind basis, suggesting excellent R&D. However, on a branded basis, manufacturers I and J score highest, showing the impact of advertising and promotion.

(4) Consumers perceive differences among the products on a blind basis. These differences, coupled with the power of advertising, allow the Admiral Foods Co. to develop and advertise a superior product. Consumers can perceive the superiority, if present.

TABLE 16.5
RELATION BETWEEN BRAND SHARE IN THE MARKET AND BOTH PRODUCT* AND ADVERTISING/PROMOTION FACTORS**

Product	Equation	R^2
Brand Share vs. Blind Acceptance*		
Tacos	Share = − 42.2 + 1.11 (Blind)	$R^2 = 0.13$
Burritos	Share = 23.4 − 0.14 (Blind)	$R^2 = 0.04$
Enchiladas	Share = 15.8 − 0.01 (Blind)	$R^2 = 0.01$
Brand Share vs. Brand Acceptance*		
Tacos	Share = − 56.2 + 1.19 (Branded)	$R^2 = 0.13$
Burritos	Share = 25.2 − 0.16 (Branded)	$R^2 = 0.04$
Enchiladas	Share = 14.4 + 0.02 (Branded)	$R^2 = 0.01$
Brand Share vs. Promotion Expenditures*		
Tacos, Burritos, Enchiladas	Share = − 29.5 + 0.05 (Dollars)	$R^2 = 0.18$
Brand Share vs. Total Advertising Expenditure**		
Tacos, Burritos, Enchiladas	Share = − 139.9 + 0.18 (TV Dollars) + 0.19 (Print Dollars)	$R^2 = 0.60$
Brand Share vs. Print Advertisement Expenditures**		
Tacos, Burritos, Enchiladas	Share = − 22.86 + 0.17 (Dollars)	$R^2 = 0.10$
Brand Share vs. TV Advertisement Expenditures**		
Tacos, Burritos, Enchiladas	Share = − 101.6 + 0.17 (Dollars)	$R^2 = 0.48$

*Differs by product and manufacturer
**Same for all products, but differs by manufacturer

Product Response Segmentation—Looking For Segments To Satisfy

The previous analyses revealed that consumers do perceive differences among products, leading to the opportunity for R&D to develop new prototypes to satisfy consumers. It further revealed that consumers attended to advertising as a key element which influenced their impressions of products. One could generate an entirely different perception of a product by successfully positioning it, and advertising the product (especially in print form).

This section deals with segmentation, from the business point of view. The marketing research director at Admiral Foods discovered from the secondary reports that consumers fell into different segments. Some consumers absolutely disliked any hot and spicy foods. During focus group interviews these consumers stated, again and again, that they enjoyed Mexican food, but would never buy "that hot stuff". Other consumers, with just as much vehemence, retorted that they enjoyed hot Mexican food, and indeed the hotness comprised some of the attraction of the cuisine.

From a marketing point of view, one would like to target a product to the segment of consumers which holds the biggest promise for volume consumption. This desire requires that the marketing researcher consider several factors: (1) the size of the segment, (2) the number of products currently serving the segment, (3) the volume consumption by consumers in the segment, (4) the steps required by Admiral Foods to enter the segment (namely, R&D development time versus acquisition of an existing line versus heavy spending on advertising and promotion).

The initial analysis of the data looked at relative acceptance of the different entrees, using demographic "breaks" or variables, such as market, age, working versus nonworking. In terms of the absolute scores, differences do exist (e.g., consumers in one market may assign higher acceptance ratings to Mexican foods than do consumers in another market). In terms of relative ratings, however, little differences among products appeared using the demographic variables as the source of the data breaks. Products scoring high (on a relative basis) in New York also scored high (on a relative basis) in Omaha and Los Angeles. Of course, as in any research project, inversions and inconsistencies appeared, but by and large the inconsistencies in relative acceptance from market to market, or age to age, seemed relatively inconsequential, compared to the overall performance of the products, and the range of acceptance. The high scorers in New York agreed with the high scorers in Omaha and Los Angeles.

A distribution of liking ratings assigned to the various products (blind) shows variation from panelist to panelist. We can segment the population of consumers by their taste preferences, just as we did for beverages.

By segmenting the consumer panel, it quickly became clear to the marketing group and the market research director that at least three segments of consumers exist, having quite different taste preferences. As Table 16.6 shows, we can label these as "hot lovers" (who like the heat of the product, and will accept both hard and soft wrappings on the product), "cool/hard group" (who prefer hard covers), and the "cool/soft group" (who prefer soft covers). Table 16.6 shows the distribution of these segments. Note that the hot lovers account for about 1/4 of the consumers, whereas the remaining two segments of cool/non-hot lovers account for the remaining 3/4 of the consumers tested in the market.

Fitting Products To Segments

The marketing research director looked at the products by segments to determine the relevance or acceptance of each product to every segment. One product might satisfy only one segment, or else satisfy two segments. Table 16.7 reveals that of the 19 products, only 3 of 19 appealed to the hot segment. In contrast, for the cool/mild segments (comprising 3/4 of the sample), 8 of 19, or more than 40% of the products appealed to this group.

Looking at the acceptance pattern in Table 16.7, we can rapidly discern the opportunity in a category. The cool segments, while having the majority of the panelists in the study (75%), hold only modest promise. About half of the products currently in-market (10 of the 19 in the test) appeal to these segments. For Admiral Foods to make a successful entry, it has to go against stiff competition. In contrast, the hot segment, although of lesser size (25% of the market, approximately) has only 3 major products which appeal to it. It looks promising for Admiral Foods to go after this hot category, because of the size (25% of the consumers), and the relative lack of competition in terms of basic product acceptance.

Do The Consumers Know Their Own Preference Segments

The segmentation analysis reveals the existence of different segments. Do consumers know the segment to which they belong? On the surface, this seems a fairly simple question to answer; people should know their own taste preferences, even on an attitudinal basis. We can check the consumers' knowledge of their taste preferences by asking them to profile the "ideal" product, in terms of the sensory characteristics. Consumers who behaviorally fall into the hot segment should profile their ideal product as tasting relatively hot. Conversely, consumers who behaviorally fall into the mild segment should profile their ideal product as tasting fairly

TABLE 16.6
DEMOGRAPHICS OF SENSORY (PRODUCT RESPONSE) SEGMENTATION OF CONSUMERS REGARDING MEXICAN ENTREES

			SEGMENT 1	SEGMENT 2	SEGMENT 3
		Flavor:	Hot Lover	Cool Lover	Cool Lover
		Texture:	No Texture Preference	Like Soft Textures	Like Hard Textures
	AGE		25%	45%	30%
	18-24		18	21	36
	25-34		24	40	30
	35-49		38	15	19
	49+		20	24	15
	Total		100%	100%	100%
Consumption (Time/Month)					
Low	1-2		24	31	31
Medium	3-6		25	36	42
High	7+		51	33	27
	Total		100%	100%	100%

mild. Table 16.8 shows the profile of the ideal product, scaled by the panelists in each segment. Note that based upon the ideal, we conclude that consumers do have an idea of the segment to which they belong (namely, the hot segment profiles their ideal product as tasting fairly hot). At the same time, however, note that the difference between the sensory profiles of the ideal product assigned by the taste preference segments seems smaller than the differences in the sensory profiles of the products scored highest by each segment.

EVALUATING THE MESSAGES COMMUNICATED BY THE VARIOUS PRODUCTS

The previous section dealt with the responses by consumers to the different products, blind and branded. Another element in the marketing

TABLE 16.7
ACCEPTANCE RATINGS (0-100 SCALE) OF THE NINETEEN PRODUCTS FOR THE THREE SEGMENTS

	TOTAL (100%)	HOT (25%)	COOL/SOFT (45%)	COOL/HARD (30%)
Tacos				
A	54	[42]	[56]	[61
B	37	23	33	54]
C	39	19	49	46
D	38	24	38	49
E	38	31	34	[50]
F	40	29	38	[52]
Burritos				
M	61	42	[76]	[54]
N	43	36	[57]	28
O	30	[58]	21	20
P	38	28	42	40
Q	52	40	[54	[59
R	58	[47]	62]	62]
Enchiladas				
S	28	[51]	15	28
T	66	35	[72	[83
U	61	42	65]	71]
V	29	18	31	35
W	29	12	45	19
X	32	34	30	33
Y	27	33	24	27

[ ] = Denotes a viable product for that segment.

mix, the package and advertising messages, also deserve consideration in a category appraisal. By evaluating these messages or communications, without the benefit of product testing, the researcher and manager can discover the "hot buttons" or communication elements which generate consumer interest. When one focuses interest on purchasing a product, this analysis of communication helps the decision. It tells the marketer and manager whether the product communicates a unique selling proposition, or whether consumers react to the messages as just another "me-too" product.

TABLE 16.8
COMPARISON OF PROFILE RATINGS FOR THREE POLARIZING PRODUCTS APPEALING MOST TO SEGMENTS

	PERFORMANCE OF WINNING PRODUCTS			SELF-DESIGNED IDEAL PRODUCTS		
	Burrito "O"	Burrito "M"	Enchilada "T"	Hot	Cool/Soft	Cool/Hard
Best for	Hot	Cool/Soft	Cool/Hard			
Taste						
Hot/Peppery	76	31	34	59	43	31
Texture						
Soft-Hard	36	46	39	56	59	64
Liking						
Total Panel	30	61	66		Not Asked	
By Segment						
Hot	58	42	35			
Cool/Soft	21	76	72			
Cool/Hard	20	54	83			

Discovering The Communication Profile By Content Analysis

A simplistic, disciplined content analysis of products of interest quickly reveals the communication profiles of all the products in the category. For Admiral Foods, whose marketing research group had extensive experience in communication analysis, the task posed no particular difficulties. The marketing research director had a project leader assemble all print advertisements, packages and story boards (TV commercials, written down) for the frozen Mexican food category. Among these they collected material from the four main manufacturers listed in Table 16.9, along with a wide variety of material from other, smaller manufacturers.

The array of package and advertising information represents a valuable store of information about the messages sent by the different manufacturers. In essence, if one believes that manufacturers act on their best guess about consumer hot buttons, then the array of information provides a collection of these best guesses.

The project director in charge of the analysis performed a content analysis on the various advertisements and packages. She drew up a list of elements present in the array, as shown in Table 16.9. Then, she went through each of the packages and ads, and decided which particular elements that package or ad contained. For that package or ad, she then filled in a 1 if the stimulus contained the particular element, or a 0 if it did not. Table 16.9 also shows part of the data matrix which emerged from this exercise.

Looking at Table 16.9, and especially at the bottom of the table (which presents summary statistics on the elements) we can determine the following.

(1) What communication points do the various manufacturers stress?

(2) Do we see elements which appear unduly often? If so, this may indicate undue competition to occupy that "communication niche." On the other hand, we may find some communication points which seem quite attractive, but which relatively few manufacturers use. Perhaps Admiral Foods, after purchasing a product line in the category, or even developing its own line, might avail itself of that under-used communication point, as part of the marketing strategy.

Consumer Reactions To Communication Elements—Concept Development

In a previous chapter, we dealt with the issue of concept evaluation and optimization. Concepts comprise communication elements. We have seen the relative frequency of use of each communication by manufacturers (Table 16.9). Do consumers find the messages equally acceptable, or equally persuasive?

TABLE 16.9
RESULTS OF CONTENT ANALYSIS OF COMPETITORS IN THE MEXICAN FOOD CATEGORY MESSAGES PROVIDED BY PACKAGES OR ADS

STIMULUS	TOTAL WITHIN STIMULUS	COMMUNICATION ELEMENT FROM CONTENT ANALYSIS A	B	C	D	E	F
1	2	1	0	0	1	0	0
2	2	0	1	0	0	1	0
3	2	1	1	0	0	0	0
4	2	0	0	1	1	0	0
5	1	0	1	0	0	0	0
6	3	0	1	0	0	1	1
7	2	0	0	1	0	1	0
8	2	0	0	1	0	0	1
9	2	1	0	0	1	0	0
37	2	0	0	0	0	1	1
Totals	82	12	19	15	13	11	12
Breakdown by Manufacturer							
Man H	22	5	4	3	6	2	2
Man I	17	4	2	1	3	3	4
Man J	22	1	7	4	3	4	3
Man K	21	2	6	7	1	2	3

Elements Used in Content Analysis

A = Mexican spokesman.
B = Recipe attached for extended use.
C = Line of additional items featured or mentioned.
D = Emphasis on authenticity of Mexican taste.
E = Picture of actual item on package or advertisement.
F = Emphasis on economical aspects—e.g., cost savings.

In order to answer this question, we can present concepts to consumers, for consumer evaluation of acceptance, and communication. These concepts should mirror the existing packages and advertisements, all reduced to a simple concept board or card (with graphics). By reducing all the communication media (advertisements, packages) to a common denominator (namely, concept boards) we reduce the chance of obtaining an inflated or deflated acceptance score because of degree of embellishment. Our interest focuses on acceptance of the messages, not on reactions to embellished ideas.

Table 16.10 shows the data base that this exercise generated. Note that we have an array of stimuli comprising the concept boards. The left hand side of Table 16.10 indicates the particular elements present in the print ad or package. The right hand side provides the average rating from the entire panel, in terms of communication, as well as the ratings of appeal assigned by the total panel, and the various segments.

We can relate the presence/absence of communication elements to the ratings by means of regression. Keep in mind that the independent variables assume one of two values; a 1 if the advertisement or package contains the particular communication element, or a 0 if it does not. Table 16.11 shows the outcome from running a dummy variable regression analysis, relating attribute rating (a continuous variable) against the presence/absence of the independent variables. Keep in mind that the communication elements do not all vary entirely independently of each other, because we have to make do with the existing competitive frame, and the communication elements contained therein.

Key Learning From The Evaluation Of Communication

(1) The elements in the advertisements and packages generate different purchase intent ratings. Specifically, products presented in color generate the highest contribution purchase intent. Consumers like to see the products portrayed in color.

(2) The segments discovered from the product evaluation portion differ in their reactions to the elements. Specifically, the hot lovers seem most attentive to concepts featuring a Mexican spokesman, and like the authentic Mexican emphasis. In contrast, the cool or mild lovers seem more attuned to other elements. The mild/soft lovers like the idea of a recipe. The mild/hard segment shows strong interest in communications of a line of items.

Early stage analyses of the packages and print advertisements thus increases one's knowledge about the hot buttons in the category. With this information, marketing at Admiral Foods can better plan its entry into the Mexican foods category. It now knows the types of consumers, and what general types of messages each attends to.

AN OVERVIEW

Quite often manufacturers look with greatest diligence at a company's profit and loss statement, before acquiring it, or at secondary sources of information about a category before entering it with their own products.

TABLE 16.10
PARTIAL DATABASE OF RATINGS ASSIGNED TO ADVERTISEMENTS, PACKAGES AND PROMOTIONAL PIECES BY CONSUMERS

STIMULUS	CONTENT ANALYSIS ELEMENTS IN MESSAGE						CONSUMER ATTRIBUTE RATINGS PURCHASE INTENT				COMMUNICATIONS		
	A	B	C	D	E	F	Total	Hot	Mild/Soft	Mild/Hard	Mexican	Flavor	Value
1	1	0	0	1	0	0	39	34	47	30	66	33	45
2	0	1	0	0	1	0	46	28	49	62	48	42	41
3	1	1	0	0	0	0	42	34	52	38	57	30	44
4	0	0	1	1	0	0	47	30	45	48	58	38	43
5	0	1	0	0	0	0	34	26	49	31	45	28	43
6	0	1	0	0	1	1	51	27	52	60	49	39	63
7	0	0	1	0	1	0	53	24	46	83	54	43	44
8	0	0	1	0	0	1	43	26	49	51	48	29	63
9	1	0	0	1	0	0	39	36	45	31	66	32	42
37	0	0	0	0	1	1	47	23	47	67	47	36	64

A = Mexican spokeman.
B = Recipe attached for extended use.
C = Line of additional items featured or mentioned.
D = Emphasis on authenticity of Mexican taste.
E = Picture of actual item on package or advertisement.
F = Emphasis on economical aspects, e.g., cost savings.

TABLE 16.11
ADDITIVE MODELS RELATING PRESENCE/ABSENCE OF ELEMENTS ON PACKAGES AND ADVERTISEMENTS TO PANEL RATINGS

RATINGS	INTERCEPT	ELEMENTS FROM CONTENT ANALYSIS					
		A	B	C	D	E	F
Purchase Intent							
Total	35.0	1.6	2.5	6.5	1.9	11.2	0.8
Hot	22.6	7.2	3.6	2.9	4.5	2.1	1.6
Cool Mild/Soft	42.6	1.9	6.1	1.4	2.3	1.4	3.1
Cool Mild/Hard	34.0	-3.5	-3.8	17.1	- .9	13.4	-3.3
Communications							
Mexican	42.0	11.9	2.8	6.5	11.0	4.5	1.2
Good Flavor	26.4	1.7	3.7	6.5	5.3	11.9	3.6
Good Value	42.2	1.8	0.3	1.1	0.2	0.9	19.3

A = Mexican spokesperson.
B = Recipe attached for extended use.
C = Line of additional items featured or mentioned.
D = Emphasis in authenticity of Mexican taste.
E = Picture of actual item on package or advertisement (in color).
F = Emphasis on economical aspects—e.g., cost savings.

This chapter has presented a method by which the manufacturer can evaluate the competitive frame of products and advertisements/positionings in a category, efficiently, rapidly and inexpensively.

The information provided by such a category appraisal consists of the following:

(1) A quantitative assessment of how well the products in the category perform

(2) A measure of impact of branding on acceptance

(3) An ability to correlate acceptance and brand value to advertising and promotion expenditures (obtained from separate sources)

(4) An understanding of the types of consumers segments in the markets, and the degree to which the products currently in the market satisfy those segments

(5) A measure of reactions to communication elements present in advertisements and packages

(6) An idea of which elements to stress in a new entry.

As business becomes increasingly competitive, more and more marketers and managers turn to such category appraisals. The disciplined evaluation provides some of the information necessary to make the proper decision. Most importantly, however, the information comes in a relatively straightforward, unambiguous way from consumers who actually have a chance to evaluate the existing products on the market and report their reactions.

REFERENCES

MORGAN, K. J., METZEN, E. J. and JOHNSON, S. R. 1979. An hedonic index for breakfast cereals. J. Consumer Res. *6,* 67-75.

MOSKOWITZ, H. R., JACOBS, B., LAZAR, N. and RABINO, S. Early stage product development: Using category appraisal and competitive product testing to set targets for product development. Unpublished manuscript.

NAERT, P. and WEVERBERG, W. 1981. On the prediction power of market share attraction models. J. Marketing Res. *18,* 146-153.

NAKANISHI, M. 1973. Advertising and promotion effects on consumer response to new products. J. Marketing Res. *10,* 242-249.

SIMON, J. L. 1969. The effect of advertising on liquor brand sales. J. Marketing Res. *6,* 301-303.

INDEX